CREATING CONSPIRAC

Conspiracy theories are spread more widely and faster than ever before. Fear and uncertainty prompt people to believe false narratives of danger and hidden plots, but are not sufficient without considering the role and ideological bias of the media. This timely book focuses on making sense of how and why some people respond to their fear of a threat by creating or believing conspiracy stories. It integrates insights from psychology, political science, communication, and information sciences to provide a complete overview and theory of how conspiracy beliefs manifest. Through this multidisciplinary perspective, rigorous research develops and tests a practical, simple way to frame and understand conspiracy theories. The book supplies unprecedented amounts of new data from six empirical studies and unpicks the complexity of the process that leads to the empowerment of conspiracy beliefs.

DOLORES ALBARRACÍN is Professor of Psychology at the University of Illinois at Urbana–Champaign.

JULIA ALBARRACÍN is Professor of Political Science at Western Illinois University.

MAN-PUI SALLY CHAN is Research Assistant Professor of Psychology at the University of Illinois at Urbana–Champaign.

KATHLEEN HALL JAMIESON is Professor of Communication at the University of Pennsylvania and Director of its Policy Center.

CREATING CONSPIRACY BELIEFS

How Our Thoughts Are Shaped

DOLORES ALBARRACÍN

University of Illinois, Urbana–Champaign

JULIA ALBARRACÍN

Western Illinois University

MAN-PUI SALLY CHAN

University of Illinois, Urbana–Champaign

KATHLEEN HALL JAMIESON

University of Pennsylvania

CAMBRIDGE
UNIVERSITY PRESS

CAMBRIDGE
UNIVERSITY PRESS

University Printing House, Cambridge CB2 8BS, United Kingdom

One Liberty Plaza, 20th Floor, New York, NY 10006, USA

477 Williamstown Road, Port Melbourne, VIC 3207, Australia

314–321, 3rd Floor, Plot 3, Splendor Forum, Jasola District Centre, New Delhi – 110025, India

103 Penang Road, #05–06/07, Visioncrest Commercial, Singapore 238467

Cambridge University Press is part of the University of Cambridge.

It furthers the University's mission by disseminating knowledge in the pursuit of
education, learning, and research at the highest international levels of excellence.

www.cambridge.org
Information on this title: www.cambridge.org/9781108845786
DOI: 10.1017/9781108990936

First published 2022

A catalogue record for this publication is available from the British Library.

ISBN 978-1-108-84578-6 Hardback
ISBN 978-1-108-96502-6 Paperback

Additional materials are available to view at cambridge.org/creatingconspiracybeliefs

To our families for their inspiration and unconditional support.

Contents

Figures

Tables

Preface

What is a conspiracy belief, and how is one created and sustained? How does a narrative that both harnesses and justifies recipients' general anxiety increase susceptibility to the belief in a hidden plot that powerful agents have orchestrated to harm the believer? Or do anxious feelings from other sources (e.g., one's mood) create a predisposition to think about conspiracies? What is the role of social networks and media in trafficking such accounts to susceptible individuals? How do psychological and sociopolitical influences play out?

In *Creating Conspiracy Beliefs*, we use survey, experimental, and social media data to test the utility of a theory of psychological and sociopolitical influences on conspiracy beliefs. Our objects of interest range from hoary beliefs that Barack Obama was not born in the United States and assertions that the dangers of vaccination have been covered up by self-interested agents to beliefs about the existence of a deep state within the American governmental bureaucracy bent on subverting the presidency of Donald J. Trump, first by engineering his impeachment, later by undermining his efforts to bring the COVID-19 pandemic under control, and finally by preventing his reelection.

Our theoretical framework acknowledges psychological and sociopolitical influences that have been looked at in past research on conspiracy beliefs, including anxiety (e.g., an anxious mood), the need for closure, and the motives that arise from feeling isolated and disenfranchised. More important, however, is our goal of describing the proverbial "elephant in the room" for conspiracy theories, how these non-falsifiable beliefs spread through social interaction and are validated by others in like-minded communities. When thoughts of conspiracy are socially shared, what are their sources? How do discussions with other people and exposure to media contribute to creating these beliefs? What is the influence of media, and is their influence enhanced by feelings of anxiety in their audiences? Do the media contribute to this anxiety as well?

The book draws on data from three cross-sectional surveys and one longitudinal panel. Collectively, these surveys investigated distal psychological and sociopolitical predispositions, anxiety, and the important social and media influences at play. The first three surveys tested beliefs in four conspiracy theories, all involving secret activities by a powerful Individual or group:

1. Barack Obama was not born in the United States; he faked his birth certificate to become president (for an analysis of the theory, see Politico, 2011).
2. Undocumented immigrants voting illegally prevented Republicans from winning the popular vote in 2016 (for more information, see Business Insider, 2018).
3. The US government created the HIV epidemic by experimentally injecting the virus in people of African descent (see Heller, 2015).
4. The MMR vaccine causes autism, but this link has been covered up by the US government (see Eggertson, 2010).

Each of the surveys examined psychological and sociopolitical precursors of beliefs in the theories as well as the role of anxiety and media. The longitudinal panel concerned the belief that unelected state officials have conspired against Donald J. Trump by illegally undermining his candidacy and presidency. This survey, which examined the role of feelings of anxiety and media exposure, was conducted while the United States Congress determined whether he should be impeached, and, after impeachment, convicted and removed from office. An experiment gauged the causal impact of anxiety focused on the conspiracy theory that 5G technology caused the COVID-19 pandemic (Satariano & Alba, 2020).

We also obtained 407,697 relevant, publicly available tweets from the United States (i.e., 391,935 tweets with hashtags and keywords) alluding to conspiracy theories and 15,762 tweets, including their hashtags and keywords, that attempted to debunk some of them. This study involved the theories we just listed, the deep state theory, and an additional set of the following science relevant conspiracy theories:

1. Lizard aliens hybridized with humans who now secretly occupy positions of power ("The reptilian elite," 2020)
2. The earth is flat, but an elaborate deception explains the popular belief that the earth is not flat ("The Flat Earth Society," n.d.).
3. "Chem" trails, as the condensation ("con") trails from airplanes are labeled, are evidence of large-scale, secret spraying with pesticides to

control the population and modify the environment (Fraser, 2009; Van Assche et al., 2018).

4. Agenda 21, a secret United Nations plan to control population growth, is in effect, in violation of American sovereignty (Dickson, 2017).

Our social media analyses were used to determine the degree to which conservative, liberal, and mainstream media account handles (i.e., @[username]) disseminated these theories online, and whether the anxiety-inducing content of the material contributed to this dissemination.

The book is organized around a set of theoretical principles that guided our review and empirical research. The appendix describes all methods and our samples. An online supplement contains the research instruments, as well as the data and code used in our analyses.

Our work is indebted to a number of books that deal with specific conspiracy theories or areas of inquiry. These include *UFOs, Conspiracy Theories, and the New Age* by David G. Robertson (Bloomsbury, 2017), *I Heard It through the Grapevine* by Patricia Turner (University of California Press, 1993), *Conspiracy Theory and American Foreign Policy* by Tim Aistrope (Manchester University Press, 2016), and *Textual Conspiracies* by James Martel (University of Michigan Press, 2011).

In the substantial body of existing scholarship on conspiracy beliefs, five books have special relevance to our arguments. *Conspiracy Theory in America* by DeHaven-Smith (University of Texas Press, 2013) provides a thorough theoretical analysis of the intellectual development of conspiracy theorizing. Particularly impressive is his attempt to conceptualize the "conspiracy theories" as a mechanism to bring state crimes against democracy (SCAD) to light.

American Conspiracy Theories by Joseph E. Uscinski and Joseph M. Parent (Oxford University Press, 2014) develops an impressive general theory of why people believe in conspiracy theories. According to them, these include conspiratorial predispositions, ideologies, group identity, and loss of political power. While their model concerns factors that we carefully incorporate when possible, these factors are not the sole focus of our book. Instead, we argue that conspiracy beliefs emerge from the intersection of anxiety and specific social influences, which, in the case of many of the beliefs we explore, include those circulating in the conservative media (e.g., Fox News, Breitbart, and InfoWars).

Like our work, *Empire of Conspiracy* by Timothy Melley (Cornell University Press, 2000) argues that fears and anxieties are drivers of conspiratorial beliefs that are expressed in many venues including film, fiction, sociology, political writing, and self-help literature. To this understanding, we add the general argument that anxiety and conspiracy theorizing cut across areas and, in particular explore the creation of the content of *specific* beliefs and why some ideas take hold and others do not.

A Culture of Conspiracy by Michael Barkun (University of California Press, 2013, 2nd ed.) discusses how conspiracy theories seek to reveal the real loci of power. To that insight, we add the argument that anxiety and other psychological and sociopolitical factors increase susceptibility to conspiracy beliefs.

In *Conspiracy Theories*, Mark Fenster (University of Minnesota Press, 1999) makes the important argument that by raising the alarm about threats to democracy, conspiracy theories serve a social and political purpose. We agree both that conspiracy theories are not always marginal and pathological and that some suspicion about the government and the powerful may be beneficial for democracy.[1]

---

[1] There is also an interesting, general audience, brief book by Jan-Willem Van Prooijen (2015).

Acknowledgments

We owe a debt of gratitude to the Center for Advanced Study at the University of Illinois at Urbana–Champaign for appointing the first author as a faculty associate during which the research for this book was developed, as well as to Dr. Kenneth Winneg, who supervised the fielding of most of the survey research reported in this book, and to the research assistants who helped with other aspects of the book. Minh Pham checked some of our data, and Lucy Park and Kevin Qin provided invaluable help with the literature review. Ellen Peters, Chadly Stern, Annie Jung, Bita Fayaz-Farkhad, and Sandra Gonzalez-Bailón provided excellent comments on chapters of this book. Also, we thank members of the Social Action Lab at the University of Illinois at Urbana–Champaign, and Martin P. Repetto at Purdue University for informal feedback on important aspects of this work. Finally, we are grateful to David Repetto, our editor and one of the publishers at Cambridge University Press, for his invaluable feedback and encouragement throughout the process.

CHAPTER I

Introduction

Creating Conspiracy Beliefs focuses on making sense of *how and why* some people respond to their fear of a threat by creating and, especially, accepting conspiracy stories. It also concerns why and how embrace of such beliefs is affected by people's interactions with others and with media content, both on- and offline.

The experience of anxiety (i.e., the feeling of imminent threat and/or uncertainty about the future, which involves cognitive feelings and may involve the bodily reactions associated with fear) is often diffuse (i.e., an anxious mood) and thus easy to misattribute to narratives of danger and hidden plots contained in communications from other people or media sources. The fear-inducing contents of messages can also produce an anxious mood as well as specific fears that can predispose people to believe in conspiracy theories.[1] Anxiety alone, however, does not account for beliefs such as the following, which was advanced in 2018 by Robert F. Kennedy Jr., nephew of President John F. Kennedy and son and namesake of the former New York senator assassinated during his presidential bid in 1968:

> The CDC has systematically [within its vaccine branch] ordered its scientists to destroy data, to manipulate data, to massage it, to dump it in garbage cans [if it uncovers] links between development diseases and vaccines. Do I think everyone at the CDC is corrupt? Of course not. There is a tiny handful of corrupt scientists and leaders. . . . The rest of the public health community is not part of any conspiracy, but it has [become part of] the orthodoxy. (Mills, 2018)

Explaining why some beliefs take hold requires that we account for the content of communications. In the case of the MMR (measles, mumps,

---

[1] The term "anxiety" is used to refer to an anxious mood, a diffuse feeling that is thus easy to attribute to any object. "Fear" is an emotion with a specific object, and we use the term when we describe emotional contents contained in a communication (e.g., fear sentiments within a tweet).

and rubella) vaccine beliefs, this environment involves the legitimation of the original assertion of an MMR vaccine–autism association by the *Lancet*, a major science journal. It also involves a more than 10-year delay by the journal in the retraction of that article as well as ongoing advocacy of the discredited claims by the senior author, Dr. Andrew Wakefield (Eggertson, 2010). It also involves the retransmission and amplification of Wakefield's claims on social media and among groups of parents whose children had been diagnosed with autism. It further involves a popular online video in which Wakefield asserted the existence of a cover-up of evidence by the Centers for Disease Control and Prevention (CDC) that the MMR vaccine was associated with an increased rate of autism in Black male children (YouTube, 2020).

This book addresses these questions: What are the specific communications that create such beliefs? How do close others and acquaintances foster them? Does exposure to media content about them interact with anxiety? Do such synergies cut across sociopolitical, health, or environmental theories? How can one integrate psychological and sociopolitical factors, which create a predisposition to these beliefs, into this landscape?

This book presents a theory of psychological and sociopolitical influences on conspiracy beliefs at a time when some of these beliefs are consequential and held by more than one in ten in the United States, a threshold that Aizen and Fishbein argued establishes that a belief is salient in a population (Ajzen & Fishbein, 1980; Jamieson & Albarracín, 2020). Among the COVID-19-related conspiracy beliefs that exceeded that level in March 2020 was one that averred that the US government created the virus, which was accepted by 10 percent of a national sample (Jamieson & Albarracín, 2020). That belief was problematic because it called into question the integrity of the US government at a time in which public confidence was required to mount a national defense against the pandemic. At the same time, nearly one in five (19 percent) reported believing that some in the CDC were exaggerating the seriousness of the virus to undermine the Trump presidency, a conclusion with the potential to engender distrust in a US government agency tasked not only with protecting public health but also with communicating accurate information about ways to protect oneself and others (Jamieson & Albarracín, 2020). Meanwhile in 2020, a widely circulated conspiracy theory linking 5G technology to the 2020 SARS-CoV-2 pandemic led to more than 100 attempts to burn down cell phone towers in the United Kingdom (Satariano & Alba, 2020).

The book begins with definitions and a presentation of our theoretical framework, followed by a detailed qualitative analysis of the origin of a conspiracy theory that both led to an attack on a Washington, DC, pizza parlor and is an expression of the deep state conspiracy theory. Then six chapters describe our studies and their results, along with a detailed review of the relevant past literature. The book concludes by advancing criteria for determining which theories to debunk and forecasting directions that future research might productively take.

Our conceptualization of conspiracy beliefs and their implications contributes to the interdisciplinary scholarship on conspiracy theories by doing the following:

(1) Drawing on survey and experimental data to place anxiety and social influence at the center of conspiracy beliefs.

(2) Explaining how the media, as a particular form of social influencer, confer seemingly irrational ideas with the plausibility and circulation necessary to spread in the population.

(3) Integrating and charting the pathways of previously identified psychological and political factors that can influence conspiracy beliefs by affecting (a) general anxiety (i.e., uncertainty, worry, and fear) and its precursors of belief defense, belief accuracy, and social integration motivation; (b) the theories' perceived plausibility; and (c) the theories' perceived unfalsifiability. The belief defense motivation is the set of needs and goals to preserve one's self-views and a coherent sense of the self and the world. The belief accuracy motivation involves relatively stable needs and goals that encourage individuals to form a realistic representation of the world. The social integration motivation entails needs and goals of social connection, trust, and status.

(4) Integrating data from four surveys on both various conspiracy beliefs and comparable accurate ones with similar content to act as controls. For conspiracy beliefs stating that undocumented immigrants decided the popular vote in the 2016 presidential election in the United States, or that there is a cover-up of the link between MMR and autism, the controls included accurate beliefs that, for example, some undocumented immigrants obtain other people's credentials to gain employment in the United States, and that the link between tobacco use and cancer was once covered up.

(5) Presenting Big Data social media analyses on the spread of conspiratorial and anxiety-inducing contents.

(6)   Formulating theoretical principles that allow readers to parse the
      material and theoretical assumptions.

1.1   Context of This Work

Past studies of conspiracy theories have often involved college students.
WEIRD (white, educated, industrialized, rich, and democratic) is an
appropriate acronym when it comes to characterizing a sizable body of
the conspiracy literature as indexed by PsycInfo and summarized by the
scoping review in the Online Supplement. Of the first 50 entries summarized in the Online Supplement, 28 percent included at least one sample of
college students. Thirty-two percent of those entries included a specialized
sample of, for example, patients or members of a given ethnic group,
8 percent participants from Mechanical Turk, 8 percent a convenience
sample, and 8 percent respondents from a sample intended to represent a
particular nation. All in all, from the review in the Online Supplement,
only 16 of the 287 studies included nationally representative samples, and
none of them had the same goals as our book. By contrast, we collected an
initial study on Mechanical Turk followed by online samples of the adult
American population that are nationally representative. We also included a
national probability-based sample surveyed by phone.

Our research contributes to the interdisciplinary literature on
conspiracy theories by testing our hypotheses with large, general population studies while also advancing the methodology used to reach
conclusions about our hypotheses. Our work makes two assumptions.
First, reaching conclusions about conspiracy beliefs requires distinguishing a dynamic that operates for conspiracy beliefs in contrast to verifiable
beliefs of similar content. Second, reaching conclusions about conspiracy
beliefs requires a diversity of topics to maximize the generalizability of
the research.

We developed our measures of beliefs and pretested them over several
surveys, leading to the ones we report in the book. In addition, we
included established measures of anxiety, media use, need for closure,
need for cognition, need to belong, political knowledge, political ideology,
and trust in government (see Appendix). We also measured recent financial loss, employment, income, and education, and included a battery of
demographic questions (see Appendix).

Cross-Sectional Studies 1–3: We conducted three original cross-
sectional surveys reported in this book. Study 1 was conducted with a
convenience online panel (i.e., Mechanical Turk) and served to validate

measures and obtain preliminary data. Studies 2 and 3 included nationally representative samples drawn from Dynata online panels.

The research process began with our interdisciplinary team identifying a set of conspiracy theories centered around political and health issues:

(1) Barack Obama was not born in the United States; he faked his birth certificate to become president.
(2) Undocumented immigrants voting illegally in 2016 prevented the Trump–Pence ticket from winning the popular vote.
(3) The US government created the HIV epidemic by experimentally injecting the virus in people of African descent.
(4) The MMR vaccine causes autism, but this has been covered up by the US government.

The theories in the study were selected to represent different views and domains. In addition, the cross-sectional surveys measured accurate control events within similar political or health domains. For example, the HIV conspiracy theory was paired with the belief that the Tuskegee experiment was veridical. Matched controls are useful to distinguish the dynamic of misconceptions from the dynamic of correct understanding of events.[2]

Longitudinal Panel: In addition to the cross-sectional surveys, we conducted a panel survey with a probability sample of 1,000 US adults. We concentrated on Americans' beliefs in the notion that the "deep state," an alleged secret network of unelected government officials and intelligence officers, was conspiring against President Donald Trump. This study allowed us to further test our model with a conspiracy theory that biased interpretations of the political events unfolding at the time, including the impeachment trial of President Trump. The first wave of the survey was conducted in November 2019, the second in December 2019, and the third in February 2020. The surveys measured belief in the deep state theory, anxiety, and media use, along with demographics.

Experiment: We also conducted an experiment manipulating anxiety elicited by unrelated events to determine if manipulated fear induced greater agreement with conspiracy beliefs. This experiment was conducted with a nationally representative sample from Dynata and supplemented

---

[2] When past research has used controls (e.g., Swami et al., 2010), they are typically used to show that conspiratorial tendencies lead to beliefs in conspiracies that do not exist and thus that participants could not have heard. In our case, the control beliefs are important to assess for differences in the processes leading to conspiracy beliefs and similar but accurate beliefs.

the correlational evidence with data that are best poised to address causality. The belief in question was the alleged involvement of 5G technology in creating the novel coronavirus pandemic.

Social Media Study: To examine the social media networks associated with conspiracy theories studied in the surveys, we first used Twitter's Full Archive API to identify messages that were in English and originated in the United States. The social media study included the five conspiracy theories investigated in the surveys in addition to the following theories:

(1) Lizard aliens hybridized with humans now occupy positions of power.
(2) The earth is flat, but an elaborate deception explains the popular belief that it is not.
(3) "Chem" trails, which denote condensation ("con") trails from airplanes, are evidence of large-scale spraying with pesticides to control the population and modify the environment.
(4) Agenda 21, a United Nations plan to control population growth, is, in effect, in violation of American sovereignty.

Tweets were selected on the basis of hashtags and keywords representing a particular conspiracy theory. For example, posts about Obama's birth certificate were obtained using #fakebirthcertificate, "obamafakebirthcertificate," #obamafakebirthcertificate, "fakeobama," #fakeobama. As a control set of tweets, we also obtained posts countering this conspiracy theory using "#birther." The same was done for the deep state conspiracy theory, which had both conspiracy tweets and control ones. Next, we recorded the account handles that authored each tweet (e.g., @CNN). With that in hand, we were able to determine whether the tweet came from a conservative media account handle, a liberal media account handle, or a mainstream media account handle. Finally, we analyzed the fear sentiments within the tweets, recorded the number of retweets, and, in some cases, compared the conspiratorial tweets with the non-conspiratorial ones.

1.2 International Contexts

These issues may be important outside the United States, too, because beliefs in conspiracy theories continue to spread all over the world in the twenty-first century (Bruder, Haffke, Neave, Nouripanah, & Imhoff, 2013). Recent conspiracy theories have revolved around the 9/11 attacks, the death of Princess Diana, Osama bin Laden, and the scientific evidence of climate change (Bruder et al., 2013). According to Räikkä (2009), such political conspiracy theories can be divided into global, local, and total conspiracy theories. A conspiracy theory is global when it aims at explaining international events or when the explanation it provides refers to international affairs. For instance, a conspiracy theory that explains John F. Kennedy's murder in reference to a Central Intelligence Agency (CIA) plot, with connections to the Mafia and Cuba, is a global conspiracy theory because even if it explains a local event, it does so by using international factors (Räikkä, 2009). A conspiracy theory is local when the events and alleged causes occur within a country (Räikkä, 2009). For example, the theory that the Democratic Party was involved in fraud during the 2020 election is local. A conspiracy theory is total when it aims at explaining the course of world history or global politics by referring to a conspiracy or a series of conspiracies that have widespread implications for humanity as a whole (Räikkä, 2009). Total conspiracy theories claim that past or present events are the results of actions by powerful groups such as the Illuminati or the Templars, or that lizard aliens who arrived in unidentified flying objects (UFOs) decades ago control human affairs.

Conspiracy theories are neither American nor new (Mancosu, Vassallo, & Vezzoni, 2017). In Ortmann and Heathershaw's (2012) terminology, some of the world's oldest conspiracy theories are "total" and were born outside the United States. One of the most notorious conspiracy theories of all time, the "Protocols of the Elders of Zion," was used to justify the Holocaust. It emerged in Russia and was most likely fabricated by an Okhrana officer using French sources trying to discredit the reform party by manipulating widespread anti-Semitic sentiments (Ortmann & Heathershaw, 2012). Or, as Karl Popper put it, the most influential nineteenth- and twentieth-century ideological narratives (Marxism and Nazism) were based on or incorporated a "conspiracy theory of society" (Mancosu et al., 2017, p. 328). Likewise, conspiracy theories are used today by populist leaders who want to mobilize latent anti-establishment biases and boost their own support (Castanho Silva, Vegetti, & Littvay, 2017).

Conspiracy theories are prevalent in many countries around the world and, in some cases, present mainstream views of political and social life (Mancosu et al., 2017). Transnational COVID-19 conspiracy theories included ones alleging that the pandemic was a hoax concocted for various potential ends and that philanthropist Bill Gates had implanted microchips in vaccines. In turn, every pandemic provides fertile ground for conspiracy theories, from the Black Death in 1348 to the H1N1 influenza outbreak in 2009 (Smallman, 2018) to the more recent COVID-19 pandemic (Detoc, Bruel, Frappe, Botelho-Nevers, & Gagneux-Brunon, 2020). In South Africa, the government's former embrace of HIV denialism as part of a conspiracy may have contributed to approximately 330,000 deaths, as people delayed or ignored preventive measures (Thresher-Andrews, 2013). Conspiracy theories are also prevalent among extremist groups from across the spectrum: religious, far-right and -left, eco, anarchic, and cult-based (Bartlett & Miller, 2010).

An important question is whether the model and research we present in this book apply to contexts outside the United States. We think the answer is yes. First, our review of research is systematic and includes more international research than it does research from the United States. The higher representation of international research is due to the fact that more research on conspiracy theories has been conducted in Europe, Australia, and Asia than in the United States. Second, even though the research we present was conducted with US inhabitants and US tweets, the theories that we studied include global and total theories in Räikkä's (2009) framework. The alleged cover-up of the effects of the MMR vaccine, the pernicious effects of 5G technology, and the alleged cover-up of the HIV virus being a CIA creation are all global. The theories about the Agenda 21 and Chemtrails conspiracies to control the world's population are also global. In Ortmann and Heathershaw's (2012) terminology, the theories about lizard people and flat earth are "total," and as such apply to many international contexts as well.

Granted, we worked with political theories that are unique to the United States. These involve Obama falsifying his birth certificate to become president, undocumented immigrants voting illegally, and the deep state undermining Donald Trump's candidacy and presidency. Of these, the deep state and QAnon notions have connections with lizard people (Winter, Kosner, & Wong, 2010). The ones that do not have connections with either global or total theories, such as the theory about Obama's birth certificate, are tied to racist and xenophobic attitudes that exist in virtually every country (see, for example, the case of "Brexit," Sloan, n.d.).

1.3   Brief Summary of Upcoming Chapters

Following this introduction and overview of our theoretical model in Chapter 2, Chapter 3 describes the consequences of conspiracy beliefs, including analyses of our own data on their effects on voting intentions, past vote, and policy support. Chapter 4 introduces our theoretical and empirical analyses of the role of anxiety in conspiracy beliefs, and its relation to the belief defense motivation (e.g., need for closure), belief accuracy motivation (e.g., need for cognition), and social integration motivation (e.g., need to belong) Chapter 5 reviews classic works on sociopolitical variables, including the notion of paranoid political style, as well as education and political knowledge, disenfranchised and minority populations. Chapter 6 discusses the relation between media and anxiety, Chapter 7 covers social influences (e.g., norms and close others) on conspiracy beliefs, and Chapter 8 focuses on media influences, both independently and in combination with anxiety. Chapter 9 presents criteria for the selection of conspiracy theories worthy of debunking, discusses the likely applicability of our conclusions in international contexts, and outlines a future research agenda. More details appear below.

Chapter 2. A Framework for Understanding How Conspiracy Beliefs are Created. We outline the overarching framework through a figure and principles that integrate important prior contributions and advance new ones. The second chapter also presents a qualitative analysis of a conspiracy theory, including its informational sources and a concrete illustration of the theoretical concepts undergirding the book.

Chapter 3. The Consequences of Conspiracy Beliefs. In this chapter, we argue that the beliefs on which we focus raise real-world concern because of their implications for behavior and important political considerations. Among other factors, we examine data on the associations between conspiracy theories and voting intentions, past vote, as well as policy support.

Chapter 4. Anxiety, Psychological Motivations, and Conspiracy Beliefs. We review the psychology of anxiety, and literatures that shed light on the belief defense motivation (e.g., need for closure), the belief accuracy motivation (e.g., need for cognition), and the social integration motivation. In particular, we examine anxiety, personality traits, and cognitive styles connected to these motives in prior literatures and through our own data, including the experiment.

Chapter 5. Sociopolitical Factors and Conspiracy Beliefs. We review classic works that are relevant to conspiracy beliefs and address political variables, including the notion of paranoid political style in American politics, as well as political ideology, political knowledge, cynicism, and the points of view of ethnic minorities. We also discuss our survey data.

Chapter 6. The Relation between Media and Anxiety. We begin our analysis of media effects by reviewing the American media landscape, considering how media use influences affective responses, including anxiety.

In so doing, this chapter provides a foundation for understanding the affective influences of the media, and how these outlets may contribute to conspiracy beliefs through indirect impacts on anxiety.

Chapter 7. The Influence of Norms and Social Networks on Conspiracy Beliefs. We report our analyses of associations between conspiracy beliefs and conspiracy norms and interactions with other people. We also review the literature on the social networks on which conspiracy beliefs spread, and discuss our own data on the dissemination of tweets authored by media account handles (e.g., @NBC and @CNN) and with varying levels of fear language.

Chapter 8. Influences of Media and Anxiety in a Psychological and Sociopolitical Context. We review our empirical evidence for the premises of our framework through path analyses of cross-sectional data and longitudinal analyses of the deep state belief over the 2019–2020 impeachment trial. We then present our results on the sources of subjective plausibility of conspiracy beliefs and the role of perceived unfalsifiability.

Chapter 9. Conclusions. We draw conclusions and present criteria for the selection of conspiracy theories worthy of debunking. Specifically, we argue for the need to balance accessibility of the beliefs in memory, the risks they pose for those who believe them and society at large, and their relative weight within a larger system of beliefs associated with risky behaviors. We also describe possible ways of debunking the various conspiracy beliefs on which the book has focused.

CHAPTER 2

A Framework for Understanding How Conspiracy Beliefs Are Created

Actual conspiracies do, in fact, exist, some involving the "cover up" of secret activities by perpetrators and accomplices. For example, Richard Nixon conspired with his aides to obscure his complicity in Watergate (Sapphire & Gardner, 2005; Schudson, 1993). But there are also patently false narratives about conspiracies that undermine our health (Bogart et al., 2016; Nyhan, Reifler, Richey, & Freed, 2014) and our democracy (Einstein & Glick, 2015; Invernizzi & Mohamed, 2020). A case in point is the false notion that, over several administrations, the federal government conspired with the pharmaceutical companies to gull Americans into purchasing dangerous vaccines against MMR (Eggertson, 2010) or against the SARS-CoV-2 virus (Mooney, 2020).

This chapter introduces the notions of conspiracy theory and their belief counterparts. It then describes our theoretical model and a concrete example of how a conspiracy theory is born and how it can spread. In doing so, we consider political and psychological definitions of conspiracy theories and beliefs, and describe the principles tested in this book.

2.1 Definitions

The book concerns conspiracy theories, which constitute a type of misinformation. Like other literatures connected to psychology (Douglas et al., 2019), the focus of our book is also on *conspiracy beliefs*. We define conspiracy *belief* as "a judgment of the probability that an actor or a group of actors (e.g., government, corporations, and other organizations) is secretly working to produce an unlawful or harmful outcome for others in society." However, before dissecting this definition and the decisions that led to our adoption of it, a brief review of the notion of conspiracy theory in past literatures is in order.

2.1.1   Conspiracy Theories as Totalitarian and Pathological

At times, conspiracy theories have been viewed as totalitarian and pathological. In the 1940s, Karl R. Popper (2012) cast them as an artifact of
totalitarian regimes to control society. In his words, "whatever happens in
society – including things which people as a rule dislike, such as war,
poverty, shortages – are the results of direct design by some powerful
individuals or groups." Conspiracy theories are "the typical result of the
secularization of religious superstitions" in which "the place of the gods on
Homer's Olympus is now taken by the Learned Elders of Zion, or the
monopolists, or the capitalists, or the imperialists" (Popper, 1949).

The pathological connotation was added by Hofstadter's classic
1964 formulation in "The Paranoid Style in American Politics"
(Hofstadter, 1964, 2008). In this work, conspiracy beliefs again presuppose a "vast, insidious, preternaturally effective international conspiratorial
network designed to perpetrate acts of most fiendish character"
(Hofstadter, 1964). Hofstadter borrowed "paranoid style" from clinical
psychology to characterize the fear of communism and the right wing
during the McCarthy era of the early 1950s in the United States. His
choice of "paranoid style" was justified "because no other word adequately
evokes the sense of heated exaggeration, suspiciousness, and conspiracist
fantasy that I have in mind" (Hofstadter, 1964, p. 1).

According to this view, conspiracy theories can be a means of sustaining
established power. They accomplish this end by focusing attention on
supposed powerful, secret malevolent forces that threaten the wellbeing of
those within the established power structure who are portrayed as attempting to keep the believer safe. The deep state conspiracy theory espoused by
Donald J. Trump represents an example of use of a conspiracy theory by a
person who is in power (for the notion of deception in conspiracy theories,
see Basham, 2003, 2006).

2.1.2   Conspiracy Theories as a Device to Monitor and Control
the Political Order

Although conspiracy theories were initially seen as an instrument of
totalitarianism, in more recent decades, they have been conceptualized as
instruments to challenge the established political order. DeHaven-Smith
and Witt (2013) defined conspiracy theories as those that involve "an
allegation that an event affecting national political priorities was the result
of a secret plot by political insiders who have used their power and

influence to keep their intrigues hidden." Taking issue with Popper's (2006) portrayal of conspiracy theories as anti-democratic, they (2013) view conspiracy theories as an instrument to counter state crimes against democracy (SCAD), which refer to concerted actions or inactions by government insiders intended to manipulate democratic processes and undermine popular sovereignty. Among the questions these authors ask is: How can a nation wary of power, and structured around the division of powers and proper checks and balances, dismiss all conspiratorial suspicions? To them, conspiracy theories can enhance democracy by shining a light on unlawful manipulations of the democratic process.

For Mark Fenster (2008, p.1), who defined conspiracy theory as "the conviction that a secret, omnipotent individual or group controls the political and social order or some part thereof," conspiracy theories are "cultural practices and signifying systems through which the social and political order is communicated, reproduced, experienced, and explored." Similar to Fenster (2008), Timothy Melley (Melley, 2000) traced the expression of conspiracy theories in postwar American culture, and proposed that conspiracy theories can be democratic and even necessary. According to him, conspiracy theories grow as a result of the fear that individuals can be controlled by powerful external forces. As such, they offer a master narrative capable of explaining numerous complex unfortunate events outside of the control of the individuals. People thus rely on these theories to explain their loss of autonomy and to understand and resist control by mass-communication systems, bureaucracies, and regulatory discourses (Melley, 2000).

Another way of characterizing this democratic function of conspiracy theories is as a form of counter discourse (M. Gray, 2010) that challenges dominant understandings of social power and political legitimacy (Sapountzis & Condor, 2013). From a similar perspective, Uscinski and Parent (2014) define conspiracy theory as the notion that "a secret arrangement between a small group of actors to usurp political or economic power, violate established rights, hoard vital secrets, or unlawfully alter government institutions" (p. 31). According to them, by highlighting the potential for actual conspiracies, conspiracy theories increase citizen vigilance and hence play an important role in democratic societies.

2.1.3 *Conspiracy Beliefs*

All definitions agree that conspiracy theories entail the conspirators: a group of actors that is a faction in society at large, who conduct secret work with unlawful or harmful outcomes. The group of actors can be part of government, corporations, or other organizations and is relatively smaller than the society as a whole. Different disciplines, however, have highlighted two distinct aspects of conspiracy theories.

The political science literature has addressed conspiracy theories as social devices used to negotiate power. Some of the literature generated by law scholars and political social psychologists has also addressed the functions of conspiracy theories but with a focus on their utility to the regular citizens who end up believing in them. For example, Sunstein and Vermuele (2009, p. 205) define conspiracy theory as "an effort to explain some event or practice by reference to the machinations of powerful people, who attempt to conceal their role (at least until their aims are accomplished)." Similarly, Douglas and her colleagues cast "conspiracy theories" as "attempts to explain the ultimate causes of significant social and political events and circumstances with claims of secret plots by two or more powerful actors" (Douglas et al., 2019).

In contrast to the emphasis on how conspiracy theories are crafted in response to political power in political philosophy, the political psychology literature has concentrated on why people who do not create these theories come to believe in them. In this book, we explicitly distinguish "conspiracy theory" as the content of propositions within a body of knowledge from "conspiracy belief." "Conspiracy theory" is an epistemic entity, which according to Keith Harris (2018, p. 3), has the following defining features:

1. Posits an explanation for a target event or set of target events that is alternative to the official account of the event(s).
2. Claims that the event(s) was/were brought about by one or more conspirators.
3. Posits that the architects of the event(s) are involved in promoting the official account.
4. Has greater explanatory power than the official account

By comparison, "conspiracy belief" is the internalized equivalent of a conspiracy theory. We define "conspiracy belief" as "the subjective conviction that a small group of powerful actors is secretly working together to produce an unlawful and/or harmful outcome for others in society." This definition comports with ones in which an event or happening is thought to be the result of plotting by actors, often unlawfully and clandestinely, who have malign intent and a clear goal (Swami, Voracek, Stieger, Tran, & Furnham, 2014). It also dovetails well with Uscinski and Parent's (2014) definition of conspiracy belief as pertaining to "a secret arrangement between a small group of actors to usurp political or economic power, violate established rights, hoard vital secrets, or unlawfully alter govern-ment institutions" (2014, p. 31).

Whereas a conspiracy theory exists as an object of knowledge in the cultural world, a conspiracy belief involves a mental representation (i.e., in permanent memory) and a judgment (i.e., in the present moment). A *belief* is defined as a judgment of the probability that an event is true or that a referent has certain features (Ajzen, Fishbein, Lohmann, & Albarracín, 2018; D. Albarracin, 2021; Fishbein & Ajzen, 1975; R. S. Wyer & Albarracín, 2005). Thus, a conspiracy belief describes the weaker or stronger internalization of a conspiracy theory by a person and is specific to an event or a set of events. In this sense, we are not interested in a general disposition to believe any conspiracy, which is the focus of research on a "generic conspiracist belief" (Brotherton, French, & Pickering, 2013), a "conspiracy mentality" (Franks, Bangerter, & Bauer, 2013; Stojanov & Halberstadt, 2019), or "conspiracy ideation" (Barron et al., 2018), all of which generalize across ideas and are thus trait-like. Variability in different theories suggests (e.g., Jamieson & Albarracín, 2020) that even though a person may endorse multiple conspiracy beliefs, many will only endorse one favorite theory. For example, people who espouse conspiracy beliefs about the MMR vaccine typically do not hold the belief that the Earth is flat.

Like any other body of knowledge, conspiracy theories can be studied through manifestos and other cultural expressions. In this chapter, for example, we present a qualitative study of sources that gave birth to a conspiracy theory. In addition, we measured conspiracy theories on social media by tracking hashtags and keywords (e.g., #fakebirthcertificate, #obamafakebirthcertificate, #obamafakebirthcertificate, fakeobama, and #fakeobama) that have come to represent a specific theory and exist beyond individuals. These results can also show how the theories spread (see Chapter 6) but say very little about subjective *belief* in the theories. Thus, our surveys and experiment directly measured these beliefs.

Conspiracy beliefs can be studied by analyzing the discourse of believers. In addition, however, conspiracy beliefs can be studied with psychological scales to measure beliefs as reported by people. Thus, over a series of surveys and one experiment, conspiracy beliefs were measured by present-ing participants with a proposition such as, "Undocumented immigrants voting illegally prevented Republicans from winning the popular vote during the 2016 Presidential Elections," and asking them to rate the degree to which this proposition is "definitely false," "probably false," "neither true nor false," "probably true," and "definitely true."

By definition, the secret operation depicted in a conspiracy theory makes it impossible to disprove it. This element of conspiracy theories has a subjective, conspiracy belief counterpart, which is *perceived unfalsifiability*. Thus, we also developed measures of perceived unfalsifiability. Specifically, we assessed the degree to which people believe that the evidence that could confirm the theory has been covered up or distorted, and the degree to which sources challenging or contravening the supposed conspiracy are considered untrustworthy. For example, participants were asked to report the degree to which they felt that "No evidence can conclusively demonstrate if Obama was born in the United States or not," and "There are no reliable sources to determine if Obama was born in the United States or not." As a result, we could examine whether the belief in the conspiracy theory that Obama faked his birth certificate to become president correlates with the belief that the proposition is unfalsifiable. Whereas a verifiable epistemology (e.g., science) would result in weaker beliefs when a proposition is unverifiable, the conspiratorial epistemology changes this dynamic and sustains or bolsters beliefs in the absence of proof and even in the presence of evidence to the contrary.

2.1.4 Studying Demonstrably False Conspiracy Beliefs

Although we recognize that conspiracy beliefs may turn out to be correct, we were interested in studying beliefs that are not tenable given current evidence. Beliefs that are factually incorrect and yet upheld with certainty are ideal to study beliefs that are unfalsifiable. These incorrect but seemingly certain beliefs exist within the closed knowledge system of a social group and epitomize misinformation transmitted through social communication.

Our distinction is akin to "real" and "imagined" conspiracies and is important if we are ever to try to debunk them (Jarche, 2020). Thus, even though we recognize that the absence of proof of a relation cannot logically prove that a conspiracy does not exist (Popper, 2005), there is currently no credible evidence that the MMR vaccine causes autism, that widespread illegal voting by undocumented immigrants cost Donald Trump the popular vote in 2016, that the CIA created the HIV virus, or that Obama was born outside the United States. However, there is evidence about genetic predispositions to autism, that the 2016 election had no widespread voting by undocumented immigrants, and that the two HIV viruses originated in African primates (Sharp & Hahn, 2011). There is also a birth certificate for Barack H. Obama on file in governmental offices in

Hawaii as well as a birth announcement in a Honolulu newspaper, and satellite evidence that the Earth is spherical, or, more exactly, an oblate ellipsoid. Drawing on these understandings, in the remaining chapters, we will treat the conspiracy beliefs on which we focus as unwarranted and the statements that we use as controls as warranted or "accurate."

Despite our focus on conspiracy beliefs that are false, we do not typecast conspiracy beliefs as irrational. For example, we agree with Sunstein and Vermuele's (2009) point that acceptance of false conspiracy theories "may not be irrational or unjustified from the standpoint of those who adhere to them within epistemologically isolated groups or networks, although they are unjustified relative to the information available in the wider society, especially if it is an open one" (Sunstein & Vermeule, 2009). However, for those in the wider society who are open to scientific evidence, the conviction that the Earth is flat should collapse in the face of vast amounts of evidence that our planet is in fact spherical. The belief that the MMR vaccine causes autism is also resistant to correction, thus providing an interesting case to study social influences from other believers or the media.

Our interest in beliefs not supported by the preponderance of evidence does not mean that we consider all conspiracy theories as false. What is known as "The Iran-Contra Affair" was initially an unproven conspiracy theory (Räikkä, 2009). Over time, however, the evidence showed that the United States government had indeed secretly sold weapons to the Khomeini government of Iran with the goal of funding the right-wing Contra Nicaraguan guerrillas in violation of the Boland Amendment, which prohibited any further assistance to the Contras with the purpose of overthrowing the Nicaraguan government. More recently, the notion that Russia had hacked Democratic servers and insinuated troll content into American social media in the 2016 election to undercut the candidacy of Democratic Party presidential nominee Hillary Clinton may have initially been an unsubstantiated claim, but evidence uncovered by the Mueller investigation showed that it did indeed take place (Jamieson, 2018). Thus, unproven conspiracy theories are sometimes subsequently convincingly supported.

In sum, the conspiracy theories on which we focus are either unproven (and largely unprovable) or face preponderant evidence against them. Although we know that the Centers for Disease Control and Prevention (CDC) did not exaggerate the COVID-19 spread or death count, we do not know whether a group within the government or CDC worked to undermine the presidency of Donald J. Trump. We do know that the available evidence confirms that Barack Obama was born in Hawaii. We also know that there is no credible evidence that the MMR vaccine causes autism, and hence that the CDC is unlikely to be covering up evidence that it actually does. Finally, as multiple manual recounts have confirmed, there is no reason to believe that the 2020 presidential election was stolen from Donald J. Trump by software that flipped millions of votes for him and awarded them instead to Joe Biden.

Although we recognize that some conspiracy theories can turn out to be true, and that they play an important cultural role of surveillance of government activities, our book is not geared toward adjudicating their accuracy but rather toward identifying how conspiracy beliefs are formed, with anxiety as well as social and media influences at the center of our analysis. For that reason, our empirical analyses concentrate on beliefs that are unwarranted by available evidence and compare them with psychological and political processes that apply to accurate beliefs. For example, there is no historical question that Barack H. Obama was born in Hawaii, which is a state in the United States. Thus, the notion that someone faked his birth certificate to make it possible for him to be eligible to become president of the United States is a false conspiracy belief. By contrast, the belief that Barack H. Obama's foreign policy facilitated a crisis in Syria has evidence to deem this claim as correct. For this reason, Obama's inaction in Syria was used as a comparison belief that allowed us to determine what is unique to the mechanisms of conspiracy beliefs.

2.2   Our Theoretical Framework

This book advances a model of how conspiracy theories gain traction and tests it through surveys of United States inhabitants, an experiment, and a Big Data study of social media. We depart from the personality literature (Cichocka, Marchlewska, & Golec de Zavala, 2016; Goreis & Voracek, 2019; Green & Douglas, 2018). This literature focuses on fixed traits, often connected to evolutionary pressures of the ancestral human environment (van Prooijen & van Vugt, 2018), which are proposed to influence conspiracy beliefs and other similarly irrational beliefs (i.e., beliefs in the paranormal) (c.f. Darwin et al., 2011). We also depart from the political science literature that has focused on public support for the theories (Oliver & Wood, 2014), analyzed conspiracy theories as attempts at derailing democratic processes and accumulating power, or viewed them as the "byproduct of political extremism" (Popper, 2006; Sapountzis & Condor, 2013).

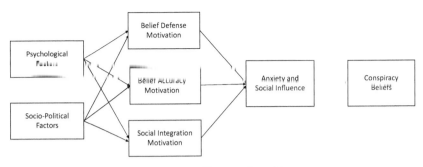

Figure 2.1. Theoretical model

In our perspective, however, understanding conspiracy beliefs requires understanding how deep psychological motivations and political factors combine to create specific beliefs promoted by social groups, whether a person's immediate network, social media networks, or the media. Understanding conspiracy beliefs also requires gauging how an audience's anxiety can make social norms or media messages appear more credible as an explanation of the fear, thus understanding the role of anxiety beyond correlations between conspiracy beliefs and negative emotions (c.f. Tomljenovic, Bubic, & Erceg, 2020). We also ask: Do norms, social networks, and the media contribute to conspiracy beliefs? How does an audience's anxiety amplify the impact of media messages on conspiracy beliefs, an issue not addressed in past research on conspiracy beliefs (cf. Douglas et al., 2017)? When do beliefs appear most plausible, and what makes conspiracy beliefs unfalsifiable?

2.2.1 Theoretical Principles

The model we advance in this book appears in Figure 2.1. Although it integrates past research on conspiracy theories and assumptions shared by many researchers (Stephan Lewandowsky, Gignac, & Oberauer, 2015; Swami, Chamorro-Premuzic, & Furnham, 2010; Uscinski & Parent, 2014; van Harreveld, Rutjens, Schneider, Nohlen, & Keskinis, 2014; van Prooijen, Douglas, & De Inocencio, 2018; van Prooijen & Jostmann, 2013), it advances the field by explaining the proximal mechanisms of conspiracy beliefs. The model presents basic human motivations of belief defense, belief accuracy, and social integration as distal factors that predispose a person to endorsing conspiracy beliefs. We define the belief defense motivation as the set of needs and goals to preserve one's self-views and a coherent sense of the self and the world. We define the belief accuracy motivation as relatively stable needs and goals that encourage individuals to form a realistic representation of the world. We define the social integration motivation as comprising needs and goals of social connection, trust, and status.

When the needs for belief defense, belief accuracy, and social integration are not met, we maintain that the natural response is anxiety, which acts as a more immediate determinant of conspiracy beliefs. However, as will be discussed presently, anxiety alone is not sufficient to create conspiracy beliefs. Instead, if these beliefs are to be socially shared, communications that characterize a conspiracy are necessary. The principles below which guide this book synthesize these processes. Following these principles, we present a qualitative analysis of a conspiracy theory that emerged during the 2016 election. The theory alleged that Comet Ping Pong, a pizza parlor in Washington, DC, was used by Democratic candidates to perpetrate abuse of children exchanged as part of a sex ring (Lipton, 2016).

2.2.2 Principle of Anxiety

As mentioned before, one premise of our model is that anxiety, either due to chronic psychological or sociopolitical factors, or induced by communications, constitutes an important basis for conspiracy beliefs. People who experience a mood often have difficulty pinpointing a source and thus attribute these feelings to objects or events that appear as reasonable sources for their feelings (D. Albarracin, 2021; Albarracín & Kumkale, 2003a; Schwarz & Clore, 1983, 2007). For example, people often feel happy when the weather is sunny. When asked to evaluate how satisfied they are with their lives, they report being more satisfied when the weather is sunny than when it is cloudy (Schwarz & Clore, 1983). The psychological mechanism underlying this effect is that people have a diffuse positive feeling, and being asked about their life satisfaction leads to their belief that they must feel happy *because* they are satisfied with their lives (D. Albarracin, 2021; Albarracín & Kumkale, 2003a; Schwarz & Clore, 1983, 2007). In the case of anxiety and conspiracy beliefs, one can propose the same mechanism. People who experience anxiety and hear about a conspiracy may believe that the conspiracy made them fearful, particularly because the anxiety is diffuse and difficult to localize. Therefore, because they have engaged in an attributional process that itself creates the belief, they conclude that the conspiracy is credible. In addition, people who experience anxiety may pay greater attention to conspiracy news and thus be more influenced by the news because the content is processed more extensively.

The first principle of our book is as follows:

> **Principle of Anxiety** Anxiety is a perception of threat and depends on relatively stable psychological motivations of belief defense, belief accuracy, and social integration, as well as sociopolitical factors and situational factors such as communications and media exposure. Experiencing anxiety at a particular time motivates a search for an explanation and can lead to misattributing the anxiety to a conspiracy story.

Past scholarship on the origins of conspiracy beliefs has invoked the need for closure, cognition, and social belonging as explanations. On the one hand, need for cognition, which we view as part of the belief accuracy motivation, reduces the tendency to believe in conspiracies (Freeman & Bentall, 2017; Garrett & Weeks, 2017; Georgiou, Delfabbro, & Balzan, 2019). On the other, the belief defense and social integration motivations (e.g., need for closure and need to belong) may increase this tendency. A first assumption is that a higher (vs. lower) need for closure makes people string random events into a conspiracy story (van Prooijen & Acker, 2015; van Prooijen & Jostmann, 2013; but see Fahlman et al., 2009). A second is that a higher (vs. lower) need for social integration turns disenfranchised people to conspiracy theories as an explanation for why they are marginalized (Mashuri & Zaduqisti, 2015; Uscinski & Parent, 2014; van Prooijen, 2016). Take, for example, the notion that a deep state threatens the freedoms and wellbeing of American citizens and their president. Although clearly unsettling, as Uscinski and Parent (2014) argue, this idea reassures believers of their social value and embeds them within a social group tightly allied against an external threat (Hetherington & Nelson, 2003; J. E. Mueller, 1970). These premises imply that these motivations can influence conspiracy beliefs but that this influence is mediated by anxiety, a point summarized in the principle of anxiety.

Socioeconomic conditions like a financial loss, political knowledge, political ideology, and cynicism of government have all been identified as factors affecting conspiracy beliefs (Barkun, 2013; deHaven-Smith, 2010; Swami, Barron, Weis, & Furnham, 2018; Uscinski & Parent, 2014; van Prooijen & Krouwel, 2015). In this book, we integrate this literature into our model by recognizing that sociopolitical factors are connected with the belief defense, belief accuracy, and social integration motivation. As shown in Figure 2.1, political ideology, income, or financial loss may also influence conspiracy beliefs through indirect effects on anxiety and exposure to specific social communications. This notion is also summarized in the principle of anxiety.

2.2.3 Principle of Social Influence

Anxiety is often not sufficient to create new beliefs, including new conspiracy beliefs. Either or both informal social influences from other people in a social network or more formal influences from media outlets are necessary to create thoughts of conspiracy. Spontaneous conversations with others, exposure to persuasive attempts within one's social network, and exposure to media can provide conspiracy-based stories that create conspiracy beliefs. Hence, the media are likely to play an important role in the inculcation of conspiracy beliefs (e.g., Dickinson, 2020; Gabbatt, 2020; Stelter, 2020). This idea appears in the principle of social influence, which is as follows:

> **Principle of Social Influence.** Social influence (e.g., other people within a person's social network as well as the media) provides the content or stories of conspiracy beliefs. Exposure to these influence sources may also stem from relatively stable psychological motivations of belief defense, belief accuracy, and social integration, as well as sociopolitical factors and situational factors.

As described, this principle further recognizes that exposure to different types of communications is also likely to depend on more or less stable psychological and sociopolitical factors. For example, need for cognition and political ideology are likely to affect media choices.

2.2.4 Principle of Synergy

An interesting possibility is that the influences of anxiety and social influence could be synergistic. For example, conspiratorial messages containing fear language may be disseminated more widely than conspiratorial messages without such language. Furthermore, conspiracy contents broadcast in the media may find more fertile ground when audiences experience higher (versus lower) levels of anxiety and thus find the theories to be a plausible explanation for their feelings. This possibility leads to proposing the principle of synergy.

> **Principle of Synergy.** The social influence on conspiracy beliefs may be amplified by anxiety. That is, social communications that promote conspiracy theories may be even more influential when an audience experiences anxiety.

2.2.5 Principle of Perceived Plausibility and Perceived Unfalsifiability

The communications that create conspiracy beliefs require contents that confer stories of conspiracy with plausibility and unfalsifiability. The conspiracy narratives must establish plausibility by anchoring a claim in facts or commonly accepted assumptions that create a sense of reality. People may see a particular theory as plausible because they perceive it as historically, psychologically, or normatively similar to other beliefs and prior knowledge (D. Albarracín, 2021; Wyer & Albarracín, 2005).

As an illustration, consider how people make judgments of plausibility based on historical precedent. For example, the existence of secrecy in some domains of government (e.g., intelligence) is an anchor for conspiracy beliefs and a reason for their proliferation (Stempel, Hargrove, & Stempel, 2007). As another example, the Tuskegee experiment failed to treat African Americans infected with syphilis as part of a study of the natural course of the disease (Daugherty-Brownrigg, 2013; Jaiswal, Singer, Siegel, & Lekas, 2018; Mays, Coles, & Cochran, 2012). How far-fetched is it, then, to believe that the American government created HIV to eliminate racial and sexual minority groups? Or that the CDC is covering up evidence that the MMR vaccine is a cause of autism in Black children?

Plausibility beliefs are also based on psychological and normative similarity. Stories may also seem plausible when the perceiver can imagine why people would act the way they do in a story (for theory of mind, see Higham et al., 2016; Tomasello et al., 2005). They may also seem plausible when people close to the perceiver find the stories to be credible (for other considerations about norms, see Albarracin, 2021; Cialdini & Goldstein, 2004; Fishbein & Ajzen, 2011). If others within our group believe that people in power have ill intentions, we are more prone to consider conspiracies as well.

Finally, as mentioned earlier, we typically come to believe in phenomena that make sense and that can be falsified, as is the case in scientific reasoning and general forms of learning. However, we are all exposed to magical thinking and learn that appearances are frequently deceptive. From this standpoint, we are all psychologically prepared to switch from falsifying to defending beliefs, and we all form some beliefs ungrounded in evidence (Albarracin & Vargas, 2010; Chaiken, 1980; Fiske & Taylor, 1991). This book analyzes the degree to which different forms of perceived plausibility correlate with conspiracy beliefs. This point is summarized in the principle of perceived plausibility and unfalsifiability.

Principle of perceived plausibility and unfalsifiability. Conspiracy beliefs become plausible through (a) historic similarity (i.e., the similarity between the story of conspiracy and historic precedent), (b) psychological similarity (i.e., the audience's ability to understand the motives of others), and (c) normative plausibility (i.e., the audience's knowledge that others hold these beliefs). However, the device that protects conspiracy beliefs from falsification is the proposition that evidence confirming the conspiracy has been covered up and that sources of disconfirming information are untrustworthy.

2.3   A Case Study of the Deep State Theory

A case study of a version of the deep state conspiracy theory in the United States, an important focus of the book, illustrates the role of anxiety and the media in disseminating a theory that outsiders might judge a fantasy. In the coming sections, we describe the theory's origins and explain how it might have responded to and reflected the anxieties of its adherents. We also outline some of the ways in which the theory's proponents constructed evidence to increase its plausibility and insulate it from rebuttal. This case also shows how conspiracy theories retain relevance and sustain audience involvement by mutating, in this case from alleged pedophilia ring at a pizza restaurant in Washington, DC, to incorporate the notion that President Donald J. Trump secretly battled this cabal and elicited deep state attacks in retribution. Even though the details of the case are specific to this theory, the case will help the reader visualize the likely social and historical context of beliefs we measure later in this book.

We begin by analyzing the words and actions of Edgar Maddison Welch, who believed and acted on the Pizzagate theory, and of Alex Jones, founder of the conservative media outlet InfoWars, who purveyed it. Fueled by exposure to the conspiracy theory on media sites such as Jones's *Infowars* and probably the financial insecurity of working-class individuals in 2016, Welch acted on the theory in a reckless fashion. Weapons at the ready, on December 4, 2016, he barged into a Washington, DC pizza place and live music venue named Comet Ping Pong to rescue the children that the theory alleged were being imprisoned and tortured in the restaurant's basement. The case also shows the theory's hold on Welch even in the face of direct evidence that the key premise of it – the existence of a basement – was false. It illustrates how the theory was presented to audiences and how it achieved acceptance.

This case study makes it possible for us to explore the interplay of anxiety, media exposure, beliefs, and behavior that occurred in an identifiable individual and to tie actual exposure to a conspiracy theory to a belief in it and that belief to action. Although this kind of evidence is not generalizable, it can link media exposure to belief in specific ways that the surveys and experiments reported in this book cannot. The theory in question, although clearly far-fetched, has some popularity among Americans. A December 2020 NPR/Ipsos poll (Ipsos, 2020) found that 17 percent of Americans accepted as true the statement that "A group of Satan-worshipping elites who run a child sex ring is trying to control our politics and media." Thirty seven percent reported being unsure.

2.3.1   The Backstory of the Pizzagate Conspiracy Theory, Welch, and Jones

Pizzagate began when 4chan denizens and Trump-supporting Reddit devotees mined a conspiracy theory from illegally acquired, Russian-hacked Democratic content in the closing weeks of the 2016 election. As emails stolen by Russian operatives from the account of Clinton campaign manager John Podesta were dropped week by week into public view by Wikileaks from October 7 until election day, "[s]ocial media users on a popular Reddit forum dedicated to Donald J. Trump and 4chan's far-right fringe message board searched the releases for evidence of wrongdoing" (Aisch, Jon, & Kang, 2016). The task was daunting. In the period between October 7 and Election Day 2016, WikiLeaks' Julian Assange released more than 20,000 pages of messages sent or received by Podesta (Stein, 2016). Unsurprisingly, among the emails were some discussing dining preferences or plans. In them, the cyber-sleuths divined ominous subtextual messages. For the 4channers, an aside about cheese pizza was a reference to "child pornography" (Tuters, Jokubauskaité, & Bach, 2016). The *New York Times* reports that pedophiles use "CP," coincidentally the initials of cheese pizza, to signal that aberration (Kang & Frenkel, 2020).

According to the code that the 4chan and Reddit groups used, high-ranking Democrats, including Podesta and New York Senator and 2016 Democratic Party presidential nominee Hillary Clinton, were operating a Satan-worshipping child-sex-trafficking and torture ring. The individuals deciphering the subtexts assumed that the child abusers disguised their activities by expressing them in benign shapes, symbols, and words that actually were analogizing types of foods to categories of children and forms of abuse. Hotdog, for example, meant "boy," "pizza" meant "girl," "cheese" meant "little girl," and "pasta" meant "little boy" (Collett, n.d.).

Filtered through this glossary, a WikiLeak'd April 11, 2015 exchange between Podesta and a friend was actually about feasting on tasty little boys.

> Hey John,
>
> We know you're a true master of cuisine and we have appreciated that for years ...
>
> But walnut sauce for the pasta? Mary, plz tell us the straight story, was the sauce actually very tasty?
>
> FROM: John Podesta
>
> It's an amazing Ligurian dish made with crushed walnuts made into a paste. So stop being so California.

It is not difficult to imagine how the suspicious 4channers, who already believed that the discussion was about little boys, would see references to "a true master," "straight story," "cuisine," "sauce," "dish," and "walnuts" as ominous as well.

The Podesta emails also mentioned "pizza," hence interpreted as "girls." One, for example, referenced a misplaced handkerchief that may have had "a map that seems pizza-related" (September 2, 2014 Podesta exchange). Separately, the WikiLeak's trove contained a September 9, 2008 query in which James Alefantis, the owner of Comet Ping Pong, invited Podesta to drop by an Obama fundraiser at his establishment. When a 4chan user amalgamated the pizza references to the invitation to that specific pizza place, the link between the supposed sex trafficking ring and Comet Ping Pong was forged.

Among the official sources that the adherents of the theory used to legitimize their inferences about the existence and meaning of Podesta's presumed code was a 2007 FBI document headlined "Symbols and Logos Used by Pedophiles to Identify Sexual Preferences" leaked by Wikileaks (Collett, n.d.; "Symbols and Logos Used by Pedophiles to Identify Sexual Preferences," 2016). With that single page in hand, the theory proponents concluded that Comet Ping Pong's promotional material, signage, and menu were brimming with cues signaling pedophilia. To their eyes, the crossed ping pong paddles on the restaurant's menu resembled the butterfly symbol designating child love (Tempey, 2016). The picture of a slice of pizza was code for a triangle meaning group sex.

Scouring Alefantis's Instagram account for evidence that top Democrats frequented the restaurant, the Pizzagate proponents located a photo of President Obama at a ping pong table. Noting that the environment shown in the photo was clearly in the White House, the *Washington Post* concluded that, contrary to the label the theory's proponents superimposed on it, the photo did not show "Obama at Comet Ping Pong." In a similar fashion, Alefantis's Instagram post of a walk-in freezer that he was considering leasing was construed as evidence of "a secret kill room" in the "basement" of Comet Ping Pong. The restaurant's actual freezer was stocked with food, and, as mentioned, the pizza place itself had no basement.

A first indication that internet imaginings can turn into real-world behavior followed in the form of threatening Instagram, Twitter, and Facebook messages sent to Alefantis and his employees. In the closing days of the 2016 election, Alefantis identified the cause. Exploring the Internet, he located Facebook pages such as one from *The Vigilant Citizen* proclaiming: "Pizzagate: How 4Chan Uncovered the Sick World of Washington's Occult Elite"(Kang, 2016).

2.3.2 Edgar Maddison Welch

Shortly thereafter, on December 4, 2016, Edgar Maddison Welch, a 29-year-old resident of Salisbury, North Carolina, armed with an AR-15 rifle and a 0.38 revolver, entered Comet Ping Pong to rescue children he thought were being imprisoned and tortured in its basement. Frustrated at his inability to open a locked door in the back of the pizza shop, he attempted to force it open "first using a butter knife and then discharging his assault rifle multiple times into the door" (United States Department of Justice, 2017). Court documents indicate that when he failed to locate a basement and "found no evidence that underage children were being harbored in the restaurant," Welch surrendered peacefully. As the police body camera footage of his arrest confirms (NBC News, 2019), he informed the arresting officers that he was there to investigate a pedophilia ring. Hearing that explanation, an officer who was apparently familiar with the conspiracy theory circulating online, responded, "Pizzagate." In a handwritten apology filed with the court, Welch claimed he had not intended to "harm or frighten innocent lives" and characterized his actions as foolish and reckless (Buchman, 2017). The court sentenced him to a four-year prison term.

2.3.3 The Media and Anxiety

The alternative reality of Pizzagate confronted palpable reality in a second way when Alefantis threatened Infowars' Alex Jones with legal action. The cause of action was straightforward. As the Comet Ping Pong owner's letter of complaint argued, Jones had urged his audience "to go out and investigate the 'Pizzagate' conspiracy theory, to come to my restaurant and investigate lies" (Fahri, 2017). Jones's focus on Pizzagate had been pronounced. Our internet search of Alex Jones and Pizzagate October 7, 2016–December 3, 2016 elicited 64,000 results. Faced with defending the Pizzagate conspiracy with the kind of evidence required in a court of law or facing litigation, Jones conceded that his advocacy of the Pizzagate theory was not based on evidence.

Jones's six-minute video apology was issued on the day in 2017 on which Welch pleaded guilty to the charges resulting from his actions in Comet Ping Pong ("Alex Jones apologizes for propagating pizzagate conspiracy theory," n.d.; Shelbourne, 2017). The recantation cast his purveying of the conspiracy theory as an act of relaying information from others. He claimed to be simply commenting on others' accounts, relying on third-party reports and on the work of others, some now separated from his employ. His statement contended that "neither Mr. Alefantis, nor his restaurant Comet Ping Pong, were involved in any human trafficking as was part of the theories about Pizzagate that were being written about in many media outlets and which we commented upon" (Doubek, 2017). "I made comments about Mr. Alefantis that in hindsight I regret, and for which I apologize to him," Jones noted. "We relied on third-party accounts of alleged activities at the restaurant. We also relied on accounts of [two] reporters who are no longer with us" (Fahri, 2017).

Another important factor to consider is the situation of deprivation many men like Welch perceived in 2016. As a warehouse worker, Welch was probably among the 78 percent of Trump supporters who perceived that their financial situation was worse than before (New York Times, n.d.). Anxiety derived from one's financial situation deteriorating is, as this book will show, a likely source of uncertainty and worry for men like Welch.

2.3.4   Why the Theory Could Have Been Plausible for Welch and Others

Every conspiracy belief has some tie to reality. The realities of Pizzagate are that children are vulnerable and child sex trafficking exists. "Children make up 27% of all human trafficking victims worldwide," (Save the Children, n.d.). Welch told the court he went to Comet Ping Pong "with the intent of helping people I believed were in dire need of assistance, and to bring an end to a corruption that I truly felt was harming innocent lives" (Hsu, 2017).

To lend plausibility to their evolving theory, Pizzagate proponents interwove conjecture and undisputed facts. In addition to the existence of child sex abuse, those facts included that: President Bill Clinton was impeached for lying about his relationship with Monica Lewinsky, a White House intern in her early twenties; Jeffrey Epstein was convicted in 2008 of procuring a child for prostitution and in 2019 was arrested for sex trafficking of minors; and Bill Clinton was a social acquaintance of Epstein's and took trips in his private jet. Unmentioned by the Pizzagate followers was the sundered but once-friendly relationship between Trump and his Palm Beach neighbor and one-time partygoing pal, Epstein (Bohrer, 2019). The fabulations included the claim that the Clintons had murdered those able to frustrate their political ambitions, (Jamieson, 2018) and intimations about Hillary Clinton's sexuality, complete with manufactured images on the web of her as a dominatrix or demon (Jamieson & Dunn, 2008) and a Conservative Action Network ad insinuating in foreboding tones that she is a lesbian.

The first-generation Pizzagate conspiracy theory that prompted Welch's sojourn to Comet Ping Pong was scaffolded on one known as "Orgy Island" that was already circulating on 4chan. It "alleged the Clintons flew to a secret island for sex tourism aboard a private jet called 'Lolita Express' owned by Jeffrey Epstein, an American financier who had served 13 months in prison for soliciting an underage prostitute" (Tuters et al., 2016). In the same vein, Epstein's 2019 arrest for sex trafficking of minors is used in a YouTube film titled "Out of the Shadows" to create a "See I told you so" argument saying that the jailing of Epstein proved that Pizzagate is real.

2.3.5   *Factors that Insulate the Pizzagate Theory from Falsification*

Among the factors that protect conspiracy theories from efforts to correct them are (a) believers who distrust in the sources of knowledge likely to debunk them, (b) a network of like-minded others focused on contorting disconfirming evidence into confirmation of the theory, and (c) adherents who are enveloped in media that reinforce the theory.

Distrust of those likely to debunk the theory. Consistent with scholarship showing that conspiracy beliefs are "extremely resistant to correction" (Sunstein & Vermeule, 2009), Welch's eyewitness evidence that there was neither a basement at the site nor children at risk did not disabuse him of his belief in Pizzagate. When asked by a reporter, "What did he think when he discovered there were no children at the pizzeria?"

Welch responded, "The intel on this wasn't 100 percent." However, added the reporter, "he refused to dismiss outright the claims in the online articles, conceding only that there were no children 'inside that dwelling.'" In short, for Welch, the conspiracy theory was not undercut by direct evidence that a key claim about it was false.

Other believers were not dissuaded either. Instead, they asserted that media coverage of Welch's activities suggested that reporters were covering up the crimes perpetrated at the pizza place. Rationalizations that discredited Welch emerged as well. Drawing on a past resume of Welch's that listed some acting experience, some conspiracy believers surmised that he was a "crisis actor" involved in a false flag operation designed by the deep state to persuade the credulous that Comet Ping Pong was crime-free (Gillin, 2016).

Disconfirmation becomes confirmation of the extent of the conspiracy and guile of the conspirators. As these examples illustrate, "every debunking . . . has only convinced its believers that they must be right, and that the circle of pedophiles and sympathizers trying to cover up their findings must be even bigger and more powerful than they imagined" (Ohiheiser, 2016). Neither Welch's imprisonment nor the recantation of Alex Jones succeeded in interring the Pizzagate theory. Instead, a group of Pizzagate diehards responded to Jones's apology by protesting in Lafayette Park across from the White House with signs saying, "We demand a criminal investigation now!" and "Fake news? Decide for yourself" ("Alex Jones apologizes for propagating pizzagate conspiracy theory," n.d.). In a similar vein, a small January 2019 fire at Comet Ping Pong (Romero, 2019) elicited a post on the public Facebook group "PizzagateUncompromised" that read "To destroy evidence or vengeance? I hope the latter." "Burn baby burn that evil place of debauchery of children, torture and murder down," noted another user (Zadrozny, 2019).

Efforts to read signals of sex trafficking into the culinary preferences of Democrats persisted as well. In a September 2020 video on Instagram that since has been removed by the platform, believers argued that this light-hearted exchange between 2020 Democratic vice-presidential nominee Kamala Harris and former Democratic President Barack Obama confirmed that Democratic Party presidential nominee Joe Biden was also a pedophile (Ford, 2020):

HARRIS: So tell me about Joe and your relationship with Joe and what do I need to know? Like what's the thing about the ice cream? He loves ice cream. Tell me about that.

OBAMA: Ice cream is big. Pasta with red sauce. He can go deep on that
   (Campaign, 2020)

As the 4chan code breakers believe that ice cream is to "male prostitute" ("Hacker News," 2016) what pasta is to "little boy," for them the subtext is problematic.

Being enveloped in a media ecosystem that reinforces conspiracy beliefs. Welch's online activity reinforced beliefs that he fashioned into a mission that gave him a new identify "Standing up against a corrupt system that kidnaps, tortures and rapes babies and children in our own back yard" (Hsu, 2017). From the court record, we know that "Welch binge-watched YouTube videos about the alleged child-trafficking ring on December 1, setting a plan" (Hsu, 2017). Related sleuthing revealed that "the would-be shooter likes both InfoWars and its host Alex Jones" (Mak, 2016). In an interview with a *New York Times* reporter, Welch "said he did not believe in conspiracy theories, but then added that the September 11, 2001, attacks needed to be re-examined." The reporter learned as well that Welch "has listened to Alex Jones, whose radio show traffics in conspiracy theories and who once said that Mrs. Clinton 'has personally murdered and chopped up' children" (Goldman, 2016). Jones has actually alleged complicity of the United States government in the 9/11 attacks (Shelbourne, 2017).

The algorithmic structures of many online platforms draw those who enter a conspiracy site into deeper engagement with such content. For example, a February 2019 *NBC News* investigation revealed that Facebook users "who find their way into a Pizzagate interest group named after Hillary Clinton's campaign chairman, John Podesta – whose stolen emails are misread in a way to inform much of the Pizzagate conspiracy" are prompted by "a right rail labeled 'Suggested Groups' [which] includes the group 'Pizzagate Reports,' the header image for which is prominent Democrats including Hillary Clinton and Barack Obama and George Soros, photoshopped with glowing red eyes in what appears to be a Satanic ritual" (Zadrozny, n.d.).

This underlying referral structure of the online platforms increases exposure to other conspiracy theories. Those who happen upon the

> private group "Pizzagate," topped with an image that points to Comet's owner James Alefantis as the ringleader of a child sacrifice ring – are pushed to join other fringe groups including, "Real UFO Sightings & Strange Phenomenon," "Official Flat Earth & Globe Discussion," and "Q Angels," a group dedicated to an unfounded conspiracy theory involving

Donald Trump and a secret war against a cabal of alleged child abusers and
the Deep State (Zadrozny, n.d.)

Although, long before these algorithms were invented, scholars knew
that individuals holding one conspiracy belief are likely to believe in others
as well (Brotherton & Eser, 2015; Brotherton et al., 2013; Hofstadter,
1964; Rocklage et al., 2017), the underlying architecture of the platforms
now exacerbates that tendency.

Changing the settings of online platforms eliminates that spiral. In late
November 2016, the subreddit, r/Pizzagate "banned the pizza gate groups
from the platform" (Durden, 2016). Subsequently, Facebook, Instagram,
and Twitter banned Jones (Haselton, 2019; Schneider, 2018). Before
Facebook shut them down, Pizzagate had "over 30 different open and
closed Facebook groups, boasting more than 40,000 collective members"
(Zadrozny, n.d.).

An analysis of CrowdTangle data conducted by the *New York Times*
found 512,000 Pizzagate mentions, likes, and shares on Facebook and
93,000 on Instagram during the first week of December 2016, but under
20,000 from the beginning of 2017 through January 2020. However, "[i]n
the first week of June [2020], comments, likes and shares of PizzaGate . . .
spiked to more than 800,000 on Facebook and nearly 600,000 on
Instagram" (Kang & Frenkel, 2020).

2.4   Discussion

Despite the idiosyncrasies of Pizzagate, our case study vividly illustrates the
intense media engagement of an extreme supporter of a conspiracy theory
that unfolded in the United States around the time of the 2016 presidential
election. The model in Figure 2.1 starts with psychological and political
factors associated with the belief defense, belief accuracy, and social
integration motivation. These variables on the left side of our model have
been extensively studied in the literature and are also important in this
book. Furthermore, this book examines the more immediate determinants
of conspiracy beliefs and how the motives on the left exert their influence
via anxiety and social influence. Thus, we begin with consequences of
conspiracy, then go into the role of stable psychological and sociopolitical
factors, and then turn to social influences and the media.

CHAPTER 3

The Consequences of Conspiracy Beliefs

Conspiracy theories in the Trump era have assumed increased significance. The combination of lows in campaign rhetoric and the rise of fake news has led some to suggest that we are living in an age of "post-truth politics" (Rose, 2017). A search on Trump and conspiracy theories in Google Scholar since 2019 shows more than 8,000 hits. The prevalence of conspiracy theories in the phenomenon of Trump and Trumpism has been termed what Hofstadter (1964) called "American paranoid style" (Hellinger, 2018). During the COVID-19 pandemic, conspiracy theories fused health and political conspiracies more so than ever. For example, in May 2020, Eric Trump appeared on Fox News and pushed conspiratorial ideas suggesting that Democrats were secretly using the coronavirus crisis as an opportunity to expand mail-in voting and thereby steal elections from Republicans (Rupar, 2020).

Examples abound that the belief in conspiracy theories can have negative implications for important social issues, including health and prejudice against Asians, as well as political ones, including decreased trust in government and democratic attitudes. COVID-19 conspiracy theories likely led Trump's supporters to take COVID-19 less seriously than public health officials had hoped and to put millions of Americans at risk. According to a research report, one-quarter of Americans see some truth in the theory that alleges that powerful people intentionally planned the coronavirus outbreak (Schaeffer, 2020). During the pandemic, more than 2,000 rumors and conspiracy theories have been linked to thousands of hospitalizations (Rettner, 2020). From the idea that drinking bleach can kill the coronavirus to the theory that the virus was created in a lab as a bioweapon in China, to references to the "Chinese Virus," the COVID-19 pandemic has generated rumors and conspiracy theories with serious consequences (Jamieson & Albarracín, 2020; Rettner, 2020). Further, anti-COVID-19 vaccine attitudes and movements are challenging the effectiveness of the fight against the pandemic in 2021, putting the lives of millions around the world at risk (Arti & Gandhar 2021).

To be sure, conspiracy theories may allow citizens to question social hierarchies and thus encourage governments to be more transparent (Jolley & Douglas, 2014b). Some conspiracy theories do indeed reveal anomalies or inconsistencies in official accounts of political events. Such cases include the Watergate and Iran Contra affairs, which led to thorough official investigations with important benefits for democracy (DeHaven-Smith, 2013). Negative consequences of conspiracy theories are, however, more prevalent than positive ones.

The medical implications of potential conspiracy theories are many. Conspiracy believers are likely to have negative attitudes toward prevention behaviors that are advocated by experts. People who believe that the MMR vaccine causes autism and that the government hides this fact are less likely to vaccinate their children (Nyhan et al., 2014). After being exposed to information about the lack of evidence that the MMR vaccine causes autism and the dangers of illnesses like MMR, their intent to vaccinate a future child does not increase (Nyhan et al., 2014). Also, a belief in the claim that HIV was created in a laboratory with the sole purpose of eliminating African Americans can affect responsiveness both to prevention campaigns and HIV treatment (Bogart, Galvan, Wagner, & Klein, 2011; Bogart et al., 2016; Simmons & Parsons, 2005). By the same token, distrust of experts' recommendations such as social distancing, due to suspicions that the pandemic is a Democratic Party plot, can lead conspiracy believers to engage in risky behaviors (Biddlestone, Green, & Douglas, 2020). Finally, belief in conspiracy theories can increase distrust in medical authorities and decrease the extent to which people seek out medical attention (Oliver & Wood, 2014).

Belief in conspiracy theories can also be associated with less egalitarian human rights attitudes (Swami et al., 2014), more prejudice (Jolley, Meleady, & Douglas, 2020), more racism (Berkowitz, 2014; Pollard, 2016), and more discrimination (Kofta, Soral, & Bilewicz, 2020). Belief in conspiracy theories about Jewish domination of the world is associated with anti-Semitic attitudes and discrimination toward Jewish people (Kofta et al., 2020). Conspiracy theories can also have an deleterious impact on democracies. Exposure to conspiracy theories can undermine confidence in government (Einstein & Glick, 2015; Invernizzi & Mohamed, 2020), democracy and governability (Hernáiz & Antonio, 2008), and promote cynicism and dangerous extremist movements (Banas & Miller, 2013; Bartlett & Miller, 2010; McGregor, Hayes, & Prentice, 2015). Moreover, conspiracy theories disputing the validity of scientific claims about climate change decrease intentions to reduce one's carbon footprint (Douglas & Sutton, 2015). This chapter presents an overview of these consequences.

3.1   Medical Conspiracy Theories

Although it is common to dismiss adherents of conspiracy theories as delusional and paranoid cranks, medical conspiracy theories are widely circulated, broadly endorsed, and predictive of many common negative health behaviors (Oliver & Wood, 2014). Studies confirm that acceptance of conspiracy beliefs is associated with reduced intention to engage in behaviors that can contain the spread of COVID-19, including intent to vaccinate (Romer & Jamieson, 2020).

Dr. Anthony Fauci, director of the National Institute of Allergy and Infectious Diseases, is among those who have publicly denounced the anti-science sentiments and beliefs that vaccines are being used to hurt people (AJMC, 2020). The disbelief in vaccines tied to claims about the existence of a conspiracy to hide their dangerous effects has helped undermine the effectiveness of the fight against COVID-19. A study ($N = 2,259$) in France showing that only 78 percent of participants intended to get vaccinated when the COVID-19 vaccine become available, concluded that vaccination hesitancy would be a major barrier in COVID-19 vaccine uptake (Detoc et al., 2020). A study conducted in Australia showed that 86 percent of respondents intended to get vaccinated when the COVID-19 vaccine became available (Dodd, Cvejic, Bonner, Pickles, & McCaffery, 2020). Similarly, a study conducted in the United States found that 20 percent of respondents reported that they would decline the vaccine (Thunstrom, Ashworth, Finnoff, & Newbold, 2020). This study concluded that a vaccine would benefit public health by saving many lives but nevertheless may fail to achieve herd immunity (Thunstrom et al., 2020). In 2021, COVID-19 vaccination these predictions have acquired a new meaning (Arti & Gandhar 2021).

Pre-pandemic, vaccination rates in some regions around the world had declined, declines foreshadowing reduced receptivity to the combined MMR (Douglas & Sutton, 2018) and COVID-19 vaccines (Arti & Gandhar, 2021). Over the last decade, outbreaks of vaccine-preventable diseases have been reported in developed countries around the world (Siani, 2019). Measles outbreaks have been ongoing in the European Union since 2017, especially in Italy and Romania (Siani, 2019). Although the reemergence of measles outbreaks is a multifaceted phenomenon reinforced by a variety of factors, there is increasing proof indicating that the main reason for it is an accumulation of a large pool of measles-susceptible populations due to suboptimal uptake of the measles vaccine over the years.

The existing regional differences in access to healthcare in Italy, combined with feelings of skepticism and hostility towards the practice of vaccination, can result in the formation of pockets of at-risk populations as vaccine coverage drops significantly below the effective immunity threshold (Siani, 2019). One likely contributor to this problem was the 1998 publication in the *Lancet* of an article by Andrew Wakefield that linked MMR vaccination with autism (Douglas & Sutton, 2018). Although this research was discredited and retracted, conspiracy theories about the topic are still common (Douglas & Sutton, 2018). These include the idea that the pharmaceutical companies bribe researchers to fake pro-vaccination data (Jolley & Douglas, 2014a) and conceal evidence that their vaccines are ineffective and/or unsafe in order to preserve their outsized profits (Douglas & Sutton, 2018). Even though there may be other reasons for the plateauing of vaccination rates around the world, conspiracy theories likely play a role (Jolley & Douglas, 2014a).

Our research included a question on conspiracy beliefs related to the MMR vaccine in several surveys. These data appear in Table 3.1. Participants were asked to assess the truthfulness of the statement, "The MMR vaccine causes autism but this fact has been covered up," with possible answers being, "definitely false," "probably false," "neither true nor false," "probably true," and "definitely true." The percentage of participants who believed that this statement was probably or definitely false ranged from 51 to 63 percent, and the percent who believed that it was probably or definitely true ranged from 21 to 24 percent (see Table 3.1). The rest of the participants declared that they considered this statement neither true nor false. As these results show, the proportion of participants who believed that evidence that the MMR vaccine causes autism had been covered up was comparable to the proportions who believed that the United States government created the HIV epidemic, that Obama was not born in the United States, and that the illegally cast votes of undocumented immigrants cost Trump the popular vote in the 2016 election (see Table 3.1).

The effects of conspiracy theories on vaccination were examined in two noteworthy studies (Jolley & Douglas, 2014a). The first used a correlational design and asked participants to rate their agreement with a number of statements related to anti-vaccine conspiracy theories. Participants were asked to imagine that they faced the decision to vaccinate their children or not for a specific made-up disease, were given information about the disease and vaccine, and were asked to indicate their intention to have their child vaccinated. As predicted, regression analyses revealed that

Table 3.1. *Distribution of conspiracy beliefs among residents of the United States: Studies 1–4*

	MMR vaccine	HIV virus cover-up	Obama's birth certificate	Undocumented immigrants decided popular vote
	N (%)	N (%)	N (%)	N (%)
Study 1				
Definitely true	54 (7)	59 (8)	60 (8)	51 (7)
Probably true	116 (16)	92 (12)	89 (12)	121 (16)
Neither true nor false	114 (15)	101 (14)	91 (12)	117 (16)
Probably false	181 (25)	193 (26)	147 (20)	158 (21)
Definitely false	273 (37)	296 (40)	354 (48)	293 (40)
Study 2				
Definitely true	77 (8)	86 (9)	93 (9)	93 (9)
Probably true	133 (13)	158 (16)	126 (13)	174 (17)
Neither true nor false	265 (26)	215 (21)	158 (16)	219 (22)
Probably false	183 (18)	192 (19)	160 (16)	182 (18)
Definitely false	348 (35)	357 (35)	468 (47)	340 (34)
Study 3				
Definitely true	72 (7)	82 (8)	87 (9)	95 (10)
Probably true	153 (16)	162 (16)	127 (13)	146 (15)
Neither true nor false	259 (26)	219 (22)	158 (16)	219 (22)
Probably false	178 (18)	204 (21)	145 (15)	174 (18)
Definitely false	325 (33)	319 (32)	469 (48)	354 (36)

Note: N: Sample size.

anti-vaccine conspiracy beliefs were a significant negative predictor of vaccination intentions, an effect mediated by feelings of powerlessness, disillusionment, distrust of authorities, and perceived dangers of the vaccine (Douglas, Sutton, Callan, Dawtry, & Harvey, 2016; Jolley & Douglas, 2014a).

Jolley and Douglas's (Jolley & Douglas, 2014a) second study exposed participants to material supporting anti-vaccine conspiracy theories (versus anti-conspiracy materials or a control condition) and asked them to indicate whether, if they had a child, they would have him or her vaccinated. Results showed that vaccination intentions were significantly lower in the pro-conspiracy condition than the anti-conspiracy condition and the control condition. This effect was mediated by feelings of powerlessness (Jolley & Douglas, 2014a), which were significantly higher in the pro-conspiracy condition than the anti-conspiracy condition.

In other words, exposure to conspiracy theories affected vaccination intentions and also had other negative consequences such as increasing feelings of powerlessness.

Another experimental study investigated the effects of vaccine-related conspiracy theories on perceptions of the HPV vaccine among young Chinese adults (Chen, Zhang, Young, Wu, & Zhu, 2020). Relying on the theory of planned behavior (Aizen, Fishbein, Lohmann, & Albarracín, 2019; Madden, Ellen, & Ajzen, 1992), the online experiment examined the impact of exposure to conspiratorial social media messages on HPV vaccine perceptions among young Chinese adults. In the treatment group, participants read an article that described typical conspiracy theories about the HPV vaccine common in social media. Three perspectives on the vaccine were emphasized: (a) Cervical cancer should not be considered a prominent health threat because it is not common, but the science community has exaggerated its prevalence and severity; (b) the HPV vaccine has severe side effects that have been covered up by the pharmaceutical industry; and (c) the Chinese government's advocacy of the HPV vaccine, which is driven by profitmaking motives, is placing millions of citizens at risk. In the control group, participants read an article that was not relevant to the HPV vaccine, namely, an introduction to a public university.

Consistent with the theory of planned behavior, the results showed that attitude ($\beta = .48, p < .001$), subjective norms ($\beta = .17, p < .001$), and self-efficacy ($\beta = .48, p < .001$) significantly predicted participants' behavioral intentions (Chen et al., 2020). Respondents who had more knowledge about the HPV vaccine also had more favorable attitudes toward it, more positive norms, higher perceived behavioral control, and greater vaccination intentions. Finally, analyses revealed a statistically significant interaction between the effects of the experimental condition and knowledge on attitudes and behavioral intentions. These interactions implied that preexisting knowledge about the HPV vaccine might have had a protective effect against exposure to online conspiracy theories.

Another experiment, this time conducted in the United States, tested how to reduce vaccine misperceptions and increase vaccination rates for MMR. The study involved a web-based nationally representative two-wave survey of parents who had children aged 17 years or younger living with them (Nyhan et al., 2014). Parents were randomly assigned to one of five conditions, including four interventions: (a) information explaining the lack of evidence that MMR causes autism; (b) textual information about the dangers of the diseases prevented by MMR; (c) images of children who have diseases prevented by the MMR vaccine; (d) a dramatic narrative about an infant who almost died of measles; or (d) a control group. The condition correcting the alleged link between the vaccine and autism was most effective in reducing agreement with the autism misperception, although other conditions also changed some perceptions.

Despite some effects on perceptions of the vaccine–autism link, none of the interventions in Nyhan et al.'s (2014) study increased parental intent to vaccinate a future child. Refuting claims of an MMR–autism link successfully, for example, actually decreased intent to vaccinate among parents who had the least favorable vaccine attitudes (Nyhan et al., 2014). This is a cautionary tale for simplistic views that a change in perceptions may necessarily lead to a change in behavior (D. Albarracin, 2021; Albarracín et al., 2003), and shows that the current public health communications about vaccines may in some cases be counterproductive (Nyhan et al., 2014).

Belief in conspiracy theories about HIV has also produced harmful effects. The belief that HIV was created by scientists or the American government to depopulate certain groups, such as the Black population, is widespread (M. W. Ross, Essien, & Torres, 2006). Treatment-related conspiracies also are common, including the idea that "people who take new medications for HIV are human guinea pigs for the government" (Brooks et al., 2018, p. 376). One study investigated conspiracy beliefs and their consequences among Black men who have sex with men (MSM), one of the groups most affected by the HIV epidemic in the United States (Brooks et al., 2018). Pre-exposure prophylaxis is an important HIV prevention strategy that may help reduce new HIV infections among Black MSM. In this context, Books et al. (Brooks et al., 2018) studied the association between HIV conspiracy beliefs and intentions to adopt pre-exposure prophylaxis among 224 Black MSM and assessed the likelihood of engaging in it. HIV genocidal and treatment-related conspiracies were assessed using scales previously validated with Black MSM.

Sixty-three percent of participants in this study endorsed at least one of eight HIV conspiracy beliefs. In multivariate analyses, Black MSM who endorsed the genocidal or treatment-related conspiracy theories had a lower intention to adopt PrEP (Pre-Exposure Prophylaxis). All in all, the study indicated that preexisting HIV conspiracy beliefs might deter some Black MSM from adopting PrEP, and led to recommending strategies to address the lack of trust in the healthcare system and conspiracy beliefs in the Black population (Brooks et al., 2018). These data appear in Table 3.2.

Table 3.2. *Odds ratios for intentions to adopt PrEP*

	PrEP Adoption Intention OR (95% CI)
HIV/AIDS conspiracy beliefs – genocidal subscale[a]	0.73 (0.54, 0.99)
HIV/AIDS conspiracy beliefs – treatment-related subscale[a]	0.37 (0.24, 0.56)

Note: Table 3.2 shows reduced probability of adapting PrEP when exposed to conspiracy beliefs and 95% confidence intervals. [a]Average agreement on scale (1 = strongly disagree; 2 = disagree; 3 = neither agree nor disagree; 4 = agree; 5 = strongly agree). Brooks et al. (2018).

In March of 2020, the global COVID-19 outbreak was labeled a "pandemic" (Biddlestone et al., 2020). Since then, governments around the world have encouraged a number of mitigation strategies, including social distancing, the wearing of masks, improving hygiene practices, and more recently, vaccination campaigns (Pal & Gosh, 2021). all of them dependent on the cooperation of their populations. Further, the recent rise of anti-Chinese rhetoric and xenophobia likely affects the wellbeing of millions of Chinese overseas (Sun, Lin, & Operario, 2020). The urgent need to stop the spread of the disease has motivated research on factors that influence compliance with mitigation strategies as well as impact on groups blamed for the disease. A 2020 study investigated the cultural and psychological factors associated with intentions to reduce the spread of COVID-19 (Biddlestone et al., 2020). Participants completed measures of individualism/collectivism, beliefs in conspiracy theories about COVID-19, feelings of powerlessness, and intentions to engage in behaviors that reduce the spread of this disease.

Cultural orientations were associated with intentions to mitigate COVID-19 in four ways. First, vertical individualism predicted lower intentions to engage in social distancing, both directly and indirectly, through a stronger belief in COVID-19 conspiracy theories and stronger feelings of powerlessness (Biddlestone et al., 2020). Second, vertical and horizontal collectivism predicted greater social distancing, an effect that was direct in both cases and also mediated by lesser feelings of powerlessness for horizontal collectivism, standardized indirect effect = 0.04. Third, horizontal collectivism predicted stronger hygiene intentions, both directly and indirectly, through lower feelings of powerlessness. Lastly, horizontal individualism predicted stronger social distancing intentions, both directly and indirectly, through greater feelings of powerlessness. The study concluded that promoting collectivism would be a way to increase compliance with mitigation strategies (Biddlestone et al., 2020).

3.2 Prejudice, Racism, and Discrimination

Some of the oldest conspiracy theories are anti-Semitic, and conspiracy beliefs frequently find their way into debates about immigration. Below, we consider both anti-Semitic and Islamophobic beliefs, as well as xenophobic ones.

3.2.1 Anti-Semitic and Islamophobic Conspiracy Beliefs

Although conspiracy theories have been common throughout history, their characteristics changed after the French Revolution. Anti-Semitic conspiracy theories, the oldest among those promoting racism and discrimination against a specific group of people, also took a new form. "In the nineteenth century, 'the Jew' was thus no longer perceived as, in a literal sense, the 'spawn of Satan' and 'a diabolic beast fighting the forces of truth and salvation with Satan's weapon' (which was a common view in the Middle Ages) but rather as a political force using money, influence and arcane knowledge 'to conquer the world, to refashion it in its own craven image, enslave it to his own alien ends'" (Byford, 2011, 48). The wave of Jewish emancipation in Europe in the 1860s and 1870s contributed to the proliferation of anti-Semitic conspiracy beliefs (Byford, 2011). Russian authorities engaged in a campaign to reduce the size of the Jewish community through a combination of restrictive administrative measures and violent pogroms.

The concocted anti-Semitic text known as "The Protocols of Zion," a pamphlet of no more than a hundred pages first published in the early 1900s in Russia, laid out a supposedly secret plan for world domination allegedly drawn up by a group of Jewish elders. The Protocols' simple framework drew on deeply engrained anti-Semitic stereotypes and had the potential to accommodate popular anxieties about the upheaval in Russia (Byford, 2011). American industrialist Henry Ford helped to popularize the Protocols in the 1920s in his newspaper, the *Dearborn Independent* (Berkowitz, 2014). Belief in conspiracy theories about Jews is an example of how a baseless theory can serve as a universal explanation of "all the bad things happening in society." Theories of this type often arise in times of political unrest that tend to breed feelings of uncertainty in politics and a lack of control over politics. More recently, statements against Muslims ranging from the discriminatory to the openly hateful also have been expressed in diverse political milieus (Shooman, 2016).

Using an experimental design, Jolley et al. (2020) tested the effects of exposure to intergroup conspiracy theories on prejudice and discrimination. Study 1 in this series focused on popular conspiracy theories relating to Muslim immigration and attempts to "Islamicize" Europe (Jolley et al., 2020). After being exposed to a conspiracy narrative about immigrants' involvement in terrorist organizations and plots to attack Britain, participants were assigned to one of three conditions: (a) conspiracy arguments, (b) anti-conspiracy arguments, or (c) a control condition with no information. Results demonstrated that exposure to conspiracy theories concerning immigrants to Britain exacerbated xenophobia (Jolley et al., 2020). More specifically, findings demonstrated that prejudice was significantly higher in the pro-conspiracy condition than in both the anti-conspiracy ($d = .43$) and the control ones ($d = .50$).

Study 2 of Jolley et al.'s (2020) article sought to determine whether exposure to conspiracy theories about Jews can increase prejudice toward this group. Participants were asked whether or not they would vote for a Jewish candidate in an election. Findings indicated the same effect in the context of conspiracy theories about Jewish people. Specifically, belief in conspiracy theories about Jews was higher in the conspiracy condition than the anti-conspiracy condition ($d = .87$) and the control condition ($d = .68$).

Study 3 (Jolley et al., 2020) examined whether the prejudice-enhancing effect of conspiracy theories generalizes beyond the group implicated in them. It demonstrated that prejudice towards Jewish people was higher in the experimental condition compared to the control ($d = .38$), and that the prejudice extended to other groups as well. In short, exposure to intergroup conspiracy theories can directly increase prejudice and discrimination in two different contexts: conspiracy theories about immigrants and conspiracy theories about those who are Jewish (Jolley et al., 2020). Further, exposure to conspiracy theories can lead to an attitude generalization effect, by which exposure to conspiracy theories about one outgroup can lead to prejudice against outgroups beyond the one targeted in the theories (Jolley et al., 2020).

Anti-Semitic conspiracy theories in Malaysia have also led to the scapegoating of ethnic minorities, thus unifying Muslims around a political argument about threats to their nationhood (Swami, 2012). Swami (2012) studied theories that have been promoted by the Malaysian state to strengthen nationalism and reinforce the state as a source of protection against external threats. In Study 1, participants completed a measure of belief in a Jewish conspiracy theory, along with a measure of general conspiracist ideation. Findings indicated that the belief in the conspiracy theory and conspiracist ideation were significantly but weakly correlated, standardized direct effect − .22 (p < .001). In Study 2, participants completed the earlier measure of belief in the Jewish conspiracy theory, along with measures of general conspiracy ideation and ideological attitudes. Findings showed that the belief in the conspiracy theory was no longer significant once other factors were included in the analyses. More specifically, in Study 2, modern racism ($\beta = 0.17, p < .001$), right-wing authoritarianism ($\beta = 0.15, p = .002$), and social dominance orientation ($\beta = 0.14, p = .006$) were more important than conspiracy beliefs, implying that conspiracy beliefs somehow activate these dormant traits.

Anti-Semitism and Islamophobia both cast their target population as a separate and antagonistic "race" (Zia-Ebrahimi, 2018). Conspiracy theories of the 'world Jewish domination' type or their Islamophobic equivalent 'Islamization of Europe' type are powerful enablers of racialization – the process of ascribing a racial identity to a relationship, practice, or group that does not self-identify that way – something that the race literature has so far neglected (Zia-Ebrahimi, 2018). Zia-Ebrahimi presented a textual comparison of two conspiracy theories featuring Jews and Muslims. The first is the Protocols of the Elders of Zion, the notorious forgery claiming that the Jewish leaders were planning to take over Europe and the world, a Hitlerian premise common among the justifications for the Holocaust. The second is Eurabia: The Euro–Arab Axis (2005), a pamphlet by Bat Ye'or claiming to have uncovered a similar conspiracy about a Muslim plot to turn Europe into "Eurabia," a dystopic land in which jihad and sharia rule, while non-Muslims live in a state of subjugation (Zia-Ebrahimi, 2018). Zia-Ebrahimi argued that, despite some differences in format, the two texts display similar discursive dynamics in their attempt to racialize Jews and Muslims as the ultimate "Other" determined to destroy "Us."

Before the Norwegian mass murderer Anders Behring Breivik committed his attacks in July of 2011 in Oslo and on the island of Utøya, leaving 77 people dead, he uploaded a manifesto of more than 1,500 pages containing international anti-Muslim theories onto the Internet and simultaneously sent it by email to more than 1,000 recipients (Shooman, 2016). After analyzing several cases of internet activism promoting racist conspiracy theories, the impact of this hatred of Muslims on the everyday lives of internet users is still unclear (Shooman, 2016). What is evident, according to the author, is that these weblogs offer a forum in which participants mutually reinforce each other's hostility, construct their own informational universe, and immunize themselves against a change of mind (Shooman, 2016).

3.2.2   Xenophobia

The 2016 campaign and Trump presidency were extremely divisive, pitting different ethnic and racial groups against each other. A number of critics predicted that President Trump's divisive rhetoric would embolden white supremacists, thereby contributing to more hate crimes (Edwards & Rushin, 2018). Supporting this prediction, Trump's tweets about Islam-related topics have been shown to be associated with increases in xeno-phobic tweets by his followers, cable news attention paid to Muslims, and hate crimes on the days following his tweets (Müller & Schwarz, 2019). On August 3, 2019, in a Walmart Supercenter in El Paso, Texas, a gunman opened fire with an AK-47, killing 23 people and leaving more than two dozen others wounded (Stewart, 2020). The perpetrator's manifesto echoed comments on immigration made by President Trump, who during a rally stated, "You look at what is marching up, that is an invasion! That is an invasion!" (Baker & Shear, 2019). As another study showed, such presidential communications legitimized, normalized, and amplified the racist and xenophobic anti-Latinx discourses perpetrated by hate groups and conspiracy theorists, bringing fringe beliefs into the communicative mainstream (Wiedeman, 2020).

Trump's embrace of racist and racializing conspiracy theories raised their visibility during his presidency and two campaigns for that office. Donald J. Trump is perhaps the most publicly conspiratorial president in recent American history (Uscinski, 2016). For starters, the belief that Obama is a Muslim is a way to construct Obama as a racialized "other" in a society where explicit anti-Black prejudice is publicly unacceptable (Bouie, 2016). Our studies included a question to assess the belief in the statement, "Obama was not born in the United States and faked his birth certificate to become president," with possible answers being "probably true/most definitely true," "neither true nor false," and "probably false/ most definitely false." Between 62 and 68 percent of respondents believed that this statement was probably false or definitely false; the percentage who believed that it was true or definitely true ranged from 19 to 22 percent (see Table 3.1). Consistent with racialized anxiety is the degree to which white Americans now see "reverse discrimination" as a serious problem in national life. A 2017 NPR survey conducted with the Robert Wood Johnson Foundation and the Harvard's Chan School of Public Health found that roughly one in two Americans think that today there is discrimination against white Americans (Harvard T.H. Chan, 2017).

Trump exploited the anxiety of a non-college-educated white electorate. Immigration was a major theme of Trump's campaign from the moment he announced his candidacy on August 1, 2015, when he accused undocumented immigrants from Mexico of being criminals and rapists bringing crime to the United States (Hellinger, 2018). After describing several crimes allegedly committed by such immigrants and blaming them for costing the jobs of vulnerable American workers, he accused liberals of a cover-up when he stated that these facts are never reported and that Democrats only discuss the needs of immigrants and not the social and economic costs of undocumented immigrants (Hellinger, 2018). Trump promised to build a wall to put an end to the "problem" of Mexican immigration, a wall that he inaccurately insisted Mexico would fund. Also, Trump suggested that "Syrian refugees and Muslims more generally are secret ISIS terrorists, and that there are giant networks of Muslim-Americans who aided, abetted, and continue to cover-up terrorist attacks" (Uscinski, 2016). In addition to his conspiracy theories, Trump's rhetoric blamed foreigners and immigrants for taking "our jobs and our money," and after the 2016 elections, of "stealing the popular vote" from him.

At the end of November 2016, President Elect Trump tweeted: "I won the popular vote if you deduct the millions of people who voted illegally" (BBC, 2017). However, he offered no evidence to support this assertion. Although Trump won the Electoral College vote, he received 2.86 million fewer votes than his rival Hillary Clinton (BBC, 2017). Thus, if, as his team asserted, between 3 and 5 million unauthorized immigrants voted in favor of Clinton in the election, Trump would have been the winner of the popular vote as well. He later announced an investigation that disbanded after locating no such evidence (BBC, 2017).

Our studies included a question to assess the belief in the statement, "Undocumented immigrants voted illegally preventing Republicans from winning the popular vote during the 2016 election," with possible answers being "probably true/most definitely true," "neither true nor false," and "probably false/most definitely false." The percentage of participants who believed that this statement was probably or definitely false ranged from 52 to 64 percent; the percent believing that it was true or definitely true ranged from 22 to 26 percent (see Table 3.1). During Trump's time as president, this rhetoric was accompanied by drastic changes in immigration policies designed to restrict both documented and undocumented immigration (Pierce, Bolter, & Selee, 2018). Trump's rhetoric and subsequent immigration policies have affected immigrants' mental health. In a recent study with Latinx adolescents in California, besides overwhelmingly rejecting Trump's immigration policies, participants reported feeling afraid and/or anxious, expressing anger, contempt, and/or disgust, and recognizing and experiencing racism (Wray-Lake et al., 2018).

3.3   Science and Environmental Attitudes and Behaviors

A considerable number of studies have explored the consequences of exposure to conspiracy theories on participants' intentions to engage in pro-social behavior to reduce their carbon footprint. Jolley and Douglas (2014b) speculated that the presence of conspiracy theories about secret government operations might decrease intentions to participate in political activities, namely, voting and contributing money to political candidates, political parties, or an organization supporting candidates, as well as intentions to reduce carbon footprint. In Study 1, undergraduate and postgraduate students at a British university were exposed to a range of conspiracy theories concerning government involvement in significant events such as the death of Princess Diana. The independent variable was the nature of the article presented (pro-conspiracy versus anti-conspiracy), which was different across conditions. Findings showed that exposure to information supporting conspiracy theories reduced participants' intentions to participate in political activities, relative to participants who were given the anti-conspiracy information (Jolley & Douglas, 2014b). This effect was mediated by feelings of political powerlessness, $g^2 = .07$, and uncertainty, $g^2 = .06$.

In Study 2, student participants were exposed to conspiracy theories about climate change (Jolley & Douglas, 2014b). The authors investigated whether this exposure influenced intentions to purchase energy-efficient light bulbs or use means of transport other than driving a car. Using a similar design to Study 1, the authors exposed participants to conspiracy theories involving climate change (versus anti-conspiracy material) and measured the extent to which they intended to engage in efforts to reduce their carbon footprint, as well as in political activities, the same measures used in Study 1 (Jolley & Douglas, 2014b). In this case, exposure to information supportive of conspiracy theories decreased intentions to reduce carbon footprint, relative to participants who were given the anti-conspiracy information, or those in the control condition. Furthermore, climate powerlessness, uncertainty, and cynicism were significantly higher in the pro-conspiracy condition than the anti-conspiracy condition, and either marginally or significantly higher than the control (Jolley & Douglas, 2014b).

Several other studies have explored the impact of conspiracy theories on intentions to engage in carbon footprint diminishing activities. Douglas and Sutton (2015) have proposed that there is uncertainty around the public understanding of conspiracy theories and that this uncertainty creates a fertile ground for them. Conspiracy theories about climate change, which argue that global warming is a scam created by those who have something to gain from it (Douglas & Sutton, 2015; Inverse, n.d.),[1] also challenge our view of humans as moral. The authors reviewed previous research and found that evidence suggests that climate change conspiracy theories may be harmful, steering people away from environmentally friendly initiatives. Most people chose to believe that they are part of an enduring and moral social group and they are themselves moral (Douglas & Sutton, 2015). When climate change challenges these moral beliefs, people engage in motivated reasoning and end up endorsing conspiracy beliefs. In this form of reasoning, information that challenges valued beliefs is discounted, whereas information that supports them is accepted uncritically (Douglas & Sutton, 2015).

Whereas most research has assessed the effect of conspiracy theories on environmentally-related behaviors that lead people to reduce their carbon footprint, Van der Linden (2015) explored the impact of climate change conspiracy theories on pro-social behavior and science acceptance. This work set out to investigate this effect in a survey study, where participants were recruited from Amazon Mechanical Turk and randomly assigned to a conspiracy, pro-climate, or control condition. In the conspiracy condition, participants watched a short video of a popular conspiracy movie. In the pro-climate condition, participants saw a United Nations video clip about climate change. In the control condition, participants were asked to solve a neutral word puzzle.

As expected, exposure to conspiracy arguments affected the belief that global warming is a hoax. Participants in the conspiracy condition agreed more with the statement that global warming is a hoax than did those in

---

[1] Climate change claims either deny that changes in temperature are significant and/or claim that fossil fuels are not responsible for variations in temperature in our planet. In this sense, climate change denial represents an "anti-conspiracy theory" that denies the damage produced by a group within society.

the control condition (Van der Linden, 2015). In addition, those who were exposed to the conspiracy video judged the scientific consensus on human-caused climate change to be significantly lower than did those in the control group and the pro-climate video condition. Van der Linden (2015) measured pro-environmental behavior by asking participants to sign an online "stop global warming" petition. Less than 23 percent of participants agreed to sign the petition in the conspiracy condition vs. 43 percent in the pro-climate and 34 percent in the control group, respectively. Pro-social intentions were also measured by the willingness to make donations to a charitable organization and volunteer time to a local community and charitable organization in the following six months. Compared to the control or pro-climate condition, those who were exposed to the conspiracy video were less likely to have pro-social intentions (Van der Linden, 2015).

3.4   Political Participation

Democratic societies need informed citizens who can participate intelligently in the democratic process. What citizens want and do in the political arena depends on what they know (Luskin, Sood, & Blank, 2013). Ample evidence, however, shows that the average citizen is not highly knowledgeable about politics (Converse, 1964). Conspiracy theories both misinform citizens and act as an obstacle for educating them (Kuklinski, Quirk, Jerit, Schwieder, & Rich, 2000). The shock and awe style of Donald J. Trump marked a turning point in American politics. Trump's election was said to represent a rhetorical watershed moment, due not only to his embrace of innuendo and smear but also because of the avid way in which public audiences consumed his norm-shattering rhetoric (Neville-Shepard, 2019). Some content that Trump spread was the "harbinger . . . of a 'post-truth' political imaginary" (Goodstein 2017, cited in Neville-Shepard, 2019, p. 1). This cultural shift was so significant that Oxford Dictionaries designated "post-truth" the word of the year for 2016, to describe "circumstances in which objective facts are less influential in shaping public opinion than appeals to emotion and personal belief" (Neville-Shepard, 2019).

Many conspiracy theories feature the "shady and sinister actions of government operations," a representation that is likely to influence the extent to which people engage in politics (Douglas & Sutton, 2018). Further, conspiracy theories can lead to collective preferences that are different from those people would exhibit if they had the correct information (Jolley, 2013; Kuklinski et al., 2000). From its inception as a modern nation, the United States has been rife with conspiracy theories (DeHaven-Smith, 2013). The "Birther" conspiracy theory stating that Obama was not born in the United States was debated across electoral cycles from 2008 to 2016 (Invernizzi & Mohamed, 2020). After the 2020 presidential election in the United States, Trump propagated another false theory, arguing that the election results had been secretly and illegally manipulated by the Democratic Party and others (Roose, 2020). Trump's presidential campaign and presidency have both been plagued by conspiracy theories, many of which have been created, propagated, or augmented by Trump himself. For example, on August 22, Trump tweeted that "The deep state, or whoever, over at the FDA is making it very difficult for drug companies to get people in order to test the vaccines and therapeutics" because they were "hoping to delay the answer under after November 3rd." Also, after the election, Trump alleged that the announcement of the success of the Pfizer COVID-19 vaccine had been deliberately delayed with the same intent (Alexander, 2020).

Another important consideration is QAnon (see Chapters 1 and 9), which was once a peripheral phenomenon but has more recently swamped Twitter, Facebook, and other social networks with conspiratorial falsehoods about Covid-19, the Black Lives Matter protests, and the 2020 election (Roose, 2020). QAnon is the umbrella term for an expansive set of internet conspiracy theories built on Pizzagate, which asserts that the world is run by a cabal of Satan-worshiping pedophiles who are plotting against Donald Trump while operating a global child sex-trafficking ring (Roose, 2020). Conspirators include Hillary Clinton, Barack Obama, and George Soros, as well as a number of entertainers and Hollywood celebrities like Oprah Winfrey, Tom Hanks, Ellen DeGeneres, and religious figures like Pope Francis and the Dalai Lama (Roose, 2020). According to QAnon folklore, Mr. Trump was recruited by military generals to run for president in 2016 as a way of breaking up this criminal cabal, end its control of politics and the media, and bring the conspirators to justice (Roose, 2020).

A related, overlapping conspiracy theory holds that a deep state, although not one of Satanist pedophiles, is plotting against Donald Trump (Roose, 2020). The plotters, in this case, are parts of the United States government that wield real power outside the conventional checks and balances of the system (Illing, 2020). Applied to the United States for the first time in 2007, the term "deep state" originated in references to the Turkish military's alleged effort to slow the spread of democracy there

(Illing, 2020). In 2019, Trump argued that deep state antics were responsible for special counsel Robert Mueller's investigation into Russia's interference in the 2016 election (Illing, 2020). Among its rhetorical purposes, some scholars argue that the use of the machinations of a "deep state" is a way for Trump and his supporters to divert criticism (Illing, 2020).

Some of Trump's supporters contend that the COVID-19 pandemic was a hoax concocted by the deep state and that the Black Lives Matter protests were engineered to damage Trump's reelection prospects. The Black Lives Matter protests were revived by the murder of George Floyd in Minneapolis, MN at the hands of police in May 2020 and spread across the United States and later the world. Trump combined the virus and the protests during one weekend in August 2020, in 89 posted or reposted messages between 5:49 a.m. and 8:04 a.m. on Sunday, in addition to 18 such posts the night before. Among their claims were ones alleging that the coronavirus death toll had been exaggerated and that street protests were actually an organized coup d'état against him (Baker, 2020).

Study 4 in this book was designed to assess the belief in the deep state. We asked participants whether they believed that some statements were true, including "Unelected U.S. government officials including some in the U.S. intelligence services have secretly conspired to illegally undermine the candidacy and presidency of Donald Trump," with possible answers being "probably true/most definitely true," "probably false/most definitely false," and "not sure." These results appear in Table 3.3. As shown, participants were almost evenly split between the 43 percent who thought that this conspiracy belief was definitively true/probably true, and the 45 percent who thought that it was definitely false/probably false. This finding shows that President Trump and his supporters have been successful in spreading the Deep State conspiracy. The proportion of participants

Table 3.3. *Belief in deep state among residents of the United States: Study 4*

Response categories	N (%)
Definitely true	178 (20)
Probably true	253 (29)
Probably false	170 (19)
Definitely false	276 (31)

Note: N = Number of participants.

who believed in it was almost double that of those who believed in the other conspiracy theories assessed in our studies, namely that there is a cover-up of the link between the MMR vaccine and autism, that the United States government created the HIV epidemic, that Obama was not born in the United States, and that undocumented immigrants decided the 2016 popular vote (see Table 3.1). What our studies suggest is that the influence of a mainstream political figure such as President Trump to propagate non-truths persists, despite debunking by the mainstream media and factcheckers (Neville-Shepard, 2019).

Our studies also allowed us to test associations between conspiracy beliefs and vote in the 2016 presidential election. These analyses appear in Table 3.4 and show that in most cases, conspiracy beliefs were associated with lower participation. For instance, participants who believed that the United States government created the HIV epidemic and that there is a cover-up of the link between the MMR vaccine and autism were less likely to have voted in this election in all but one case (see Table 3.4). Likewise, in Study 2, those who believed that Obama was not born in the United States were less likely to have voted, and those who thought undocumented immigrants decided the popular vote were less likely to have voted (see Table 3.4). In contrast, those who believed that the tobacco industry covered up the harmful impact of smoking were more likely to have voted

Table 3.4. *Correlations of conspiratorial and control beliefs and voting*

	Study 1	Study 2	Study 3
Conspiracy belief about Obama's Birth Certificate (Birther)	0.03	−0.09**	−0.03
Control belief about Obama's inaction and crisis in Syria	0.07	−0.02	−0.02
Conspiracy belief that undocumented immigrants decided the 2016 popular vote	0.05	−0.11***	−0.05
Control belief that undocumented immigrants use false documents to work	−.02	−0.02	0.10**
Conspiracy belief about the HIV virus	−0.07*	−0.13***	−0.09**
Control belief about the Tuskegee study	−0.07	−0.02	0.02
Conspiracy belief about the MMR vaccine cover-up	−0.03	−0.13***	−0.10**
Control belief about the tobacco effects cover-up	−0.02	0.11***	0.18***

Note: *r:* Pearson correlation. *: $p < .05$; **: $p < .01$; ***: $p < .001$.

in Studies 2 and 3, suggesting that accurate, control, beliefs were a different phenomenon (see Table 3.4). As these results show, our studies supported the notion that conspiracy beliefs can lower political participation. However, our results were correlational.

Other research demonstrates the effects of conspiracy beliefs on trust of public institutions. By decreasing trust in political institutions and raising uncertainty about the trustworthiness of the informational environment, conspiracy theories can undermine democratic accountability (Invernizzi & Mohamed, 2020). This general distrust can lead to unwarranted punishment of politicians by voters or to ignoring their blameworthy behavior. Conspiracy theories may also create noise and confusion in the informational environment, which undermines voters' ability to incorporate new information into their evaluation (Invernizzi & Mohamed, 2020). To test these contentions, Invernizzi and Mohamed ran an online experiment with American participants who identified as Republicans or Democrats. In it, participants were exposed to a short video on a conspiracy theory unrelated to the current American government, namely alternative explanations of the burning of Notre Dame Cathedral.

Participants in the control group watched an equivalent length video discussing reasons why people cannot ride zebras. After viewing the conspiracy video, participants either read about news of Trump's achievements or about scandals in his administration. They then answered questions regarding their support for the government and trust in different institutions. Participants in the conspiracy treatment group expressed significantly lower trust in political institutions, by about two percentage points (Invernizzi & Mohamed, 2020). This result suggests that even unrelated conspiracy theories about the burning of Notre Dame Cathedral can undermine trust in the American Government. This study also showed that conspiratorial narratives can increase voters' mistrust towards public institutions and affect intentions to vote for the incumbent.

Another study used surveys to assess whether exposure to a conspiracy theory claim influences conspiratorial beliefs and trust in government (Einstein & Glick, 2015). Building on the ideas that exposure to conspiracy theories diminishes political participation and belief in conspiracy induces negative attitudes toward the government, this study tested whether exposure to conspiracy theories could cause a general distrust in government institutions. The authors worked with two trust hypotheses: (a) Exposure to conspiracy theory will decrease trust in government, and this decrease will even affect trust in institutions not directly implicated in the allegations; and (b) among those who have already been exposed to a conspiracy claim, those asked a question relative to their belief in the claim will have relatively higher trust in government.

The authors used a pair of experiments to evaluate their hypotheses (Einstein & Glick, 2015). In both experiments, exposure to a conspiracy theory was done by giving participants a newspaper article describing the view that the Bureau of Labor Statistics manipulated recent unemployment data and rebutting the conspiracy claim. Participants were asked a question about their trust in the Bureau of Labor Statistics, *"Do you think that recent monthly unemployment data from the Bureau of Labor Statistics are calculated as accurately as possible or are they politically manipulated?* Possible responses included, *calculated as accurately as possible* and *politically manipulated.* They collected the data using Amazon's Mechanical Turk (Einstein & Glick, 2015).

The results showed that respondents who were asked if they believed in a specific conspiracy claim after reading a specific allegation reported lower beliefs than those not exposed to the specific claim (Einstein & Glick, 2015). In addition, exposure to a conspiracy claim had a strong negative effect on trust in government and institutions, including those not connected to the allegations. Moreover, the findings indicated that asking participants if they believed in the conspiracy mitigated the negative trust effects. The study concluded that conspiracy exposure increases conspiracy beliefs and reduces trust, but that asking about beliefs provokes additional thinking about the claims, softening the effect on beliefs and trust (Einstein & Glick, 2015). Our data assessing the influence of cynicism and trust in government in conspiracy beliefs are reported in Chapter 5.

3.5 Discussion

Conspiracy theories can have important implications for health, intergroup relations, policy, political participation, and trust in institutions. Conspiracy theorists who argue, for instance, that evidence that the MMR vaccine causes autism has been covered up can negatively affect intentions to vaccinate children, and theories that argue that HIV was created by the government can thwart prevention and treatment efforts. Similarly, research about the connection between conspiracy beliefs and environmental attitudes and behaviors has shown that conspiracy theories related to climate change can impair efforts to reduce carbon in the atmosphere.

As this chapter showed, conspiracy theories can also lead to discrimination and scapegoating of different groups. Our data show that 22–26 percent of participants held the belief that undocumented immigrants voted in the 2016 election (purportedly, leading Trump to lose the popular vote). Conspiracy beliefs have also been shown to decrease trust in government and political participation, and our own studies showed that they are negatively associated with voting. Chapter 5 returns to cynicism of government as not only a consequence but also a precursor of conspiracy beliefs.

Although conspiracy theories have been at play across the history of the United States, their pervasiveness in the Trump era has combined with his unprecedented level of deception. President Trump made 8,158 false or misleading claims in his first two years (Kessler, Rizzo, & Kelly, 2020). After promoting the notion that a deep state had fabricated evidence against him that led to his first impeachment in 2019, President Trump was impeached a second time for spurring some who accepted the QAnon conspiracy to storm the nation's Capitol on January 6 in an unsuccessful attempt to disrupt certification of the 2020 election for the Democratic ticket (BBC Reality Check team, 2020).

Conspiracy theories are easy to propagate and difficult to refute. As Goertzel (2010, p. 493) puts it, "Responding to conspiracy theories and 'sceptics' draws scientists into arenas where objective information matters less than emotional appeals, unsupported allegations and unverified speculations." Even if a conspiracy theory is improbable, it can be used as a rhetorical device to appeal to the public's emotions (Goertzel, 2010). As this chapter has shown, belief in conspiracy theories can have tragic consequences.

CHAPTER 4

Anxiety, Psychological Motivations, and Conspiracy Beliefs

4.1 The Belief Defense, Belief Accuracy, and Social Integration Motivations

Human beliefs, including beliefs about conspiracies, are closely connected to human motivations. Motivations include needs and goals. Needs are psychological states of deprivation. In the case of biological needs, an organism needs water when it is dehydrated and cannot maintain basic biological processes without it. In the case of psychological needs, a woman who does not know what role she will play on a project may need to feel more certain before conducting herself effectively in that role.

Needs can, in turn, create goals, which are forward-looking. Needs create goals that mobilize behavioral, cognitive, and affective processes to satisfy future needs. In this sense, needs and goals are neighboring concepts and are all relevant to conspiracy beliefs. These beliefs may last for long periods of time; some people have maintained the belief that the MMR vaccine creates autism for decades. Likewise, the needs and goals associated with these beliefs are often chronic, spanning months, years, and even decades. For this reason, in this book, we chose the term *motivation* as an umbrella term to denote relatively stable needs and goals implicated in the creation of conspiracy beliefs.

Defense, accuracy, and social integration motivations are conceptual categories that align well with past theories about goals in the area of attitudes (Albarracin, 2021; Hart et al., 2009). The defense motivation allows human beings to maintain stability in their environments and is the set of needs and goals to preserve one's self-views and a coherent sense of the self and the world. All living creatures respond to their surrounding through processes of organization (i.e., development of cells, organs, systems), homeostasis (i.e., equilibrium fostered by positive and negative feedback mechanisms), metabolism (i.e., transformation of energy into matter and dissolution of matter), growth (i.e., increase in size), and adaptation (i.e., exchange with and change in response to the environment) (Albarracin, 2021). Human beings respond to their social world by maintaining their self-views and sense of self-worth and by defending their beliefs (Albarracin, 2021; Baumeister, 1997; Eagly & Chaiken, 1993; Kunda, 1990; Tesser, 2001).

The belief accuracy motivation is important because properly understanding one's environment is critical to survival (Albarracin, 2021). A unicellular organism such as an amoeba receives chemical information from its surroundings, and these signals allow the organism to accurately understand its world. Human beings do the same through their senses of sight, hearing, audition, smell, taste, proprioception, and touch, as well as through a cognitive system that allows them to form beliefs and theories about the world. In our book, we presuppose that the *belief accuracy motivation* involves relatively stable needs and goals that encourage individuals to form a realistic representation of the world.

In addition to the belief defense and belief accuracy motivations, humans strive to be integrated within a society. The social integration motivation entails needs and goals of social connection, trust, and status. To achieve collective milestones and survive as eminently social beings, we synchronize our actions and beliefs with others, trust close others and institutions, and strive to feel valued and to have a place in society. We pay attention to signals of social value, which involve status and income, and defend against a loss of these signals (Husting & Orr, 2007; Leary & Baumeister, 2000; Mutz, 2018)

In this chapter, we discuss the associations of conspiracy beliefs with the motivations of belief defense, belief accuracy, and social integration. We review the evidence about psychological traits and states that are related to the belief defense, belief accuracy, and social integration motivations. In addition to organizing research findings within our own framework of motivations, we propose that these motivations influence conspiracy beliefs by affecting anxiety. Figure 4.1 presents our book's model about the pathway from belief defense, belief accuracy, and social integration motivation to anxiety to belief in conspiracy. To present the model, this chapter first covers the relations between conspiracy beliefs and anxiety. Anxiety has been studied as "anxiety," "uncertainty," "fear," and "feelings of being out of control," all terms that have been used interchangeably. The subsequent sections of this chapter cover the associations of conspiracy beliefs with the belief defense, accuracy, and social integration motivation, and ultimately the intervening role of anxiety. The following

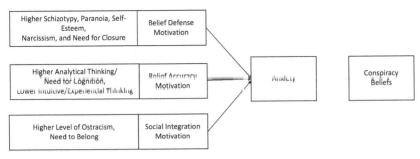

Figure 4.1. Theoretical model focusing on motivations, anxiety, and conspiracy beliefs

principle is the focus of this chapter. In Chapter 6, we will deal more specifically with the role of the media in relation to anxiety.

Principle of Anxiety. Anxiety is a perception of threat and depends on relatively stable psychological motivations of belief defense, belief accuracy, and social integration, as well as sociopolitical factors and situational factors like communications and media exposure. Experiencing anxiety at a particular time motivates a search for an explanation and can lead to misattributing the anxiety to a conspiracy story.

4.1.1 Anxiety, Uncertainty, and Fear

Anxiety involves both emotional and cognitive feelings. We may feel visceral fear, which is accompanied by a physical response controlled by the autonomic nervous system. We may also worry, or feel uncertainty, in a more cerebral, cognitive way. Emotional and cognitive feelings are often intertwined, which leads us to use the term "anxiety" as a broad label that encompasses both.

According to Gray and colleagues (2000; 1991), behavior is regulated by three systems: (a) the behavioral approach system, (b) the behavioral inhibition system, and (c) the fight-flight-freezing system. The behavioral approach system regulates approach by initiating behavior that may lead to positive outcomes, rewards, or relief from punishment (Gray & McNaughton, 2000; Gray, 1991). As such, the behavioral approach system correlates with impulsivity, risk taking, and predisposition for mania (Gray & McNaughton, 2000; Gray, 1991). In contrast, the behavioral inhibition system inhibits behaviors that may lead to negative outcomes, punishment, pain, and novelty (Gray & McNaughton, 2000; Gray, 1991), and correlates with high anxiety, generalized anxiety disorder, and obsessive-compulsive disorder (Gray & McNaughton, 2000).

The fight-flight-freezing system regulates escape/avoidance behavior as responses to aversive stimuli and correlates with fear, avoidant personality disorder, phobias, and panic attacks (Gray & McNaughton, 2000). The behavioral inhibition system and the fight-flight-freezing system are clearly relevant to conspiracy theories in that they regulate anxiety and fear. Anxiety and fear involve the same type of experience of unease, except that the threat is mild in anxiety and more extreme in fear. Anxiety also involves cognitive manifestations experienced as worry, doubt, and uncertainty, whereas fear always involves a physiological experience of arousal (e.g., palpitations, changes in breathing).

4.1.1.1   Uncertainty

Research conducted by van Prooijen and Jostmann (2013) has shown that uncertainty fosters conspiracy beliefs without affecting other beliefs. In the first experiment by van Prooijen and Jostmann (2013), participants were induced to experience uncertainty or not by writing about either an experience of uncertainty or watching television. They then read either an excerpt about either ethical or unethical personnel policies of oil companies (labeled "immoral" and "moral" in the article). Even though the excerpts did not cite a conspiracy, an actor described as immoral provides the ideal terrain to infer a conspiracy belief, a hypothesis that the researchers tested with questions such as, "To what extent do you believe that people who are associated with oil companies gave the order to start the war in Iraq?" Agreement with these statements constituted a measure of conspiracy beliefs.

The hypothesis van Prooijen and Jostmann's (2013) tested in Experiment 1 was that states of uncertainty would lead to spontaneous inferences of a conspiracy, provided the actors in the story are unethical. Accordingly, participants were more likely to *deduce* a conspiracy when an actor was described as generally unethical (vs. ethical), but this effect was only present when uncertainty was salient. This pattern was replicated in a second experiment with the same uncertainty manipulation but describing the government of an African city as corrupt or law-abiding. Participants learned that a candidate for presidential elections who opposed the incumbent group had died in a car accident. Again, if people who feel uncertain construct a conspiracy theory as a way of reducing uncertainty, positing a corrupt government may lead to more conspiracy inferences than positing a law-abiding one. As shown by the summary of their results in Table 4.1, this was in fact the case.

Table 4.1. *Spontaneously deduced conspiracies for unethical and ethical actors under uncertainty and control conditions*

Experiment and condition	Uncertainty condition	Control condition
Experiment 1		
Unethical actor	4.69 (1.29)	4.11 (1.25)
Ethical actor	3.80 (1.10)	4.49 (0.98)
Experiment 2		
Unethical actor	4.67 (0.74)	4.56 (1.03)
Ethical actor	3.42 (1.13)	4.24 (1.33)

Note: Table entries are Means (*SD*s). The data are from Prooijen and Jostmann (2013).

More indirect evidence of the effect of uncertainty comes from work on ambivalence and conspiracy beliefs. In research by Van Harreveld, Rutjens, Schneider, Nohlen, and Keskinis (2014), participants described an issue or opinion that personally elicited either ambivalent or unequivocal points of view. They then judged the degree to which work or financial events were related to the actions of people. As expected, the ambivalence manipulation produced negative affect, which in turn strengthened the tendency to attribute events to the actions of others.

4.1.1.2 Feeling Out of Control

Loss of control over specific and general aspects of the environment has been identified as a key factor in the endorsement of conspiracy beliefs (Heine, Proulx, & Vohs, 2006; Park, 2010; van den Bos, 2009). Presumably, conspiracy beliefs help the powerless cope with their disadvantages (see also Bale, 2007; Hofstadter, 1964), and, in doing so, help communities manage the psychological impact of threatening events (van Prooijen & van Dijk, 2014; see also van Prooijen & van Lange, 2014). The more disturbing an event is, the greater the loss of control and the more likely people are to endorse conspiracy beliefs about the event (Pipes, 1997; Robins & Post, 1997; Shermer, 2011; van Prooijen & van Dijk, 2014).

Perceptions of personal control protect us from the disorienting randomness of life (Lerner, 1980). According to Kay et al. (2009), humans deploy compensatory psychological mechanisms to preserve a sense of order when they cannot control events. Perceiving a disorienting world as orderly can mitigate the experience of anxiety and the sense of limited control that often accompanies anxiety. To test this hypothesis, Whitson and Galinsky (2008) asked their research participants to recall experiences of feeling out of control and crossed this factor with a self-affirmation manipulation. Self-Affirmation (Steele, 1988) is often induced by recalling one's important values and is a proven way of reducing anxiety. Therefore, for people who feel a low sense of control, self-affirmation should reduce the motivation to engage in compensatory control strategies. According to Whitson and Galinsky's (2008) results, participants in the out of control condition who were not self-affirmed had stronger conspiracy beliefs than did those in self-affirmation conditions. In other words, reaffirming one's value eliminated the need to impose order on random events and reduced anxiety.

One limitation of Whitson and Galinsky's experiment is the absence of a baseline with which to compare feeling out of control. Research by van Prooijen and Acker (2015), however, addressed this issue. The researchers conducted a similar experiment in which participants wrote about a time when they had felt out of control, in control, or neither. They then read information about the construction of a subway line in Amsterdam and answered questions about corruption in the construction contract. As in Whitson and Galinsky's (2008) research, participants in the low control condition had stronger conspiracy beliefs than did those in the high control condition. Furthermore, participants in the baseline condition did not differ from those in the low control condition, implying that most of us feel that the world is out of control on a regular basis and are thus predisposed to believing in conspiracies.

Interestingly, van Prooijen and Acker (2015) also analyzed a prior survey of conspiracy beliefs. The survey included measures about the threat of the Y2K bug to computer systems around the world, which was relevant at the time the survey was conducted. The study also included measures of other conspiracy beliefs, including the Kennedy assassination and the cover-up of evidence of extraterrestrial life. The hypothesis, which received support, was that the threat of Y2K could lead to yet other conspiracy beliefs. The degree to which respondents felt threatened by Y2K correlated with their beliefs in conspiracy theories unrelated to Y2K, suggesting that *any* perceived threat is likely to ignite conspiratorial explanations of events. Importantly, however, it was the threat of Y2K and not the belief in it that correlated with other conspiracy beliefs. This point is important because conspiracy beliefs are well known to correlate with each other (Brotherton et al., 2013) but the reason is not always clear.

4.1.1.3 Stress and Anxiety

A study by Swami and colleagues (2016) measured anxiety in several ways, including perceived stress. The study included American adults recruited on Amazon Mechanical Turk, who completed (a) the Belief in Conspiracy Theories Inventory, as well as the (b) Perceived Stress Scale (Cohen, Kamarck, & Mermelstein, 1983), the List of Threatening Experiences Questionnaire (Brugha, Bebbington, Tennant, & Hurry, 1985), Form Y-1 of the State Trait Anxiety Inventory (Spielberger, Gorsuch, Lushene, Vagg, & Jacobs, 1983) as measures of state anxiety, (c) Y-2 of the State-Trait Anxiety Inventory (Spielberger et al., 1983) as measures of trait anxiety, and (d) the Profile of Mood States (Shacham, 1983). As expected, perceived stress, stressful life events, and trait anxiety each correlated positively with conspiracy beliefs (rs = .10 to .29).

Stress has been the focus of other research on conspiracy beliefs. A study with a sample from the US, the UK, and Australia (Georgiou et al., 2019) included a 10-item self-report measure that assesses perceptions that life situations are stressful. The items assessed how unpredictable, uncontrollable, and overloaded respondents found their lives on scales from 0 ("Never") to 4 ("Very often"). This stress measure was analyzed in relation to Swami et al.'s (2011) conspiracy belief scale. Results indicated that perceived life stress was positively associated with conspiracy beliefs.

A specific form of anxiety that has also received attention in the literature is insecure attachment. Whereas people with an anxious attachment style avoid (avoidant attachment) or seek proximity with others (insecure attachment), people with secure (vs. insecure) attachment seek instrumental and emotional support from others (Florian, Mikulincer, & Taubman, 1995; Larose, Bernier, Soucy, & Duchesne, 1999). Anxiously attached individuals tend to exaggerate the threats they encounter as a way of gaining support from others and are hypervigilant in interpersonal domains (Cassidy & Berlin, 1994; Cassidy & Kobak, 1988; Mikulincer, Shaver, & Pereg, 2003). This pattern suggests that people with an anxious attachment style may be prone to conspiracy beliefs as well. This hypothesis was tested by Green and Douglas (2018) (see also Douglas et al., 2017), who measured conspiracy beliefs and the perception that powerful groups conspire, as well as attachment styles. As hypothesized, anxious attachment predicted more conspiratorial thinking above and beyond other interpersonal and political variables.

Another anxiety linked to conspiracy beliefs in the literature has been death anxiety. A study by Newheiser, Farias, and Tausch (2011), for example, found an association between belief in the Da Vinci Code conspiracy and experiencing existential threat and death-related anxiety. In this work, anxiety of death was measured by asking participants how anxious they felt about "The total isolation of death" and "How it will feel to be dead," among other items. The role of death-related anxiety is further discussed in Chapter 5, in relation to political ideology.

Our studies for this book also investigated the connections between reported anxiety (e.g., affective feeling of worry and uncertainty in the present moment) and conspiracy beliefs. Participants were asked to express their agreement with items such as "I feel calm" (reversed-scored), "I am worried," "I am confused," and "I sometimes don't feel safe." Responses were given on Likert scales, as follows: "Strongly Agree," "Somewhat Agree," "Neither Agree nor Disagree," "Somewhat Disagree," and "Strongly Disagree." This scale was scored from 1 ("Strongly Disagree") to 5 ("Strongly Agree") (for more details, see Appendix).

The relevant correlations appear in Table 4.2, and consistently show the predicted positive correlations between these two variables. In fact, anxiety was significantly and positively correlated with conspiracy beliefs 12 out of 12 times (see left column). In contrast, only three of our accurate, control beliefs, were significantly and positively correlated with anxiety (see right column). The implication of these correlations is that anxiety predisposes individuals to believe in baseless conspiracies without increasing belief in real, similarly threatening events such as the Tuskegee study.

Table 4.2. *Correlations between anxiety and conspiracy beliefs in our studies*

	Conspiracy belief	Accurate, control belief
Study 1		
Obama's birth certificate	0.10**	0.06
Undocumented immigrants decided popular vote	0.09*	−0.06
HIV virus as a government creation	0.23***	0.18***
MMR vaccine cover-up	0.14***	−0.05
Study 2		
Obama's birth certificate	0.08*	0.03
Undocumented immigrants decided popular vote	0.07*	−0.05
HIV virus as a government creation	0.22***	0.13***
MMR vaccine cover-up	0.10**	0
Study 3		
Obama's birth certificate	0.16***	0.06
Undocumented immigrants decided popular vote	0.17***	0
HIV virus as a government creation	0.27***	0.12***
MMR vaccine cover-up	0.23***	−0.07*

Note: r. Pearson correlation. *: $p < 0.05$; **: $p < 0.01$; ***: $p < 0.001$.

We were also interested in seeing whether general or specific anxiety correlates with conspiracy beliefs. Study 1 in this book included measures of anxiety that were general and ones specific to health or political issues, thus allowing us to compare these different measures. Specifically, for political anxiety, participants were asked to report their agreement with "When it comes to politics, I feel calm," "When it comes to politics, I am worried," "When it comes to politics, I am confused," "Politics makes me anxious," and "I am worried about contemporary politics." For health anxiety, the items were "Health issues make me anxious," and "I am worried about health issues." As for the more general anxiety items, participants used Likert scales to report their answers.

We were able to separate general anxiety from political anxiety. The correlations with political anxiety appear in Table 4.3. This political anxiety measure correlated positively with the conspiracy belief that HIV was created by the American government and with the accurate beliefs in the Tuskegee experiment and the cover-up of the effects of smoking by the tobacco industry. However, the measure of general anxiety had much stronger associations with all conspiracy beliefs. These results suggest that, overall, anxiety is more conducive to conspiracy beliefs than anxiety associated with specific events, probably because specific anxieties are more

Table 4.3. *Correlations between general anxiety and domain-specific anxiety (Study 1)*

	Conspiracy belief			Accurate, control belief		
	Anxiety	Political anxiety	Health anxiety	Anxiety	Political anxiety	Health anxiety
Obama's birth certificate	0.21**	0	0.09*	0.11**	−0.01	0.04
Undocumented immigrants decided popular vote	0.21***	−0.001	0.10**	−0.06	−0.05	0.07*
HIV virus as a government creation	0.32****	0.08*	0.14****	0.14****	0.16***	0.05
MMR vaccine cover-up	0.24****	0.03	0.11**	−0.17***	0.05	0

Note: r. Pearson correlation. *: $p < 0.05$; **: $p < 0.01$; ***: $p < 0.001$.

circumscribed and thus more difficult to misattribute to false conspiracies as an explanation for the anxiety.

Table 4.3 reports the correlations between health anxiety and beliefs. As shown, both the general measure and the health anxiety measure were similarly correlated with conspiracy beliefs, again implying that general feelings rather than health worries are sufficient to produce conspiracy beliefs. To further test this interpretation, we next conducted a multilevel regression predicting conspiracy beliefs from both the general and the health specific measure. This regression was conducted by predicting conspiracy beliefs from the general and health specific measures of anxiety. Because, in the study, each participant responded to two political beliefs and two health beliefs, the multilevel linear regressions were clustered by participant, and the specific conspiracy theory (i.e., within the political beliefs: Obama's birth certificate and voting by undocumented immigrants, and HIV and MMR within the health ones) was introduced as a random factor (see equations in the Appendix and code in Online Supplement). Specifically, the outcome of the multilevel model is belief in a specific conspiracy theory (i.e., level 1 unit) nested within participant (i.e., level 2 unit), and belief was predicted from both general and health anxiety, introduced as fixed effects at the level of the participant. We repeated the multilevel regression for political and health beliefs analyzed separately. When this analysis was done, only the general anxiety measure predicted conspiracy beliefs. These analyses appear in Table 4.4.

4.1.1.4   Our Experimental Evidence on the Impact of Anxiety on Conspiracy Beliefs

Affective or emotional feelings are an intuitive basis for beliefs and attitudes about any topic, even though many of them are objectively irrelevant to the judgments people make. Uncertainty about one's financial future is objectively unrelated to the possibility that a deep state conspiracy is working to undermine Donald J. Trump's presidency. However, when people feel uneasy or afraid, they may attempt to explain their feelings by finding a possible cause. In this case, if a particular conspiracy is a topic of discussion in their social milieu, people might conclude that they are anxious because of this conspiracy. In other words, affect elicited by irrelevant sources, such as experiencing an anxious mood, can influence judgments (Schwarz & Clore, 2007). These feelings can then influence judgments about products (Pham, 1998), personal risks (Gasper & Clore, 2000), and politics (Forgas & Bower, 1987).

Table 4.4. *Associations of general measure of anxiety and health anxiety with conspiracy beliefs (Study 1)*

	b(SE)	p	b(SE)	p
Fixed Effects	Sociopolitical		Health	
(Intercept)	2.21 (0.04)	<0.001	2.27 (0.04)	<0.001
Anxiety^	0.30 (0.05)	<.001	0.37 (0.05)	<0.001
Health anxiety^	−0.01 (0.05)	0.91	0.01 (0.04)	0.85
Random Effects				
σ^2		0.55		0.77
τ_{00}		1.12 pid		0.80 pid
ICC		0.67		0.51
N_{pid}		734 pid		734 pid
N		1467		1465
Marginal R^2 / Conditional R^2		0.050 / 0.686		0.0794 / 0.549

Note: Entries correspond to a multilevel regression conducted separately for political and health beliefs. Within each type of belief (political or health), the specific conspiracy theory (e.g., about HIV and the MMR vaccine) was introduced as a random factor. *b*: regression coefficient. *SE*: standard error of regression coefficient. *p*: p value. *N*: sample size. ^ denotes that the variable was centered. Sigma squared refers to the within-group (residual) variance. Tau-oo refers to the between-group variance. The marginal R^2 considers only the variance of the fixed effects, whereas the conditional R^2 takes both the fixed and random effects into account.

People who become aware that affect may bias their judgments may use this affect as information or correct for it. A now classic study of correction for the biasing influence of affect took place in the political domain. In this research conducted by Isbell and Wyer (1999), participants induced to experience a happy or sad mood read an article about the positions of political candidates. Participants varied in their partisan intensity and were told that they would vote on the candidates or not, allowing the researchers to separate participants on the basis of their level of motivation to think about the candidates. When participants had low motivation to process this information, mood had a contagion effect. That is, happy participants judged the candidates more positively, whereas sad participants judged the candidates more negatively. In contrast, when participants had high motivation to think about the information, there was evidence that participants corrected for the influence of their mood. Specifically, happy participants rated the candidates less favorably than did sad ones.

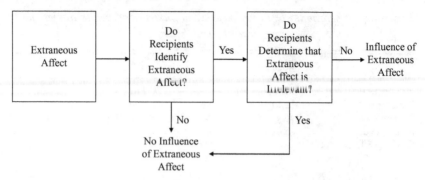

Figure 4.2.   Selection and identification of affect in persuasion (reproduced from Albarracin, 2020)

Even though being motivated to think about the information can make people set their feelings aside as irrelevant, some attention to one's feelings is still necessary for mood to influence judgments. Albarracín and Kumkale (2003) proposed that information identification and selection processes guide the use of feelings as information. As shown in Figure 4.2, no feelings can bias judgment unless people first identify or direct attention to them and then use them as a basis for judgment. Hence, we were interested in examining attention to feelings within our research on conspiracy beliefs.

The existence of the two processes of affect identification and selection impacts how ability and motivation influence the use of affect as information. Moderate decreases in ability and motivation may increase the impact of feelings people see as irrelevant when they can carefully consider relevance. Further decreases in ability and motivation, however, prevent the identification of feelings when making judgments. When this happens, the influence of affective feelings goes away.

Individuals' level of attention to their feelings varies according to individual differences or to situational factors. External inducements to consider affect can make people attend and use their feelings as information, or attend and then ignore them (Albarracín & Kumkale, 2003c). Albarracín and Kumkale (2003b) relied on this idea in research we report presently, which was designed to shed light on the cognitive processes by which anxiety can bias conspiracy beliefs in the moment.

The original research reported in this book included an experiment to determine if extraneous affect could influence conspiracy beliefs. In this experiment, we recruited a nationally representative sample of 606 participants from Dynata. Participants were first induced to experience anxiety or not according to random assignment. Those in the anxiety condition were told:

> Today we are collecting personal experiences for use in the development of personality inventories. You have been assigned to writing about a time when you experienced fear. Please write about it in a letter to somebody you feel close too, making sure to describe exactly how you felt during this experience. Do not worry about grammar or style.

Participants were also asked to indicate the truth or falsity of the statement that "The novel coronavirus is caused by cell towers delivering 5G connectivity" on a scale from 1 ("definitely true") to 5 ("definitely false"), which we reverse-scored. However, we manipulated attention to their anxiety with the position of a question about how calm, worried, and confused they felt, as well as how much they experienced fear and how much fear and anxiety dominated their feelings. For example, participants were first asked: "How did you feel while writing about the experience?" They then provided their response to "While I was writing, I felt anxious" on a scale from 1 ("strongly disagree") to 5 ("strongly agree"). For participants in the anxiety-attention condition, these items preceded the belief measure; for participants in the no-anxiety-attention condition, they followed the belief measure.

Preliminary analyses indicated that participants had not guessed our hypothesis and that the anxiety manipulation made them more anxious. If participants were thinking moderately (e.g., they had ability but no motivation to think) to begin, being asked about their feelings might lead them to discount those feelings. However, if participants were thinking minimally (i.e., they had neither ability nor motivation to think) to begin, being asked about their feelings might lead them to identify and thus use those feelings as a basis for their beliefs. Thus, the anxiety-attention manipulation could have either decreased or increased the influence of the anxiety manipulation on the 5G conspiracy belief.

Findings from our experiment suggested that the anxiety-attention manipulation actually increased the use of anxiety as a basis for judgment. The findings for the belief measure appear in Table 4.5. As shown, when participants had been prompted to think about their feelings, their conspiracy beliefs aligned with them. On a 5-point scale, they reported their conspiracy beliefs to be 2.22 and 1.95 in the anxiety and no anxiety condition, respectively. These results suggest that participants were relatively unmotivated to think about their anxious feelings at the beginning

Table 4.5. *Results from our experiment manipulating anxiety*

	Anxiety	No anxiety
N		
Questions about affect before beliefs	153	156
Questions about affect after beliefs	150	152
Conspiracy belief Ms		
Questions about affect before beliefs	2.22 (1.39)	1.95 (1.34)
Questions about affect after beliefs	1.84 (1.22)	2.26 (1.40)

Note: *N*: Sample sizes for each cell. *M:* Mean. Standard errors appear in parentheses.

of the study. However, when a prompt allowed them to identify how they felt, the anxiety manipulation had an impact.

One aspect we did not anticipate, however, was that when participants were not prompted to think about their anxiety, having written about an anxiety-inducing event actually led to weaker conspiracy beliefs (Ms = 1.84 versus 2.26). These participants might still have been thinking about the event and could not clearly label their feelings. As a result, they may have still been distracted by the episode, thus paying less attention to the judgments that followed. Whatever the case, it is clear that inducing extraneous anxiety had implications for conspiracy beliefs: When people thought about their anxiety, it affected their beliefs about the alleged coronavirus conspiracy.

4.1.1.5 Our Longitudinal Evidence on the Reciprocal Impact of Anxiety on Beliefs

Even though affect can shape beliefs as we demonstrated experimentally, beliefs in conspiracies could also exert causal effects on anxiety. On the one hand, conspiracy beliefs may increase anxiety by making our world appear more dangerous. On the other, they may provide an explanation that reduces anxiety (Whitson & Galinsky, 2008). By providing longitudinal measures on both anxiety and the belief in the deep state conspiracy, Study 4 in this book, which we conducted during the 2019–2020 impeachment process, allowed us to examine the direction of influence.

The anxiety item in Study 4 was "Thinking about feeling calm or worried. In the past week, would you say you felt." Participants provided responses on the following scale: 1 ("Very calm most of the time"), 2 ("Fairly calm most of the time"), 3 ("Fairly worried most of the time"), 4 ("Very worried most of the time"), and 5 ("Neither calm nor worried"). Responses were rescored onto a 1 ("Very calm most of the time") to 5 ("Very worried most on the time"), with "Neither calm nor worried" scored a 3.

The conspiracy belief item was "Unelected U.S. government officials including some in the US intelligence services have secretly conspired to illegally undermine the candidacy and presidency of Donald Trump." This belief item was introduced at baseline and reintroduced in the two follow-ups of the survey. Ratings were provided on a scale with the following points 1 ("Definitely true"), 2 ("Probably true"), 3 ("Probably false"), 4 ("Definitely false"), and 8 ("Not sure"). "Not Sure" was scored as the middle point of the scale and everything was mapped onto a 1 ("Definitely false") to 5 ("Definitely true").

We used the three time points in the study to conduct a cross-lagged panel analysis that modelled the directional influence that beliefs and anxiety have on each other over time. Results of the cross-lagged panel analysis, which constrained the relations to be the same across time under the stationarity assumption, can provide evidence about the relative influence of earlier beliefs on later anxiety and of earlier anxiety on later beliefs. The analyses showed a nonsignificant association between earlier anxiety and later conspiracy beliefs (between anxiety at Time 1 and the belief in the deep state conspiracy at Time 2, and between anxiety at Time 2 and belief in the deep state conspiracy at Time 3) ($\beta = -0.02$, *ns*, in both cases). However, there were significant associations between the belief at Time 1 and anxiety at Time 2, and between the belief at Time 2 and anxiety at Time 3. However, these associations were negative ($\beta = -0.09$, $p < .001$, in both cases). These results then suggest that the belief might have provided an explanation that later reduced anxiety.

In sum, even though experimentally we found effects of manipulated anxiety/fear on conspiracy beliefs, the longitudinal data did not show that anxiety at the beginning of the study had an influence on later beliefs. These seemingly inconsistent data point to the complexity of these processes and our argument that anxiety is insufficient to produce conspiracy beliefs. As discussed in later chapters, it is social influence that provides the content of conspiracy beliefs, and in the case of the deep state, the contribution of the media and of anxiety varied at different points of the impeachment process (see Chapter 8).

4.2 Conspiracy Beliefs, Human Motivations, and Anxiety

Conspiracy beliefs have been linked to various needs related to the belief defense, belief accuracy, and social integration motivations. We first review this evidence and then move to the role of anxiety in possibly mediating effects of the motivations on conspiracy beliefs.

4.2.1   Conspiracy Beliefs as a Means to Meet the Belief Defense Motivation

A key psychological function of the ego is to defend us from perceptions that are unpleasant or that may undermine effective action. Our self-views, including our self-esteem, and psychopathological ego-defensive distortions common in schizotypy (i.e., odd or eccentric personality characteristics that range from dissociation to psychosis) and paranoia (i.e., the belief that one is being threatened, watched, or persecuted when no facts support it) can trigger defensive processes to protect our beliefs. Self-esteem (i.e., a positive evaluation of oneself) and narcissism (i.e., exaggerated feelings of self-worth) develop to preserve a defined sense of self with which to respond to the challenges the world presents. Paranoid ideas preserve the view that the ego is benevolent, whereas other people and outside forces are not. Thus, self-esteem and narcissism and paranoia are different forms of defending important self-beliefs. Each has been studied in the conspiracy theory literature.

4.2.1.1   Schizotypy and Paranoia

In psychoanalysis, the ego is the psychological structure in charge of effective action and adaptation to reality (Freud, 1961; Hartmann, 1958). Maladaptive forms of ego defense include schizotypal personality and paranoia, both of which have been investigated in relation to conspiracy theories for decades. Schizotypal personality is characterized by omnipotence, idealization (i.e., exaggerated positive views), devaluation (i.e., sudden and exaggerated negative views), denial (i.e., inability to perceive an uncomfortable aspect of reality), projection (e.g., attributing undesirable aspects of oneself, such as one's hostility, to another person), and splitting (i.e., inability to have a balanced view of the self or other people as having both positive and negative characteristics). These defenses are consistent with a presence of autistic fantasy and an absence of repression (i.e., the defense mechanism by which undesirable contents are removed from one's awareness), all consistent with a failure of the ego to maintain contact with reality and consequently regulate healthy interactions with the environment (Perry, Presniak, & Olson, 2013). These defense mechanisms allow people to believe that they are all-powerful and protect them from shame or fear by imagining that others have aggressive thoughts and emotions that in reality they themselves have. When people with a

Table 4.6. *Paranoia and conspiracy beliefs*

Short reference	r
Barron et al. (2014)	0.24
Brotherton and Eser (2015)	0.52
Bruder et al. (2013), Study 2	0.45
Bruder et al. (2013), Study 3	0.5
Cichocka, Marchlewska, and Golec de Zavala (2016)	0.37
Darwin, Neave, and Holmes (2011)	0.47
Grzesiak-Feldman and Ejsmont (2008)	0.62
Grzesiak-Feldman (2015)	0.3
Wilson and Rose (2014), Study 1	0.27
Wilson and Rose (2014), Study 2	0.27
Wilson and Rose (2014), Study 3	0.29
Wilson and Rose (2014), Study 4	0.3

Note: Imhoff and Lamberty (2018).

schizotypal personality lose contact with reality, paranoia is apparent in their delusions of persecution, unwarranted jealousy, or exaggerated self-importance.

Saying that people who are paranoid believe in conspiracies is to some extent tautological. However, whereas people who experience paranoia have unique beliefs about who threatens them and why, conspiracy beliefs are socially shared and thus common to many people. In this sense, correlations between the two may reveal common mechanisms, one occurring at the level of individuals and the other at the level of groups. Imhoff and Lamberty (2018) characterized the size of the correlations between paranoia and conspiracy beliefs. These correlations appear in Table 4.6, and suggest that paranoia and conspiracy beliefs are distinct, a finding confirmed via factor analysis in two primary studies reported by Imhoff and Lamberty (2018).

Among the studies in Table 4.6, Darwin et al. (2011) measured conspiracy beliefs with ad-hoc statements like "There are specialized government services who attempt to harass UFO witnesses into silence." The paranormal belief scale (Tobacyk & Milford, 1983) measured traditional religious belief, psi beliefs, witchcraft, superstition, spiritualism, extraordinary life forms, and precognition. The paranoid ideation scale (Fenigstein & Vanable, 1992) measured thoughts of others wanting to harm the respondent; and the schizotypal personality questionnaire measured cognitive-perceptual deficits, interpersonal deficit, and disorganization. The correlations of conspiracy beliefs and these personality measures

Table 4.7. *Correlations between conspiracy beliefs, religious beliefs, various paranormal beliefs and abnormal perceptions*

	Conspiracy Beliefs (N = 120)
Total paranormal belief score	
Religious belief	0.26*
Parapsychology	0.53**
Witchcraft	0.40**
Spiritualism	0.43**
Superstition	0.22*
Extraordinary life forms	0.30*
Precognition	0.22**
Total paranormal belief score	0.47**
Paranoid ideation scale	0.47**
Schizotypal personality questionnaire	
Cognitive-perceptual deficits	0.31**
Interpersonal deficit	0.19*
Disorganization	0.27*
Total schizotypy score	0.34**

Note: r: Pearson correlation. *: $p < 0.05$; **: $p < 0.01$; ***: $p < 0.001$. N: Sample size. Darwin et al. (2011).

appear in Table 4.7 and suggest some shared variance between conspiracy beliefs and each of these scales, particularly parapsychology and paranoid ideation. Causal modeling further showed that the best-fitting model was one in which the overall schizotypy score influenced conspiracy beliefs, both directly and via mediating influences on paranoid ideation.

4.2.1.2   Self-Esteem and Narcissism

The degree to which people value themselves has also been posited as an important predictor of conspiracy beliefs (Robins & Post, 1997). For example, in a study conducted in the UK and Austria (Swami et al., 2011), participants completed measures of conspiracy beliefs and self-esteem. Belief in a conspiracy surrounding the London bombings on July 7, 2005 and a general conspiracy theory inventory had negative correlations with self-esteem $r = -.16$ and $-.20$ (Galliford & Furnham, 2017). Although this finding is interesting and replicated in a second study with a fictitious conspiracy belief, the direction of causality could not be ascertained. On the one hand, having low self-esteem may strengthen conspiracy beliefs with the unconscious objective of projecting negative self-representations and feelings onto an outside threat. On the other, having low self-esteem may correlate with viewing all aspects of the world in a negative light.

The connection between self-esteem and conspiracy beliefs has received considerable attention in relation to narcissism. The rationale for studying narcissism is that the more narcissistic people are, the more likely they are to believe that others envy and conspire against them, which is a core characteristic of conspiracy beliefs. In research by Cichocka, Marchlewska, De, and Olechowski (2016), the zero-order correlations between self-esteem and conspiracy beliefs were not statistically significant. However, their studies supported the hypothesis that *narcissism* correlates positively with conspiracy beliefs (e.g., $r = .25$ in Study 2) and paranoia (e.g., $r = .18$ in Study 2). Moreover, some of the influence of narcissism on conspiracy theories was mediated by paranoia. In contrast, self-esteem correlated negatively with paranoia, possibly because perceiving plots against oneself assumes that one is important and valuable.

The research on self-esteem and narcissism is, by necessity, correlational. Research on the need for uniqueness, however, has employed experimental procedures. Need for uniqueness is the desire to differ from others and stand out for individualizing characteristics and ideas (Lynn & Snyder, 2002). Because they are relatively unconventional and suggest access to privileged knowledge, conspiracy beliefs can signal uniqueness (Douglas & Sutton, 2018; Lantian, Muller, Nurra, & Douglas, 2017). In research by Lantian et al. (2017), participants completed a scale measuring need for uniqueness. This scale contains items such as "I prefer being different from other people," and responses to it were positively correlated with belief in conspiracy theories. In a later study by Lantian et al., participants who wrote about being individual were more likely to believe in conspiracies than were ones who wrote about conforming to norms. Thus, the positive association between narcissism and conspiracy theories could also be explained by the tendency of narcissists to see themselves as intellectually superior and, as a result, more skilled at detecting plots compared to other people.

4.2.1.3   *Tendency to Perceive Patterns*

Connecting the dots when no clear shape exists is an important characteristic of conspiracy theories, and has led researchers to study the tendency to perceive patterns as a possible predictor of conspiracy beliefs. A study by Moulding et al. (2016) included various measures of conspiracy beliefs as well as the intolerance for uncertainty and the need for cognitive closure scales. Conspiracy beliefs were measured with the Belief in Conspiracy

Table 4.8. *Beliefs that events are not random and conspiracy beliefs*

	Belief that events are not random
Belief in Conspiracy Theories Inventory	0.42**
Belief in Conspiracy Theories Inventory-True	0.36**
Belief in Conspiracy Theories Inventory-False	0.27**
Generic Conspiracist Beliefs Scale	0.44**
Conspiracy Mentality Questionnaire	0.26**

Note: r: Pearson correlation. **: $p < 0.01$. Moulding et al. (2016).

Theories Inventory (Swami et al., 2010) and involved rating such state-ments as "The Apollo moon landings never happened and were staged in a Hollywood film studio." The study also included statements about ficti-tious conspiracy theories such as Red Bull containing extract of bull testicles (i.e., Belief in Conspiracy Theories Inventory-False), and items about historical or real conspiracies like "The CIA attempted, through chemical, biological and radiological means, to develop mind control as part of what is a project designated MKUltra" (Belief in Conspiracy Theories Inventory-True, Swami et al., 2010). Furthermore, the study included the Generic Conspiracist Beliefs Scale (Brotherton, French, & Pickering, 2013), which measures government and scientific malfeasance, global conspiracies, and extraterrestrial cover-ups, as well as the Conspiracy Mentality Questionnaire, which contains items such as "many very impor-tant things happen in the world, which the public is never informed about." This study also measured the tendency to perceive a pattern of social relations and the concept of beliefs in a just world. Specifically, the World Assumptions Scale (Janoff-Bulman, 1989) was used to assess per-ceptions of randomness ("bad events are distributed to people at random"). The correlations from this study appear in Table 4.8 and show that the sense that events do not happen at random had consistent, moderate correlations with every measure of conspiracy belief.

4.2.1.4   *Need for Closure*
Uncertainty would have little impact if humans could be content without certainty and individuals and situations did not vary in the need to reduce uncertainty. Conspiracy beliefs may emerge when people try to reduce anxiety, much in the same way as they do in response to the need for control. The need to reduce uncertainty is often measured with the Intolerance of Uncertainty Scale (Carleton, Norton, & Asmundson,

Table 4.9. *Correlations with intolerance for uncertainty and need for closure*

	Intolerance for uncertainty scale	Need for closure
Belief in Conspiracy Theories Inventory	0.09	0
Belief in Conspiracy Theories Inventory-True	0.16	0.04
Belief in Conspiracy Theories Inventory-False	0.09	−0.03
Generic Conspiracist Beliefs Scale	0.13	0.08
Conspiracy Mentality Questionnaire	0.30**	0.17

Note: r. Pearson correlation. **: $p < 0.01$. van Prooijen and Jostmann (2013).

2007; Freeston, Rhéaume, Letarte, Dugas, & Ladouceur, 1994), which includes statements like "I can't stand being taken by surprise" on a 5-point scale (1 = "not at all characteristic of me" to 5 = "entirely characteristic of me"). Another popular measure is the Need for Cognitive Closure Scale (Roets & Van Hiel, 2011; Webster & Kruglanski, 1994), which includes statements such as "I dislike unpredictable situations" measured on a 6-point Likert-type scale (1 = "Strongly Disagree" to 6 = "Strongly Agree"). There is also the very similar Uncertainty Orientation Scale (Sorrentino & Short, 1986), which was created in an initial collaboration between Kruglanski and Sorrentino.

The support for a direct association between conspiracy beliefs and the need to reduce uncertainty has been mixed. Take, for example, van Prooijen and Jostmann's (2013) study, which included no less than five conspiracy belief scales. Results with these scales appear in Table 4.9. The correlations of those five scales with the intolerance for uncertainty scale and the Need For Closure Scale revealed only one significant correlation out of ten.

Weak associations between need for cognitive closure and conspiracy beliefs may be due to either the absence of association or the presence of a nonlinear one. For example, the effect of the need for closure may be apparent only among people who have chronic conspiracy beliefs, a hypothesis that Leman and Cinnirella (2013) investigated. They used the Swami et al.'s (2010) Belief in Conspiracy Theories Inventory as a measure of chronic conspiracy beliefs and the Need for Closure Scale with a sample of college students in the United Kingdom. They then presented ostensible evidence about a plane crash leading to five fatalities, one of whom was a political figure the opposition wanted to block. The material presented to participants appears in Table 4.10.

Table 4.10. *Experimental materials*

Conspiracy material	Control material
The accident investigation report could not identify a cause for the crash.	The accident investigation report cited mechanical failure as the cause of the crash.
Some interested parties have expressed concern that the crash may not have been an accident. The plane had been given a full engineering check only the day before the crash, and was judged to be in excellent working order.	All interested parties were satisfied that the crash had been an accident.
The emergency services arrived late because they had received contradictory evidence from anonymous witnesses concerning the location of the plane.	Three months prior to the crash an identical fault had been detected on another plane of the same model, type, and make.
The "safety concerns," which had necessitated the change in travel plans, related to intelligence suggesting that an assassination attempt on Sir – was imminent.	The late arrival of the emergency services had been due to the restricted information concerning the location of the plane.
	The security threat, which had necessitated the change in travel plans, was deemed to be unfounded.

Note: Leman and Cinnirella (2013).

People with high need for closure may reach a definitive conclusion even from ambiguous evidence provided they normally believe in conspiracies. The results from Leman and Cinnirella's (2013) experiment showed that habitually suspecting conspiracies and receiving information favoring a conspiracy led to conspiracy beliefs. However, the need for closure moderated the influence of chronic conspiracy beliefs. People high in need for closure had stronger conspiracy beliefs when they scored higher (vs. lower) on the Belief in Conspiracy Theories Inventory, which, as explained previously, measures chronic conspiracy beliefs (approximately $Ms = 34$ vs. 30 on a scale of 0–50). In contrast, people with lower need for cognitive closure were not affected by the information they read (approximately $M = 28$ in both cases). In conclusion, the need for closure correlated the tendency to habitually rely on conspiratorial hunches when the new information was conspiratorial.

A study by Marchlewska, Cichocka, and Kossowska (2017) conceptually replicated the finding by Leman and Cinnirella (2013) with an immigration theme. In one of their studies, participants read information about the arrival of refugees into Poland. Generally, need for closure correlated with the belief that the arrival of refugees was part of a conspiracy against Poland ($r = .22$). Moreover, the association with need for closure was stronger when participants heard a conversation suggesting that the refugee arrival was part of a European Union conspiracy to harm Poland. These effects were replicated in a second experiment in which, similar to Leman and Cinnirella's (2013) one, participants were exposed to information about a plane accident.

Need for closure is a factor we analyzed in the surveys we report in this book. Studies 1 and 2 contained a short measure of need for closure (Kossowska, Van Hiel, Chun, & Kruglanski, 2002). The two items were (a) "I don't like situations that are uncertain," and (b) "I enjoy having a clear and structured mode of life." Study 3 included the full Need for Closure Scale. Responses were provided on Likert scales, as follows. "Strongly Agree," "Somewhat Agree," "Neither Agree nor Disagree," "Somewhat Disagree," and "Strongly Disagree." This scale was scored from 1 ("Strongly Disagree") to 5 ("Strongly Agree").

We thus estimated the correlations between need for closure and the conspiracy beliefs we studied. These analyses appear in Table 4.11.

Table 4.11. *Correlations with need for closure (Studies 1–3)*

Conspiracy beliefs	r with conspiracy beliefs	r with accurate, control beliefs
Study 1		
Obama's birth certificate	0.09[*]	0.04
Undocumented immigrants decided popular vote	0.04	0.23[***]
HIV virus as a government creation	0.01	0.05
MMR vaccine cover-up	0.01	0.16[***]
Study 2		
Obama's birth certificate	−0.03	0
Undocumented immigrants decided popular vote	0.01	0.17[***]
HIV virus as a government creation	−0.08[*]	0
MMR vaccine cover-up	0.06	0.13[***]
Study 3		
Obama's birth certificate	−0.03	0.04
Undocumented immigrants decided popular vote	−0.02	0.09[**]
HIV virus as a government creation	−0.08[*]	0.01
MMR vaccine cover-up	−0.02	0.13[***]

Note: r. Pearson correlation. *: $p < 0.05$; **: $p < 0.01$; ***: $p < 0.001$.

Table 4.12. *Correlations of beliefs and general and specific need for closure (Study 1)*

	Conspiracy beliefs		Accurate, control beliefs	
	General need for closure	Political need for closure	General need for closure	Political need for nlosure
Obama's birth certificate	0.08*	0.05	0.02	0.04
Undocumented immigrants decided popular vote	0.06	−0.01	0.19***	0.20***
HIV virus as a government creation	−0.02	0.03	−0.01	0.11**
MMR vaccine cover-up	−0.01	0.03	0.13***	0.17***

Note: r. Pearson correlation. *: $p < 0.05$; **: $p < 0.01$; ***: $p < 0.001$.

As shown, our findings differed from some others in that need for closure was minimally associated with conspiracy beliefs, and, if anything, was positively correlated with some control, accurate beliefs. That is, being motivated to reach closure was uncorrelated with the tendency to believe that Obama was not born in the United States, that undocumented immigrants decided popular vote, or that the link between the MMR vaccine and autism was covered up. However, being motivated to reduce uncertainty correlated with the accurate beliefs that undocumented immigrants falsify work documents to secure a job and that the tobacco industry covered up the evidence that smoking causes cancer and other diseases.

In Study 1, we also analyzed whether need for closure in a specific domain correlates with conspiracy beliefs in that same arena. Thus, we included items to measure the need for political closure. The correlations appear in Table 4.12. As shown, the need for closure was uncorrelated with conspiracy beliefs, irrespective of whether we measured it as a general trait or in relation to political information. In combination with other studies showing little evidence that need for closure matters, we concluded that other forces, including anxiety, play a more important and immediate role in the production of conspiracy beliefs.

4.2.2   Conspiracy Theories and the Accuracy Motivation

The type of cognitive style that gives way to conspiracy beliefs has received considerable attention, often in research that measures rational and experiential/intuitive thinking. A preference for rational thought is associated with higher academic achievement (GRE scores and grade-point average), self-esteem, openness to experience, and conscientiousness. Rational thinking (Pacini & Epstein, 1999) is typically measured with items similar to those in the need for cognition scale, which includes "I enjoy solving problems that require hard thinking" and "I enjoy thinking in abstract terms." The experiential/intuitive thinking scale (Pacini & Epstein, 1999) involves items such as "Intuition can be a useful way to solve problems" and "I tend to use my heart as a guide for my actions." A number of studies have obtained correlations between conspiracy beliefs and cognitive styles. Using these scales, Swami, Voracek, Stieger, Tran, and Furnham (2014) found that rational thinking style correlated $r = -.25$ with conspiracy beliefs. They also found that experiential cognitive style correlated $r = .21$. Similarly, the study by Georgiou et al. (2019) included these measures and found that, as expected, rational thinking correlated negatively with two measures of conspiracy beliefs: $r = -.29$ and $-.31$. In contrast, experiential/intuitive thinking correlated positively with two measures of conspiracy beliefs: $r = .37$ and .35.

Systematically inducing a rational or analytic cognitive style has also been shown to reduce conspiracy beliefs. Swami, Voracek, Stieger, Tran, and Furnham (2014) manipulated analytic thinking in several ways. First, in one of their studies (Study 2), they used scrambled sentences to prime cognitive style. The analytical condition included words like "analyse," "reason," "ponder," "think," and "rational." The control condition included words like "chair" and "shop." In other studies (Studies 3 and 4), participants were given a text in a difficult or easy to read font. Researchers hypothesized that a difficult to read font would induce people to be more analytical, which was actually the case. The results from Studies 2 and 3 supported the hypothesis that priming an analytical thinking style weakened conspiracy beliefs.

More recent work has replicated the finding of a negative association of conspiracy beliefs with an analytic thinking style and need for cognition. In a study conducted by Barron et al. (2018), participants rated items like "US agencies intentionally created the AIDS epidemic and administered it to Black and gay men in the 1970s," which are part of Swami et al.'s Belief in Conspiracy Theories Inventory. Findings indicated that belief in conspiracy correlated $r = -.14$ with analytical thinking and $r = -.19$ and cognitive insight. This work also showed that paranoid ideas of reference influenced conspiracy beliefs via corresponding influences on analytical thinking.

Table 4.13. *Analytical thinking and epistemically suspect beliefs*

		1	2	3	4	5	6
1	Scientific reasoning	1					
2	Cognitive ability	0.37	1				
3	Analytical thinking	0.20	0.23	1			
4	Dogmatism	−0.26	−0.26	−0.09	1		
5	Epistemically suspect beliefs	−0.21	−0.21	−0.09	0.13	1	
6	Susceptibility to cognitive biases and heuristics	−0.38	−0.44	−0.18	0.20	0.15	1

Note: Entries are Pearson correlations. Čavojová et al. (2020).

Similar work has been conducted to understand the connection between conspiracy beliefs and not only analytical thinking but also scientific reasoning, cognitive ability, and dogmatism. In a study by Čavojová, Šrol, and Jurkovič (2020), the researchers used Raven's progressive matrices to measure cognitive ability, the Pacini and Epstein's (1999) analytic thinking scale, and a measure of dogmatism (Altemeyer, 2002). They estimated the associations of these measures with "epistemically suspect beliefs," which were a combination of beliefs in the paranormal as well as conspiracy beliefs about global warming and the effectiveness of wearing crystals, among others. They also estimated associations with 18 different cognitive biases and heuristics as an indication of the tendency to commit fallacies. The correlations among the study measures appear in Table 4.13. As one might expect, higher levels of scientific reasoning and cognitive ability were negatively correlated with epistemically suspect beliefs. Moreover, analytical thinking had a weak, nonsignificant negative correlation with epistemically suspect beliefs. The study also showed a positive association between epistemically suspect beliefs and susceptibility to cognitive biases and heuristics, suggesting that conspiracy beliefs increase as a function of nondeliberative judgment.

In addition to conspiracy beliefs being linked to heuristics and biases more generally, there also is evidence that they are connected to conjunction errors. Conjunction errors occur when people are likely to rate the co-occurrence of two events as more likely than one even though the probability of each alone is higher. Rogers, Fisk, and Lowrie (2018) used scenarios such as:

(a)   Erica feels uneasy driving her car for such a long distance.
(b)   Whilst on the motorway, Erica's car breaks down.

(c) Erica feels uneasy driving her car for such a long distance and whilst on the motorway, Erica's car breaks down.

People who choose (c) judge the conjunction as more likely and may resemble people who perceive causal events are connected. The researchers measured a variety of epistemically suspect beliefs such as extrasensory perception and psychokinesis. As hypothesized, participants who believed in conspiracies were more prone to conjunction errors than nonbelievers. In addition, the beliefs correlated negatively with need for cognition ($r = -.24$, $-.29$, and $-.24$ for extrasensory perception, psychokinesis, and life after death, respectively) and positively with faith in intuition ($r = .30$, $.24$, and $.34$ for extrasensory perception, psychokinesis, and life after death, respectively). Finally, the errors and thinking style were correlated such that the fallacy was more pronounced when people were lower in analytical thinking (i.e., need for cognition).

Our own surveys considered whether an analytical cognitive style, measured as need for cognition, reduces the tendency to explain events by resorting to conspiracies. Studies 1 and 2 included short measures of need for cognition (Cacioppo, Kao, Petty, & Rodriguez, 1986) with the following items: (a) "I like to have responsibility for handling situations that require a lot of thinking," and (b) "I prefer simple to complex problems." Study 3 included the complete need for cognition scale (Cacioppo, Kao, Petty, & Rodriguez, 1986). In all cases, responses were given on Likert scales, as follows. "Strongly Agree," "Somewhat Agree," "Neither Agree nor Disagree," "Somewhat Disagree," and "Strongly Disagree." This scale was scored from 1 ("Strongly Disagree") to 5 ("Strongly Agree").

Table 4.14 presents the correlations involving need for cognition. Studies 1 and 2 included a short version of the need for cognition scale, whereas Study 3 employed the complete version (for more details on methods, see Appendix). As expected from prior research, the table shows that the correlations with conspiracy beliefs generally tended to be negative. However, these correlations were only significant with the complete scale included in Study 3. In addition, need for cognition correlated positively with accurate beliefs, implying that an analytical style facilitates discrimination of true and false information.

Our own surveys also allowed us to analyze whether the accuracy motivation in specific domains is more relevant to conspiracy beliefs than is the general need for cognition. Specifically, our first study included measures of need for cognition with the items being specific to politics or

Table 4.14. *Correlations with need for cognition (Studies 1–3)*

Belief	Conspiracy belief r	Accurate control belief r
Study 1		
Obama's birth certificate	0.02	0.08*
Undocumented immigrants decided popular vote	−0.03	0
HIV virus as a government creation	0.04	0.15***
MMR vaccine cover-up	−0.03	0.13***
Study 2		
Obama's birth certificate	0	0.09**
Undocumented immigrants decided popular vote	−0.04	−0.05
HIV virus as a government creation	0.07*	0.22***
MMR vaccine cover-up	0.02	0.06
Study 3		
Obama's birth certificate	−0.18***	−0.03
Undocumented immigrants decided popular vote	−0.17***	−0.04
HIV virus as a government creation	−0.07*	0.10**
MMR vaccine cover-up	−0.19***	0.13***

Note: r: Pearson correlation. *: $p < 0.05$. **: $p < 0.01$. ***: $p < 0.001$.

to health (for more details, see Appendix). Thus, we were able to correlate political conspiracy beliefs with specific measures of need for political cognition. These analyses appear in Table 4.15 and showed that the general need for cognition was associated with weaker conspiracy beliefs, implying that a general analytical thinking style was sufficient for people to form more accurate beliefs. Political need for cognition did not show such negative correlations with conspiracy beliefs, and, for the belief that the HIV virus is a CIA creation, a higher need for cognition was associated with stronger endorsement of that notion.

4.2.3   Conspiracy Beliefs as Means to Fulfill the Social Integration Motivation

Many of the social factors implicated in conspiracy beliefs are political (see Chapter 5), but isolation and exclusion are also prominent predictors of conspiracy beliefs in the psychological literature. On the one hand, isolation and social exclusion appear to strengthen belief in conspiracies by increasing anxiety and the desire to simplify the world. Graeupner and

Table 4.15. *Correlations with general and specific need for cognition (Study 1)*

	Conspiracy beliefs		Accurate control beliefs	
Belief	General need for cognition	Political need for cognition	General need for cognition	Political need for cognition
Obama's birth certificate	−0.04	0.06	0.07	0.08*
Undocumented immigrants decided popular vote	−0.10**	0.03	0.01	−0.01
HIV virus as a government creation	−0.02	0.08*	0.16***	0.13***
MMR vaccine cover-up	−0.09*	0.01	0.16***	0.09*

Note: r. Pearson correlation. *: $p < 0.05$; **: $p < 0.01$; ***: $p < 0.001$.

Coman (2017) investigated this possibility in two studies. They found that the correlation between feelings of exclusion and endorsement of conspiracy theories was $r = .19$. On the other hand, being concerned about groups can heighten social threats and thus strengthen conspiracy beliefs. Accordingly, Graeupner and Coman's second study showed that being selected to be a partner for an experimental task led to greater conspiratorial attributions than not being selected, an effect equal to $r = .25$. Also, in real life, a reduction of social interaction provides little opportunity to verify one's ideas vis-à-vis the corrective opinions of others.

There is, however, evidence that endorsing conspiracy theories is a source of social stigma. To begin, people who actually endorse conspiracy theories are reluctant to label their beliefs as conspiratorial (M. J. Wood & Douglas, 2013). They also object to other people labeling their own ideas as such. Apparently, even though belonging to groups with strong beliefs might promote a sense of social acceptance, being labeled as a "conspiracy theorist" creates a stigma. Lantian et al. (2018) tested this notion in two studies. Participants were randomly assigned to either a condition in which they advocated a conspiracy as an explanation of a shooting, or a condition in which they advocated against the conspiracy. After a brief reminder of the Charlie Hebdo shooting, participants were informed that some people called into question the official story about the group accused of causing the event, claiming instead that it was planned in secret by foreign secret services or secret societies. In the pro-conspiracy condition, participants were asked to argue against those explanations, which were explicitly labeled

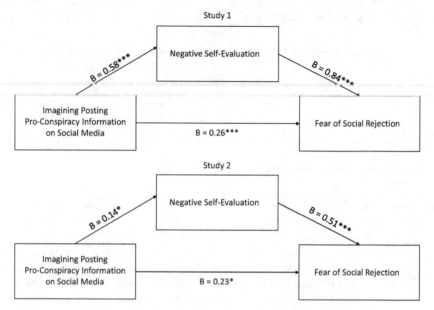

Figure 4.3.   Mediational analyses for the stigmatizing effects of advocating conspiracy theories online (results from Lantian et al., 2018)

"conspiracy theories." They then imagined that they publicly posted what they had written on their Facebook profiles, available for all to view. Imagining posting pro-conspiracy materials on their Facebook profile led participants to anticipate a negative evaluation and ultimately to fear social exclusion. The mediational analyses from this study appear in Figure 4.3. Moreover, the effect was stronger among participants who did not endorse conspiracy beliefs at the beginning of the study. Presumably, participants who did not endorse these beliefs had more to lose from being derogated as "conspiracy theorists" by others, an effect that people who endorsed the same beliefs before the study might not have minded because they were used to it.

In a second study, Lantian et al. (2018) conducted a conceptual replication of their previous study. Participants again argued either in favor of or against a conspiracy theory and imagined presenting this material to an audience. The bottom half of Figure 4.3 presents the mediational analyses for this study. The results were similar to the ones from Study 1. Imagining posting pro-conspiracy materials on one's Facebook profile led participants to anticipate a negative evaluation and ultimately to fear social exclusion. However, the coefficients in Figure 4.3, which are stronger from the manipulation to fear of social rejection than negative self-evaluation, suggest that fear of rejection might have arisen first, giving way to negative expectations as a result. It could be that the presence of a physical audience in Study 2 triggered a more visceral reaction, whereas the online audience in Study 1 could have triggered more reflection and thus expectations of negative evaluations. Regardless, the studies provided evidence that endorsing beliefs in conspiracy can create a stigma.

Our own surveys included measures of need to belong (M. R. Leary, Kelly, Cottrell, & Schreindorfer, 2013), an ideal measure to assess correlations with the social integration motivations. Need to belong was measured with the following items: (a) "I do not like being alone," and (b) "I want other people to accept me." Study 3 included the full Need to Belong scale. Responses were provided on Likert scales, as follows: "Strongly Agree," "Somewhat Agree," "Neither Agree nor Disagree," "Somewhat Disagree," and "Strongly Disagree." This scale was scored from 1 ("Strongly Disagree") to 5 ("Strongly Agree").

The correlations between need to belong and conspiracy beliefs in Studies 1–3 appear in Table 4.16. As shown, there were consistent positive

Table 4.16. *Correlations of social integration motivation (need to belong)*
with conspiracy beliefs (Studies 1–3)

Belief	Conspiracy beliefs r	Accurate control beliefs r
Study 1		
Obama's birth certificate	0.15***	0.06
Undocumented immigrants decided popular vote	0.10**	0.06
HIV virus as a government creation	0.08*	0.02
MMR vaccine cover-up	0.09*	0.06
Study 2		
Obama's birth certificate	0.09*	0.10**
Undocumented immigrants decided popular vote	0.09**	−0.04
HIV virus as a government creation	0.05	0.08*
MMR vaccine cover-up	0.04	0.05
Study 3		
Obama's birth certificate	0.11**	0.04
Undocumented immigrants decided popular vote	0.12***	−0.04
HIV virus as a government creation	0.05	−0.02
MMR vaccine cover-up	0.10**	−0.06

Note: r: Pearson correlation. *: $p < 0.05$; **: $p < 0.01$; ***: $p < 0.001$.

Table 4.17. *Correlations with general and specific need to belong (Study 1)*

	Conspiracy beliefs		Accurate, control beliefs	
Belief	General need to belong	Political need to belong	General need to belong	Political need to belong
Obama's birth certificate	0.09*	0.16***	0.02	0.08*
Undocumented immigrants decided popular vote	0.04	0.13***	0.04	0.06
HIV virus as a government creation	0.08*	0.06	−0.01	0.08*
MMR vaccine cover-up	0.10**	0.06	0.03	0.07

Note: r: Pearson correlation. *: $p < 0.05$; **: $p < 0.01$; ***: $p < 0.001$.

correlations with conspiracy beliefs, indicating that the more motivated participants were to connect with others, the stronger their beliefs that Obama was not born in the US, that undocumented immigrants decided the popular vote in the 2016 election, and that there is a cover-up of the effects of the MMR vaccine. Moreover, the need to belong was relatively uncorrelated with the accurate control beliefs, suggesting that people with a strong need to belong seek fringe beliefs and/or that the groups disseminating these beliefs offer strong social rewards for participation in conspiracy-theorizing groups (see Chapters 7 and 8).

As with the other motivations, we also analyzed the correlations of belief in conspiracy with the general and political need to belong. These correlations appear in Table 4.17. As Table 4.17 shows, the correlations were similar regardless of whether the measure was general or specific to political issues. Thus, the social integration motivation appears to predispose people to believe in conspiracies regardless of whether the motivation is related to politics or not.

4.2.4   *How the Defense, Accuracy, and Social Integration Motivations Influence Conspiracy Beliefs via Anxiety*

The principle of anxiety presented in this book states that the defense, accuracy, and social integration motivations correlate with conspiracy beliefs primarily because they correlate with anxiety. In our surveys, we measured need for closure, need for cognition, and need to belong, and found that the need for cognition and the need to belong were associated with conspiracy beliefs. The key question, however, is whether the

Table 4.18. *Correlations of anxiety with need for closure and need for social integration (Studies 1–3)*

Survey	Need for closure	Need to belong
Study 1	0.21***	0.25***
Study 2	0.17***	0.22***
Study 3	0.09**	0.33***

Note: r. Pearson correlation. ***: *p < 0.001.*

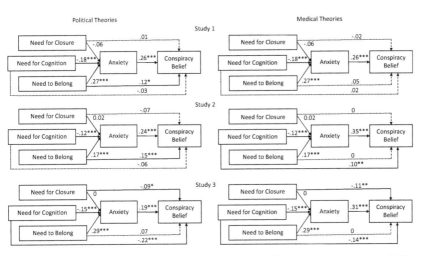

Figure 4.4. Anxiety as a mediator of the motivational influences on conspiracy beliefs

associations between motivations and conspiracy beliefs are mediated by anxiety. As shown in Table 4.18, anxiety was positively correlated with the needs for closure and social integration in all cases.

The positive correlations of anxiety with the need for closure and the need to belong and between anxiety and conspiracy beliefs are consistent with the hypothesis that anxiety is the intervening mechanism linking these motivations to conspiracy beliefs. The next stage, however, was to statistically show mediation within our studies. This goal was achieved by testing the path model in Figure 4.4. The path model was multilevel, clustered by participant, and was conducted separately for political and health beliefs. Within each type of belief, the specific conspiracy theory (i.e., Obama's birth certificate and voting by undocumented immigrants

Table 4.19. *Indirect effects of motivations on conspiracy beliefs as mediated by anxiety (Studies 1–3)*

	Estimate	SE	z
Study 1			
Political beliefs			
Need for cognition	−0.03	0.01	−3.19***
Need to belong	0.02	0.01	2.57**
Medical beliefs			
Need for cognition	−0.05	0.01	−4.06***
Need to belong	0.03	0.01	2.97**
Study 2			
Political beliefs			
Need for cognition	−0.03	0.01	−3.27***
Need to belong	0.03	0.01	3.38***
Medical beliefs			
Need for cognition	−0.04	0.01	−3.59***
Need to belong	0.04	0.01	3.92***
Study 3			
Political beliefs			
Need for cognition	−0.01	0.01	−2.28*
Need to belong	0.03	0.01	3.10**
Medical beliefs			
Need for cognition	−0.02	0.01	−2.69**
Need to belong	0.05	0.01	4.59***

Note: Analyses conducted with multilevel path analyses conducted separately for political and health beliefs. Within each type of belief, the specific conspiracy theory (e.g., about HIV and the MMR vaccine for health beliefs) was introduced as a random factor. *: $p < 0.05$; **: $p < 0.01$; ***: $p < 0.001$. The same effects for accurate, control beliefs were *ns* in Studies 1, 2, or 3. These estimates were obtained from path analyses that are described in more detail in Chapter 8.

for political beliefs and HIV and the MMR vaccine for health beliefs) was introduced as a random factor (see code in Online Supplement), and anxiety, need for cognition, and need to belong were introduced as fixed effects at the level of the participant.

As shown in Figure 4.4, need for cognition and need to belong, but not need for closure, influenced anxiety, which in turn influenced conspiracy beliefs. This finding implies that the motivation to achieve an accurate understanding of reality (e.g., the need for cognition) decreases anxiety, and consequently decreases conspiracy beliefs. In contrast, the motivation

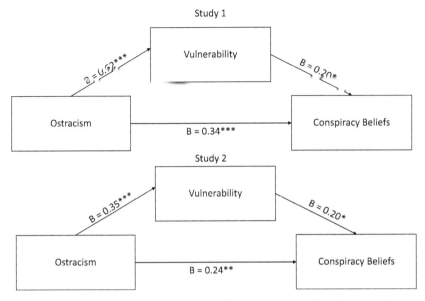

Figure 4.5.   Impact of ostracism on vulnerability and conspiracy beliefs (adapted from Pool et al., 2020)

to be socially integrated (i.e., the need to belong) increases anxiety, and consequently increases conspiracy beliefs. In addition, the motivation to achieve an accurate understanding of reality also had direct effects on conspiracy beliefs, implying that an analytical style ensures better understanding and attention to information. These conclusions were supported by formal tests of mediation for those models. As shown in Table 4.19, anxiety was a significant mediator of the effects of need for cognition and need to belong on both political and medical beliefs in every one of our studies. However, need for closure was uncorrelated with anxiety (see Figure 4.4).

A recent series of studies by Poon et al. (2020) led to similar conclusions about the impact of the social integration motivation on conspiracy beliefs. In a first study, participants completed a measure of ostracism with items such as "In general, others do not look at me when I'm in their presence" (1 = hardly ever, 7 = almost always). Participants also reported whether they felt vulnerable and whether they agreed or disagreed with 14 different political conspiracy theories. One of these beliefs involved whether SARS (Severe Acute Respiratory Syndrome) was produced in the laboratory as a bioweapon, a belief that has resurfaced in relation to COVID-19.

Figure 4.5 presents the results. Feeling ostracized correlated with feeling vulnerable and in turn with believing in false conspiracies. In a second study, the researchers manipulated ostracism by having participants recall an instance in which they felt ostracized. Once again, as shown in Figure 4.5, ostracism produced feelings of vulnerability, which in turn increased endorsement of conspiracy beliefs.

Poon et al. (2020) were also interested in finding mechanisms that might offset the negative impact of ostracism on conspiracy beliefs. They considered self-affirmation as a possible way of coping with stressful situations. Out of a list of 12 values, participants selected two that were either important (self-affirmation condition) or unimportant (no self-affirmation condition) to them. They then explained why they were important or not important to them. Consistent with other research reviewed in this chapter, participants who were not self-affirmed believed in conspiracy theories more after recalling a past instance of ostracism than after recalling a control instance. However, this difference disappeared when participants were self-affirmed.

4.3   Discussion

This chapter reviewed the degree to which experiencing anxiety, or the closely connected feelings of being stressed out or out of control, correlate with conspiracy beliefs. We found that these feelings show consistently positive correlations with conspiracy beliefs in many domains. In addition, we analyzed the extent to which conspiracy beliefs are connected to the defense, accuracy, and social integration motivations. There are several important conclusions. First, the literature has argued that the belief defense motivation instills conspiracy beliefs. Naturally, paranoia correlates with conspiracy beliefs, but conspiracy beliefs are so similar to paranoia that the relation is almost tautological. In contrast, some past work and our findings about need for closure generally do not support a relation with conspiracy beliefs. Our surveys constitute a thorough examination of that relation and across four different conspiracy theories, but none supported a consistent relation between need for closure and conspiracy beliefs. Similarly, work by van Prooijen and Jostmann (2013) showed only one significant positive correlation between need for closure or need for uncertainty and conspiracy beliefs out of a total of 10 correlations.

What the need for closure can do, however, is to encourage people to align with information consistent with their preexisting conspiracy beliefs, just as need for closure does in any domain. Research by Leman and

Cinnirella's (2013) and by Marchlewska, Cichocka, and Kossowska (2017) converged in pointing out that the need for closure makes people interpret new information in ways consistent with their prior conspiracy beliefs or information about a conspiracy. However, there was little evidence for a direct influence from need for closure to conspiracy beliefs in the absence of prior conspiracy beliefs.

The belief accuracy motivation has typically been measured with the need for cognition scale or the closely related measure of analytical thinking. The need for cognition clearly reduces vulnerability to conspiracy beliefs in several areas, both in studies conducted by other researchers and in our own. Likewise, the opposite counterpart of analytical thinking, which is intuitive/experiential thinking, consistently and positively correlated with conspiracy beliefs in past research.

The social integration motivation is clearly a determinant of conspiracy beliefs. In combination, past studies, including our own, show that feelings of exclusion, feelings of ostracism, and the need to belong are positively correlated with conspiracy beliefs. Moreover, both ostracism and the need to belong affect conspiracy beliefs through mediating influences on feelings of vulnerability or anxiety. The motivation to be socially accepted appears to be central to the fears that end up creating conspiracy beliefs. However, the actual content of the conspiracy beliefs is not explained by the social integration motivation, making the origin of conspiracy stories an open question. We turn to different forms of social influence as a possible source in later chapters.

CHAPTER 5

Sociopolitical Factors and Conspiracy Beliefs

Both stable and situational psychological dynamics affect conspiracy beliefs. The research in our book added to this literature by highlighting the role of anxiety, which is a feeling that goes from mild uncertainty about the future to more extreme manifestations of fear. As described in Chapter 4, people with higher need for cognition are less likely to feel anxious and in turn endorse conspiracy beliefs less. People with higher need to belong are more likely to feel anxious and in turn endorse conspiracy beliefs more.

This chapter builds on the prior ones by considering sociopolitical influences on conspiracy beliefs. As shown in Figure 5.1, sociopolitical factors are critical to the endorsement of conspiracy theories. As proposed in the principle of anxiety below, sociopolitical factors can influence conspiracy beliefs, in part by corresponding influences on anxiety.

> **Principle of Anxiety.** Anxiety is a perception of threat and depends on relatively stable psychological motivations of belief defense, belief accuracy, and social integration, as well as sociopolitical factors and situational factors such as communications and media exposure. Experiencing anxiety at a particular time motivates a search for an explanation and can lead to misattributing the anxiety to a conspiracy story.

This chapter presents alternative political approaches and, using our survey data, tests the influences of sociopolitical factors underlying conspiracy beliefs. The main goal is to organize a dispersed body of knowledge into our motivations of belief defense, belief accuracy, and social integration. Under factors associated with the belief defense motivation, we include paranoia (Hofstadter, 1964; Pipes, 1997; Robins et al., 1997; see also Chapter 4) and political ideology or party identification (Gaines, Kuklinski, Quirk, Peyton, & Verkuilen, 2007; McHoskey, 1995). Under factors associated with the belief accuracy motivation, we include political knowledge and education (van Prooijen, 2017). Under factors associated

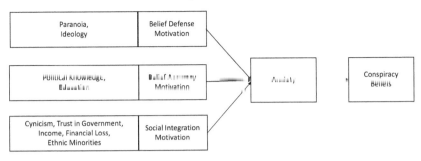

Figure 5.1. Theoretical model

with the social integration motivation, we include cynicism and trust in government institutions (Goertzel, 1994; Jolley, Douglas, Leite, & Schrader, 2019), ethnic minorities, and economic factors such as income and financial loss. In addition to organizing this long list of factors typically studied in isolation into a parsimonious framework, we empirically examine their influence by proposing anxiety as a factor that, being proximal to conspiracy beliefs, can explain some of their impact.

5.1 Sociopolitical Factors Associated with the Belief Defense Motivation

The belief defense motivation allows humans to preserve stability in their environments. Human beings respond to their self-views and sense of self-worth (Baumeister, 1997; Eagly & Chaiken, 1993; Kunda, 1990) by defending their beliefs (Albarracin, 2021). In this section, we describe and assess the ways in which conspiracy beliefs are influenced by paranoia (Hofstadter, 1964; Pipes, 1997; Robins et al., 1997; see also Chapter 4) as well as by political ideology and party identification (Gaines et al., 2007; McHoskey, 1995). Our own analyses appear in Table 5.1.

5.1.1 *Paranoia in American Politics*

As we noted in the opening chapter, influenced by Hofstadter's work (1964), early accounts of conspiracy theories proposed that conspiracy beliefs are the product of extreme paranoia, delusional thinking, or narcissism (See also, Swami & Furnham, 2014) (see Table 7.2). The underlying motivation of Hofstadter's scholarship (see also Popper, 2006, 2012) was to explain the rise of the "New American Right" or

Table 5.1. *Correlations between beliefs and political variables (Studies 1–3)*

Theory	Republicans vs. Democrats	Political Knowledge	Education	Cynicism	Voted in Last Election	Income	Financial Loss
Study 1							
Political conspiracy beliefs							
Obama's birth certificate	−0.38***	−0.13***	0.01	−0.25***	0.03	−0.03	0.11**
Undocumented immigrants decided popular vote	−0.34***	−0.10**	0.10**	−0.26***	0.05	0.04	0.07
Health conspiracy beliefs							
Obama's inaction and crisis in Syria	−0.30***	−0.05	0.02	−0.03	0.07	−0.04	0.09*
Undocumented immigrants use false documents to work	−0.20***	0.01	−0.10**	0.01	−0.02	0.04	−0.02
Health conspiracy beliefs							
HIV virus cover-up	−0.09	−0.10**	0.06	−0.13***	−0.07*	−0.04	0.20***
MMR vaccine cover-up	−0.27***	−0.11**	0.01	−0.19***	−0.03	−0.08*	0.19***
Health control beliefs							
Tuskegee study	−0.02	0.03	0.03	0.14***	−0.07	−0.05*	0.13***
Tobacco effects cover-up	0.15***	0.09*	−0.14***	0.27***	−0.02	−0.03	0.01
Study 2							
Political conspiracy beliefs							
Obama's birth certificate	−0.38***	−0.15***	−0.13***	−0.15***	−0.09**	−0.10**	0.10**
Undocumented immigrants decided popular vote	−0.35***	−0.15***	−0.11***	−0.17***	−0.11***	−0.07*	0.04
Health conspiracy beliefs							
Obama's inaction and crisis in Syria	−0.40***	0.03	−0.04	−0.05	−0.02	0.01	0.03
Undocumented immigrants use false documents to work	−0.25***	−0.04	−0.05	0.02	−0.02	0.02	0
Health conspiracy beliefs							

HIV virus cover-up	0.07*	-0.22***	-0.14***	-0.16***	-0.13***	-0.17**	0.21***
MMR vaccine cover-up	-0.08*	-0.21***	-0.14***	-0.22***	-0.13***	-0.12**	0.21***
Health control beliefs							
Tuskegee study	0.07*	-0.02	0.04	-0.07*	-0.02	0	0.11***
Tobacco effects cover-up	0.05	0.16***	0.15***	0.16***	0.11***	0.11***	0.01
Study 3							
Political conspiracy beliefs							
Obama's birth certificate	-0.41***	-0.16***	-0.14***	-0.08*	-0.03	-0.07*	0.19***
Undocumented immigrants decided popular vote	-0.31***	-0.16***	-0.13***	-0.08**	-0.05	-0.03*	0.18***
Obama's inaction and crisis in Syria	-0.42***	-0.07*	-0.03	0.03	-0.02	-0.02	0.09**
Undocumented immigrants use false documents to work	-0.21***	-0.06	-0.08*	0.07*	0.10**	-0.04	0.07*
Health conspiracy beliefs							
HIV virus cover-up	0.04	-0.25***	-0.19***	-0.15***	-0.09**	-0.17**	0.17***
MMR vaccine cover-up	-0.11**	-0.26**	-0.23***	-0.19***	-0.10**	-0.15**	0.19***
Health control beliefs							
Tuskegee study	0.11**	0.02	0.03	0.05	0.02	-0.06*	0.07*
Tobacco effects cover-up	0.03	0.10**	0.15***	0.17***	0.18***	0.08*	-0.04

Note: r: Pearson correlation. *: $p < 0.05$; **: $p < 0.01$; ***: $p < 0.001$.

McCarthyism, and, later, Barry Goldwater and other groups (Fenster, 1999). Nonetheless, the theorizing itself remains influential in today's academic and popular culture, as demonstrated by the more recent use of the term "paranoid style" to refer to the Republican and Democratic Parties and to George W. Bush and Dick Cheney in the 2000s (Fenster, 1999). The term has also been used more recently to characterize Donald J. Trump's beliefs and behavior (Lynch, 2016)

In his foundational 1964 essay, Hofstadter compared different paranoid styles throughout American history, from the Illuminati to McCarthyism. His notion of paranoid style was not clinical because in the paranoid beliefs of a conspiracy theory, the plot is not directed to the individual, as it is in classic paranoia, but to a nation, culture, or political group (Hofstadter, 1964). Despite this caveat, Hofstadter introduced clinical terminology into the discourse about conspiracy beliefs and was deeply influenced by psycho-analytic thinking (D. W. Howe & Finn, 1974). After Hofstadter's work (1964), "paranoia" has been used both metaphorically (Byford, 2011) and in the stricter, clinical sense (Byford, 2011; Robins et al., 1997).

For instance, a recent study by Larsen et al. (2020) assessed paranoia in the clinical sense using the Revised Green et al.'s (2008) Paranoid Thought Scale among young participants (Freeman et al., 2019). The study examined the predictors of conspiracy beliefs about COVID-19. Findings indicated that endorsement of COVID-19 conspiracy theories was associated with higher levels of intolerance of uncertainty as well as anxiety (see Chapter 4), delusion-proneness, and paranoid ideation. Furthermore, delusion-proneness and paranoia explained the relation between intolerance of uncertainty and conspiratorial thinking and were partial predictors of conspiratorial thinking. In contrast, anxiety did not explain the relation between intolerance for uncertainty and conspiratorial thinking, implying a stronger role of paranoid traits as opposed to affective factors.

As explained previously, a common critique of the use of the term "paranoia" is that the widespread acceptance of conspiracy beliefs makes a mental disorder an implausible cause. For instance, a number of con-spiracy theories have surrounded COVID-19. A recent survey showed that nearly 60 percent of Nigerians thought that the statement that COVID-19 deaths "have been deliberately and greatly exaggerated" was definitely or probably true, along with more than 40 percent in Greece, South Africa, Poland, and Mexico (Henley & McIntyre, 2020). About 38 percent of Americans, 36 percent of Hungarians, 30 percent of Italians and 28 percent of Germans shared the same belief.

5.1.2   Party Identification and Political Ideology

Because partisanship and ideology often yield belief defense processes, scholars of political science and political psychology have investigated its role in abetting conspiracy theorizing. Political scientists traditionally assumed that citizens can acquire information in an unbiased way (Gerber & Green, 1999). After the 1970s, however, despite certain disagreement (Abrams & Fiorina, 2012; Fiorina & Abrams, 2008; Kinder & Kalmoe, 201), scholars agree that the American public has become increasingly more partisan and ideological along liberal–conservative lines on a wide range of issues (Shapiro & Bloch-Elkon, 2008). This polarization has led to research showing how partisanship and ideology bias voters' perceptions of information relevant to political decisions (Shapiro & Bloch-Elkon, 2008).

The assumption that party identification would not preclude impartiality in information interpretation was common in the 1960s. The *American Voter* (Campbell, Miller, Converse, & Stokes, 1960) was an important book that launched the field of political behavior (Lewis-Beck & Stegmaier, 2009). This study found two distinct, uncorrelated attitude structures: one for foreign policy issues and one for domestic socioeconomic issues. Of interest to our analysis, the positions on policy issues were not correlated with the respondents' party identification. Accordingly, Campbell, Miller, Converse, and Stokes (1960) concluded that issue attitudes were neither derived nor correlated with ideology.

In contrast to the impartiality assumption of scholarship such as *The American Voter*, more recent research on political science *has* speculated that party identification raises a perceptual screen through which the individual sees what is favorable to her partisan orientation (Gaines et al., 2007; McHoskey, 1995). Political scientists have further contended that the more politically aware segments of the population develop a partisan resistance that causes them to filter out information that conflicts with their views (Zaller, 1992). This characterization of partisan biases reflects extensive social psychological research on attitude persistence, selective exposure, and motivated reasoning (Gerber & Green, 1999; Hart et al., 2009; Howe & Krosnick, 2015; Kunda, 1987; Kunda & Sanitioso, 1989; Lord, Ross, & Lepper, 1979).

An example of biased processing was provided by Gaines and colleagues (2007). These authors examined whether and how partisans updated factual beliefs, interpretations of beliefs, and opinions about the handling of the Iraq War over a dynamic period of time (Gaines et al., 2007). According to this study, partisans tended to support their party's position in a conflict independently of their personal values about war and international conflict. In all of their studies but one the authors found, significant majorities of strong Democrats interpreted the number of casualties they believed to be correct as "large" or "very large," thus adopting interpretations compatible with their party's opposition to the conflict in Iraq. Similarly, strong Republicans also adopted interpretations that were consistent with their party's position about the conflict in Iraq. About 80 percent of strong Republicans judged the number of casualties as "moderate," "small," or "very small" at the beginning of the study. In terms of the mechanisms that prevent updating beliefs to match reality, extremely high numbers of casualties may trigger a more critical interpretation among Republican perceivers, who supported the war. In addition, the distortion may escalate in response to perceived biases of the other side, and elites may dictate what "small" and "large" number of casualties entail.

The existence of bias in perceptions of reality was actually present across a wide range of political topics during the 1990s and 2000s (Jerit & Barabas, 2012). To begin, Democrats and Republicans offered different answers to objective questions related to the unemployment rate, inflation, and how effective the party in power was at governing the nation. In addition, however, Democrats and Republicans had more information about topics that had positive implications for their own party and correspondingly less information about topics that had negative ones. These results, which appear in Table 5.2, show that, for instance, the overall proportion of correct information for Democrats was 0.41. However, this figure was 0.45 for topics that have positive implications for the Democratic party, but 0.35 for topics that have negative implications for the Democratic party. The results for Republicans mirrored those for Democrats (Jerit & Barabas, 2012). The overall proportion of correct information for Republicans was is 0.43. However, the same figure was 0.52 for topics that had positive implications for Republicans.

Table 5.2. *Levels of knowledge across partisan groups*

	All topics	Positive implications for the party	Negative implications for the party
Democrats	0.41 [0.40 0.41]	0.45 [0.44 0.45]	0.35 [0.34 0.36]
Republicans	0.43 [0.43 0.44]	0.52 [0.52 0.53]	0.43 [0.41 0.44]

Note: Entries represent proportion of correct items with 95% confidence intervals between brackets. Jerid and Barabbas (2012).

Jerit and Barabas (2012) have shown similar biased patterns for learning new political information. They directly measured participants' readiness to learn information that was congenital or uncongenial to the views of their political party. As hypothesized, partisans were more likely to learn facts that had positive implications for their party than ones with negative implications. Democrats were 32 percent more likely to learn facts that had positive implications for their party, and Republicans were 17 percent more likely to do the same with facts advantaging theirs. By contrast, exposing partisans to information with negative implications for their own party produced virtually no learning.

A study of the assassination of President Kennedy led to similar conclusions about partisan bias (McHoskey, 1995). The central thesis was that biased assimilation and attitude polarization (Lord et al., 1979; McHoskey, 1995) would lead the different sides to interpret information about the assassination in opposite ways consistent with their initial beliefs. Biased assimilation implies that evidence that supports one's position tends to be uncritically accepted, whereas evidence that contradicts one's position tends to be critically scrutinized and rejected. Attitude polarization is a common result of biased assimilation. In practice, this means that considering evidence that challenges one's initial position tends to strengthen rather than undercut that position (Lord et al., 1979; McHoskey, 1995). In McHoskey's (1995) research, participants rated the evidence consistent with their own position about the Kennedy assassination as stronger. Participants who initially thought that Oswald was responsible for the assassination judged the evidence about him and his actions to be more credible than the evidence contained in conspiracy theories about JFK's death. In contrast, participants who initially believed in a conspiracy judged the conspiracy evidence to be more credible than the evidence indicating that Oswald was the lone assassin. (For other work on political biases, see McHoskey, 1995; Sunstein, 2014; Swire, Berinsky, Lewandowsky, & Ecker, 2017).

The surveys we conducted allowed us to test whether Republicans versus Democrats and those who are more or less ideologically conservative are more likely to believe in specific conspiracy theories and accurate control ones. For party identification we asked the question, "Generally speaking, do you usually think of yourself as a Republican, a Democrat, an Independent, or something else? And the possible answers were, Republican, Democrat, Independent, or something else. The "something else" category was dropped, and the answers were coded, Democrat (1), Independent (2), Republican (3). For ideology, we asked the question,

"Do you think of yourself as liberal, conservative, or neither?" We later coded the answers as liberal (1), neutral (2), and conservative (3).

Our correlational analyses showed a strong association between party identification as well as ideology and beliefs, such that Republicans and conservative respondents were more likely to believe several accurate, control beliefs that are consonant with conservative opinions, including that: President Obama's inaction facilitated the humanitarian crisis in Syria and that undocumented immigrants often falsify documents to work in the United States (see Table 5.1). Republicans and conservative respondents were also more likely to accept a number of conspiracy beliefs, including that Obama faked his birth certificate to become president of the United States, and that undocumented immigrants voted in large numbers in 2016, deciding the popular vote. In addition, Republicans and conservative respondents were more likely to report that the United States government caused the HIV epidemic, and that the link between the MMR vaccine and autism has been covered up (Table 5.1). In turn, Democrats and liberals were more likely to endorse the accurate beliefs that the tobacco industry covered up the damaging effects of smoking and that the Tuskegee experimentation happened (Table 5.1).

Our own data thus supported the notion that partisanship and ideology shaped beliefs. Republicans/conservatives were more likely than Democrats/liberals to believe claims by President Trump and negative facts about President Obama. Less clear, however, is why Republicans were also more likely to endorse health conspiracy theories about the HIV virus or the MMR vaccine. Of note is the fact that the correlations between partisanship and health conspiracy beliefs were considerably smaller than the ones between partisanship and political conspiracy beliefs. In addition, our analyses showed that Democrats were more likely to endorse accurate control health beliefs, including that the Tuskegee experiment occurred and that the tobacco industry covered up the damaging effects of smoking. This is unsurprising insofar as Democrats are more likely than their ideological counterparts to distrust large corporations (Pew Reasearch Center, 2017). In addition, Black Americans, the group victimized by the Tuskegee deceptions, are a core Democratic constituency (Pew Research Center, 2016). Whether media use explains these patterns is a focus of Chapter 8.

5.2   Belief Accuracy Motivation

As forecast by the research on cognitive style synthesized in Chapter 4, individuals who have a belief accuracy motivation should be less likely to endorse conspiracy beliefs. However, in domains associated with political or other strong values, the same factors that can trigger unbiased processing may instead heighten bias. For this reason, whether factors such as political knowledge and education correlate with conspiracy beliefs was an open question for us.

5.2.1 Political Knowledge

Belief accuracy motivation (see Chapter 4) refers to the needs and goals that help individuals maintain a realistic representation of the world and make correct decisions (Jerit & Zhao, 2020). Political knowledge is widely viewed as a foundation for a representative democracy, and knowledge about the political system and politics is assumed to be crucial for participation in politics (Jerit & Zhao, 2020). However, there is disagreement as to whether cognitive sophistication decreases or magnifies politically biased information processing (Pennycook & Rand, 2019). In this section, we present this research.

Drawing on the literature on motivated reasoning, which posits that endorsement of a belief endorsement is a process that serves both ideological and psychological needs (Kunda, 1987; Kunda & Sanitioso, 1989; Lord et al., 1979), a study of self-identified conservatives and liberals tested endorsement of conspiracy theories when people have political knowledge but also the motivation to believe in the conspiracy because of their conservative ideology (Miller, Saunders, & Farhart, 2016). Consistent with the main prediction of motivated reasoning, among conservatives, political knowledge was positively correlated with endorsement of conspiracy theories ($bs = .07$ and $.10$ for Mturk and ANES, respectively). In contrast, among liberals, political knowledge was negatively correlated with conspiracy beliefs ($bs = -.30$ and $-.34$ for Mturk and ANES, respectively). In sum, the authors' hypothesis that knowledge exacerbates ideologically motivated reasoning in the domain of conspiracy endorsement was confirmed, but only for conservatives.

Despite research suggesting that political knowledge should increase conspiracy beliefs by increasing one's ability to rationalize those beliefs, other work has not supported this hypothesis. Work by Tappin et al. (2020) gave American partisans new information about factual political questions, and measured their beliefs, and their analytic thinking. Here, cognitive sophistication was operationalized as analytic thinking (see Chapter 4) inferred from participants' performance on the Cognitive Reflection Test. There was little evidence that analytic thinking magnified politically biased deviations from an unbiased benchmark. Rather the beliefs reported by participants suggested that greater analytic thinking was associated with beliefs closer to an unbiased benchmark.

Our own studies allowed us to examine associations between political knowledge and conspiracy beliefs. Political knowledge was based on a measure of knowledge of American government (A filibuster in the US Senate can be used to prevent legislation from coming to a vote. Who casts a tie-breaking vote in the US Senate? Of the 100 US senators, how many votes are needed to end a filibuster? How is the number of terms a president can serve determined?) and a higher value represents a higher number of correct answers to these questions (Pew Research Center, April 26, 2018). The level of political knowledge was generally negatively correlated with conspiracy beliefs and positively correlated with the accurate belief that the Tuskegee experiment occurred (see Table 5.1). More specifically, participants who had higher levels of political knowledge were less likely to hold conspiracy beliefs. However, to understand if motivated reasoning was at stake, it is necessary to analyze if political knowledge is used differently as a function of political ideology. We thus considered interactions between political ideology and political knowledge and found no significant interactions for either the conspiracy or the control beliefs. We concluded that motivated reasoning was unlikely to explain endorsement of conspiracy beliefs.

5.2.2   Education

The effects of education on conspiracy beliefs have been generally expected to be directionally negative because education also imparts knowledge about how to verify claims (Douglas et al., 2019; Goertzel, 1994; Oliver & Wood, 2014). Although generally a higher level of educational attainment predicts a lower likelihood of conspiracy beliefs, some null findings exist as well (Douglas et al., 2016; Georgiou et al., 2019; Hoftyzer, 2013; van Prooijen, 2017). Furthermore, if motivated thinking were at stake, it should increase conspiracy beliefs when these beliefs are consistent with one's ideology, much in the same way as political knowledge could.

A study by Douglas et al. (2016) examined whether education correlated with a general tendency to endorse conspiratorial explanations for events (Douglas et al., 2016). In two studies, the authors examined the association between education and conspiracy belief. They found that conspiracy beliefs were negatively correlated with education level (e.g., $r = -.26 \, p < .01$). Of particular note, however, education predicted conspiracy beliefs because less educated people were more likely to see intentionality and agency where there is none (Douglas et al., 2016).

Our own studies also found support for the idea that education is a protector against conspiracy beliefs. Binary correlations (see Table 5.1) showed that education was negatively associated with endorsement of conspiracy theories. In general, those with lower levels of schooling were more likely to believe that President Obama was not born in the United States, undocumented immigrants decided the popular vote in the 2016 election, the United States government caused the HIV epidemic, and the link between the MMR vaccine and autism has been covered up (see Table 5.1). In contrast, education generally correlated positively with endorsement of accurate beliefs (see Table 5.1). We also investigated the interactions between party identification or ideology and education, as such interactions are the hallmark of motivated reasoning. These interactions were not significant with two exceptions. In Study 1, the interaction between knowledge and ideology was $\beta = 0,13$ ($p < .05$) for the belief that Obama falsified his birth certificate to become president and $\beta = 0,14$ ($p < .05$) for the accurate belief that Obama's inaction contributed to the Syrian crisis. Our research thus demonstrated that education protected individuals from believing conspiracies and that this benefit applied independently of political ideology.

5.3 Social Integration Motivation

Politically, social integration should be facilitated by trust in politicians and institutions which is usually associated with increased participation in democracy (J. Albarracin & Valeva, 2011). In turn, social integration should be more challenging for members of underrepresented groups, and persons in fragile economic situations, either because of the social class to which they belong or because a detrimental change in their financial status.

5.3.1 Political Cynicism

A considerable amount of past research has treated conspiracy theories as a product of cynicism, defined as lack of trust and disenchantment with political authority or disaffection from the political system (Swami & Furnham, 2014), a disposition that suggests low integration into society. For example, a survey of residents of New Jersey showed that belief in conspiracy theories was associated with anomia ($r = .43$), lack of interpersonal trust $(r = -.37)$, and insecurity about employment $(r = .21)$ (Goertzel, 1994). These correlations suggest that conspiracy beliefs are associated with cynicism (Goertzel, 1994).

Saunders (2017) hypothesized that trust in government would serve as a moderator of the impact of different ways of casting climate-relevant conspiracy beliefs. He reasoned that, because "climate change" (CC) is perceived to be less severe than "global warming" (GW), the CC frame would pose less identity threat for Republicans and, as a result, trust in government would have a larger negative effect on the belief that CC is a hoax than the belief that GW is. For Democrats, trust was hypothesized to have either no effect (because of the potential floor in endorsement) or a negative one in both the CC and GW question frames. The study found a positive and statistically significant interaction among party identification, trust, and question frame. Supporting the hypothesis, Democrats were unaffected by frame. High-trust Republicans were more likely to endorse anthropogenic global warming when the GW frame rather than the CC one was used (Saunders, 2017).

Our studies included measures related to disenchantment with political authority and cynicism. We measured cynicism in a nuanced way, by asking participants to rate their agreement with the statements "Politicians are honest," "Politicians genuinely try to keep campaign promises," and "Politicians are incompetent. Answers were recorded in a 5-point scale, ranging from "strongly disagree" to "strongly agree." We then reverse-scored these items. Our Study 3 also included a set of questions on trust in government, "The US House of Representatives can be trusted," "The US Senate can be trusted," "The Centers for Disease Control and Prevention (CDC) can be trusted," "The police can be trusted," "The Federal Bureau of Investigation (FBI) can be trusted." Answers were also recorded on a 5-point scale, ranging from "strongly disagree" to "strongly agree." These results appear in Table 5.1.

Our results showed (see Table 5.1) that, contrary to prior research, participants who were more cynical endorsed all conspiracy theories less than participants who were less cynical. More cynical respondents were less likely to report that President Obama was not born in the United States, that undocumented immigrants voted illegally in the 2016 election, that the HIV epidemic was caused by the American government, and that there is a cover-up of the effects of the MMR vaccine. The variable of trust in government, however, had few significant results. People who trusted the government less were more likely to believe that the Tuskegee experiment was true ($r = -0.06, p < .05$) and that the United States government created the HIV virus ($r = -0.08, p < .05$). However, although the other correlations were not significant, in general they had the negative signs predicted in the literature implying that less trust may be associated with stronger conspiracy beliefs.

One important aspect interpreting these data is that Donald Trump was president of the United States during our studies. As Trump has promoted both conspiracy theories and the idea that politicians are dishonest, participants who trusted Trump might have endorsed conspiracy theories more as well. This was in fact the case. Trust in the president correlated positively with all conspiracy beliefs in all studies. As trusting the president could be a reason to believe in conspiracies and could at the same time increase cynicism, we then regressed conspiracy beliefs on both trust in the president and cynicism. In these regressions, cynicism either had less weight or its regression coefficient was positive, thus approximating the past literature more closely.

The results for accurate beliefs, however, were different. Respondents who were more cynical about politicians and government institutions were more likely to endorse the accurate beliefs in the cover-up of the damaging effects of tobacco and the Tuskegee study (see Table 5.1). It seems that overall, being cynical was associated with increased agreement with statements reporting wrongdoings by the government and corporations.

5.3.2 Ethnic Minorities

Past scholars have argued that embrace of conspiracy beliefs is a byproduct of perceived exclusion from the power structure, as is the case among members of racial or ethnic minorities in the United Stated (Parsons, Simmons, Shinhoster, & Kilburn, 1999). Bird and Bogart (Bird & Bogart, 2005) analyzed conspiracy beliefs among African Americans related to HIV from their previous work. They showed that substantial numbers of respondents believe in different conspiracy theories, including, "Whites want to keep the numbers of African-American people down," "Poor and minority women are sometimes forced to be sterilized by the government," "The government is trying to limit the African-American population by encouraging the use of condoms" and "Medical and public health institutions use poor and minority people as guinea pigs to try out new birth control methods." These data are summarized in Table 5.3. A small proportion, however, endorsed the belief that "Birth control is a form of Black genocide." In addition, Parsons et al.'s (1999) analysis of conspiracy beliefs

Table 5.3. *Beliefs in conspiracy theories about African Americans and HIV*

Belief	Somewhat or strongly agree (%)
Having children is the key to the survival of the African American population	37
Whites want to keep the numbers of African-American people down	49
Poor and minority women are sometimes forced to be sterilized by the government	27
The government is trying to limit the African-American population by encouraging the use of condoms	21
Medical and public health institutions use poor and minority people as guinea pigs to try out new birth control methods	35
Birth control is a form of Black genocide	6

Note: Bird and Bogart (2005).

among African Americans has demonstrated that one reason African Americans endorse various conspiracy theories is their perception that they lack the ability to influence government actions. The researchers analyzed 11 government-related conspiracies (e.g., that AIDS was created to wipe Black people from the face of the earth). The most important determinant of conspiracy beliefs was perceived lack of influence of African Americans in government.

Our studies also enabled us to explore associations between minority status and conspiracy beliefs. Our results, which appear in Table 5.4, were consistent with previous findings that persons of color are more likely to believe conspiracy theories (Bird & Bogart, 2005; Parsons et al., 1999). Specifically, non-White participants were more likely to conclude that Obama was not born in the United States, undocumented immigrants decided the popular vote in 2016, the United States government created the HIV epidemic, and the link between the MMR vaccine and autism has been covered up. Also, non-White participants were more likely to believe the facts that the United States government left African Americans untreated in the Syphilis Tuskegee study and that Obama's inaction facilitated the humanitarian crisis in Syria. Finally, Whites were more likely to believe that the tobacco industry covered up the detrimental effects of smoking, an effect that persisted after controlling for education.

Table 5.4. *Table difference in means conspiracy beliefs non-Whites versus Whites (Studies 1–3)*

Belief	Means Non-Whites	Whites	*t*-test	*df*
Study 1				
Obama's birth certificate	2.45	2.06	2.98**	231.33
Undocumented decided popular vote	2.67	2.21	3.64***	226.71
Obama's inaction and crisis in Syria	2.88	2.89	−0.08	239.70
Undocumented immigrants use false documents to work	3.42	3.56	−1.16	244.92
HIV virus cover-up	2.87	2.05	6.61***	228.40
MMR vaccine cover-up	2.93	2.17	6.41***	241.75
Tuskegee study	3.21	3.01	1.55	249.90
Tobacco effects cover-up	3.80	4.15	−3.06**	222.89
Study 2				
Obama's birth certificate	2.15	2.26	−1.02	383.38
Undocumented decided popular vote	2.53	2.51	0.26	363.84
Obama's inaction and crisis in Syria	2.87	3.02	−1.65	384.07
Undocumented immigrants use false documents to work	3.53	3.72	−2.06*	361.31
HIV virus cover-up	2.95	2.28	6.75***	370.40
MMR vaccine cover-up	2.89	2.26	6.49***	369.99
Tuskegee study	3.47	3.15	3.39***	377.28
Tobacco effects cover-up	3.92	4.17	−2.81**	340.36
Study 3				
Obama's birth certificate	2.07	2.26	−1.78	375.90
Undocumented decided popular vote	2.52	2.42	0.98	373.57
Obama's inaction and crisis in Syria	2.65	3.03	−3.9***	365.06
Undocumented immigrants use false documents to work	3.60	3.73	−1.49	355.22
HIV virus cover-up	3.04	2.29	7.43***	350.24
MMR vaccine cover-up	2.90	2.32	5.82***	352.25
Tuskegee study	3.56	3.17	4.08***	354.89
Tobacco effects cover-up	3.98	4.15	−2.05*	353.54

Note: The table presents means and results from an independent sample *t* test. *: $p<.05$; **: $p < 0.01$; ***: $p<.001$.

5.3.3 *Income and Financial Loss*

Besides introducing the idea of paranoia as a characteristic of conspiracy theorizers, Hofstadter introduced social factors, stating that conspiracy theories are more likely to emerge when people feel powerless, disadvantaged, or voiceless (Hofstadter, 1964; see also, Sunstein & Vermeule, 2009). Some approaches (Swami, 2012) have proposed that Karl Marx's concept of alienation (Marx et al., 2013), defined as powerlessness, meaninglessness, normlessness, isolation, or self-estrangement, is implicated in conspiracy beliefs (Nettler, 1957, Swami, 2012)

One study set out to explain the emergence of the Tea Party, which promoted conspiracy theories (Enders, 2017; Newsweek, 2010), based on perceived social threats and negatively impactful changes (Barreto, Cooper, Gonzalez, Parker, & Towler, 2011). Barreto et al. argued that the Tea Party represented a right-wing movement distinct from mainstream conservatism, which reacted to the social and demographic changes in America over the past few decades and anxiety over loss of power. These changes included a dramatic growth of the immigrant population and the election of many prominent African-American, Latino, and Asian-American candidates to office. The beliefs endorsed by the Tea Party were presumably a response to these social threats.

Our surveys included several variables that captured the social position of people in society, including income and deterioration of the respondent's financial loss in the recent past. Specifically, income captured annual income and financial loss whether a person's financial situation had deteriorated in recent years. These data also appear in Table 5.1. As shown, income had several negative significant associations with conspiracy beliefs. That is, those with lower incomes believed that Obama was not born in the United States, that undocumented immigrants decided the 2016 popular vote, that the United States government created the HIV virus, and that the MMR vaccine causes autism. In turn, the same participants believed one of the control beliefs, namely that the United States government left African Americans untreated during the Tuskegee experiment. In turn, those with higher incomes believed that the tobacco industry covered up the effects of smoking. Altogether, income correlated more with conspiracy than accurate beliefs, supporting the idea that social exclusion explains them.

We also speculated that people who experienced a negative change in their social position may be more likely to endorse conspiracy beliefs. In general, participants who reported a financial loss in the previous few years were more likely to believe in the events we measured, both conspiracy and control ones. These individuals were more likely to believe that Obama was not born in the United States, that undocumented immigrants decided the popular vote in 2016, that President Obama's inaction facilitated the humanitarian crisis in Syria, that undocumented immigrants obtain fake social security number to work, that United States government caused the HIV epidemic, that the MMR vaccine causes autism, and that the government left African Americans untreated during the Tuskegee experiments (see Table 5.1). Clearly, financial loss matters for both conspiracy beliefs and agreement with beliefs in all of the negative events we measured.

5.4 Involvement of Anxiety

Our review up to this point in the chapter has served to organize a diverse literature about the belief defense, belief accuracy, and social integration motivation. We have also looked at some of these factors within our studies. As this chapter has shown, party identification and ideology, political knowledge, education, cynicism, income, and financial loss all predicted at least some of the conspiracy beliefs, as well as some control ones. In addition to the goals of organizing the literature and testing prior hypotheses within our data, we proposed that sociopolitical factors may affect conspiracy beliefs because they produce anxiety. In Chapter 4, factors such as the need for cognition and the need to belong were associated with anxiety and with conspiracy beliefs, and anxiety mediated the influence of those two needs on conspiracy beliefs. Similarly, as we propose, sociopolitical factors associated with the belief defense, belief accuracy, and social integration motivations may influence conspiracy beliefs via mediating influences on anxiety (see principle of anxiety).

To test the presuppositions in this principle, we first explored associations between the sociopolitical factors we considered in our surveys and anxiety. The correlations in Studies 1, 2, and 3 were, for political ideology: $r = .01$, $-.10$, $p < .01$, and 0.07, $p < .05$; for education: $r = .16$, $p < .001$, $-.18$, $p < .001$, and $-.19$, $p < .001$; for political knowledge: $r = -.14$, $p < .001$, $-.15$, $p < .001$, and $-.20$, $p < .001$; for cynicism: $r = -.12$, $p < .001$, $-.07$, $p < .05$, and $-.06$ *ns*; for financial loss: $r = .42$, $p < .001$, $.40$, $p < .001$, and $.41$, $p < .001$; and for having a job: $r = .08$, $p < .05$, $-.05$, *ns*, and $-.01$, *ns*.

We then conducted analyses to determine whether the associations between sociopolitical variables and conspiracy beliefs were mediated by anxiety. We fit a multilevel path model clustered by participant (see code in Online Supplement) in which belief was the outcome or endogenous variable, anxiety was the mediator, and sociopolitical variables were the external variables. Within each type of belief, the specific conspiracy theory (i.e., Obama's birth certificate and voting by undocumented immigrations for political beliefs and HIV and the MMR vaccine for health beliefs) was introduced as a random factor (see code in Online Supplement). These analyses, which appear in Table 5.5, show that anxiety mediated the influence of education, political knowledge, and having experienced a financial loss on conspiracy beliefs. Participants who were more (versus less) educated and had higher (versus lower) levels of political knowledge felt less anxious and therefore were less likely to endorse conspiracy beliefs. In contrast, participants who had (versus had not) experienced a financial loss felt more anxious and therefore were more likely to endorse conspiracy beliefs.

According to our analyses in Table 5.5, political ideology had a negative indirect effect mediated by anxiety on conspiracy beliefs in Study 1 and nonsignificant but directionally negative indirect effects in Studies 2 and 3. This finding may appear to conflict with past reports that conservatives are more anxious than liberals (for an excellent review, see Jost, Stern, Rule, & Sterling, 2017). However, the meaning of "anxiety" in the political literature differs from that in social psychological studies. In the classic work by Adorno, Frenkel-Brunswik, Levinson, and Sanford (1950), "anxiety" is used to refer to social, intergroup anxiety, as illustrated by the following quotes:

> These items, presented in Table 2(111), describe the Jews as a dangerous, dominating, corrupting social group. They are asserted to have great power economically and politically, and to be unscrupulous and conniving in their dealings with Gentiles. They do not like hard work (Item 1I–i) but at the same time they lower the general standard of living by doing menial work and by living under low standards (Item I–I 4). In addition to being simultaneously rich and poor, powerful and parasitic, they are also at once capitalists and revolutionaries. In their lack of patriotism, they are a threat to the nation, and in general they are a threat to civilization. (Adorno et al., 1950, p. 63)

> Apart from the enormous complexity of "the Jew" so described, there is something fantastic in the idea that a group so small numerically can be so powerful and so basic a social threat. This imagery in extreme cases seems to be an ideological expression of underlying paranoid trends; in Mein Kampf, for example, the Jews are regarded not only as "base and inferior" but also as having "germicidal potency" and "devilish cunning." However, most American anti-Semites are undoubtedly not psychotic or paranoid in the usual psychiatric sense." (Adorno et al., 1950, pp. 63–64)

Table 5.5. *Indirect effects of sociopolitical factors on conspiracy beliefs as mediated by anxiety (Studies 1–3)*

	Estimate	SE	z-value
Study 1			
Political beliefs			
Political ideology	−0.01	0.01	−2.25*
Education	0.03	0.01	1.96
Political knowledge	−0.01	0.01	−2.01*
Cynicism	0	0.01	0.5
Financial loss	0.06	0.02	3.44***
Having a job	0.01	0.01	0.88
Medical beliefs			
Political ideology	−0.02	0.01	−2.43*
Education	0.04	0.02	2.31*
Political knowledge	−0.02	0.01	−2.28*
Cynicism	0	0.01	0.5
Financial loss	0.1	0.02	5.26***
Having a job	0.01	0.01	0.89
Study 2			
Political beliefs			
Political ideology	−0.02	0.01	−1.76
Education	−0.02	0.01	−2.42*
Political knowledge	−0.01	0.01	−1.63
Cynicism	0	0.01	0.02
Financial loss	0.08	0.01	5.49***
Having a job	−0.01	0.01	−1.03
Medical beliefs			
Political ideology	−0.02	0.01	−1.72
Education	−0.03	0.01	−2.57*
Political knowledge	−0.02	0.01	−1.69
Cynicism	0	0.01	0.02
Financial loss	0.11	0.02	6.83***
Having a job	−0.01	0.01	−1.06
Study 3			
Political beliefs			
Political ideology	−0.01	0.01	−1.62
Education	−0.01	0.01	−1.63
Political knowledge	−0.01	0.01	−2.19*
Cynicism	0.01	0.01	1.64
Financial loss	0.04	0.01	3.48***
Having a job	0	0	0.57
Medical beliefs			
Political ideology	−0.02	0.01	−1.55
Education	−0.02	0.01	−1.68
Political knowledge	−0.02	0.01	−2.37*
Cynicism	0.01	0.01	1.82
Financial loss	0.07	0.01	5.57***
Having a job	0	0.01	0.58

Note: Analyses conducted with multilevel path analyses conducted separately for political and health beliefs. Within each type of belief, the specific conspiracy theory (e.g., about HIV and the MMR vaccine for health beliefs) was introduced as a random factor. *: $p < 0.05$; **: $p < 0.01$; ***: $p < 0.001$. The same effects for accurate, control beliefs were *ns* in Studies 1, 2, or 3. These estimates were obtained from path analyses that are described in more detail in Chapter 8.

Adorno and colleagues saw these socially anxious, prejudicial attitudes as related to obsessive compulsive types of traits, which they attributed to psychodynamic forces. For example, they wrote:

> Rigid repression of hostility against parents may be accompanied by an occasional breaking through of drives in a crude and unsocialized form; under certain circumstances this may become dangerous to the very society to which there seems to be conformity". (Adorno et al., 1950, p. 482)

If one were to assume that the negative feelings toward parents involved anxiety and fear, then Adorno et al.'s "anxiety" would be at best repressed rather than experienced. At the level of conscious experience, however, Adorno et al. characterized the social anxiety of conservative ideology as "fear of being a sucker" (Adorno et al., 1950, p. 484)

By contrast, recent uses of the term "anxiety" in the area of political ideology have sometimes denoted feelings of vulnerability in response to uncertainty. For example, according to Wilson (1973), the common basis for the conservative attitude syndrome is a generalized susceptibility to experiencing threat or anxiety in the face of uncertainty. The concept of uncertainty is employed by Wilson in the information theory sense, and includes both *stimulus uncertainty* (i.e., innovation, complexity, novelty, ambiguity, risk, anomie, etc., as states of the physical and social environment), and *response uncertainty* (i.e., freedo m of choice and conflicting needs). However, it is important to note that even though Wilson's definition is similar to ours, we are not aware of empirical tests using the sorts of measures of state anxiety that we employed.

A widely employed operationalization of threat in studies of its relation to political ideology casts it in such terms as fear of death or subjective perception of a dangerous world. These responses correlate with conservative ideology (Altemeyer, 1988; Jost et al., 2017; Jost, Glaser, Kruglanski, & Sulloway, 2003). A meta-analysis by Jost et al. (2003) found that political conservatism correlated with death anxiety ($r = .50$) and fear of threat and loss ($r = .18$). However, neither of these involves the feelings of being worried or anxious that we measured. Instead, fear of death involved mortality salience, and fear of threat and loss involved perceptions that life is changing for the worse, neuroticism, perceptions of a dangerous world, response latency to danger-related words, and persuasive impact of threatening messages. In a more recent meta-analysis by Jost et al. (2017) political conservatism correlated $r = .11$ with fear of death and $\sim.21$ with perceptions of threat, which again included measures of perceptions of a dangerous world.

Differences between our definition and measurement of anxiety and those of other authors notwithstanding, we were interested in conducting supplementary analyses of the association between our anxiety measures and political ideology. To begin, Studies 1 and 2 included a 3-point measure of political Ideology. For consistency, the 5-point ideology scale in Study 3 was rescored onto the same 3-point scale. To verify the associations between ideology and anxiety, we performed supplementary correlations with the 5-point scale, which correlated $r = .02$. This ruled out the possibility that a more sensitive measure of ideology might reveal an association.

In addition to the measures of general anxiety discussed earlier in this chapter, Studies 1 and 2 also included items measuring political and health anxiety. Political anxiety was measured in the following items (a) "When it comes to politics, I feel calm" (Reverse-scored); (b) "When it comes to politics, I am worried;" (c) "When it comes to politics, I am confused;" (d) "Politics makes me anxious;" and (e) "I am worried about contemporary politics." Health anxiety was assessed with (a) "Health issues make me anxious" and (b) "I am worried about health issues." Responses were given on Likert scales, as follows. "Strongly Agree," "Somewhat Agree," "Neither Agree nor Disagree," "Somewhat Disagree," and "Strongly Disagree." This scale was scored from 1 ("Strongly Disagree") to 5 ("Strongly Agree").

The results with the different measures of anxiety were illuminating. As the earlier analyses implied, the correlation between political ideology and the general measure of anxiety was nonsignificant in Studies 1 and 2 ($r = -.04$ and, 06, *ns* in both cases). In contrast, in both studies, the correlation between political ideology and political anxiety was significant and positive ($r = .19$ and, 11, $p < .001$ in both cases). The correlation between political ideology and health anxiety was significant and positive in Study 2 ($r = .14, p < .001$) but not in Study 1 ($r = .04$, *ns*). Our earlier literature review and these analyses thus support the notion that at the points in time in which our work fielded (i.e., 2018–2020), conservatives felt anxious about political issues, manifested as worry and anxious affect. Their general anxiety in the moment, however, was uncorrelated with political ideology.

5.5 Discussion

This chapter was dedicated to organizing the sociopolitical predictors of conspiracy beliefs into three categories depending on their relevance to the belief defense, belief accuracy, and social integration motivation. In parallel with Chapter 4, which addresses psychological factors, this one first covered a sociopolitical factor broadly connected with the belief defense motivation, particularly party identification and ideology (Altemeyer, 1988; McHoskey, 1995; Sunstein, 2014). Our findings showed a strong effect of party identification and ideology on the conspiracy beliefs on which we focused, with Republicans being more likely to accept several of the conspiracy theories and control, accurate beliefs that comported with their partisan dispositions. These data are consistent with the supposition that biased assimilation may influence Republican's adherence to conspiracy theories that speak poorly of President Obama and were promoted by President Trump. However, more research needs to be conducted to understand why Democrats were more likely to endorse control, true beliefs in the health domain. Chapter 8 will argue that patterns of media use provide a partial answer.

In the current chapter, we also asked whether sociopolitical factors broadly linked to the belief accuracy motivation correlate with conspiracy beliefs and tested associations between holding conspiracy beliefs and political knowledge and education. One of our findings was that people with higher levels of political knowledge were less likely to endorse conspiracy beliefs. These data dovetail well with our findings for need for cognition (see Chapter 4), indicating that higher levels of political knowledge might act as a buffer against the influence of conspiracy theories. Similarly, our analysis of the impact of education on conspiracy beliefs confirmed past findings that those with higher education levels are less likely to believe in conspiracy theories. However, we did not find support for the possibility that motivated reasoning might be at the root of conspiracy beliefs.

This chapter also addressed a number of factors that we relate to the social integration motivation. For starters, we reviewed the research on the hypothesis that conspiracy beliefs are associated with cynicism. Our literature review found little support for the contention that cynicism makes people more likely to believe in conspiracy theories except for one study (Goertzel, 1994). Our work found that, surprisingly, people with lower levels of cynicism about politicians were more likely to believe in political conspiracy theories. However, supplementary analysis suggest that the more cynical respondents were those who trusted the president in power, who has personally promoted conspiracy beliefs. The finding that those with higher levels of cynicism were more likely to endorse our accurate control health beliefs is less surprising since two of them involved cover-ups – by the tobacco industry and the other by the governmental scientists who developed and superintended the Tuskegee experiment. This effect persisted after controlling controls were in place.

We also reviewed the contention that conspiracy theories are more prevalent among people who are disadvantaged economically and racial minorities, specifically, African Americans, who are likely to feel they have limited influence in the political system. Our chapter also assessed the influence of race on conspiracy beliefs and found that non-White people were more likely to believe a number of conspiracies, hinting that experiences of exclusion are a precursor, as previously argued. Finally, White participants were more likely to believe in the Tobacco industry cover-up of the harmful effects of smoking, and this effect persisted after controlling for education.

Treating conspiracy beliefs as a way for people to make sense of unequal power relations seems appropriate given our own data and research by others. In general, our data showed that people in underprivileged social positions were more likely to believe in conspiracy theories. However, the best predictor of belief in health conspiracy theories was the perception that compared to that of others, one's financial situation had deteriorated in recent years. Interestingly, some scholars have attributed Donald Trump's Electoral College victory over Hillary Clinton in 2016 to a shift toward him among lower-educated White voters who were feeling undeservedly socially or economically displaced by others who are unlike them. Our results align with this argument.

In this chapter, we also conducted analyses to determine if the sociopolitical factors associated with belief defense, belief accuracy, and social integration motivations influenced conspiracy beliefs via the mediation of anxiety. Our findings indicated that this was the case. The influences of education, political knowledge, and having experienced a financial loss were due to the fact that these factors made individuals more anxious. Participants with higher levels of education and political knowledge felt less anxious and were therefore less likely to endorse conspiracy theories. However, political ideology had a negative indirect effect on conspiracy beliefs, and this negative effect was mediated by anxiety, contesting the point that conservatives are necessarily more anxious than liberals. We also conducted further review of the literature and supplementary analyses of the association between our anxiety measure and political ideology. Our review of past research indicated that conservatives are more pessimistic about our future way of life, believe the world is dangerous, and are anxious about political issues. However, as shown by our data, their general anxiety in the moment was not correlated with political ideology.

In conclusion, our chapter reviewed a heterogeneous literature applicable to our model to provide some guiding principles about the processes that make some sociopolitical factors similar to and different from others. Our review and data suggest that some of the direct psychological phenomena we observed in Chapter 4 stem also from sociopolitical factors. For example, political knowledge and education are negatively associated with conspiracy beliefs, and having had a financial loss or being African American correlate with stronger endorsement of conspiracy beliefs. However, in the case of African Americans, this finding focuses on health beliefs, for which history has provided a high level of plausibility. We return to sociopolitical factors in Chapter 8, which revisits their relation with anxiety and examines them in context.

CHAPTER 6

The Relation between Media and Anxiety

People who feel a loss of control over important aspects of their lives also are more likely to endorse conspiracy beliefs (Heine, Proulx, & Vohs, 2006; Park, 2010; van den Bos, 2009). The more they experience events that are threatening, the greater the loss of control and the stronger the embrace of conspiracy beliefs about such events (Landau, Kay, & Whitson, 2015; Mccauley & Jacques, 1979; Pipes, 1997; Robins & Post, 1997; Shermer, 2011; van Prooijen & van Dijk, 2014). The more they feel emotionally anxious for whatever reason, the stronger their conspiracy beliefs even if they are unrelated to their anxiety (see Chapter 4). In our own research, Americans who are more anxious are more likely to believe that Obama faked his birth certificate, that undocumented immigrants decided the 2016 popular vote, that HIV was created by the CIA, and that, athough covered-up by the government, administering the MMR vaccine to children leads to development of autism (see Chapter 4).

To begin with, feelings (e.g., emotions, which have a specific object, and mood states, which do not have a specific object) entail two dimensions: (a) they are positive or negative and (b) elicit high or low arousal (Albarracin, 2021; Albarracín & Vargas, 2010; Bradley, Codispoti, Cuthbert, & Lang, 2001; Clore & Schnall, 2005; Russell, 2003; Schimmack & Crites, 2005). In terms of emotions, people may feel sad, fearful, angry, content, or excited about a particular object, person, or event; in terms of mood, they may be in a sad, anxious, or happy mood unrelated to any specific objects. Sadness, anger, contentment, and elation vary not only in their negative or positive valence but also in their arousal level (Russell, 2003). Arousal involves bodily changes in such phenomena as skin conductance, heart rate, or brain waves (Bradley, Hamby, Löw, & Lang, 2007; Cacioppo, Gardner, & Berntson, 1997). Feeling fearful, anxious, tense, alert, or excited involves high arousal (e.g., high heart and breathing rate), whereas feeling sad or content involves low arousal

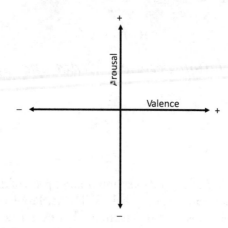

Figure 6.1.   Valence and arousal dimensions (adapted from Albarracín, 2020)

(e.g., lower heart and breathing rate; somnolence). The valence and arousal dimensions are represented in Figure 6.1.

Affective feelings are a natural basis for beliefs because many beliefs are subjective (for the affect as information perspective, covered in Chapter 4, see Clore & Schnall, 2005; Martin et al., 1993; Schwarz & Clore, 1983; Schwarz & Lee, 2019). If one is unsure of whether a "deep state" conspired against Donald J. Trump, feelings of fear and anxiety may function as a source of information. In the case of conspiracy theories, people's feelings of uncertainty might stem from their mood or personal circumstances unrelated to the alleged deep state conspiracy. However, one's access to the true source of one's feelings is typically limited. Accordingly, even though the actual reason a person feels anxious is that they feel that their status in society is being threatened, the deep state conspiracy theory may lead them to conclude instead that they are anxious because of the existence of a deceptive "deep state." This attributional process, which was demonstrated experimentally in Chapter 4, can then fortify conspiracy beliefs.

In addition to the anxiety related to personal circumstances, exposure to media portrayals of a dangerous world and conspiracy-tied fear appeals may also induce anxiety. This influence occurs when messages produce diffuse anxiety, which may translate into stronger conspiracy beliefs, but may also occur for more specific fears about a particular topic such as disease anxiety and beliefs in an MMR vaccine conspiracy. This chapter asks whether, and if so when, media can function as a source of

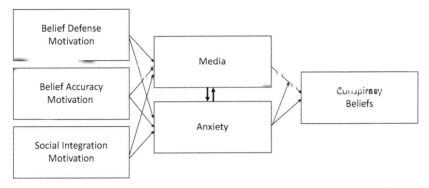

Figure 6.2. Theoretical model focusing on relations between media and anxiety (thicker lines represent focus of the chapter)

anxiety: What is the role of media cultivation and fear appeals in the creation of anxiety? Can the media create anxiety? And do people who feel anxious seek out media relevant to those feelings? These questions stem from our theoretical model, which we present again in Figure 6.2.

In this chapter, we first synthesize how media can affect diffuse emotional feelings, including anxiety. We then turn to three bodies of literature, one on the effects of media portrayal of self-inflicted death, and the others on the capacity of fear appeals to persuade and media cultivation of fear of crime. Finally, we review the effects of partisan media and report our evidence about media use and anxiety.

6.1 Media Effects on More Diffuse Feelings

Media can affect our feelings in fairly diffuse ways. Film and music can change our moods and our emotions, evoking fear, compassion, sadness, hope, and excitement in specific contents. These feelings may also influence conspiracy beliefs that may be salient for other reasons. Before describing our insights on these associations, we review the effects of music as well as television and film, the effects of media on depression and anxiety among youth, and the effects of media coverage of suicide.

6.1.1 Effects of Music

Evidence of the effects of music on feelings comes from the use of music to reduce pain. In a meta-analysis of the effects of music with patients in intensive care units (Richard-Lalonde et al., 2020), the association between music and reduction of pain was $d = -.63$, suggesting a moderately beneficial impact on patients. Also, the association was dose dependent. Music interventions of 20–30 minutes were associated with larger decreases in pain than were music interventions of less than 20 minutes ($d = -0.66$ vs. -0.10). Moreover, music has been used successfully for pain reduction outside of intensive care units (e.g., Wu, Liu, Pang, & Cheng, 2020), confirming that media can impact feelings in a number of contexts.

The effects of music on emotions have also been demonstrated by examining the impact of music interventions of patients undergoing cancer treatment (Koehler et al., 2020). Koehler and colleagues selected 19 studies and estimated the impact of the interventions on a combination of measures related to emotional wellbeing (e.g., less depression and anxiety and more hope). The results of this meta-analysis showed that effects of all but one intervention were positive and altogether yielded a positive average effect ($d = 0.35$).

6.1.2   Affective Effects of Film and Television

Like music, film and television can have powerful emotional effects. For example, a meta-analysis of 45 studies showed a large impact of film clips on emotions. The effects of the clips on negative emotions were $d = 1.49$ for valence and 1.77 for arousal; and the corresponding effects on positive emotions were $d = 1.22$ for valence and 1.34 for arousal.

The effects of scary films and television among children have also received attention. For instance, another meta-analysis estimated the effects of this genre on children's fear, worry, sadness, and depression, as measured by clinically validated measures (Pearce & Field, 2016). This meta-analysis estimated the overall effect size as a $d = 0.37$, which implies that children exposed to scary films and television shows are twice as likely to experience negative emotions as their unexposed counterparts. Although the effects on these emotional manifestations were considerable, effects on more severe psychopathology were weaker. For example, effects on post-traumatic stress disorder were smaller despite being statistically significant. Overall, however, the effects of film and television on specific emotions were medium-specific, applying to TV only and to a combination of film and television but not to film alone. They did, however, apply equally to factual content as well as fantasy.

6.2 Associations between Media Exposure to News and Anxiety

Extensive research on media coverage of violence, politics, terrorism, presidential elections, misinformation, natural disasters, and COVID-19 (Makkonen et al., 2020; McNaughton-cassill, 2001; Wormwood, Devlin, Lin, Barrett, & Quigley, 2018; Zhao & Zhou, 2020) suggests that associations between media exposure and anxiety are common. A sample of Chinese college students completed measures of media use and mental health at the beginning of the COVID-19 epidemic (Zhao & Zhou, 2020). In this study, traditional and online media use correlated positively with how much stress participants perceived in relation to COVID-19, and social media use correlated positively with reported anxiety.

Also looking at the effects of the COVID-19 pandemic, Riehm et al. (2020) surveyed American adults between March 10 and March 31, 2020. During this period, Americans were spending roughly 1 hour a day on social media, and they additionally consulted about 2.5 traditional media sources a day. However, social media time increased over time, from 0.85 hours early in March to 1.27 hours on March 31, 2020. The number of traditional media sources also increased, going from 2.38 to 3 sources during the same period. The authors found that increases in time spent on social media and the increases in the number of media sources used correlated with mental distress even after adjusting for demographic characteristics (Riehm et al., 2020).

The impact of news on anxiety appears to also depend on the level of trust in institutions within a society. This possibility was investigated in an interesting experiment conducted in five countries (Makkonen et al., 2020). The study, which was conducted in early 2017, sampled participants from Finland, Norway, Spain, France, and the United States. News coverage of a jihadist terrorist incident aroused the lowest level of fear in Finland and the highest level of fear in France, with the other countries falling in the middle. Moreover, participants' neuroticism level mattered. Specifically, participants with a higher level of neuroticism experienced greater fear than did participants with lower levels of fear.

6.3 Effects of Media Coverage on Suicide

No media effects seem as impressive as the reports that media and fictional coverage of suicide respectively increase suicide in the population (Dan Romer, Jamieson, & Jamieson, 2006; Schmidtke & Häfner, 1988).

Although the outcomes of this research are generally not emotions per se, the hypothesized effects assume that media exposure triggers negative emotions that in turn cause self-harm. In addition, the effects of suicide coverage on emotions have been measured experimentally.

The fictional portrayal of suicide has been deemed problematic since Goethe published *The sorrows of young Werther* in 1774. At the time, the novel was frequently blamed for a wave of copycat suicides by the novel's enthusiasts. Some readers shot themselves as did Werther, whereas others jumped from buildings or into rivers. However, it took another 300 years for the effect to receive serious empirical attention. Phillips studied similar copycat effects and coined the term "Werther effect" to describe an increase in suicide following well-publicized cases of suicide. An excellent review by Gould (2001) found support for the Werther effect when real suicide as opposed to fictional suicide is portrayed. In addition, the effect was reported to be stronger when suicides are covered on the front page and in large headlines than when suicides are less prominently publicized (Phillips, Lesyna, & Paight, 1992).

The size and robustness of the Werther effect, however, is a matter of debate (Hawton & Williams, 2001). Experimental effects have typically examined the impact of exposure to suicide stories on recipients' emotions. For example, Biblarz and colleagues (1991) assigned college students to films depicting teenage suicide, physical violence, or neither. They found immediate effects on affective arousal, implying that the events caused anxiety. However, the effects were short-lived and there were no effects on attitudes toward suicide.

A systematic 2012 review of the literature found that the majority of the studies support an effect of media reports on suicidal acts or ideation (Sisask & Värnik, 2012). That same year, a meta-analysis involving 10 studies of 98 celebrity suicides concluded that a change in per capita suicide rates (suicides per 100,000 population) of 0.26 occurred in the month after a celebrity suicide (Niederkrotenthaler et al., 2012; Scherr & Steinleitner, 2017). More recently, Niederkrotenthaler et al. (2020; for an earlier review, see Scherr & Steinleitner, 2017) synthesized available associations between media coverage of suicide and suicide in the pop-ulation. The synthesis included only studies comparing suicide at least one time point before and one time point after media reports of nonfic-tional suicide. The meta-analysis estimated a 13 percent increase in the probability of suicide after media coverage of suicide, an effect driven by reports of celebrity suicide. However, the sample of effects appeared to be quite biased, suggesting that studies that found no support for the effect were likely not being published and thus contributed to inflating the effect.

The plausibility of the media–behavior link increases when there is a post-exposure rise in the numbers of hospitalizations of individuals employing the suicide method depicted in a television show or series (Ostroff et al., 1985; Sandler, et al., 1986; Williams, et al. 1987) and when those hospitalized were likely to have been exposed to the media depiction. For example, self-inflicted railway deaths rose in 1981–1982 in Germany after a TV series, "Death of a Student," depicted a youth killing himself by jumping in front of a train (Schmidtke & Häfner, 1988). Also, the highly publicized 2014 death by suffocation of the celebrity Robin Williams was followed by "excess suicides" across gender and age groups (Fink, Santaella-Tenorio, & Keyes, 2018). Fink et al.'s study showed a 32 percent increase in suffocation suicides in the five months following Williams' death, compared to a 3 percent increase in the number of suicides from all other methods combined (i.e., firearms). A content analysis of 63 articles about the celebrity's death found that 46 percent detailed suffocation as the suicide method (Carmichael & Whitley, 2019), thus increasing the probability of use of the same method by the audience. Furthermore, after an embargo on coverage was established following a rash of subway suicides in Vienna from 1984 to 1987, the subway suicide attempt rate dropped by 80 percent (Etzersdorfer & Sonneck, 1998; Sonneck, Etzersdorfer, & Nagel-Kuess, 1994). A popular British TV drama portraying an overdose produced a similar effect in the form of a roughly 20-percent increase in admissions to British emergency rooms for self-poisoning (Hawton et al., 1999). For a review see Gould, Jamieson, and Romer (2003).

One of the explanations for the effects of media coverage of suicide is that audiences with depression or suicidal ideation are susceptible to this influence (U.S. Department of Health & Human Services, n.d.). For example, a laboratory experiment with Austrian participants compared the effects of exposure to a drama that ends in suicide, a drama that ends in natural death, and a film with a happy ending (Till et al., 2015). Importantly, the study included measures of identification with the protagonist as well as measures of suicidal tendencies prior to exposure to the stories. As the researchers predicted, both identification with the protagonist and suicidality played a role. When participants were suicidal and identified with the protagonist, the suicide film had stronger impact on suicidality following the film. In contrast, participants who were not suicidal showed the opposite effect and became even less suicidal after viewing the suicide film.

6.4   Fear in Cultivation Effects

Consistent with the premise of cultivation theory that heavy television viewing aligns our view of the world with the one we see on that medium (Gerbner & Gross, 1976), a meta-analysis (Morgan, M., Shanahan, 1997) of 58 samples found a small but nonetheless significant relation between frequency of television viewing and beliefs about the world ($r = .085$). The theory applies to immersion in other media as well (Cheng, Mitomo, Otsuka, & Jeon, 2016). Cultivation effects have been tied to greater fear of crime and identification of crime as a significant problem (Jamieson & Romer, 2017), for example, both of which are relevant for our analysis.

Because fear and anxiety are central concerns in this chapter, it is important to note that fear of crime is not only associated with heavy exposure to violent dramatic programming on prime-time television (Jamieson & Romer, 2017) but also to crime-saturated local television news (Chiricos, Eschholz, & Gertz, 1997; Holbert, Shah, & Kwak, 2004; Romer, Jamieson, & Aday, 2014). In sum, the media can create anxiety through a biased construction of reality.

6.5   Fear Appeals

Fearing a particular outcome motivates people to avoid it (for other specific emotions, see Graton et al., 2016; Skurka et al., 2018). For this reason, appeals to fear that highlight a threat or danger can be persuasive (Dillard, Plotnick, Godbold, Freimuth, & Edgar, 1996; Maddux & Rogers, 1983). Although using fear to promote protective behavior is common in risk communication, fear appeals also may be employed to garner political approval by presenting threatening contents and advocating a political solution. For example, fear-mongering is common among authoritarian leaders who increase their popularity by inducing fear of minority groups and casting their acquisition and retention of power as a means of securing the wellbeing of the masses (Mueller & Schulz, 2019; Rico, Guinjoan, & Anduiza, 2017).

Threatening messages and fear-inducing arguments can influence many beliefs. For example, a study of textual messages about a hypothetical hurricane compared three messages. The first simply described a storm surge as a hazard that would only affect low-lying areas; the second dramatically described devastating damage; and the third warned that people who stayed in the area would die (Morss et al., 2018a). As one might expect, beliefs that the storm was severe and that respondents could be affected were stronger when the messages discussed devastation and death. More interesting to us is the finding that the death-message condition also produced greater levels of worry and fear (Morss et al., 2018b) than messages that described the risk in unemotional ways.

A meta-analysis (Tannenbaum et al., 2015) quantified the effects of fear appeals on beliefs and attitudes, as well as intentions and behaviors. Introducing fear or risk information has an overall moderate effect on beliefs/attitudes, intentions, and behaviors. The more a message induces fear, the more recipients experience it and the more they think that the behavior recommended to address it is desirable. Also, feeling susceptible to a threat appears to be particularly important. According to Tannenbaum et al., a message that describes recipient susceptibility to a risk has more than twice the chance of influencing attitudes than a message that does not.

Fear is of course at the core of beliefs that secret sinister forces are engaging in malign behavior. In one study, anti-vaccination messages were shown to appeal to emotion and specifically fear more frequently than did pro-vaccination ones (Harvey, Thompson, Lac, & Coolidge, 2019). In our own Twitter study (see methods in the Appendix), we analyzed the fear sentiments of tweets discussing Obama's birth certificate to determine if conspiratorial tweets were more likely to employ fear appeals than were correct, nonconspiratorial ones. We searched for English-language tweets with hashtags and keywords associated with conspiratorial posts about (a) Obama's birth certificate, (b) the deep state, (c) the MMR vaccine cover-up, (d) Pizzagate, (e) chemtrail, (f) lizard people, (g) flat earth, (h) Agenda 21, (i) GMOs, and (j) Bush knew about 9/11. We also had control hashtags attempting to debunk the theory about (a) Obama's birth certificate and (b) deep state (see Appendix). Next, we filtered out retweets (i.e., direct reposting of other Twitter users' tweets) by checking "RT @." This process resulted in a total of 222,903 tweets from 2016 through 2017 in the United States (i.e., 207,141 tweets for conspiracy theories and 15,762 tweets for control hashtags and keywords). For the deep state theory, we collected additional tweets from 2018, 2019, and 2020 (i.e., 184,794 tweets, see Appendix).

On the one hand, one could expect that conspiracy tweets would highlight fear, thus leading to a higher proportion of fear words in conspiratorial than nonconspiratorial tweets. On the other hand, tweets that attempt to counter the conspiracy theory could also appeal to fear as a means of rousing resistance to the proffered deceptions. If that were the case, nonconspiratorial tweets would have similar or even greater numbers of fear-related words than would conspiratorial ones. What we found was consistent with this second possibility. That is, nonconspiratorial, control tweets ($M = 6.34, SD = 3.21$) had a higher percentage of fear words than did conspiratorial ones ($M = 6.06, SD = 3.58$), $t(5409) = -6.08$, $p < .001$. Thus, even though anti-vaccination messages have been shown to use fear language (Harvey et al., 2019), not all conspiracy tweets appear to do so, or at least not more so than attempts at debunking them.

6.5.1   Inducement of Anxiety by Other Media

Like threats in general, those conveyed in media can elicit anxiety (Gadarian & Albertson, 2014), and the subsequent emotional arousal can enhance attention to not only the source of the threat but also goal-relevant information (Levine & Edelstein, 2009). If anxiety increases information-seeking about a threat identified by a conspiracy theory, a biased search also could bolster a person's conspiracy beliefs. Indeed, Gadarian and Albertson (2014) found that the information searches of anxious individuals were biased toward threatening content. Given the opportunity to browse an online news website that contained both threatening and nonthreatening stories about immigration and nonimmigration subjects, anxious participants were more likely than non-anxious ones to read, remember, and agree with the threatening content (Gadarian & Albertson, 2014).

Also helpful in understanding the ways in which anxiety affects information-seeking is the conclusion of Valentino and his colleagues that anxiety triggers a search for information that is useful for addressing the problem at hand, in essence producing an interaction between anxiety and information utility (Valentino et al., 2009). Although one result of this interaction may be a biased information search supporting one's attitude, that is not necessarily the outcome. Valentino et al. (2008) concluded that anxiety can improve both the amount and breadth of information-seeking. In their first of two experiments, anxiety increased participants' expectations that they would paying attention to a political campaign. In the second, anxiety triggered by exposure to realistic political threats increased unbiased information-seeking and learning (Valentino et al., 2008)

In practice, by increasing openness to new information, anxiety con increase useful and problematic information-seeking depending on circumstances (Brader, Valentino, & Suhay, 2008). Problematic information-seeking occurred in a study of white participants that found greater exposure to news about the costs of immigration when the immigrants were described as Latinx but not when they were cast as European. In this study, group cues affected attitudes and support for political action not simply by changing beliefs about the extent and seriousness of the immigration "problem" but also by triggering anxiety. A second experiment confirmed that stereotypic group cues helped explain the effect, presumably by increasing group threats posed by immigrants regarded with suspicion.

Other relevant work has looked at anxiety and attention to political information. Although anxiety clearly increases information-seeking in politics at least under some circumstances (Hart et al., 2009), whether it influences recall of political content is less clear. When Valentino et al. (2011) compared responses to two ads, one devoid of emotionally evoca-tive content and one anxiety-inducing, respondents in the anxiety condi-tion had higher recall, were more likely to seek out related information, and were more favorable to the ad's sponsor than those in the control condition. Simulating exposure to a real campaign, Redlawsk, Civettini, and Lau (2007) also found that, when participants were induced to experience anxiety, using a manipulation similar to the one we used in the experiment reported in Chapter 4, then the anxiety elicited by specific political information led them to seek that information more. However, the results only held for information about candidates preferred by the respondent and not disfavored ones. Contrary both to Bader's finding and to a premise of the theory of affective intelligence and other formulations about the impact of feelings on attention (Worth & Mackie, 1987; Wyer, Clore, & Isbell, 1999), Civettini and Redlawsk (2009) found little evidence that, at least compared to enthusiasm or anger, anxiety increases the likelihood that political information would be remembered. However, one does not have to be able to recall content to be influenced by it (Chaiken & Eagly, 1976; Petty, Wells, & Brock, 1976). Nor is recall a direct function of attention (Eagly et al., 1999).

A related question is whether the fear language contained in a message can increase dissemination, an issue we assessed in our Twitter study by measuring dissemination of tweets as a function of being conspiratorial or not and of varying percentages of fear words. We assessed fear words for each tweet and then calculated the percentage of fear tokens over the total tokens of a tweet. Next, we analyzed retweets as the outcome and tested the main effects of fear and post type (i.e., conspiracy versus control), which we could analyze using the subset of tweets that had controls (i.e., the deep state and Obama's birth certificate). Based on intra-class correlations (ICCs), we analyzed the twitter data while accounting for different types of account handles as a random factor (ICCs = .59). We used multilevel Poisson regression and negative binomial regression for the analyses and chose the better-fitting negative binomial model. The results showed that control posts were retweeted less than conspiracy posts ($IRR = 0.56$, $SE = 0.06$, $p < .001$) and posts with more fear language were retweeted less than posts with less fear language ($IRR = 0.97$, $SE = 0.00$, $p < .001$). The issue of fear is revisited in Chapter 8.

6.6   Effects of Partisan and Mainstream Media on Anxiety

The popular press has often raised the point that, at least in the United States, the conservative media (e.g., Fox News and Newsmax) spread sometimes-unfounded fear. For example, the American climate during the 2016 presidential election campaign was described as "The United States of Anxiety" (WNYC Studios, n.d.). Likewise, the populist, fearmongering tactics of Donald J. Trump have been widely denounced (Watson, 2020) and their reach is amplified by the conservative media (WNYC Studios, n.d.).

A graphic depiction of Fox News was provided by Dickinson (2020) in the liberal magazine *Rolling Stone*. Describing how the successful media outlet mirrored the personality of its Nixon operative founder, Roger Ailes, he wrote,

> "To watch even a day of Fox News – the anger, the bombast, the virulent paranoid streak, the unending appeals to white resentment, the reporting that's held to the same standard of evidence as a late-October attack ad – is to see a refraction of its founder, one of the most skilled and fearsome operatives in the history of the Republican Party." A content analysis by Cappella and Jamieson (2008) in *Echo Chamber: Rush Limbaugh and the Conservative Media Establishment* showed that in his nationally-syndicated radio program, "Limbaugh evoked moral outrage at liberals, 'liberal media,' Democrats, and the Democratic Party. . . .[and roused] passion through various types of emotional appeal.' A survey of his listenership found that exposure to his program was associated with fear and anger about incumbent Democratic president Bill Clinton.

Although Fox News has been labeled a "fear factory" (Dickinson, 2020), conservative media such as Fox, Limbaugh, and the ultra-conservative Jones spread fear about only strategically chosen topics: Those that support the conservative political agenda. For example, Fox's Sean Hannity labeled the 2020 Democratic nominees "the most radical ticket of any major political party" (Gabbatt, 2020), and InfoWars' Jones transformed the Sandy Hook Elementary School shooting that resulted in the deaths of 20 children and six adults into a conspiracy. Tangible evidence of the shooting did not stop Jones (see also Chapter 2) from claiming that the shooting was a "false flag" raised by the left to oppose gun control. Nor did it stop him from asking his staff to produce a constant stream of false claims of widespread high levels of Fukushima-caused radiation in California, even though an attempt to verify the claims by Jones' staff found only slightly unsafe levels from "naturally occurring radioactive materials" in Half Moon Bay (Owens, 2019).

Other crises that could be used to spread fears, however, have been minimized by the conservative media. For example, a series of stories downplaying the potential risks from Covid-19 was broadcast by conservative media during the beginning of the pandemic, as the virus began to spread in the United States. During an appearance on Sean Hannity's show, for example, "medical contributor" Dr. Mark Siegel stated, "the virus should be compared to the flu. Because at worst, at worst, worst case scenario it could be the flu" (Fox News, March 6, 2020). Similarly, Rush Limbaugh said, "I'm dead right on this. The coronavirus is the common cold, folks" (Limbaugh, February 24, 2020), and that "The fatality rate of this virus is less than the flu, far less than the flu. But look at how it's been hyped" (Limbaugh, February 25, 2020).

Exposure to conservative outlets was associated with holding COVID-19 conspiracy beliefs, some of them fear-laden. A survey conducted in the United States on March 8, 2020 showed that 10 percent of Americans thought that the United States government created the virus as a bioweapon (Jamieson & Albarracín, 2020). Nineteen percent believed that some in the CDC were exaggerating the seriousness of the virus to undermine the Trump presidency, and 23 percent believed that the virus was created by the Chinese government as a bioweapon. This possibility had been promoted by conservative talk radio host Rush Limbaugh who said, "It probably is a ChiCom laboratory experiment that is in the process of being weaponized" (Limbaugh, 2020).

Whether reliance on conservative, mainstream, or liberal media sources was associated with general feelings of anxiety was, however, question for us.

To determine whether reported exposure to media sources correlates with anxious feelings, we began by surveying United States media sources and specific shows. To do so, we drew on past scholarship (c.f. Jamieson and Albarracín, 2020; Romer and Jamieson, 2020) and also consulted and incorporated news media lists, including those on Wikipedia (n.d. a, n.d. c, n.d. d) encompassing alternative media on the ideological left and right. Table 6.1 summarizes data on the shows and outlets, as well as information on their audiences. In addition, when available, the table presents information about the outlets' political leaning using the media bias ratings of AllSides, Media Bias / Fact Check, and Ad Fontes Media Index:

1. *Allsides*. AllSides ("Media Bias Rating Method of AllSides Index," n.d.) is a nonprofit funded by liberal and conservative sources that rates media bias with a patented process that collects and represents the average subjective judgment of Americans on a scale of "Left, Lean Left, Center, Lean Right, and Right." AllSides integrates a survey of politically diverse readers who blindly rate articles, an editorial review by AllSides staff, third party data (e.g., academic publications), an independent review of media conducted by several AllSides staff members, and community votes.

2. *Media Bias / Fact Check*. Media Bias / Fact Check ("Media Bias Fact Check Methodology," n.d.), which is identified by the Columbia Journalism Review as "an armchair media analysis" (Wilner, n.d.) and run by Dave Van Zandt, provides a bias scale with a yellow dot that represents the degree of bias of an outlet. The placement of the yellow dot is determined by considering political bias, factuality of the information, and availability of credible and verifiable sources. The bias assessment involves four categories: (a) biased wording/ headlines, (b) factual/sourcing, (c) story choices, and (d) political affiliation. Each of these four categories is rated on a 0–10 scale in which 0 indicates absence of bias and 10 indicates the maximum bias. The average of four ratings from the categories are used as the index that determines the placement of the yellow dot.

3. *Ad Fontes Media Index*. Ad Fontes Media ("How Fontes Media Ranks News Sources," n.d.) evaluates outlets by combining ratings from at least three analysts whose own political views are left, center, and right. When significant discrepancies among the analysts' ratings emerge, then a second ideologically balanced panel makes additional ratings. The ratings of bias are based on the categories of: (a) political position, (b) language, and (c) comparison with other coverage of the same topic. Of note, however, the ratings are provided on a 7-point

Table 6.1. *American media outlets, shows, and sites used for our surveys*

Name of show or source	Creation date	Founder/s	Allsides index	MB/FC index	AdFontes index	Audience characteristics	Audience size
Conservative Media							
Fox News Media	October 7, 1996	Ruper Murdoch, Roger Ailes	Lean Right	Right	Skews Right	Conservative, Republican	2.5 million
The Rush Limbaugh Show, Premiere Networks*	1984	Rush Limbaugh	NA	Extreme Right	NA	Conservative, Republican	15.5 million
The Mark Levin Show, Westwood One*	May 5, 2002	Mark Levin	NA	NA	NA	Mostly conservative	11 million
The Hugh Hewitt Show, Salem Radio Network	June 24, 2017	Hugh Hewitt	NA	NA	NA	NA	8 million
The Glenn Beck Show, Premiere Networks*	January, 2000	Glenn Beck	Right	NA	NA	87% universally conservative	10.5 million
The Savage Nation, Westwood One*	January 2, 1995	Michael Savage	NA	NA	NA	NA	7.5 million
The Michael Medved Show, KTTH	1996	Michael Medved	Right	NA	NA	NA	4.75 million
The Sean Hannity Show, Premiere Networks*	1989	Sean Hannity	NA	Extreme Right	NA	Conservatives, Republicans, majority are 50 and older	15 million
Drudge Report	1995	Matt Drudge	Lean Right	Right-Center	NA	74% right-of center, 8% left or left-of-center, roughly 18% center or mixed	1.488 million

Table 6.1. (cont.)

Name of show or source	Creation date	Founder/s	Allsides index	MB/FC index	AdFontes index	Audience characteristics	Audience size
Breitbart	2005	Andrew Breitbart	Right	Extreme Right	Hyper-Partisan Right	Majority right or right-of-center	23,725,000
The New York Post	November 16, 1801	Alexander Hamilton	Lean Right	Right-Center	Skews Right	NA	25,600,000
Washington Times	May 17, 1982	Sung Myung Moon	Lean Right	Right-Center	Skews Right	NA	3,516,900
Radix Journal	2012	Richard B. Spencer	NA	NA	NA	NA	NA
American Renaissance	November, 1990	Jared Taylor	NA	Extreme Right	NA	NA	158,000
Vdare	1999	Peter Brimelow	NA	Extreme Right	NA	NA	132,000
The Right Stuff	December, 2012	Mike Enoch	NA	Extreme Right	NA	NA	NA
Daily Stormer	July 4th, 2013	Andrew Anglin	NA	Extreme Right	NA	NA	284,000
Ben Shapiro's The Daily Wire, Westwood One*	September 21, 2015	Ben Shapiro, Jeremy Boreing	Right	Right	NA	Younger conservatives	98.9 million
National Review	November 19, 1955	William F. Buckley Jr.	Right	Right	Hyper-Partisan Right	NA	4,147,500
The Weekly Standard	September, 1995	Bill Kristol, Fred Barnes	Right	Right	NA	NA	3.2 million
American Spectator	1924	George Nathan, Truman Newberry	Right	Right	Hyper-Partisan Right	NA	567,665

American Thinker	March, 2005	Thomas Lifson	Right	Extreme Right	Most Extreme Right	NA	1,640,551
The Washington Examiner	2005	Philip Anschutz	Lean Right	Right	Skews Right	NA	6,213,600
The American Conservative	October 7, 2002	Patrick Buchanan, Scott McConnell, Taki Theodoracopulos	Lean Right	Right-Center	Skews Right	NA	658,800
Newsmax Magazine	September 16, 1998	Christopher Ruddy	Lean Right	Right	Hyper-Partisan Right	NA	4,762,200
Power Line	2002	John H. Hinderaker, Scott W. Johnson, Paul Mirengoff	NA	Right	NA	NA	NA
Captain Quarters	October, 2003	Ed Morrissey	NA	NA	NA	NA	NA
RedState, Salem Communications*	2004	Joshua Treviño, Ben Domenech, Mike Krempasky	NA	Right	Hyper-Partisan Right	NA	NA
Hot Air, Salem Communications*	2006	Michelle Malkin	Right	Right	NA	NA	1,989,300
Instapundit	August, 2001	Glenn Reynolds	NA	NA	NA	NA	NA
Blaze Media	December 3, 2018	Glenn Beck	Right	Right	Hyper-Partisan Right	85% right-of-center, 51% consistently conservative	5,986,800
Newsmax TV, Newsmax Media*	June 16, 2014	Christopher Ruddy	Lean Right	Right	Hyper-Partisan Right	NA	4,762,200
Sinclair Broadcast Group	1986	Julian Sinclair Smith	NA	Right	NA	NA	NA

Table 6.1. (cont.)

Name of show or source	Creation date	Founder/s	Allsides index	MB/FC index	AdFontes index	Audience characteristics	Audience size
Conspiracy Media							
Davidlcke.com	NA	David Icke	NA	Conspiracy-Pseudoscience	NA	NA	NA
WhatReallyHappened.com	1994	NA	NA	Conspiracy-Pseudoscience	NA	NA	NA
thetruthseeker.co.uk	NA	NA	NA	Conspiracy-Pseudoscience	NA	NA	NA
bilderbergmeetings.org	May 29, 1954	Józef Retinger	NA	NA	NA	NA	NA
nexusmagazine.com	1986	Ramses H. Ayana	NA	NA	NA	NA	NA
conspiracyarchive.com	NA	NA	NA	NA	NA	NA	NA
serendipity.it	NA	NA	NA	NA	NA	NA	NA
propagandamatrix.com	NA	Paul Joseph Watson	NA	NA	NA	NA	NA
www.infowars.com	March 6, 1999	Alex Jones	Right	Conspiracy-Pseudoscience	Most Extreme Right	NA	4,850,000
Mainstream Media							
New York Times	September 18, 1851	Henry Jarvis Raymond, George Jones	Lean Left	Left-Center	Skews Left	Democrats, moderates or liberals	162,890,000
USA Today	September 15, 1982	Al Neuharth	Center	Left-Center	Neutral	Centrists, highest reader age group: aged 30–49	44,075,000
Wall Street Journal	July 8, 1889	Charles Dow, Edward Jones, Charles Bergstresser	Center	Right-Center	Neutral	Politically independent, moderate audience	39,430,000

Liberal Media

Vox	April, 2014	Ezra Klein, Matt Yglesias, Melissa Bell	Left	Left	Skews Left	NA	13,948,400
HuffPost	May 9, 2005	Arianna Huffington, Andrew Breitbart, Kenneth Lerer, Jonah Peretti	Left	Left	Skews Left	59% left or left-of-center, 17% right or right-of-center, 23% mixed or center	46,900,000
slate.com	1996	Michael Kinsley	Left	Left	Hyper-Partisan Left	76% left-of-center	10,530,000
Indymedia (IMC)	November 24, 1999	Unknown	NA	Left-Center	NA	NA	NA
truthdig	2005	Zuade Kaufman, Robert Scheer	Left	Left	NA	NA	NA
US Uncut	February, 2011	Ryan Clayton, Joanne Gifford, Carl Gibson	NA	Left	NA	NA	NA
World Socialist Web Website	February 14, 1998	International Committee of the Fourth International (ICFI)	NA	Left	NA	NA	NA
The Real News	2007	Paul Jay	NA	Left	Hyper-Partisan Left	NA	582,300
Pacifica Radio*	April 15, 1949	Lewis Hill	NA	NA	NA	NA	NA
The David Pakman Show	August 17, 2005	David Pakman	NA	NA	NA	NA	NA

Table 6.1. (*cont.*)

Name of show or source	Creation date	Founder/s	Allsides index	MB/FC index	AdFontes index	Audience characteristics	Audience size
Democracy Now!, Pacifica Radio Network*	February 19, 1996	Amy Goodman, Juan González, Larry Bensky, Salim Muwakkil, Julie Drizin	Left	Left	Hyper-Partisan Left	NA	2,739,000
The Majority Report with Sam Seder	March 31, 2004	Sam Seder	NA	NA	NA	NA	NA
Chapo Trap House	March 13, 2006	Will Menaker, Matt Christman, Felix Biederman, Amber A'Lee Frost, Virgil Texas	NA	NA	NA	NA	NA
The Jimmy Dore Show, Pacifica Radio Network	June, 2009	Jimmy Dore	NA	NA	NA	NA	811,000

scale from most extreme left to most extreme right. In 2018, the Index was critiqued for its failure to report the raw and processed data used to obtain the index (Hamada, n.d.).

Table 6.1 presents information and media bias classifications of the media outlets we measured in our surveys, ratings that we used to classify media sources as conservative, mainstream, and liberal. We constructed media use variables consistent with the media bias indexes and research by Hilgard and Jamieson (2017), Jamieson and Albarracín (2020), and Romer and Jamieson (2020). All of our surveys included measures of media exposure that were scored so that higher numbers indicated more frequent exposure to each type of media. Studies 1–3 (see Appendix) included individualized measures of exposure to (a) cable news channels Fox News or One America News (classified as conservative), (b) cable news channel MSNBC (classified as liberal), (c) Cable news channel CNN (classified as liberal), (d) broadcast news (such as ABC, CBS, or NBC) (classified as mainstream), (e) your local (e.g., county) television news (classified as mainstream), (f) public radio (such as NPR) (classified as mainstream), (g) talk radio (such as The Rush Limbaugh Show, The Mark Levin Show, the Hugh Hewitt Show, The Glenn Beck Show, The Michael Savage Show, The Michael Meded Show, or The Sean Hannity Show) (classified as conservative), (h) your local (e.g., county) newspaper (including online) (classified as mainstream), (i) national newspapers (such as the New York Times, USA Today, or the Wall Street Journal, including online) (classified as mainstream), (j) online news and blogs such as the Drudge Report or Breitbart (classified as conservative), and (k) online news and blogs such as Vox, or HuffPost (classified as liberal). The frequency of exposure reported for each answer was averaged into conservative, mainstream, and liberal (see classification between parentheses; see also Appendix).

Although Studies 1–3 measured exposure to the detailed media outlets we just described, following past research by Hilgard and Jamieson (2017), Jamieson and Albarracín (2020), and Romer and Jamieson (2020), Study 4 included streamlined media-use measures. We combined all conservative media items into one question, and did the same for liberal media and mainstream media. Participants could then report their overall exposure to each type of media on a scale from 0 to 7 days a week.

Table 6.2. Correlations between anxiety and media use (Studies 1–3)

	Anxiety	Social media use	Conservative media use	Mainstream media use	Liberal media use	Watch movies	Watch sports
Study 1							
Anxiety							
Social media use	0.13***						
Conservative media use	0.27***	0.30***					
Mainstream media use	0.23***	0.34***	0.51***				
Liberal media use	0.30***	0.35***	0.57***	0.68***			
Watch movies	0.03	0.03	0.01	0.01	0.07		
Watch sports	0.09*	0.12***	0.27***	0.22***	0.23***	0.23***	
Watch fiction	0.11**	0.06	0.08*	0.18***	0.16***	0.27***	0.15***
Study 2							
Anxiety							
Social media use	0.15***						
Conservative media use	0.07*	0.26***					
Mainstream media use	−0.03	0.27***	0.45***				
Liberal media use	0.07*	0.31***	0.53***	0.56***			
Watch movies	0.08**	0.15***	0.20***	0.12***	0.23***		
Watch sports	−0.11***	0.08*	0.31***	0.28***	0.30***	0.16***	
Watch fiction	0.10**	0.07*	0.16***	0.20***	0.24***	0.22***	0.15***
Study 3							
Anxiety							
Social media use	0.16***						
Conservative media use	0.21***	0.24***					
Mainstream media use	0.04	0.25***	0.52***				
Liberal media use	0.13***	0.28***	0.64***	0.63***			
Watch movies	0.10**	0.22***	0.23***	0.16***	0.24***		
Watch sports	−0.06	0.10**	0.32***	0.32***	0.33***	0.16***	
Watch fiction	0.03	0.16***	0.21***	0.18***	0.23***	0.17***	0.13***

Note: r: Pearson correlation. *: $p < 0.05$; **: $p < 0.01$; ***: $p < 0.001$

Table 6.3. *Regression coefficients for the prediction of anxiety from use of different media (Studies 1–3)*

	Study 1	Study 2	Study 3
Conservative media	0.15[†††]	0.07	0.23[***]
Mainstream media	0	−0.12[**]	−0.12[**]
Liberal media	0.21[***]	0.09[*]	0.06

Note: Entries are standardized regression coefficients from a multiple regression equation.
[*]: $p < 0.05$; [**]: $p < 0.01$; [***]: $p < 0.001$

We measured political and health beliefs alongside conspiracy beliefs, as well as beliefs about accurate control statements. The analyses were done separately for political and health beliefs because replicating findings across domains can tell us if our findings apply to conspiratorial beliefs in general or are simply a result of political factors such as ideology. Political theories included both the belief in Obama falsifying his birth certificate and the belief in undocumented immigrants deciding the popular vote in the 2016 presidential election. Similarly, health theories included the beliefs that the HIV virus was a CIA creation and that the link between the MMR vaccine and autism was covered up. We correlated our indexes of media use with the level of anxiety participants reported. The simple correlations of anxiety with social versus traditional media use, exposure to conservative, mainstream and liberal media, and consumption of movies, sports, and fiction appear in Table 6.2 (for relevance of fiction, see Boltanski, 2014). At face value, these simple correlations suggest that all media use is positively associated with anxiety. However, because one form of media use may correlate with other forms of it, it was necessary to control for all measures simultaneously.

To better determine if the ideological slant of the media correlated with anxiety, we next considered the relations between these two variables in the context of a broader path model reflecting the theory advanced in this book. Of relevance to this discussion are the path coefficients going from conservative, mainstream, and liberal media to anxiety. These coefficients, which appear in Table 6.3, show that only conservative media use was associated with more anxiety whereas the other media had either negative or null associations.

6.7   Reciprocal Relations between Anxiety and Media Use

In addition to media influencing our emotions, our feelings can determine our choices of media (see Figure 6.2). According to Shoemaker and colleagues (Shoemaker & Cohen, 2006), human beings are "hardwired for news" because they survey their environment for threats (Alford & Hibbing, 2004; Carver & White, 1994). The public's desire to learn about crime, violence, and accidents rewards outlets that feature them with larger audiences (Grabe & Kamhawi, 2006; Shoemaker & Reese, 2014; Wise et al., 2009).

The model in Figure 6.2 shows that affective reactions can influence information-seeking and thus direct people to specific media. Marcus, Neuman, and MacKuen (2000) proposed three fundamental emotions linked to attention to new information: (a) enthusiasm, (b) anger/aversion, and (c) anxiety. Enthusiasm is associated with (a) reward, anger/aversion with (b) threat, and anxiety with (c) ambiguity about whether rewards or threats are involved. Marcus et al. showed that news stories can activate anger and aversion but also enthusiasm and anxiety. Thus, different stories can engage an audience by eliciting different reactions.

Even though media stories evoke a wide range of emotions, fear and anger are particularly relevant for politics and conspiracy theories. In a study sampling respondents from California, New Jersey, and Tennessee, research by Coan et al. (2020) compared fear and anger in the domain of terrorism. After completing baseline measures, participants received touristic information about a country with potential for Al-Qaeda attacks, another that described the country as one in which travelers can have a good time, or a control with minimal information about a country. This manipulation was supposed to induce perception of threat, which can entail fear or anger as the dominant emotional response. However, prompts were introduced to instill either anger or fear. Specifically, participants were asked to detail whether the threat of terrorism made them feel either (a) angry/hostile or (b) nervous/scared. The researchers then compared the story about (a) having a good time, (b) terrorism with anger induction, (c) terrorism with fear induction, and a control condition. As part of an ostensibly unrelated study, participants were then presented with fictitious candidates in an upcoming election. They could click on specific news titles appearing on the screen. For example, one of the titles read "Candidate A's religion," but all together the titles covered candidates' stances on a broad set of issues ranging from terrorism to global warming. Four pieces of information about the candidates were relevant to terrorism: (a) their stance on terrorism policy, (b) their position on military intervention, (c) their position on the defense budget, and (d) their level of military experience. The dependent measure was the proportion of clicks of these terrorism-relevant items out of the first 5 and first 10 clicks.

The experiment by Coan et al. (2020) yielded relevant findings. Being primed to think about terror led to more clicks than having received a control prime. However, different negative emotions led to different selections of information. Participants in the terrorism/anger condition were more likely to seek information about the candidate's stance on military intervention than were those in the terrorism/fear condition. In contrast, participants in the terrorism/fear condition were more likely to seek information about a candidate's stance on the defense budget than were those in the terrorism/anger condition.

As Marcus et al.'s (2000) contended, negative arousal can drive interest, attention, and selection of information. However, media choices also can be used to achieve positive affective states, a phenomenon that leads to prioritizing positive information (Zillmann, 1988a, 1988b, 2000; Zillmann & Bryant, 1985; for an excellent review, see Reinecke, 2017). People are motivated to seek positive affect and to avoid negative affect, and media exposure is one efficient way of arranging stimuli to optimize positive affect. Not only can individuals strategically access media without having to leave the comfort of their own homes, but the media also provide an unlimited supply of new stimuli.

Table 6.4. *Mood management through music selection*

Measures	Bad mood	Neutral mood	Good mood
Preference for energetic/joyful music	5.25^a	4.82^a	3.78^b
Frequency of music sampling	7.23^a	7.68^a	9.05^b

Note: Data obtained from Knobloch and Zillmann (2002). Within a row, different superscripts indicate statistically significant differences across the means.

Evidence of the ways in which people manage their feelings through their media choices comes from research on music choices. An experiment conducted by Knobloch and Zillmann (2002) provided participants with positive, negative, or inconclusive feedback about their ostensible performance on a task that involved identifying emotions from facial expressions. After positive, negative, or neutral feelings were induced by this feedback, participants were asked to choose songs for a listening task. The songs were described based on ratings of each song as "active," fearful," "tense," and "sleepy." The results from this experiment appear in Table 6.4. Participants in a bad or neutral mood were more likely to choose energetic and joyful music than were those in a good one. Unexpectedly, participants in a bad or neutral mood were also less likely to consume music overall.

The use of music to regulate mood has received attention across different disciplines. One finding is that people who are high in neuroticism are more likely to use music to regulate their emotions than are people who are low in this trait (Chamorro-Premuzic & Furnham, 2007). A meta-analysis of research (Miranda & Blais-Rochette, 2020) testing this possibility supported this conclusion. Miranda and Blais-Rochette synthesized correlations between neuroticism and use of music for mood regulation. These correlations resulted in an average effect of $r = .17$, which is small but still supportive of an association between neuroticism and managing mood through media choices.

Knobloch and Zillmann's (2002) research provided evidence that people often choose media with a positive valence to reduce their negative feelings. Other research has shown that the choices can be quite nuanced. In particular, Zillmann et al. (1980) manipulated frustration by providing merely negative feedback or by providing ridiculing feedback. Participants then chose whether they would view hostile and nonhostile comedic shows. For provoked participants, hostile comedy could serve as a reminder of the ridicule, whereas nonhostile comedy could allow them to repair their moods. Not surprisingly, participants who received ridiculing feedback were more likely to choose regular comedy than were participants who received negative but non-ridiculing feedback.

A growing number of media research studies have begun exploring the media coverage of emotional content on social media (Al-Rawi, 2019; Hendriks Vettehen & Kleemans, 2018; Kilgo & Sinta, 2016; Newman,

2011; Welbers & Opgenhaffen, 2019). In the analyses of Twitter threads about false and true news stories, replies to false stories showed higher levels of fear, disgust, and surprise, whereas replies to tweets about truthful information showed higher levels of anticipation, sadness, joy, and trust (Vosoughi et al., 2018). The analyses of the top shared Twitter stories from five major UK news organizations, including the BBC, Channel 4, the *Guardian*, Sky, and the *Telegraph*, over a four-month period in 2011 showed that emotions such as humor, surprise, and fear were commonly present (Hendriks Vettehen & Kleemans, 2018; Newman, 2011).

Our own studies focused on anxiety. In the case of conspiracy beliefs, anxiety can stem from threats to one's social and economic security, including those associated with the need to belong and having experienced a financial loss (see Chapters 5 and 6). In addition, anxiety correlated negatively with education, need for cognition, and political knowledge (see Chapter 5). Presumably, higher motivation and ability to solve problems reduce free-floating anxiety, whereas lower motivation and a lesser ability to solve problems can make people feel uncertain and fearful.

The correlations in Table 6.2 are consistent with prior findings that anxiety affects media selection and also suggest the possibility that the conservative media might influence global levels of anxiety. However, the correlations reveal nothing about the direction of effects, an aspect of interest in this book. Thus, we investigated direction in the context of a broader path model reflecting the theory advanced in this book.

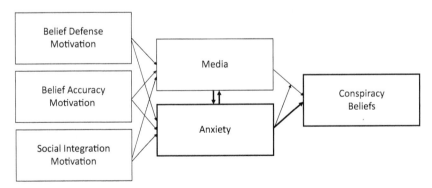

Figure 6.3. Model tested in Studies 1–3 (thicker lines indicate focus of the analyses)

Table 6.5. *Model fit with anxiety or media use as the cause (Studies 1–3)*

Study & Theory	X^2	df	CFI	RSMEA	SRMR between
Definition	Chi-square test		Comparative fit index	Root mean square error of approximation	Standardized root mean square residual
Threshold	*Ns, or lower*		*>0.90*	*<0.08*	*<0.08*
Study 1					
Anxiety Use➡ Media					
Political	260.79***	26	0.90	0.08	0.07
Health	234.93***	26	0.90	0.08	0.07
Media Use➡ Anxiety					
Political	280.68***	26	0.89	0.08	0.07
Health	254.82***	26	0.89	0.08	0.07
Study 2					
Anxiety Use➡ Media					
Political	216.5***	26	0.91	0.07	0.04
Health	191.05***	26	0.92	0.06	0.04
Media Use➡ Anxiety					
Political	216.42***	26	0.91	0.07	0.04
Health	190.97***	26	0.92	0.06	0.04
Study 3					
Anxiety Use➡ Media					
Political	271.55***	26	0.91	0.07	0.05
Health	230.10***	26	0.93	0.07	0.05
Media Use➡ Anxiety					
Political	272.85***	26	0.91	0.07	0.05
Health	231.40***	26	0.92	0.07	0.05

Note: Analyses conducted with multilevel path analyses conducted separately for political and health beliefs. Within each type of belief, the specific conspiracy theory (e.g., about HIV and the MMR vaccine for health beliefs) was introduced as a random factor. ***: $p < 0.001$.

A schematic representation of the model appears in Figure 6.3. Specifically, this model included paths from psychological and sociopolitical factors to media and anxiety, and then ones from media and anxiety to conspiracy beliefs. The analyses were conducted as a multilevel path model (see code in Online Supplement). Specifically, within each type of belief, the specific conspiracy theory (i.e., Obama's birth certificate and voting by undocumented immigrations for political beliefs and HIV and the MMR vaccine for health beliefs) was introduced as a random factor (see code in Online Supplement).

Importantly we were interested in testing the fit of the model when media influences anxiety, as well as the fit of the model when anxiety influences media use. Accordingly, this model was fitted twice, the first time with the path going from media use to anxiety and the second from anxiety to media use. These analyses were conducted for the relation between conservative media and anxiety because we found that the two were related to each other.

The model fit results in Study 1 appear in Table 6.5. As guidance, the models fit better when the chi-square test is lower, when the Comparative Fit Index (CFI) is higher, when the Room Mean Square Error of Approximation (RMSEA) is lower, and when the Standardized Mean Residual (SRMR) is lower. The analyses of Study 1 showed that the model in which conservative media influence anxiety fits better than the model in which anxiety influences conservative media.

However, in Studies 2 and 3, the similar fit of the models suggested that both models were plausible.

In sum, our surveys provided an opportunity to assess reciprocal influences between media use and anxiety. In Study 1, there appeared to be a stronger pathway from conservative media use to anxiety than from anxiety to conservative media. However, the other surveys suggested that both directions probably occur, which is consistent with the literatures we reviewed. Thus, exposure to the news media can trigger anxiety, and anxiety can also drive a search for anxiety-provoking content.

6.8 Discussion

This chapter was dedicated to reviewing the reciprocal relations between media use and anxiety. To begin, the media can exert effects on feelings that are relatively independent of content. Music can provide relief for pain and other negative emotions; scary films and television can produce anxiety; and media coverage of news about tragic events such as a pandemic can produce anxiety and reduce the audience's sense of wellbeing. This chapter also covered evidence about the possible influence of conservative, mainstream, and liberal media on anxiety. We found that the use of conservative media is most strongly correlated with anxiety. This correlation, however, cannot be interpreted to imply that the influence goes solely from media use to anxiety. On the contrary, anxiety also influences our choice of media, with more anxious audiences tending to rely on the conservative media for news and entertainment. The role of anxiety is thus key However, its full impact can only be assessed in the context of social influence, an issue to which we turn in Chapters 7 and 8.

CHAPTER 7

The Influence of Norms and Social Networks on Conspiracy Beliefs

Much of the work on conspiracy beliefs has belonged to a tradition that conceptualizes beliefs as the byproduct of traits (e.g., need for closure), enduring sociopolitical factors (e.g., SES), or situational changes that trigger need for closure or a loss of status. Anxiety is an explicit or implicit part of these perspectives but neither anxiety nor its bases are sufficient to account for the content of conspiracy beliefs. Nevertheless, scholars have largely ignored the social influences that can serve as the basis of conspiracy beliefs.

Anxiety can create a predisposition to believing in conspiracies but is insufficient to explain why people believe in some conspiracy theories and not others. We propose instead that the specific substance creating these beliefs comes from formal or informal communications with other people or exposure to media, a notion expressed in the following principle:

> **Principle of Social Influence.** Social influence (e.g., other people within a person's social network as well as the media) provides the content or stories of conspiracy beliefs. Exposure to these influences may also stem from relatively stable psychological motivations of belief defense, belief accuracy, and social integration, as well as sociopolitical factors and situational factors.

This chapter considers these social processes, beginning with the influence of social norms and discussions with others, before moving to the influence of social media networks and the conditions that lead to the spread of conspiracy theories on social media. Within the model advanced in this book, this chapter addresses the specific influence of social norms, other people, and networks, as part of the social influence component. The model in Figure 7.1 shows the focus of this chapter in thicker lines.

7.1 Estimating Associations with Social Norms

The influence of the beliefs and behaviors of other people has interested researchers for many decades and is critical to understand conspiracy

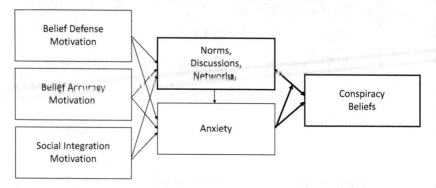

Figure 7.1.   Theoretical model emphasizing focus of the chapter

beliefs. People know what others think about well-known issues, and can also imagine what others would think about less well-known ones. For example, in a study by Patry and Pelletier (2001), Canadian college students described their intentions to report a hypothesized abduction by extraterrestrials. They also rated (a) whether they thought that people who were important to them would want them to report such an occurrence to authorities, (b) whether they thought that specific people would want them to do so, and (c) whether participants were willing to do what those people wanted. Despite the unlikely nature of the researchers' choice of incident, 49 percent of the sample was willing to report to authorities that they were abducted by aliens, and this intention was strongly correlated with the perceived norms to report the incident.

Social consensus appears to affect beliefs most when the judgments are subjective (Crano & Hannula-Bral, 1994; Wood et al., 1994), a condition that conspiracy beliefs undoubtedly meet. As demonstrated in the field of social psychology, social consensus biases beliefs when the object being judged is ambiguous (Festinger, 1954; Turner, 1985). Often, consensus implies correctness, particularly among members of a well-liked group (Wood et al., 1996), thus operating as a heuristic to make a judgment. Other times, however, consensus influences beliefs only after an in-depth discussion of the issues at hand (Wilder, 1977).

Consensus appears to determine what positions will meet approval by members of a social group. As such, an idea endorsed by multiple group members tends to lead to greater consensus. In a study by Schachter (1951), groups of naïve participants and confederates discussed an issue. The confederates advocated a range of positions, with only one being common within the group. Of these positions, only those that were close to the consensus received support, essentially demonstrating a social pressure towards conformity.

Norms influenced beliefs by means of compliance or internalization of arguments that support the beliefs. Deutsch and Gerard (1955; for a review, see Prislin & Wood, 2005) distinguished normative and informational influences. Normative influence entails conforming to a norm even when one does not agree with it (i.e., compliance; Deutsch & Gerard, 1955). Informational influence (i.e., internalization) entails becoming persuaded that a position is valid. Normative influences on conspiracy beliefs are likely to be either or both normative or informational in nature.

Despite the likely importance of norms for conspiracy beliefs, our literature review did not identify studies that assessed the association between acceptance of conspiracy theories as a norm and conspiracy beliefs. However, we studied these associations in our surveys. In Study 2, we included measures related to the belief in the alleged falsification of Obama's birth certificate, the alleged illegal voting by immigrants deciding the 2016 popular vote, and the alleged cover-up of a connection between the MMR vaccine and autism. We first presented participants with statements such as "Obama was not born in the United States and faked his birth certificate to become president." Participants then rated each of these statements on a five-point scale from "people close to me believe this is definitely false" to "people close to me believe this is definitely true." We rescored these items so that higher numbers represented stronger normative perceptions for each conspiracy belief.

The correlations between the three conspiracy beliefs measured in Study 2 and our measures of norms appear in Table 7.1. As shown, there were strong positive correlations between norms and the beliefs in Obama's false birth certificate, illegal voting by immigrants deciding the popular vote, and the cover-up of the connection between the MMR vaccine and autism. Thus, it is possible that either norms influenced participants beliefs, that participants assumed that their own beliefs were shared by others, or both.

In Study 4, participants were asked whether "Unelected U.S. government officials including some in the U.S. intelligence services have secretly conspired to illegally undermine the candidacy and presidency of Donald Trump," an item answered on a five-point scale from "definitely false" to "definitely true." Immediately after this question, participants were asked "How about people close to you? Do people who are close to you believe this is...," which they answered on the same five-point scale from "definitely false" to "definitely true." We calculated correlations

Table 7.1. *Associations between norms, discussing beliefs, and conspiracy beliefs (Studies 3 and 4)*

	Norms	Average report of discussions
Study 3		
Obama's birth certificate	0.69***	–
Undocumented immigrants voted in 2016 election	0.53***	0.34***
HIV virus cover-up	0.61***	–
MMR vaccine cover-up	0.57***	0.33***
Study 4		
Deep state	0.71***	0.05**

Note: *r*. Pearson correlation. **: $p < 0.01$. ***: $p < 0.001$

between these two items, which appear in Table 7.1 as well. As shown, there was a very strong correlation between conspiracy beliefs and conspiracy norms, again suggesting a potentially strong social influence at play.

Although simple correlations cannot disentangle the direction of influence between norms and individually held beliefs, longitudinal analyses can. To assess directionality, Study 4 included three longitudinal measures of beliefs in the deep state conspiracy that contends that unelected administrative officials and intelligence officers have conspired against President Trump. Using a cross-lagged panel model to examine the directional influence that beliefs and norms exert on each other over time, we analyzed the mutual influences of participants' belief in the deep state at Time 1 on their deep state norm at Time 2 and of the deep state norm at Time 1 on the belief in the deep state at Time 2. In the same way, we analyzed the mutual influences of participants' belief in the deep state at Time 2 on their deep state norm at Time 3 and of the deep state norm at Time 2 on the belief in the deep state at Time 3. The results from the crossed-lagged model, which constrained relations of variables to be the same across time under the stationarity assumption, were $\beta = 0.36$, $p < .01$ and $\beta = 0.13$, $p < .05$. These associations suggest that people assumed social consensus for the deep state belief if they themselves believed in it. However, their perceived norms also influenced their own beliefs.

Another important question is whether people form these norms from direct discussions with other people. To obtain an answer, both Studies 2 and 4 gauged the degree to which respondents discussed the conspiracy theories of interest with others. In Study 2, participants were asked "Regardless of whether you believe this to be true or not, have you ever talked about the issue of immigrants voting illegally in the 2016 election with the following people?" and "Regardless of whether you believe this to be true or not, have you ever talked about the issue of the autism effects of the MMR vaccine being covered up, with the following people?" Respondents then provided their answers about (a) "friends and people close to you," (b) "people you only interact with online," and (c) "acquaintances." Their answers were captured on a scale from "very frequently" to "never," which we reverse-scored so that higher numbers reflected a higher frequency of discussion. In Study 4, participants were asked "Regardless of what you believe with respect to this group of unelected U.S. government officials, how frequently, if ever, have you talked about this issue with other people before today?" and recorded their responses on a four-point scale from "never" to "frequently."

We first analyzed the average score of the three items in Study 2 by combining discussions with friends and close others, people online, and acquaintances. The correlations between these two measures and beliefs in the different conspiracies appear in Table 7.1. As shown, there were moderate correlations for illegal voting in 2016 and the MMR vaccine conspiracy and a very small, significant correlation for the deep state conspiracy.

Another question of interest to us was: Among those who are part of an individual's social network, which kinds of individuals influence one's conspiracy beliefs the most? Because Study 2 had separate items for different social relationships, we were able to study discussions with friends, close others to and those conducted with acquaintances and people they interacted with online. Table 7.2 presents results of correlations as well as multiple regressions. As shown, all reported discussions correlated with both the belief in the illegal voting conspiracy and the belief in the MMR vaccine one. The multiple regressions, however, suggest that different social relationships mattered for different beliefs. For the belief in illegal voting by immigrants in the 2016 election, discussions with family and close others as well as acquaintances had the strongest associations. The standardized regression coefficients were respectively 0.13 and 0.16 ($SE = 0.05$ in both cases). By comparison, people on social media had a weaker association, with a standardized regression coefficient of 0.10 and a corresponding SE of 0.04. In contrast, for the belief in the MMR vaccine conspiracy, discussions with people on social media seemed most important. The standardized regression

Table 7.2. *Associations between conspiracy beliefs and discussions with other people (Study 3)*

	Undocumented Immigrants voted in 2016		MMR vaccine cover-up	
		Multiple regression		Multiple regression
	r	coefficient	*r*	coefficient
Intercept in multiple regression	–	1.51***	–	1.68***
Discussions with friends and people close to you	0.31***	0.13*	0.26***	−0.01
Discussions with people you only interact with online	0.28***	0.10*	0.34***	0.26***
Discussions with acquaintances	0.31***	0.16**	0.29***	0.12*
R^2		0.118		0.118

Note: *r*: Pearson correlation. Multiple regression coefficients are standardized regression weights (β). *: $p < 0.05$; **: $p < 0.01$; ***: $p < 0.001$. –: Not applicable.

coefficient for them was 0.26 ($SE = 0.04$), whereas for family and close others it was −0.01 and for acquaintances, 0.12 ($SE = 0.05$ in both cases).

If one's network was correcting conspiracy beliefs, we should find a negative correlation between beliefs and discussions with others. Instead, the positive correlations between beliefs and discussions with others suggest that people are sometimes discussing these off-the-mainstream ideas with like-minded others. There is nonetheless variability in these positive associations, with beliefs in illegal voting during the 2016 election and the MMR vaccine cover-up showing stronger associations with discussions with others than beliefs in the deep state conspiracy. This finding suggests that discussions about the deep state belief may have included both supporters and detractors. Alternatively, the media may have had greater influences on the belief in the deep state than on other conspiracy beliefs.

7.2   Social Media Networks

In recent years, a number of studies have examined the spread of conspiracy theories, including many studies about social networks (Liang, 2018; Pierri, Piccardi, & Ceri, 2020; Walter, Ophir, & Jamieson, 2020). In research by Bogart et al. (2016), people living with

HIV who were prescribed ART (Anti-Retroviral Treatment) reported their HIV conspiracy beliefs and responded to questions assessing their social networks (see Valente, 2010 for survey methods of network assessment). These questions involved listing the initials of up to 20 members of their social networks with whom the respondents had contact (in person, or by phone, mail, or email) in the past year and then reporting how often they thought each pair of people in that network interacted. At baseline, 63 percent of participants endorsed conspiracy beliefs, and 55 percent reported hearing at least one social network member express conspiracy beliefs about the HIV virus. Over time, when network members resembled the respondent in age, gender, HIV status, sexual orientation, or race/ethnicity, exposure to expression of conspiracy beliefs by others in the network was associated with lesser treatment adherence. Furthermore, network members were more likely to express conspiracy beliefs when they themselves were HIV-positive, knew the participants' serostatus, and interacted frequently with the participant.

There are, however, limitations to the use of self-report about social network activity. Like other self-report data, respondents may forget to list some members of their networks and make inaccurate reports. Although these issues are sometimes addressed through modeling (Feehan & Salganik 2016), many researchers have moved to collecting observational data from the Internet and social media platforms. Online publishing on personal websites, forums, and social media allows researchers to observe network interactions using application-programming interfaces (Walter et al., 2020). These observations are based on such relatively objective measures of social relations as following, liking, mentioning, reposting, and replying to posts.

Unhindered by editorial norms or the need to ensure the accuracy and credibility of information (Lazer et al., 2018), the social media have the potential to allow conspiracy theories to reach millions, including people who do not seek the information to begin with (Klein, Clutton, & Dunn, 2019). First, the Internet has produced what has been called *information laundering* (Barnes & Sanger, 2020; Klein, 2012; Korta, 2018). Specifically, it provides an interconnected web that enables conspiracy groups to disguise and launder their questionable content into seemingly acceptable web-based knowledge. Second, as conspiracy theories often appear in the reply threads of posts on forums and social media, even posts from outside one's network can be influential (Harambam & Aupers, 2015; Zollo et al., 2017). Posts about the QAnon movement, for example, emerged from the fringes of the Internet a few years ago and now reach millions of individuals on social media (Lerman & Dwoskin, 2020; Sen & Zadrozny, 2010). Followers of QAnon have explicitly promoted the ideas of "information warfare" since 2019 (Thomas, 2020) and made a concerted effort to bias social, political, and health narratives on social media (Izadi, 2020; Menn, 2020; Ross, 2020; Spring & Wendling, 2020).

But which social processes within a network lead to the spread of conspiracy notions such as claims that COVID-19 is caused by 5G technology (Ahmed et al., 2020; Bruns et al., 2020; for other conspiracy beliefs about COVID-19, see Gruzd & Mai, 2020)? Although the design of algorithms and user engagement features on social media sites may facilitate the spread, the software architecture alone cannot explain why false information such as conspiracy theories and rumors spread six times faster than the truth (Vosoughi et al., 2018). Hence, recent research has investigated network characteristics (e.g., the depth, size, maximum breadth, and diffusion dynamics) that contribute to the dissemination of conspiracy theories online. This type of work has relied on collecting messages and assessing patterns of following and being followed by specific user account handles. For example, Wood (2018) analyzed over 25,000 tweets about conspiracy theories pertaining to the Zika virus as well as posts debunking those theories. Relative to the debunking tweets, tweets about the Zika conspiracy theories spread through a more decentralized network, implying that different subgroups of users were interested in specific conspiracy claims. For readers who are interested in the study of networked communication, see Welles and González-Bailón (2020)'s *Oxford handbook of networked communication*.

Other studies have examined the relations between the user and message characteristics and retweets of posts about conspiracy or other types of misinformation. These studies typically attempt to determine the authors of the information and characteristics of the retweeted posts. For example, a recent study of coronavirus misinformation compared the retweeting behavior of ordinary social media user accounts with so-called "bots," which are automated social media accounts that impersonate humans. In this research, bots accounted for 25 percent of coronavirus misinformation and amplified conspiratorial tweets by carrying out coordinated retweets (Ahmed et al., 2020) and mentioning other influential users, such as @realDonaldTrump (Shao et al., 2018). More importantly, bots were present in both right-wing and left-wing discussions, and their interactions accounted for about 5 percent of Twitter user accounts participating in those threads (Ferrara et al., 2020).

Despite some influence of bots, another study of the conspiracy theory that the COVID-19 pandemic is a hoax (#FilmYourHospital) found that ordinary Twitter users had a greater impact on the spread of conspiracy theories than did bots. In the analyses of tweets posted from April 13–20, 2020, a tweet authored by an ordinary Twitter user, rather than a bot, was the most retweeted (Ahmed et al., 2020). Another group of researchers (Gruzd & Mai, 2020) analyzed the same hashtag #FilmYourHospital and reached a similar conclusion. The #FilmYourHospital conspiracy theory was initially triggered and fueled by some conservative politicians and far-right political activists on Twitter. Likewise, Jamison et al. (2020) examined active Twitter users who posted pro- and anti-vaccine tweets. They found that only 17 percent of active users were likely bots, and more importantly, anti-vaccine Twitter users were mostly conservative politicians and conspiracy theorists whose tweets were retweeted significantly more than were pro-vaccine tweets. Moreover, user accounts that tweeted about one conspiracy theory were likely to also tweet about another conspiracy theory (Ferrara et al., 2020). That is, there was overlap among the authors of tweets about alleged Democrats' scandals, such as "pizza-gate," COVID-19-related conspiracies, and the QAnon movement.

In addition to research on bots and ordinary user accounts, Glenski et al. (2018) classified each media account handle into one of the five types (i.e., trusted, clickbait, propaganda, conspiracy theory, and disinformation) by combining annotations from crowd-sourcing sites with records of public resources, and examined the differences in retweets across news media accounts. An analysis of over 11 million tweets revealed that tweets authored by trusted media accounts were retweeted the most (71 percent of retweets), followed by tweets conveying disinformation (15 percent of retweets), and propaganda media accounts (12 percent of retweets). Despite considerable differences in the number of retweets, tweets from conspiracy theory and disinformation media accounts were retweeted as quickly as those posted by trusted media accounts (Glenski et al., 2018).

As for message characteristics, an important study analyzed tweets about conspiracy theories. Specifically, Wood (2018) compared the content of conspiracy tweets with nonconspiracy ones using a modified version of the Rumor Interaction Analysis System (RIAS). Trained coders followed the modified RIAS coding scheme to classify tweet contents into different categories, such as reference (i.e., refers, directly or indirectly, to at least one conspiracy theory), authenticating (i.e., refers explicitly to the self or other authorities to support an argument or position), and rhetorical question (i.e., asks a leading question clearly). The content analyses revealed that tweets promoting Zika-related conspiracy beliefs contained higher percentages of authenticating (Conspiracy: $M = 25.56\%$, nonconspiracy: $M = 5.80\%$) and rhetorical questions (Conspiracy. $M = 14.90\%$, nonconspiracy: $M - 9.37\%$).

7.3   The Corrective Influence of Discussions with Others on Conspiracy Beliefs

Just as users on social media can spread misinformation, other users on the same network can also correct it. Hence, the possibility that discussions with others debunk misinformation and, more specifically, conspiracy beliefs, deserves attention. Theory and research on group decision-making have indicated that even though groups do not surpass individuals when it comes to tasks with self-evident answers (i.e., "eureka" types of tasks), they do for those related to general knowledge (Laughlin, 2011). For example, when groups solve a logical problem whose solution is self-evident, it takes a single member solving it for the group to accept the solution. For this reason, the group can never perform better than the best member of the group. In contrast, when a group discusses an issue or makes a decision, the outcome of a group discussion depends on what is shared. If members share information that is already available to all members of the group, then the group's decision is not better than that of individuals. In contrast, if members share critical information not available to all members, then the discussion leads to a better decision by combining pieces of information that no single individual would have otherwise (Engelmann & Hesse, 2011; see also Gigone & Hastie, 1993).

In the domain of political misinformation, discussions of misinformation lead to more accurate judgments even when the discussions involve people from the same political party (Becker et al., 2017; Epstein et al., n.d.; Pennycook & Rand, 2019). In the domain of health misinformation, alerting an audience that the newsfeed that contains half false and half true news headlines has been shown to improve the likelihood that users will share true information on social media (Pennycook et al., 2020). In the domain of vaccine misinformation, people who live in areas where tweets frequently contain vaccine misinformation are more likely to be affected by the tweets when they do not discuss vaccination with other people. We (Chan, Jamieson, & Albarracin, 2020) studied this phenomenon by combining a longitudinal survey of vaccine attitudes and behavior with regional tweets about vaccination. To quantify how much vaccine misinformation circulated in the county where participants lived, we linked both survey participants and tweets to counties. We found that the topic of vaccine fraud (which we labeled "Big Pharma and Children") in November–February predicted more negative attitudes and less vaccination against influenza in February–March and April–May the following year. However, these associations were absent when people reported having had discussions about vaccines with family and friends. In other words, online conspiracy beliefs had a negative impact, but this effect was eliminated when discussions presumably debunked vaccine misinformation.

7.4 The Dissemination of Conspiracy Information through Media Account Handles on Social Networks

People can communicate on Twitter just as on television or in newspapers. The main difference between social media and many of the other media outlets is that the content on social media outlets like Twitter is brief and displayed through algorithmic curation and users' following preference. The numbers of followers of media account handles can be very large and media account handles have more followers than do most of their own followers. Thus, even if the audience spreads the information, the resulting influence is likely to be lower than the direct impact of the mainstream media. This difference was demonstrated in the study of mainstream and so-called misleading social media (see Pierri et al., 2020). Mainstream news posts were broadcast with limited interactions among the followers of the source accounts. In contrast, community users shared misleading news with each other in a more symmetric way.

In the original social media study conducted for this book, we were interested in determining if different media account handles disseminate conspiratorial information on social media. In this study, we searched for English-language tweets with hashtags and keywords associated with conspiratorial posts about (a) Obama's birth certificate, (b) deep state, (c) the MMR vaccine cover-up, (d) Pizzagate, (e) chemtrails, (f) lizard people, (g) flat earth, (h) agenda 21, (i) GMOs, and (j) Bush knew about 9/11. We also had a sample of correct posts about Obama's birth certificate and deep state that we used as controls in some separate analyses. A total of 222,903 tweets were located in the search from 2016 through 2017 in the United States (i.e., 207,141 tweets for conspiracy theories and 15,762 tweets for control hashtags and keywords). For the deep state theory, we collected additional tweets from 2018, 2019, and 2020 (i.e., 184,794 tweets, see Appendix).

As we explain in the Appendix, we were first interested in determining whether conservative, liberal, and mainstream media account handles authored messages about the conspiracy theories. Thus, we developed three lists of conservative, liberal, and mainstream media account handles corresponding to the media questions asked in our national surveys. Conservative media account handles were represented in account handles such as "FoxNews" and "BreitbartNews" among many others (see Appendix). Liberal media account handles were represented by account handles like "MSNBC" and "CNN"; and mainstream media account handles were represented by account handles like "ABC" and "CBS." For each tweet, we thus coded whether the account was 1 = a conservative media account handle, 2 = a liberal media account handle, 3 = a mainstream media account handle, or −1 = another account handle.

Our outcome variable was the count of retweets of conspiratorial posts, which we analyzed with Poisson and negative binomial regressions. Because the negative binomial multilevel regression models had a better fit, we relied on these results. As explained in Chapter 6, based on intraclass correlations (ICCs), we analyzed the twitter data while accounting for different types of account handles as a random factor (ICCs = .70 − .83).

We used a multilevel linear model to analyze retweets with a specific conspiracy theory (e.g., flat earth) as a control at the level of the individual tweets (i.e., level-1 unit), and tweets were nested within account handles (i.e., level-2 unit), which had variables indicating whether they were conservative media, liberal media, mainstream media, or other types of accounts (see equations in the Appendix and code in the Online Supplement).

Results indicated that tweets about the MMR vaccine cover-up and pizzagate were the most highly retweeted. There was also a large positive effect of conservative media account handles on retweets (IRR = 30.03, SE = 0.96, p < .001). This result implies that a conspiracy tweet coming from a conservative media account handle had 30.03 times greater chance of being retweeted than a conspiracy tweet coming from other accounts. Notably, there was a similar positive trend of liberal media account handles on retweets, but this effect was highly variable and thus was not significant. We return to these analyses in Chapter 8.

7.5   Discussion

This chapter makes the argument that even though conspiracy beliefs have chronic motivational and political antecedents, thoughts about conspiracy originate in actual communications with other people. This point is illustrated by evidence of consistent correlations between conspiracy beliefs and conspiracy norms, as well as by associations between conspiracy beliefs and discussions with other people. However, discussions with others can also correct conspiracy beliefs, and as such the ultimate influence of discussions with others depends on what they endorse.

Like other communications, conspiracy beliefs spread through social networks. These influences can prove pernicious, as they do when members of a patient's social network share conspiracy theories about ART with people who are living with HIV. Within social media networks, both bots (i.e., automatic users) and ordinary users such as conservative politicians, conspiracy theorists, and news media can be authors of conspiratorial posts, as suggested by findings that they all triggered and fueled the spread of coronavirus misinformation and conspiracy theories on social media. In our study, a conspiratorial tweet was retweeted more frequently when authored by a conservative media account handle, although a similar non-significant pattern was present for liberal media accounts. Chapter 8 examines this issue in greater detail, and considers interactions with anxiety and fear as well as the effects of the media during the 2019–2020 impeachment of Donald J. Trump with its accompanying deep state conspiracy beliefs. It also considers different media, more radicalized media, and the place of the media within a broader social influence context.

Influences of Media and Anxiety in a Psychological and Sociopolitical Context

People who believe in a conspiracy such as the alleged cover-up of the link between the MMR vaccine and autism may be surrounded by others who espouse similar ideas. Believers think that people who are important to them are also believers, and skeptics think that people who are important to them are also skeptics (see Chapter 7). In addition, certain members of a social network can drive opinions within that network. These can be persons or institutions (see Chapter 7). The media, for example, carry information that can persuade recipients that a deep state conspiracy prevented Donald J. Trump from winning the popular vote in 2016 or losing his reelection campaign in 2020. This chapter explores these influences through in depth analyses of our survey and Twitter data. Similar to Chapter 7, the chapter covers associations between exposure to conservative, mainstream, and liberal media, and conspiracy beliefs, but also considers whether these influences are enhanced by anxiety, which we established as a key determinant of conspiracy beliefs in Chapter 4 and an important concomitant of media exposure. Before describing our data, considerations about exposure to a media ecosystem and media effects are in order.

8.1 Media Effects on Conspiracy Beliefs

Media effects require exposure to media, which can be "Selective" or "*de facto.*" Selective exposure (Freedman & Sears, 1966; Sears & Freedman, 1967) involves voluntary selection. Whereas de facto exposure incidental display of information to an audience that receives it by virtue of populating a particular environment. Each of these forms of selective exposure can increase the likelihood that people who believe in conspiracies will seek or otherwise receive conspiracy information. Classic research on mass communication (Klapper, 1960), sociology (Hyman & Sheatsley, 1947; Lazarsfeld, Berelson, & Gaudet, 1948) and social psychology (Festinger, 1957; Frey, 1986; Hart et al., 2009) has shown that people prefer congenial information and engage in selective exposure to preserve beliefs and attitudes they cherish. However, people are also exposed *de facto* to congenial information because they live in environments that harbor it (Bakshy, Messing, & Adamic, 2015; Freedman & Sears, 1966; Sears & Freedman, 1967).

Although selective exposure to media occurs (Stroud, 2010; but see Bakshy, Messing, and Adamic, 2015) and selection plays a role in exposure to belief-consistent media, the evidence that individuals select congenial information is stronger than the evidence that they avoid belief-discrepant content (Winter, Metzger, & Flanagin, 2016). There is debate about the proportion residing within filter bubbles, media enclaves, echo chambers, or information cocoons (Guess, Lyons, Nyhan, & Reifler, 2018). Nonetheless, within those environments, media information and user attitudes tend to align. For example, in their 2008 book *Echo Chamber: Rush Limbaugh and the Conservative Media Establishment*, Jamieson and Cappella showed that people who relied on Limbaugh's radio show, Fox News, and the *Wall Street Journal*'s editorial page expressed agreement with information consistent with the ideological bias of those media (Jamieson & Cappella, 2008). Over a decade later, Benkler, Faris, and Roberts (2018) found the same disinformation sheltering phenomenon more so on the ideological right than left (see also Allcott & Gentzkow, 2017).

Both selective and de facto exposure (Pariser, n.d.) play a role in exposure to online media as well. Although proportionately few appear to engage in selective exposure online (Bakshy, Messing, & Adamic, n.d.; Garrett, 2009), those who do drive traffic to partisan sites (Shore, Baek, & Dellarocas, 2018). After merging the ideology of accounts' followers with the available tweets posted by those accounts, Eady et al. (2019) found that liberals and conservatives had a 51 percent overlap in the accounts they followed. However, data obtained by the Pew Center showed asymmetries in individuals' willingness to follow partisan accounts, with conservatives more frequently following right-leaning accounts than liberals following left-leaning accounts (Eady et al., 2019; Jurkowitz, Mitchell, Shearer, & Walker, 2020). Those asymmetries may mean that although both liberals and conservatives may be exposed to conspiracy beliefs (Oliver & Wood, 2014), those enclaved in a conservative media bubble may be more likely to have their views consistently reinforced.

Because as Benkler et al. (2018) described it, the online and offline media integrate a large media ecosystem, it is important to construct media measures that encompass both systems. Doing so has made it possible for researchers to confirm the association between use of conservative media such as Fox News, Rush Limbaugh, Breitbart News, One America News, or the Drudge Report and embrace of COVID-19-related conspiracy theories (Jamieson & Albarracín, 2020; J. Miller, 2020; Motta, Stecula, & Farhart, 2020; Daniel Romer & Jamieson, 2020). Over and above partisanship, Albarracin and Jamieson (2020) found that reliance on a combination of on and offline conservative media was associated with the conspiracy beliefs that (a) the CDC exaggerated the danger posed by the virus to hurt President Trump (19 percent saying probably or definitely true); (b) the United States government created the virus (10 percent); and (c) the Chinese government created the virus as a weapon (23 percent).

A media ecosystem can create conspiracy beliefs through various mechanisms that include (a) persuasion, (b) cultivation, and (c) familiarity. Persuasion involves internalization of a statement advocated by the media and may take the form of arguments that are perceived as convincing, sources that are respected, or the mere attractiveness of a communicator (Albarracín, 2002, 2021; Albarracín & Shavitt, 2018; Albarracin & Vargas, 2010; Chaiken, 1980; Petty & Cacioppo, 1986). Cultivation involves the natural inclination to take an event's frequency in the media as evidence of its frequency in reality (Jamieson & Romer, 2017; Shanahan, 1997; Wyer & Adaval, 2004; Wyer Jr. & Shrum, 2015; Wyer & Albarracín, 2005). Familiarity increases perceptions of accuracy (Brashier & Marsh, 2020; De keersmaecker et al., 2020; Dunning et al., 2014; Fazio et al., 2017; Hasher, Goldstein, & Toppino, 1977; Newman et al., 2020; Prentice & Miller, 1993; Unkelbach & Rom, 2017) and is likely to increase when the public regularly encounters similar statements. When the medium that persuades, cultivates, or regularly offers conspiratorial claims is a mass one, as are cable news and talk radio, the power of these mechanisms is magnified. In 1964, Hofstadter commented as much when he wrote that social changes may be effects of the mass media (Hofstadter, 1964): "The villains of the modem right are much more vivid than those of their paranoid predecessors, much better known to the public; the contemporary literature of the paranoid style is by the same token richer and more circumstantial in personal description and personal invective."

Across four studies, we investigated associations between media use and conspiracy beliefs both cross-sectionally and longitudinally. Cross-sectionally, we used path analyses to estimate the influence of conservative, mainstream, and liberal media on beliefs in five conspiracies. Studies 1–3 measured two political beliefs (a) that Obama's birth certificate was falsified to cover-up his foreign birth and (b) that immigrants voted for Hillary Clinton illegally in 2016, deciding the popular vote. These surveys also measured two health beliefs (c) that the HIV virus was created by the

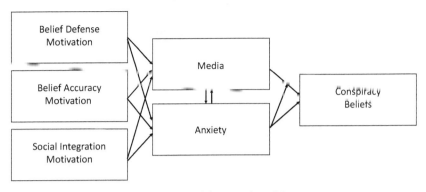

Figure 8.1. Theoretical model

CIA and (d) that the association between the MMR vaccine and autism was covered up. Study 4 concerned the deep state belief. In each case, we measured media exposure, anxiety, and conspiracy beliefs.

Up to this point, our chapters have focused on specific influences involving components of our model. Chapter 4 covered the relation between anxiety and beliefs. It also discussed underlying psychological variables connected to the belief defense, belief accuracy, and social integration motivation. Chapter 5 explicated the relation between sociopolitical factors and conspiracy beliefs. Chapter 6 addressed the relation between media and anxiety, and Chapter 7 concerned the relation between norms and conspiracy beliefs, as well as social networks and conspiracy beliefs. Although Chapter 7 discussed how media account handles disseminate conspiratorial contents online, it did not comprehensively explain how media connect to the other factors treated in prior chapters. Hence, Chapter 8 provides this integration (see Figure 8.1), which includes interactions between media exposure and anxiety. It also explains how media exposure and anxiety relate to the psychological and political antecedents discussed in Chapters 5 and 6. Finally, this penultimate chapter discusses the ways in which perceived plausibility and unfalsifiability increase conspiracy beliefs. In a nutshell, this chapter shows the interrelations among the following four principles that ground this book:

> **Principle of Anxiety.** Anxiety is a perception of threat and depends on relatively stable psychological motivations of belief defense, belief accuracy, and social integration, as well as sociopolitical factors and situational factors like communications and media exposure. Experiencing anxiety at a

particular time motivates a search for an explanation and can lead to misattributing the anxiety to a conspiracy story.

Principle of Social Influence. Social influence (e.g., other people within a person's social network as well as the media) provides the content or stories of conspiracy beliefs. Exposure to these Influence sources may also stem from relatively stable psychological motivations of belief defense, belief accuracy, and social integration, as well as sociopolitical factors and situational factors.

Principle of Synergy. The social influence on conspiracy beliefs may be amplified by anxiety. That is, social communications that promote conspiracy theories may be even more influential when an audience experiences anxiety.

Principle of perceived plausibility and unfalsifiability. Conspiracy stories become plausible through (a) historic similarity (i.e., the similarity between the story of conspiracy and historic precedent), (b) psychological similarity (i.e., the audience's ability to understand the motives of others), and (c) normative plausibility (i.e., the audience's knowledge that others hold these beliefs). However, the device that protects conspiracy beliefs from falsification is the proposition that evidence confirming the conspiracy has been covered up and that sources of disconfirming information are untrustworthy.

8.2   Our Model

The psychological, political, and communicative processes that facilitate conspiracy beliefs (see Chapter 2) appear in Figure 8.1. In this model, the basic human motivations of belief defense, belief accuracy, and social integration are distal determinants of conspiracy beliefs. As such, they create a predisposition to believe in conspiracies but by themselves are not sufficient to create specific conspiracy beliefs. Anxiety and social and media influences are the closer determinants of conspiracy beliefs, exerting both direct and synergistic effects.

This chapter brings together the evidence concerning each of the four principles. It describes our empirical tests of the assumptions that psychological and political factors associated with the motivations of belief defense, belief accuracy, and social integration precede anxiety and media exposure, which in turn precede beliefs. It also deepens our evidence that social communications and anxiety can create a synergy that strengthens conspiracy beliefs above and beyond the individual effects of social communications and anxiety.

This chapter also addresses whether and how communications create conspiracy beliefs by crafting stories of conspiracy that are plausible and unfalsifiable (see Chapter 2). *Plausibility* is defined as the resemblance of a proposition to factual data or commonly accepted assumptions. We propose that a conspiracy may be perceived as plausible due to similarity to historical events, similarity to the motives of the audience, and social norms. Unfalsifiability is conceived of as a factor that insulates a belief from disconfirmation. Lines of argument serving this self-protective function include: (a) one cannot trust those who are debunking the theory because they are part of the conspiracy and (b) disconfirming evidence simply confirms the guile and power of the conspirators who have fabricated it (see Chapter 2). Hence, we studied how perceptions of unfalsifiability correlate with beliefs in conspiracies.

All of our surveys included measures of media use that were scored so that higher numbers represented more frequent exposure to each type of media. Studies 1–3 (see Appendix) had individualized measures of exposure to (a) cable news channels Fox News or One America News (classified as conservative), (b) cable news channel MSNBC (classified as liberal), (c) cable news channel CNN (classified as liberal), (d) broadcast news (such as ABC, CBS, or NBC) (classified as mainstream), (e) your local (e.g., county) television news (classified as mainstream), (f) public radio (such as NPR) (classified as mainstream), (g) talk radio (such as The Rush Limbaugh Show, The Mark Levin Show, The Hugh Hewitt Show, The Glenn Beck Show, The Michael Savage Show, The Michael Meded Show, or The Sean Hannity Show) (classified as conservative), (h) your local (e.g., county) newspaper (including online) (classified as mainstream), (i) national newspapers (such as the *New York Times*, *USA Today*, or the *Wall Street Journal*, including online) (classified as mainstream), (j) online news and blogs such as the Drudge Report or Breitbart (classified as conservative), and (k) online news and blogs such as Vox, or HuffPost (classified as liberal). The frequency of exposure reported for each question was combined into conservative, mainstream, and liberal (see classification between parentheses and Appendix).

In Study 4, the media use measures were streamlined. We combined all conservative media items into one question, so that participants could report their overall exposure to conservative media on a scale from 0 to 7 days a week. We did the same with liberal and mainstream media questions. The analyses that we performed in Studies 1–3 were multilevel because each participant reported eight types of beliefs; they were also multilevel in Study 4 because it had different time points. In Studies 1–3, we measured political and health beliefs as well as conspiracy beliefs along with accurate control statements. The analyses were done separately for political and health beliefs because replicating findings across domains can tell us if our findings apply to conspiratorial beliefs in general or are simply a result of political factors such as ideology. However, within each analysis, we had two theories that were modeled as random slopes. Specifically, political conspiracy theories included both the belief in Obama falsifying his birth certificate and the belief that immigrants voted illegally in 2016, deciding the popular vote. Similarly, health conspiracy theories included the belief that the HIV virus was a CIA creation and the belief that the link between the MMR vaccine and autism was covered up. The accurate, control political theories stated that immigrants use inappropriate documents to work and that Obama's inaction aggravated the Syrian crisis. The accurate, control health beliefs stated that the tobacco industry covered up the health effects of smoking and that the Tuskegee study took place. Study 4 measured the belief in a deep state conspiring against President Trump.

8.2.1   Media and Anxiety as Mediators of the Influences of Psychological and Political Antecedents

The analysis of Studies 1–3 involved multilevel causal modeling. This method is ideal to try to gauge causal relations involving relatively stable factors such as a person's need for cognition or SES. Despite the limitations of modeling cross-sectional data and the superiority of longitudinal analysis, individual differences like the need for closure could require many years, perhaps decades, to change, which leaves researchers with cross-sectional analysis as a viable alternative. Hence, we used causal modeling to analyze associations involving psychological traits and sociopolitical conditions, as well as exposure to different media and anxiety. The analyses began by testing the model in Figure 8.2.

The model in Figure 8.2 shows an influence pathway that begins with psychological and sociopolitical factors related to (a) the belief defense motivation, (b) the belief accuracy motivation, and (c) the social integration motivation. Scholars have argued that these motivations affect conspiracy beliefs (for literature see Chapters 5 and 6). Our survey data support this conclusion as well. However, our model advances prior work by proposing that the impact of psychological and sociopolitical factors is mediated by the intervening influences of those factors on social influence and anxiety. Accordingly, our causal modeling tested specific mediational pathways vis-à-vis other possible mediational pathways. In particular, we compared the model in Figure 8.3 with one in which conspiracy beliefs drive media choices and anxiety.

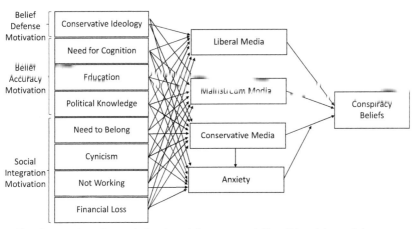

Note. Race, gender, and age controls and correlations among variables within each layer not shown.

Figure 8.2.   General causal model tested with path analyses

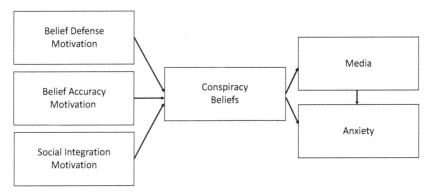

Figure 8.3.   Model with conspiracy beliefs as the antecedent of media use and anxiety

The path model operationalizing our theoretical model appears in Figure 8.2. As tested, this model had other links that are not shown for the sake of simplicity. In particular, all external variables were allowed to correlate with each other. These intercorrelations acknowledge that, for example, education probably correlates with political knowledge and that the need to belong may correlate with the need for closure. One important advantage of using path analysis is that the models provide goodness of fit indexes that determine how well a model fits the data. Accordingly, we obtained several goodness of fit indexes: (a) the Chi-square test, which indicates better fit when it is lower and, ideally, not significant; (b) the

Table 8.1. *Model fit with conspiracy beliefs as an outcome or a mediator (Studies 1–3)*

Study & Theory	X^2	df	CFI	RSMEA	SRMR between
Definition	Chi-square test		Comparative fit index	Root mean square error of approximation	Standardized root mean square residual
Threshold	*Ns, or lower*		*> 0.90*	*< 0.08*	*< 0.08*
Study 1					
Belief as the outcome					
Political	260.79***	26	0.90	0.08	0.07
Health	234.93***	26	0.90	0.08	0.07
Belief as the mediator					
Political	679.6***	59	0.72	0.09	0.09
Health	541.47***	59	0.77	0.08	0.07
Study 2					
Belief as the outcome					
Political	216.5***	26	0.91	0.07	0.04
Health	191.05***	26	0.92	0.06	0.04
Belief as the mediator					
Political	693.81***	59	0.69	0.08	0.08
Health	544.25***	59	0.75	0.07	0.07
Study 3					
Belief as the outcome					
Political	271.55***	26	0.91	0.07	0.05
Health	230.10***	26	0.93	0.07	0.05
Belief as the mediator					
Political	791.71***	59	0.74	0.08	0.09
Health	680.30***	59	0.77	0.08	0.07

Note: Analyses conducted with multilevel path analyses conducted separately for political and health beliefs. Within each type of belief, the specific conspiracy theory (e.g., about HIV and the MMR vaccine for health beliefs) was introduced as a random factor. ***: $p < 0.001$

CFI (Comparative Fit Index), which indicates a good fit above 0.90; as well as (c) the Root Mean Square Error of Approximation (RMSEA) and (d) the Standardized Root Mean Square Residual (SRMSR), both of which indicate good fit under 0.08. These indexes appear in Table 8.1, which presents the results for each study in its horizontal panels. Each study panel contains first the model with belief as an endpoint, following media and anxiety, and then a model with belief as the mediator and media and anxiety as the endpoints. Figure 8.3 presents a schematic depiction of the model with the alternate sequence. The models cannot be compared directly because they are not nested. Nonetheless, the models with conspiracy beliefs as the outcome fit very well, whereas those with conspiracy beliefs as the mediator fit poorly. These analyses thus validated the mediational assumptions of the principle of anxiety and the principle of social influence.

8.2.2 The Media and Anxiety Synergy

We proposed and empirically assessed the possibility that anxiety might enhance the impact of social and media influences on conspiracy beliefs, as proposed by the principle of synergy. To test this hypothesis, the path model in Figure 8.2 included effects of media use and anxiety, as well as an interaction between conservative media use and anxiety.

Political Beliefs
The analysis of political conspiracy beliefs in Study 1 appears in Figure 8.4. As shown, the frequency of exposure to conservative media (0 to 7 days) had

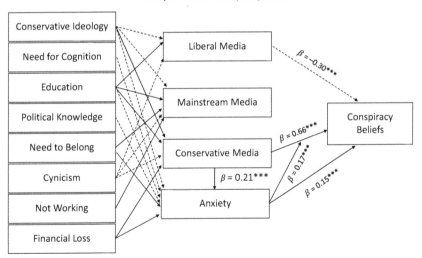

Figure 8.4. Path analysis of political conspiracy beliefs: Study 1. Links to race, gender, and age and correlations within each layer not shown. Dotted lines indicate negative associations, solid lines indicate positive associations, and no lines indicate no significant association

a strong positive effect, implying that this type of media use strengthens political conspiracy beliefs. By contrast, exposure to liberal media had a slight negative effect, implying that this type of media use weakens political conspiracy beliefs. Anxiety had a small positive association with political conspiracy beliefs, and interacted with conservative media as well. This interaction is depicted in Figure 8.6 and indicates that in addition to conservative media and anxiety increasing political conspiracy beliefs, the synergy between the two is important. In short, the combination of conservative media and anxiety was particularly powerful, affecting political conspiracy beliefs more than the simple additive effects of each variable.

It was important to compare the effects of media and anxiety on political conspiracy beliefs with political beliefs that are accurate. For Study 1, these control analyses appear in Figure 8.5, As shown, media use influenced accurate beliefs in political events such as Obama's inaction during the Syrian crisis. Because the beliefs on which we focused are more palatable to conservatives than liberals, the impact of media use depended on the outlet's ideological slant. Whereas exposure to conservative media was positively correlated with these accurate beliefs, exposure to both liberal and mainstream media was negative correlated with them. Importantly, however,

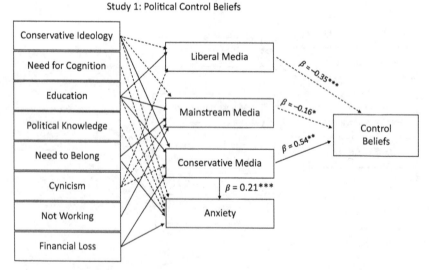

Figure 8.5.   Path analysis of accurate, control political beliefs: Study 1. Links to race, gender, and age, and correlations within each layer not shown. Dotted lines indicate negative associations, solid lines indicate positive associations, and no lines indicate no significant association. Studies 1–3.

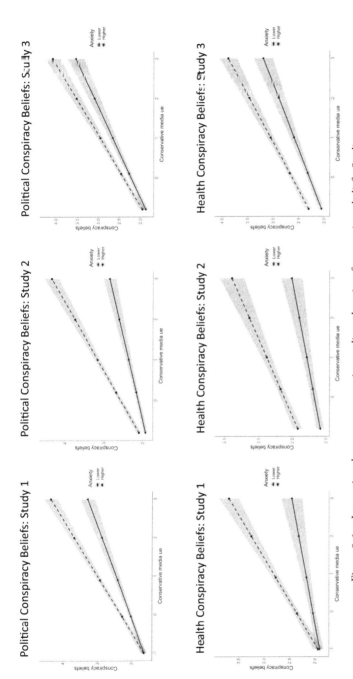

Figure 8.6.   Interactions between conservative media and anxiety for conspiracy beliefs: Studies 1–3

anxiety was not correlated with accurate political beliefs, a fact that circumscribes the contribution of anxiety to beliefs in conspiracies. In sum, anxiety may have more informational value for beliefs that are by definition unfalsifiable and thus require a leap of faith to resolve their inherent ambiguity. We consider perceived unfalsifiability later in this chapter.

The results from Study 2, which was a close replication of Study 1, were quite similar to those from Study 1. The analyses of political conspiracy beliefs appear in Figure 8.7. As depicted, use of conservative media had a strong positive effect on political conspiracy beliefs (e.g., birther), suggesting that political conspiracy beliefs increase as conservative media use does. In contrast, exposure to liberal media, and this time also exposure to mainstream media, had negative associations with political conspiracy beliefs, suggesting that increased exposure to liberal and mainstream media corrects political conspiracy beliefs. Reproducing the findings in Study 1, anxiety had a small positive association with political conspiracy beliefs, and a positive interaction with conservative media use as well. We take this result to mean that conservative media and anxiety exerted synergistic effects on political conspiracy beliefs.

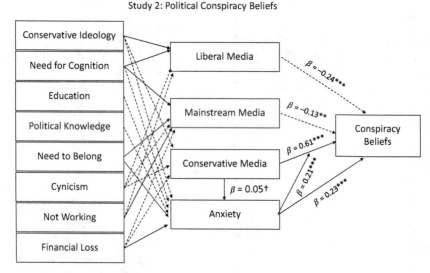

Study 2: Political Conspiracy Beliefs

Figure 8.7. Path analysis of political conspiracy beliefs: Study 2. Links to race, gender, and age and correlations within each layer not shown. Dotted lines indicate negative associations, solid lines indicate positive associations, and no lines indicate no significant association

Study 2: Political Control Beliefs

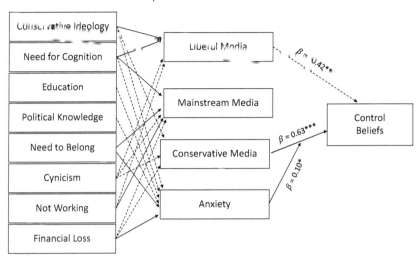

Figure 8.8. Path analysis of accurate, control political accurate beliefs: Study 2. Links to race, gender, and age and correlations within each layer not shown. Dotted lines indicate negative associations, solid lines indicate positive associations, and no lines indicate no significant association

Now compare the results of conspiracy beliefs in Figure 8.7 with the results of accurate, control political beliefs, which appear in Figure 8.8. As in Study 1, the conservative and liberal media influenced accurate beliefs about Obama's inaction in Syria and undocumented immigrants using inappropriate work documentation. Also, as in Study 1, the influence of the media reflected the likely political bias of the media outlets. As in Study 2, use of conservative media was positively correlated with these accurate beliefs, and use of liberal (but this time not mainstream media) was negatively correlated with them. In contrast to conspiracy beliefs, anxiety did not correlate with accurate political beliefs, although there was a positive interaction between conservative media and anxiety. This interaction, however, did not replicate in the other studies.

The results of Study 3, which was a replication with a different sample, were similar to those of Studies 1 and 2. The analysis of political conspiracy beliefs appears in Figure 8.9. As shown there, conservative media use had a strong positive effect on political conspiracy beliefs, further supporting the notion that conservative media use contributes to conspiracy beliefs. As in Study 2, use of both liberal and mainstream media had

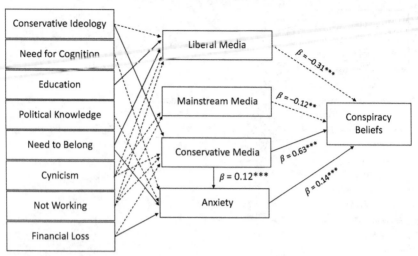

Figure 8.9.   Path analysis of political conspiracy beliefs: Study 3. Links to race, gender, and age and correlations within each layer not shown. Dotted lines indicate negative associations, solid lines indicate positive associations, and no lines indicate no significant association

negative effects on political conspiracy beliefs, further supporting the corrective effect of these information outlets. Also, as in both of the prior studies, anxiety had a small positive association with political conspiracy beliefs. However, contrary to the prior studies, anxiety did not interact with conservative media use in influencing beliefs. That is, even though conservative media use and anxiety both contributed positively to political conspiracy beliefs, their effects were additive. These effects are also represented in Figure 8.6.

Finally, the results concerning accurate political beliefs in Study 3 showed the same type of bias in interpretation of accurate beliefs that we observed in Study 2. These results appear in Figure 8.10, and show that media use affected beliefs in correct political events in line with liberal and conservative biases. On the one hand, use of conservative media had a strong positive effect on the belief that, for example, Obama's inaction produced a crisis in Syria. On the other, use of liberal media had a strong negative effect on the same belief. For example, viewers of Fox News were more likely to believe that Obama's inaction precipitated the Syrian crisis, whereas viewers of MSNBC were less likely to agree.

Study 3: Political Control Beliefs

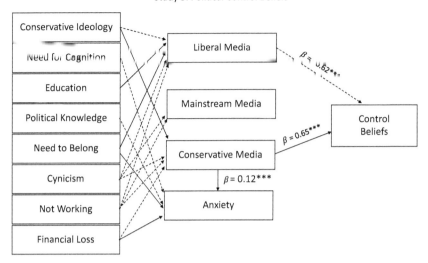

Figure 8.10.   Path analysis of accurate, control political accurate beliefs: Study 3. Links to race, gender, and age and correlations within each layer not shown. Dotted lines indicate negative associations, solid lines indicate positive associations, and no lines indicate no significant association

Health Beliefs

We also tested the synergy principle for conspiracy beliefs in the area of health. The resulting path model includes the effects of media use, as well as an interaction between conservative media use and anxiety, which was present for political conspiracy beliefs.

The findings about health conspiracy beliefs in Study 1 appear in Figure 8.11. This figure shows that, as with political beliefs, health conspiracy beliefs correlated positively with conservative media. However, the association was weaker for health beliefs than it was for political ones ($\beta = 0.38$ versus 0.66). Moreover, health conspiracy beliefs had a slight negative association with exposure to mainstream media. Similar to political conspiracy beliefs, anxiety was positively correlated with health conspiracy beliefs, and there was a positive interaction between anxiety and conservative media. This interaction (see Figure 8.6) indicated that the synergy between anxiety and conservative media is important in this domain as well. Of note, the direct associations between health conspiracy beliefs and anxiety were stronger than those between political conspiracy beliefs and anxiety (e.g., $\beta = 0.28$ versus 0.15).

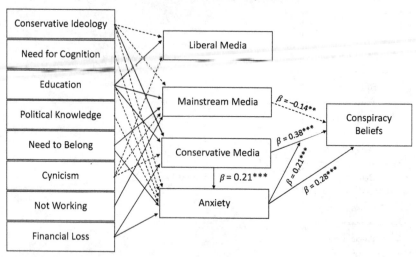

Figure 8.11.   Path analysis of health conspiracy beliefs: Study 1. Links to race, gender, and age and correlations within each layer not shown. Dotted lines indicate negative associations, solid lines indicate positive associations, and no lines indicate no significant association

Following the procedure used for political beliefs, we considered the same model for accurate health beliefs. For example, even though the theory about the link between the MMR vaccine and autism resembles the verified cover-up of the effects of smoking by the tobacco industry, only the belief that the tobacco industry engaged in a cover-up is correct. The results for the accurate control beliefs in Study 1 appear in Figure 8.12. As shown, the accurate health beliefs had a strong negative association with conservative media use, suggesting that the conservative media may also promote misinformation in this domain. However, in contrast to conspiracy health beliefs, the accurate health beliefs did not correlate with anxiety.

We next conducted the same analyses with health conspiracy beliefs in Study 2. The results from this path analysis appear in Figure 8.13, and show that, as in Study 1, health conspiracy beliefs correlated positively with conservative media, but the association was weaker than the association between conservative media use and political conspiracy beliefs in the same study ($\beta = 0.31$ versus 0.61). Moreover, health conspiracy beliefs were negatively associated with mainstream media use, which was also the

Study 1: Health Control Beliefs

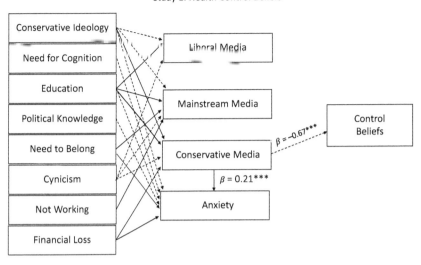

Figure 8.12.   Path analysis of accurate, control health beliefs: Study 1. Links to race, gender, and age and correlations within each layer not shown. Dotted lines indicate negative associations, solid lines indicate positive associations, and no lines indicate no significant association

Study 2: Health Conspiracy Beliefs

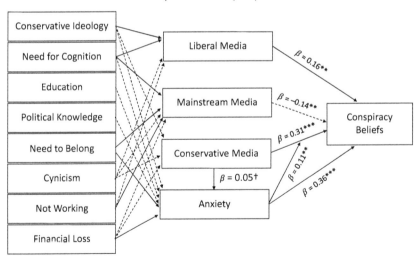

Figure 8.13.   Path analysis of health conspiracy beliefs: Study 2. Links to race, gender, and age and correlations within each layer not shown. Dotted lines indicate negative associations, solid lines indicate positive associations, and no lines indicate no significant association

Study 2: Health Control Beliefs

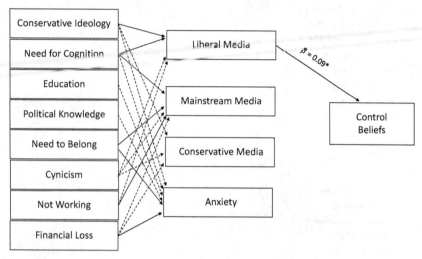

Figure 8.14.   Path analysis of accurate, control health beliefs: Study 2. Links to race, gender, and age and correlations within each layer not shown. Dotted lines indicate negative associations, solid lines indicate positive associations, and no lines indicate no significant association

case for health conspiracy beliefs in Study 1. In addition, however, these beliefs were positively associated with liberal media use, which was not what we found earlier, and also positively with anxiety, as in our prior analyses. The effects of anxiety and conservative media were also synergistic (see Figure 8.6) although weaker for health beliefs than for the political ones in the same study (e.g., β interaction = 0.11 versus 0.21 for health and political conspiracy beliefs, respectively).

The analysis of accurate health beliefs in Study 2 appears in Figure 8.14. It showed only one effect in the form of a positive association between use of liberal media and accurate health beliefs in the Tuskegee study and the tobacco industry cover-up. This effect, however, was small.

Finally, we performed the same analyses with health conspiracy beliefs in Study 3. The results appear in Figure 8.15 and again suggest a positive effect of conservative media use, although this effect was weaker than the one for political conspiracy beliefs in the same study (β = 0.46 versus 0.63). In addition, anxiety had a positive influence on health conspiracy beliefs, although only independently rather than in interaction with conservative media.

Study 3: Health Conspiracy Beliefs

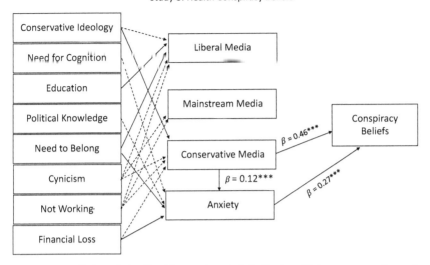

Figure 8.15. Path analysis of health conspiracy beliefs: Study 3. Links to race, gender, and age and correlations within each layer not shown. Dotted lines indicate negative associations, solid lines indicate positive associations, and no lines indicate no significant association

The findings for accurate health beliefs in Study 3 appear in Figure 8.16 and were similar to the findings for accurate political beliefs in the same study. Use of conservative media correlated negatively with accurate health beliefs. Use of liberal media correlated positively with these beliefs.

Meta-analysis
Studies 1–3 consistently showed that conservative media use and anxiety likely increase conspiracy beliefs across political and health beliefs. However, there was some variability across the studies, including the fact that the interaction between conservative media use and anxiety was significant in two out of three studies. Thus, it was desirable to quantitatively synthesize the three studies. We did that through a study level meta-analysis (Mcshane & Böckenholt, 2017) by nesting the participants from each study within the four studies we meta-analyzed. The outcome variable was conspiracy belief. Anxiety, demographics, political ideology, and time, which varied only within Study 4, were fixed-effects factors. Specifically, we assessed a three-level model with belief in either political or health conspiracy theories as the outcome, specific theory as a random

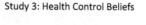

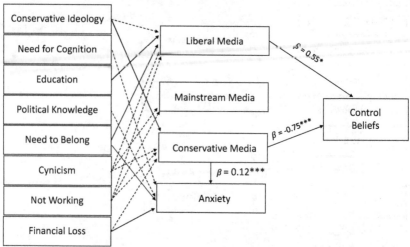

Figure 8.16.   Path analysis of health control beliefs: Study 3. Links to race, gender, and age and correlations within each layer not shown. Dotted lines indicate negative associations, solid lines indicate positive associations, and no lines indicate no significant association

factor at the first level of analysis (e.g., about HIV and the MMR vaccine cover-up; level 1 unit) nested within participant (i.e., level 2 unit) and with participants nested within study (i.e., level 3 unit). Media use, fear, as well as demographic and political variables were fixed-effects factors at the participant level (see equations in the Appendix and code in the Online Supplement). The results, which appear in Table 8.2, show that anxiety influenced conspiracy beliefs, as proposed by the principle of anxiety. The results also indicated that (a) conservative media use influenced conspiracy beliefs, as proposed by the principle of social influence and (b) the combination of anxiety and conservative media use enhanced conspiracy beliefs, as proposed by the principle of synergy. By contrast, liberal and mainstream media use were negatively associated with belief in conspiracies.

8.2.3   Media and Anxiety Effects on Dissemination of Conspiracy Information on Social Media

Surveys 1–4 provided consistent evidence that conservative media use and anxiety have interactive effects on conspiracy beliefs. However, we were

Table 8.2. *Meta-analysis of influence of conservative media use and anxiety (Studies 1–4)*

	β
Coefficients for Predictors	
(Intercept)	−0.01
Conservative media use (day)^	0.34***
General anxiety^	0.12***
Conservative media use (day)^ * general anxiety^	0.08***
Control Variables	
Gender [2]	−0.02
Age group	0.02
Education level attained	−0.07***
Political ideology	0.29***
Time	0.03**
Social media use (day)^	0.01
Liberal media use (day)^	−0.1***
Mainstream media use (day)^	−0.07***
Random Effects	
σ^2	0.6
τ_{00}	0.63 pid:study
	0.01 study
ICC	0.51
N_{pid}	3273 pid
	4 study
N	6788
Marginal R^2/Conditional R^2	0.266/0.643

Note: Analysis conducted with multilevel modeling with beliefs nested within participants and participants then nested within studies. β : Standardized coefficient estimates. N: Sample size. A caret indicates centered variables. Sigma squared refers to the within-group (residual) variance. Tau-oo refers to the between-group variance. The marginal R^2 considers only the variance of the fixed effects, whereas the conditional R^2 takes both the fixed and random effects into account. ***: $p < 0.001$.

also interested in studying if conservative media and anxiety-inducing contents affect dissemination of conspiracy information, which our social media study considered possible. As a reminder, we searched for English-language tweets with hashtags and keywords associated with conspiratorial posts about (a) Obama's birth certificate; (b) deep state; (c) the MMR vaccine cover-up, (d) Pizzagate, (e) chemtrails, (f) lizard people, (g) flat earth, (h) agenda 21, (i) GMOs, and (j) Bush knew about 9/11. We also had a sample of correct posts about Obama's birth certificate and deep state that we used as controls in some separate analyses.

As we explained in Chapter 7, we first gauged whether conservative, liberal, and mainstream media account handles authored messages about the conspiracy theories. Thus, we developed three lists of conservative, liberal, and mainstream media account handles corresponding to the media questions asked in our national surveys. Conservative media account handles were represented in account handles such as "FoxNews" and "BreitbartNews" among many others (see Appendix). Liberal media account handles were represented by account handles like "MSNBC" and "CNN"; and mainstream media account handles were represented by account handles like "ABC" and "CBS." For each tweet, we thus coded whether the account was $1 =$ a conservative media account handle, $2 =$ a liberal media account handle, $3 =$ a mainstream media account handle, or $-1 =$ another account handle.

As described in Chapter 6, we also obtained a measure of fear language for each tweet. In fact, two fear measures were obtained. The first one was a standard one and included all words linked to fear according to a preestablished dictionary (see Appendix). However, an inspection of the fear words captured by this fear index revealed that "conspiracy" and synonyms of conspiracy were included. Thus, to separate fear language from the topic of conspiracy tweets, we computed a second fear measure that excluded synonyms of conspiracy. Our analyses were replicated with the two measures.

Our outcome variable was the count of retweets of conspiratorial posts, which we analyzed with Poisson and negative binomial regressions. Because the negative binomial multilevel regression models had a better fit, we relied on these results. As explained in Chapter 6, based on intraclass correlations (ICCs), we analyzed the Twitter data while accounting for different types of account handles as a random factor (ICCs $= .70 - .83$).

In our multilevel linear model, tweets were nested within account handles (i.e., level 2 unit), which had variables indicating whether they were conservative media, liberal media, mainstream media, or other types of accounts. This multilevel model also assessed the effects of account handle type (e.g., conservative media) and fear (a level 1 variable) while controlling for the effects of different conspiracy theories (see equations in the Appendix and code in the Online Supplement) and estimating the effects of fear, both independently and in interaction with conservative media use.

As explained in Chapter 6 and shown in Table 8.3, there was also a large positive effect of conservative media account handles on retweets

Table 8.3. *Predicting retweets from media account handle types and fear index (all tweets; N = 128,401)*

Variable	Incidence Rate Ratios	SE	p
(Intercept)	0.17	0.06	<0.001
Theory: Bush knowing 9/11	1.52	0.11	<0.001
Theory: Chemtrails	1.27	0.06	<0.001
Theory: Deep state	1.71	0.06	<0.001
Theory: Obama's birth certificate	1.88	0.19	0.001
Theory: Flat Earth	1.39	0.1	0.001
Theory: GMO	1.23	0.07	0.006
Theory: Pizzagate	2.18	0.06	<0.001
Theory: Lizard people	0.53	0.07	<0.001
Theory: MMR vaccine cover-up	3.72	0.13	<0.001
Conservative media account handle	30.03	0.96	<0.001
Liberal media account handle	35.94	2.53	0.157
Fear percent^	0.9	0.01	<0.001
Conservative media account handle X fear^	9.8	1.32	0.083
Liberal media account handle X fear percent^	0.01	5.42	0.37
Random Effects			
σ^2	2.11		
τ_{00} account handles	3.42		
ICC	0.62		
N account handles	44047		
Observations	128401		
Marginal R^2/Conditional R^2	0.024/0.628		

Note: Entries correspond to a multilevel negative binomial regression with tweets nested within account handles. *SE:* Standard error. *N:* Sample size. A caret indicates centered variables. Sigma squared refers to the within-group (residual) variance. Tau-oo refers to the between-group variance. The marginal R^2 considers only the variance of the fixed effects, whereas the conditional R^2 takes both the fixed and random effects into account.

($IRR = 30.03$, $SE = 0.96$, $p < .001$). In addition, we found a marginal positive interaction effect between conservative media account handle and fear on retweets ($IRR = 9.8$, $SE = 1.32$, $p < .083$). Specifically, tweets authored by conservative media account handles that also had higher percentages of fear words were 9.6 times more likely to be retweeted than tweets from other accounts or tweets with lower percentages of fear words. A graphic depiction of the interaction appears in Figure 8.17.

Although the results in Table 8.3 were interesting, we replicated our analyses with our index of fear language that excluded synonyms of conspiracy. Table 8.4 presents these new results, again obtained with the negative binomial multilevel regression models, which had a better fit than

Table 8.4. *Predicting retweets from conservative media account handles and refined fear index (all theories; N = 128,404)*

Variable	Incidence Rate Ratios	SE	p
(Intercept)	0.17	0.06	<0.001
Theory: Bush knowing 9/11	1.46	0.12	0.001
Theory: Chemtrails	1.26	0.06	<0.001
Theory: Deep state	1.71	0.06	<0.001
Theory: Obama's birth certificate	1.9	0.19	0.001
Theory: Flat Earth	1.55	0.11	<0.001
Theory: GMO	1.21	0.07	0.01
Theory: Pizzagate	2.26	0.06	<0.001
Theory: Lizard people	0.52	0.08	<0.001
Theory: MMR vaccine cover-up	3.68	0.13	<0.001
Conservative account handle	13.47	1.25	0.037
Fear percent^	0.9	0.01	<0.001
Conservative account handle X fear percent^	5.15	1.63	0.314
Random Effects			
σ^2	2.1		
$\tau_{00 \; \text{account handle}}$	3.36		
ICC	0.62		
$N_{\text{account handle}}$	41131		
Observations	121804		
Marginal R^2/Conditional R^2	0.026/0.625		

Note: Entries correspond to a multilevel negative binomial regression with tweets nested within user account handles. *SE:* Standard error. *N:* Sample size. A caret indicates centered variables. Sigma squared refers to the within-group (residual) variance. Tau-oo refers to the between-group variance. The marginal R^2 considers only the variance of the fixed effects, whereas the conditional R^2 takes both the fixed and random effects into account.

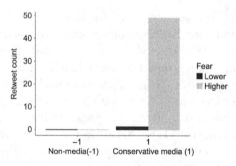

Figure 8.17.   An interaction effect between conservative-media account handle and fear on retweets of conspiratorial tweets. Results obtained from the negative binomial regression

the Poisson model. As shown in Table 8.4, there was a large positive significant main effect of conservative media account handles on retweets ($IRR = 13.47$, $SE = 1.25$, $p = .037$). Although this analysis verified the positive main effects of conservative media account handles and the negative main effect of the fear language on retweets, the interaction between the two predictors was not significant ($IR\hat{R} = 5.15$, $SE = 1.61$, $p = .314$). Similar to the results in Table 8.3, they showed that the conservative media probably played a major role in popularizing conspiracy theories and making them salient via retweets through their social networks. However, these results do not suggest that fear-inducing language beyond the conspiracy content of the tweets contributed to that dissemination. In fact, strict fear language did not interact with conservative media use and correlated with fewer rather than more retweets.

8.2.4 *Anxiety and Media Effects in the Creation of Beliefs over Time*

Up to this point, this chapter has focused on effects observed cross-sectionally. However, we were also interested in examining how a conspiracy belief forms in public opinion. For this purpose, between November 2019 and February 2020, we conducted a longitudinal study asking a nationally representative panel of participants to indicate their agreement with the conspiracy theory that a deep state of government bureaucrats was secretly and illegally undermining Donald J. Trump's presidency and candidacy. This contention was being advanced by the incumbent president as well as by many of his supporters in Congress and by proponents of conspiracy theories including the alleged Q. Participants provided their answers in November 2019, and also in December and February 2020. Their last responses were provided in the period after the impeachment trial ended in the United States House of Representatives but before the Republican-controlled Senate decided not to convict, a decision that was widely expected.

In addition to inquiring about participants' beliefs, we measured media use and level of anxiety in the population. Because the analysis was over time, we could explore whether media use was affecting conspiracy beliefs or alternatively whether conspiracy beliefs were affecting media use. We were able as well to analyze the impact of the media and of anxiety on conspiracy beliefs at different time points. In particular, we were interested in determining whether media use had an influence early in the impeachment inquiry, when the conspiracy theory was being regularly discussed in the media, relative to later in the trial. Likewise, we were interested in knowing whether anxiety was important early on, or alternatively whether it strengthened conspiracy beliefs after the information provided in the media had crystallized the beliefs.

8.2.4.1 Reciprocal Over-time Effects of Conservative Media and Political Conspiracy Beliefs

We first analyzed the reciprocal influences between conservative media use and conspiracy beliefs. We fit a cross-lagged model constraining relations to be the same across time under the stationarity assumption to investigate the directional influence of beliefs and conservative media use on each other over time. This model controls for the correlation between different measures of belief over time as well as the correlation between different measures of conservative media use over time. Once these correlations are included, the model can shed light on the relative influence of earlier media use on later beliefs and of earlier beliefs on later media use.

As judged by the correlations between each variable measured at the two time points, the cross-lagged model identified significant stability for both media use ($\beta = .69, p < .001$) and conspiracy beliefs ($\beta = .66, p < .001$). The model also showed that conspiracy beliefs influenced conservative media use at a later time ($\beta = 0.05, p < .001$). This finding implies that people seek agreeable information and thus gravitate toward outlets that support their beliefs (Hart et al., 2009). However, the analysis also showed that conservative media use influenced conspiracy beliefs at a later time ($\beta = 0.10, p < .001$), which suggests stronger influence from conservative media use to conspiracy beliefs than from conspiracy beliefs to conservative media use. This analysis supplements the causal modeling findings presented earlier in the chapter, which also supported the inference that media use affects beliefs.

8.2.4.2 Effects of Media and Anxiety at Different Points of Time

We next conducted analysis of beliefs over time analyzing beliefs as a function of media use, anxiety, and the demographic characteristics and political ideology of these participants. Specifically, using a multilevel regression, belief in the deep state conspiracy reported at each time was predicted from the media variables, anxiety, and the other factors, and belief scores at different time points were nested within participants (see Online Supplement). Liberal media use, mainstream media use, conservative media use, anxiety, and time were entered into the model as fixed effects representing the explanatory variables for each time point (i.e., level 1 unit) nested within participant (i.e., level 2 unit; see equations in the Appendix).

Table 8.5. *Analysis of deep state beliefs as a function of anxiety and media use over time (Study 4)*

	β
(Intercept)	0.61[...]
Liberal media use	−0.18***
Mainstream media use	−0.07**
Conservative media use	0.35***
Time	0
Anxiety	−0.04***
Conservative media use * Time	−0.05***
Anxiety * Time	0.04**
Conservative media use * Anxiety * Time	0.01
Random Effects	
σ^2	0.27
τ_{00} Participant	0.56
ICC	0.67
N Participants	736
Observations	1754
Marginal R^2/Conditional R^2	0.211/0.741

Note: Analysis conducted with multilevel modeling with time points nested within participants. β : Standardized coefficient estimates. N: Sample size. A caret indicates centered variables. Sigma squared refers to the within-group (residual) variance. Tau-oo refers to the between-group variance. The marginal R^2 considers only the variance of the fixed effects, whereas the conditional R^2 takes both the fixed and random effects into account. **: $p < 0.01$; ***: $p < 0.001$.

Three interaction terms between conservative media use and time, between anxiety and time, and between conservative media use, anxiety, and time, were obtained to determine whether conservative media use strengthened belief in the deep state conspiracy over time. In addition, these analyses included demographic variables and political ideologies as controls at the participant level. The results, which are summarized in Table 8.5, showed that, as in the cross-sectional analyses, conservative media use strongly influenced conspiracy beliefs. As judged by the significant negative interaction between conservative media and time, the effect of media was stronger earlier than later in the trials. This finding is graphically depicted in the left panel of Figure 8.18.

In contrast to the other studies, anxiety was overall weakly but negatively associated with conspiracy beliefs. This implies that, if anything, participants who experienced more anxiety believed in the deep state influence less than those who experienced less anxiety. However, we found

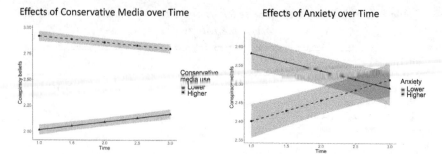

Figure 8.18.   Deep state conspiracy belief as a function of anxiety and conservative media over time

a significant positive interaction between anxiety and time. This finding appears in the right panel in Figure 8.18, and shows that, contrary to the declining impact of conservative media use over the course of the impeachment process, the impact of anxiety increased over time. All in all, it appears that conspiracy beliefs were initially fed by exposure to conservative media. Over time, however, people who were more anxious became more persuaded that a deep state was undermining President Trump than they had been in the beginning of the impeachment inquiry.

8.2.5   The Context of the Media and Anxiety Influences

A final, important question concerns the broader context of the influences of media use and anxiety preliminarily discussed in Chapter 4 and 6. These influences appeared in each of the cross-sectional path analyses we just described. In the path analysis in Figure 8.2, we included factors related to the belief defense motivation, the belief accuracy motivation, and the social integration motivation. These variables were introduced as possible causes of media use and anxiety while controlling for all demographic variables. In the path-analytic graphs (see e.g., Figure 8.5), significant positive associations are represented with solid lines, significant negative associations are represented with dotted ones, and nonsignificant paths are omitted.

The complete set of path coefficients appears in the Online Supplement. With respect to media use, generally, but not always, having a conservative ideology is associated with greater conservative media use. Also, in Study 1 and to some extent in Study 3, having a higher level of education predicted more exposure to media of all types. Similarly, factors such as cynicism, not being in the labor force at the time, and having suffered a financial loss predicted less use of media regardless of the outlet.

With respect to anxiety, first, a conservative political ideology predicted lower levels of anxiety in Studies 1 and 2, and was uncorrelated with anxiety in Study 3 (see also Chapter 5).

Factors associated with the belief accuracy and social integration motivation also mattered. In addition, a higher level of education, a higher level of political knowledge, and a higher level of need for cognition correlated with lower levels of anxiety across the board. In contrast, having experienced a financial loss had consistent positive correlations with anxiety.

Last, we reexamined the degree to which the distal variables associated with the belief defense, the belief accuracy, and the social integration motivations influenced conspiracy beliefs primarily via anxiety (see also Chapter 4), or primarily via media use. To this end, from the path analyses, we obtained indirect effect indexes of the extent to which media and anxiety mediated these influences. These coefficients are summarized in Table 8.6. As shown, both conservative media exposure and anxiety mediated the psychological and political influences associated with the belief defense, the belief accuracy, and the social integration motivation.

8.2.6 Perceived Plausibility

According to the principle of perceived plausibility, conspiracy beliefs develop when communications present conspiracy propositions as plausible (see case study in Chapter 2). For example, the CIA used weather control techniques in an attempt to extend the monsoon season over the Ho Chi Minh Trail during the Vietnam War (Department of State, 2017). In light of that operation, the belief that the United States has deliberately caused earthquakes gains plausibility. As another example, inaction by the United States government has allowed the food industry to compromise the health of American citizens (Sharma, Teret, & Brownell, 2010). Hence, it is plausible that the government has covered up evidence proving that vaccines cause autism (Eggertson, 2010).

Our first three studies measure (a) historic plausibility, (b) psychological plausibility, and (c) normative plausibility. Studies 1–3 measured different forms of subjective plausibility (see Appendix). For example, participants were told: "Independently of your beliefs as to whether this occurred, please consider the situation described in this statement and answer the questions below: The MMR vaccine causes autism but this fact has been covered up." They then rated whether each of the following statements on a 5-point scale from "clearly described my feelings" to "does not describe

Table 8.6. *Indirect effects for the influence of psychological motivations and sociopolitical factors on conspiracy beliefs as mediated by media use and anxiety (Studies 1–3)*

Mediator	Study 1 Estimate	SE	Z-value	Study 2 Estimate	SE	Z-value	Study 3 Estimate	SE	Z-value	Study 3 (with far-right and far-left media) Estimate	SE	Z-value
Political beliefs												
Anxiety	0.1	0.03	3.07**	0.04	0.02	1.64	0.06	0.02	2.58**	0.05	0.02	2.23*
Conservative media	0.24	0.07	3.21**	0.19	0.07	2.95**	0.23	0.06	3.75***	0.17	0.05	3.14**
Liberal media	−0.04	0.04	−1.15	0.02	0.02	1.03	−0.06	0.03	−1.84	−0.06	0.03	−1.71
Mainstream media	−0.02	0.02	−1.31	0	0.01	0.34	−0.01	0.01	−0.82	−0.01	0.01	−0.75
Far-right media	–	–	–	–	–	–	–	–	–	0.03	0.03	1.28
Far-left media	–	–	–	–	–	–	–	–	–	0	0.01	−0.07
Health beliefs												
Anxiety	0.15	0.04	4.25***	0.05	0.03	1.66	0.01	0.03	3.68***	0.08	0.02	3.53***
Conservative media	0.12	0.04	3.09**	0.08	0.03	2.87**	0.15	0.04	3.81***	0.09	0.03	2.99**
Liberal media	0.01	0.01	0.63	−0.01	0.01	−0.97	−0.01	0.01	−0.67	−0.02	0.01	−1.32
Mainstream media	−0.04	0.02	−1.73	0	0.01	0.34	−0.01	0.01	−0.74	−0.01	0.01	−0.69
Far-right media	–	–	–	–	–	–	–	–	–	0.03	0.02	1.15
Far-left media	–	–	–	–	–	–	–	–	–	0.01	0.01	0.72

Note: Analyses conducted with multilevel path analyses conducted separately for political and health beliefs. Within each type of belief, the specific conspiracy theory (e.g., about HIV and the MMR vaccine for health beliefs) was introduced as a random factor. *SE:* Standard error. *: $p < 0.05$; **: $p < 0.01$; ***: $p < 0.001$.

my feelings": (a) "History has provided a lot of examples of industry hiding the damage done by their products," (b) "I can imagine why the damaging effect of a product might be covered up," and (c) "People like me think it is common for industry to hide damage done by their products." Thus, the first item tapped history, the second the ability of an individual to imagine the actor's motives (psychological plausibility), and the third, social consensus (i.e., normative plausibility).

8.2.6.1 *Political Beliefs*

The plausibility results of Survey 1 appear in Table 8.7. As shown, all beliefs, whether conspiratorial or accurate, were supported by a sense of historical plausibility as well as normative plausibility. That is, participants who reported that history showed many examples of people falsifying documents to achieve power were more likely to believe that Obama had faked his birth certificate to become president. Likewise, participants who reported that people like them believed that people fake documents to achieve power were more likely to believe that Obama had faked his birth certificate to become president.

Another important conclusion from the analyses of Study 1 in Table 8.7 is that normative plausibility differentiated political conspiracy beliefs from their accurate, control counterparts. That is, normative plausibility was more strongly correlated with political conspiracy beliefs than with their accurate counterparts. In contrast, psychological plausibility was generally uncorrelated with either conspiracy or accurate political beliefs, and historical plausibility was similarly associated with both conspiracy and accurate political beliefs.

The plausibility results of Studies 2 and 3 also appear in Table 8.7 and were similar to those of Study 1. Again, all political beliefs, whether conspiratorial or accurate, were supported by a sense of historical plausibility as well as normative plausibility. That is, participants who reported that history had many examples of people falsifying documents to achieve power were again more likely to believe that Obama had faked his birth certificate to become president. Likewise, participants who reported that people like them believed that people fake documents to achieve power were again more likely to believe that Obama had faked his birth certificate to become president.

Similar to Study 1, in Studies 2 and 3, normative plausibility seemed to differentiate political conspiracy beliefs from accurate, control political beliefs. That is, normative plausibility was more strongly correlated with political conspiracy beliefs than with accurate political beliefs. In contrast,

Table 8.7. *Predicting beliefs from different sources of perceived plausibility (Studies 1–3)*

Predictor	Conspiracy beliefs			Accurate, control beliefs		
	β	β	β	β	β	β
	Study 1	Study 2	Study 3	Study 1	Study 2	Study 3
	Obama's birth certificate			Obama's inaction and crisis in Syria		
Normative plausibility	0.42***	0.40***		0.34***	0.44***	
Psychological Plausibility	−0.11**	−0.06		−0.05	−0.07	
Historical plausibility	0.19***	0.13***		0.11*	0.11**	
Observations	737	1000		730	995	
R²/R² adjusted	0.259/0.256	0.207/0.205		0.150/0.147	0.223/0.221	
	Undocumented immigrants decided popular vote			Immigrants use false documents to work		
Normative plausibility	0.52***	0.45***	0.37***	0.30***	0.30***	0.24***
Psychological Plausibility	−0.07*	0.05	0.03	0.11**	0.01	0.05
Historical Plausibility	0.15***	0.10**	0.20***	0.21***	0.23***	0.31***
Observations	733	996	976	738	993	972
R²/R² adjusted	0.361/0.358	0.292/0.291	0.282/0.280	0.301/0.298	0.237/0.234	0.256/0.253
	HIV virus cover-up			Tuskegee study		
Normative plausibility	0.45***	0.38***		0.19***	0.33***	
Psychological Plausibility	0.04	0.14***		0.01	−0.04	
Historical Plausibility	0.07	0.03		0.31***	0.16***	

	MMR vaccine cover-up			Tobacco effects cover-up		
Observations	737		1000	733		996
R^2/R^2 adjusted	0.270/0.267		0.253/0.251	0.214/0.210		0.177/0.174
Normative plausibility	0.29 ***	0.30***	0.24***	0.19 ***	0.24***	-0.36***
Psychological Plausibility	-0.04	0	-0.04	0.09	0.12***	0.07*
Historical Plausibility	0.03	0.03	0.12**	0.21 ***	0.11**	0.29***
Observations	734	999	980	733	997	976
R^2/R^2 adjusted	0.084/0.080	0.102/0.099	0.093/0.090	0.185/0.182	0.163/0.161	0.389/388

Note: Entries are standardized regression weights (β) from multiple regression questions. *: $p < 0.05$; **: $p < 0.01$; ***: $p < 0.001$.

psychological plausibility was generally uncorrelated with either conspiracy or accurate beliefs, and historical plausibility was similarly associated with both types of beliefs.

8.2.6.2   Health Beliefs

Table 8.7 also shows that health conspiracy beliefs correlated with all forms of plausibility: historical, psychological, and normative. Participants who believed that the HIV virus was created by the CIA believed there was historical precedent, understood the possible motives of the potential conspirators, and felt that other people like them thought such events do take place. Likewise, participants who believed in the MMR vaccine conspiracy believed there was historical precedent, imagined the motives of the potential conspirators, and felt that other people like them thought such events do take place.

For health beliefs, normative plausibility appeared to differentiate conspiracy from accurate, control beliefs. Interestingly, normative plausibility mattered less for conspiracy health beliefs that it did for control health beliefs. Thus, even though conspiracy health beliefs were typically anchored on perceptions of historic precedent, normative sources of plausibility were not as important.

8.2.7   Perceived Unfalsifiability

Understanding conspiracy theories implies understanding perceived falsifiability (see also case study in Chapter 2). A belief (i.e., the assignment of subjective probability to an event) can be disconfirmed through direct observation through the senses, as well as inspection of documents and interviews with credible sources. Science relies on an explicit method of verification, and investigative journalism relies on factual research and document inspection in areas of political, educational, or financial concern. Within a scientific epistemology or any system of knowledge based on verification and falsification, propositions that are unfalsifiable are set aside, at least until they become falsifiable. For example, to verify the hypothesis that diseases can be caused by germs required invention of the microscope. In contrast, conspiracy beliefs are propositions that are unverifiable by design.

Falsifiability implies that a belief can be disproven by evidence. Scientists must be able to specify observations that would disprove their hypotheses, and investigative journalists must acknowledge that absence of documentation, or documents that contradict their claims, would disprove them. Unfortunately, however, this possibility does not apply to conspiracy theories, which are forms of social fallacies. Conspiracy beliefs are hard to undermine or dislodge because they have a "self-sealing quality" that renders them immune to challenge (Sunstein & Vermeule, 2008, p. 3). The same forces that, according to a conspiracy theory, plot and cover-up a harmful event, for instance, are not reliable as sources of information that seems to undercut the theory. We call this property unfalsifiability.

Studies 1–3 measured perceived unfalsifiability. Similar to the measures of perceived plausibility, participants first read. "Independently of your beliefs as to whether this occurred, please consider the situation described in this statement and answer the questions below: The MMR vaccine causes autism but this fact has been covered up." They then reported whether each of the following statements on a 5-point scale from "clearly describes my feelings" to "does not describe my feelings": (a) "Some types of evidence (data, documents) can demonstrate if the tobacco industry covered up the damaging effects of tobacco or not," (b) "No evidence can demonstrate if the tobacco industry covered up the damaging effects of tobacco or not," and (c) "There are no reliable sources to demonstrate if the tobacco industry covered up the damaging effects of tobacco or not."

To analyze associations between perceived unfalsifiability and conspiracy beliefs, we obtained the average of our three items measuring perceived unfalsifiability and correlated these measures, which correspond to each theory, with each conspiracy belief measure. Study 1 showed that perceived unfalsifiability was either positively correlated or uncorrelated with conspiracy beliefs. In contrast, perceived unfalsifiability was negatively correlated with the control beliefs. For the conspiracy beliefs, the correlations were $r = .19$ ($p < .001$) for Obama's birth certificate, .01 (*ns*) for undocumented immigrants deciding the popular vote, .01 (*ns*) for HIV as a CIA creation, and –.006 (*ns*) for the cover-up of the link between the MMR vaccine and autism. In contrast, for the accurate, control beliefs, the correlations were $r = -.11$ ($p < .01$) for Obama's inaction in Syria, $-.18$ ($p < .001$) for immigrants using false documents, $-.28$ ($p < .001$) for the Tuskegee study, and $-.29$ ($p < .001$) for the cover-up of the link between tobacco and cancer. The implications of these associations are that perceiving that no evidence could disprove the theory was associated with less. This negative correlation belief in accurate events, This negative correlation suggests the use of the conventional logic in practical and scientific thought by each absence of evidence suggests that the event is not to be believed. However, perceiving that evidence cannot disprove the theory had little impact on conspiracy beliefs, suggesting that the need for verification had been effectively suspended.

Studies 2 and 3 also showed that perceived unfalsifiability had more positive correlations with conspiracy beliefs than it did with control beliefs. In Study 2, for conspiracy beliefs, the correlations were $r = .29$ ($p < .001$) for Obama's birth certificate, 0.02 (ns) for undocumented immigrants deciding the popular vote, 0.04 (ns) for HIV as a CIA creation, and .11 ($p < .001$) for the cover-up of the link between the MMR vaccine and autism. In contrast, for the accurate, control beliefs, the correlations were $r = -.04$ (ns) for Obama's inaction in Syria, $-.05$ (ns) for immigrants using false documents, $-.10$ ($p < .01$) for the Tuskegee study, and $-.15$ ($p < .001$) for the cover-up of the link between tobacco and cancer. The implications of these associations are that perceiving that no evidence could disprove the theory was associated with weaker control beliefs, again following the conventional logic in practical and scientific knowledge. However, unfalsifiability had little impact on conspiracy beliefs.

In Study 3, for conspiracy beliefs, the correlations were $r = .06$ ($p < .05$) for undocumented immigrants deciding the vote, and .23 ($p < .001$) for the cover-up of a supposed MMR vaccine-autism link. For control beliefs, the correlations were $r = -.15$ ($p < .001$) for immigrants using false documents to work, and $-.24$ ($p < .001$) for the cover-up of the link between tobacco and cancer. Again, perceiving that no evidence could disprove the theory was associated with weaker control beliefs, suggesting that unfalsifiability reduced endorsement of regular, accurate beliefs. In contrast, perceiving that no evidence could disprove the theory did not discount conspiracy beliefs.

8.2.8   The Relative Impact of Media in the Context of Other Social Influences

This chapter analyzed the role of the media in creating conspiracy beliefs using advanced statistical modeling and longitudinal methods. All point to the exposure to conservative media as a factor that leads people to endorse conspiracy beliefs, particularly in the political domain. Unanswered but critical questions involve where media influences fit within the broader landscape of social influences, which includes more extreme ideological media, reading or watching conspiratorial information, and discussions with other people, both close others as well as acquaintances or social network dwellers (Chapter 7).

Another question is whether the media effects reflect the media measured in all studies, or assessed use of outlets that may be more extreme in ideology that could be correlated with use of such conservative media as Fox News. Recall that in Study 3, conservative media use was an average of frequency of use of sources such as: "Fox News, Rush Limbaugh, or One America News," "Cable news channels Fox News or One America News," and "Online blogs such as the Drudge Report and Breitbart." The same study, however, included measures of far-right outlets like DavidIcke.com, WhatReallyHappened.com, thetruthseeker.co.uk, bilderbergmeetings.org, and nexusmagazine.com. To be able to distinguish the influence of conservative versus far-right media use, we conducted multiple regression analyses that jointly entered the conservative, mainstream, and liberal media use variables used previously, along with far-right and far-left media use.

The top panel of Table 8.8 presents these analyses. As shown by the results in Table 8.8, use of popular conservative outlets like Fox news continued to have an influence even after far-right media were included, and use of far-right media was not correlated with conspiracy beliefs after controlling for conservative media use. Likewise, liberal media like CNN and MSNBC continued to have a corrective influence even after including far-right and far-left outlets, the latter of which had no positive association with conspiracy beliefs. These results confirmed that the more popular conservative media played a role in producing conspiracy beliefs.

We then analyzed the detailed data obtained in Study 3, which included whether participants had read or watched information about two of the conspiracy theories of interest: (a) illegal voting by undocumented immigrants deciding the popular vote and (b) the MMR vaccine cover-up. These two variables were introduced into a multiple regression equation which appears in the second horizontal panel of Table 8.8. As shown, reading and watching information had similar influences.

Last, to understand the relative weight of media influences versus other social influences, we conducted supplementary analyses predicting conspiracy beliefs from conservative media use, mainstream media use, and liberal media use. To these media use variables, we added discussions of a particular conspiracy theory with other people, norms that endorse the conspiracy theory, and trust in President Trump. All of these factors were measured in Study 3, and were entered into a multiple regression. Study 4 measured all except for trust in the president, and these were part of in a multilevel linear regression model.

For Study 3, we conducted multiple regressions. For Study 4, the outcome was belief in the deep state conspiracy theory at a particular time

Table 8.8. *Multiple regression with media and other social influences as predictors of conspiracy beliefs (Studies 3 and 4)*

Predictors and other information	Study 3		Study 4
	Vote by undocumented immigrants in 2016	MMR vaccine cover-up	Deep state
Analyses of conservative, mainstream and liberal media use in the context of far-right and far-left media use			
Conservative media use	0.44***	0.32***	–
Liberal media use	−0.30***	−0.14**	–
Mainstream media use	−0.09*	−0.08*	–
Far-right media use	0.06	0.10	–
Far-left media use	0.11	0.10	–
	978	977	
Observations	0.167/0.162	0.142/0.137	
R^2/R^2 adjusted	0.44***	0.32***	–
Analyses of medium			
Read	0.16***	0.19***	–
Watched	0.17***	0.14**	–
N	985	980	–
R^2	0.09/0.09	0.09/0.09	–
Analyses of media use in the context of norms, discussions with other people, and trust in the president			
Conservative media use	0.19 ***	0.15***	0.24***
Liberal media use	−0.09*	−0.03	−0.13***
Mainstream media use	−0.06	−0.03	−0.05*
Discussions with others	0.11***	0.11***	0
Trust in the president	0.23***	0.11***	–
Norms	0.34***	0.48***	0.50***
Observations	974	973	–
R^2/R^2 adjusted	0.384/0.380	0.386/0.382	–
Random effects			
σ^2	–	–	0.27
τ^{00} pid	–	–	0.23
ICC	–	–	0.46
N pid	–	–	684
Observations	–	–	1495

Table 8.8. (*cont.*)

Predictors and other information	Study 3		Study 4
	Vote by undocumented immigrants in 2016	MMR vaccine cover up	Deep state
Marginal R^2/ Conditional R^2	–	–	0.557/ 0.760

Note: Entries are standardized regression weights (β). *N*: Sample size. For Study 4, the equation also included time and interactions with time as in prior analyses. –: Not available. Sigma squared refers to the within-group (residual) variance. Tau-oo refers to the between-group variance. The marginal R^2 considers only the variance of the fixed effects, whereas the conditional R^2 takes both the fixed and random effects into account. **: $p < 0.01$; ***: $p < 0.001$.

point (i.e., level 1 unit) nested within participant (i.e., level 2 unit). Media use, discussion with others, and norms were each entered as fixed-effects explanatory variables at the participant level (see equations in the Appendix and code in the Online Supplement).

Table 8.8 presents the results from these analyses and shows that the conservative media continued to have a positive effect on conspiracy beliefs after all of the other influences were entered. Finding this effect after including conspiracy norms is particularly noteworthy because norms were not just influencing beliefs but were also the result of conspiracy beliefs, possibly through mechanisms like assuming a consensus that does not exist (Monin & Norton, 2003; Sanders et al., 2014; Schroeder & Prentice, 1998). Norms continued to have a strong positive influence in all studies, and liberal and mainstream media had a corrective effect only for the deep state belief in Study 4. Moreover, trust in the president had a positive effect on conspiracy beliefs, as did discussions with other people in Study 3.

8.3   Discussion

After a series of chapters that paint parts of a landscape of diverse influences on conspiracy beliefs, this chapter provided an overview of the complex processes that create conspiracy beliefs. We showed that these beliefs are not random but rather result from the interplay of social communications, including the media, and feelings of anxiety in the population. Also at play are some more distal determinants, including need for cognition, education, political knowledge, cynicism, and having experienced a financial loss. These determinants influence beliefs by shaping people's media choices and feelings of anxiety.

Our studies also allowed us to gauge sequences of processes, including whether anxiety is a precursor or a consequence of conspiracy beliefs. Here, our evidence is primarily cross-sectional, but the path analyses support the conclusion that conspiracy beliefs are the byproduct of anxiety. Our studies also allowed us to determine whether media choices are precursors or consequences of conspiracy beliefs. Generally, the cross-sectional evidence points to media choices driving beliefs more than beliefs driving media choices. Our longitudinal study of the deep state belief suggested that, although both influences are likely present, the influence of media use on beliefs is stronger than the corresponding influence of beliefs on media use.

This chapter also examined how perceived plausibility grounds conspiracy beliefs. The sense of plausibility is primarily normative. If a person's ingroup believes in a conspiracy, the conspiracy becomes credible. If the ingroup thinks that people falsify documents to achieve power, then the notion that Obama falsified his birth certificate to become president is also believable. Interestingly, this normative plausibility is stronger for conspiracy beliefs than for similar, accurate beliefs such as Obama creating a crisis in the Middle East.

Perceived unfalsifiability also comes into play. People sustain their belief in conspiracies by adopting epistemic assumptions that make it impossible to disconfirm them. If a believer is armed with the defense system that we described in Chapter 2 and the psychological dispositions documented here, for practical purposes it is impossible to convince that person that a conspiracy theory is false. What to a non-believer is compelling evidence is taken by the believer as confirmation of the power of the conspirators to create illusions. The sources of knowledge on which the non-believer relies are seen by the believer as under the control of the conspirators and hence untrustworthy.

A media ecosystem can create conspiracy beliefs through various mechanisms: (a) persuasion, (b) cultivation, and (c) familiarity. Persuasion involves internalization of a statement advocated by the media and may be due to arguments that are perceived as convincing, sources that are respected, or the mere attractiveness of a communicator (Albarracin, 2021; Albarracín, 2002; Albarracín & Shavitt, 2018; Albarracin & Vargas, 2010; Chaiken, 1980; Petty & Cacioppo, 1986). Cultivation involves the natural inclination to take frequency of an event in the media as evidence of its frequency in reality (Jamieson & Romer, 2017; Shanahan, 1997; Wyer & Adaval, 2004; Wyer & Albarracín, 2005; Wyer Jr. & Shrum, 2015). Familiarity increases perceptions of accuracy (Brashier & Marsh, 2020; De keersmaecker et al., 2020; Dunning et al., 2014; Fazio et al., 2017; Hasher et al., 1977; Newman et al., 2020; Prentice & Miller, 1993; Unkelbach & Rom, 2017) and is heightened when the public encounters similar statements again and again. When the medium that persuades, cultivates, or ensures frequency of conspiratorial claims is a mass one, as are cable news and talk radio, the power of these mechanisms is even greater.

CHAPTER 9

Conclusions

As Chapter 2 argued, Edgar Welch's assault on Comet Ping Pong was motivated by the Pizzagate conspiracy theory. His actions were not singular. In the two-week period that ended 2020 and began 2021, two other violent events illustrated the importance of understanding the origins, evolution, effects, and need to contain the spread of conspiracy beliefs. In the first, which occurred on Christmas Eve 2020, an explosion rocked downtown Nashville Tennessee killing its perpetrator, Anthony Quinn Warner, injuring three others, and damaging surrounding buildings. Two days before the bombing, Warner sent multiple typed pages and two thumb drives to a number of individuals. The writings included speculation that "aliens have been attacking Earth since September 2011, and that the media is covering up the attacks," and endorsed the theory that "Earth is controlled by a race of reptilian lizard people." "They put a switch into the human brain so they could walk among us and appear human," Warner stated (Freiman, 2021). The theory also contends that these "shape-shifting reptilian creatures ... are bent on world domination" (Deliso & Date, 2020).

Thirteen days later, QAnon and Pizzagate believers participated in breaching the United States Capitol to disrupt the certification of the 2020 electoral college vote for the Democratic presidential ticket. In the weeks following the election, Trump, his lawyers, and his allies, and QAnon adherents had spread conspiracy theories indicting the Deep State for supposedly siphoning votes from Trump to Biden using sophisticated malware. "QAnon has gripped Trump's base and many of the people who attacked the Capitol on Wednesday wore T-shirts or held signs expressing their belief in the conspiracy theory," reported MSN (Morse, 2021). One of the signs carried by a mob member read "Pelosi is Satan."

We know that some of the insurrectionists were QAnon/Pizzagate adherents because the Twitter stream of the woman who was killed by a Capitol police officer as she tried to break through the door to the House chamber said as much. In late December, when Kamala Harris discussed Democratic plans to "to ensure Americans mask up, distribute 100M shots, and get students safely back to school," Ashli Babbitt tweeted in response, "No masks, no you, no Biden the kid raper, no vaccines . . . sit your fraudulent ass down . . . we the ppl bitch!" The day before the January 6th Trump rally at the Ellipse that incited his supporters to storm the Capitol, Babbitt had employed the argot of QAnon when she tweeted "Nothing will stop us . . . they can try and try and try but the storm is here and it is descending upon DC in less than 24 hours . . . dark to light!" (Beckett & Ho, 2021).

Conspiracy beliefs have also been associated with how people vote (see Chapter 3), attacks on cell-phone towers to prevent the spread of COVID-19 (Satariano & Alba, 2020), and donations to a fraudulent campaign to fund a wall on the United State's southern border to stop unauthorized immigration (Orden & Scannell, 2020). However, the consequences of conspiracy beliefs do not end there, expanding also to reduced adoption of vaccination recommendations (Nyhan et al., 2014) and treatment for HIV (Bogart et al., 2011; Simmons & Parsons, 2005), as well as reduced efforts to curb carbon dioxide in the atmosphere (Douglas & Sutton, 2015; Van der Linden, 2015).

In an effort to better understand the psychological underpinnings of human acceptance of conspiracy beliefs, our earlier chapters have focused on relating our work to that of others. In this final chapter, we summarize the questions we have asked and the answers we have provided and as well identify some of the issues worthy of additional study.

9.1 Our Research Questions and Answers

9.1.1 Anxiety

In ascribing a central role to anxiety, one of our central propositions (see principle of anxiety below) has much in common with prior scholarship. Anxiety is the feeling that ranges from subtle uncertainty about the future to extreme fear of imminent or future threats. As we noted in Chapters 5 and 6, scholars of psychology, political science, and communication are among those who have probed its role. However, as our formulation of the principle of anxiety below indicates, in addition to relatively stable psychological motives and sociopolitical factors that make people anxious, specific situational influences from others and the media can heighten anxiety. When this occurs, anxiety can give way to a psychological search for an explanation that can lead to misattributing anxiety to a conspiracy-based narrative.

> **Principle of Anxiety.** Anxiety is a perception of threat and depends on relatively stable psychological motivations of belief defense, belief accuracy, and social integration, as well as sociopolitical factors and situational factors like communications and media exposure. Experiencing anxiety at a particular time motivates a search for an explanation and can lead to misattributing the anxiety to a conspiracy story.

An experiment and four surveys, in addition to a large body of past research and scholarship, support the notion that anxiety plays a central role in conspiracy belief. The questions our work has addressed about that role include the following: **Does anxiety that occurs for reasons unrelated to conspiracies exert a causal influence on conspiracy beliefs?** The experiment that we reported in Chapter 4 suggests that the answer is yes. In it, experimentally inducing fear increased the belief that 5G technology is responsible for the COVID-19 pandemic. In addition, this experiment pointed to a precondition of influence: As the process established by Albarracín and Kumkale's (2003) model of affect as information suggests, for anxiety to influence, people must pay attention to their feelings.

Is there a relation between anxiety and media exposure? Our review and our surveys converge on the conclusion that individuals who feel more anxious seek different media than do those who feel less so. For example, people who regularly experience negative affect and anxiety can use music to regulate their mood (see review in Chapter 6) and those who report a higher level of anxiety have higher exposure to conservative media than do those who report a lower one (see our survey results in Chapter 6). Because they can alter people's feelings, including anxiety, media also factor in the mix. In our surveys, influence of media use on anxiety and anxiety on media use appeared to be reciprocal; a media ecosystem that is created in response to anxiety can also reinforce it.

Is there a relation between anxiety inducing posts and dissemination of tweets? Although highly or moderately emotional information has been shown to be more frequently shared on social media (Heath, 1996; Heimbach & Hinz, 2016; Towers et al., 2015), we did not find a clear association between fear and retweets. Relative to Lohmann et al.'s research (2018), which found a positive association between fear language in HIV tweets and frequency of retweets, we found either no association or a negative correlation between fear language and frequency of retweets (see Chapters 7 and 8). However, because the topic of conspiracy theories is eminently fear-inducing, added fear language may not be necessary to increase interest in the information or the motivation to disseminate it. Moreover, our analyses of fear language after excluding synonyms of "conspiracy" suggested that conspiracy tweets with fewer fear words were actually shared more than conspiracy tweets with more fear words. Together these findings suggest that the conspiracy contents were sufficiently arousing and probably optimal to gain traction without the need for more emotional language.

Is anxiety connected to the motives of belief defense, belief accuracy, and social integration? Although collectively the past psychological and political scholarship has emphasized similar motivational issues, the notion that these motivations contribute to the experience of anxiety has not been either clearly specified or empirically demonstrated. We do both in Chapters 4 and 5. Evidence of the effect is deepened by the survey analyses in Chapter 8. Our evidence that social integration motives correlate with higher levels of anxiety imply that people who are lonely or marginalized are naturally uncertain and fearful of their futures, which makes them more likely to accept conspiracy beliefs.

We also conducted analyses to determine if the sociopolitical factors associated with belief defense, belief accuracy, and social integration motivations influenced conspiracy beliefs via the mediation of anxiety. Our findings indicated that this was the case. The influences of education, political knowledge, and having experienced a financial loss were due to the fact that these factors made individuals more anxious. Participants with higher levels of education and political knowledge felt less anxious and were therefore less likely to endorse conspiracy theories. However, conservative political ideology had a negative indirect effect on conspiracy beliefs and this negative effect was mediated by anxiety, contesting the contention that conservatives are necessarily more anxious than liberals. We conducted a further review of the literature and supplementary analyses of the association between our anxiety measure and political ideology. Our review of past research indicated that conservatives are more pessimistic about our future way of life, believe the world is dangerous, and are anxious about political issues. However, as shown by our data, general anxiety in the moment was not correlated with political ideology. This finding should qualify assertions that conservatives are necessarily more anxious.

9.1.2 Social Influence

We argue that social influence is a prerequisite for the existence of conspiracy beliefs as well. For this reason, as noted in the analysis of

Pizzagate (see Chapter 2), similar processes are likely at stake for those who forge the theories. Like most other social scientists who are trying to understand conspiracy beliefs, our work centers not on the creators of the conspiracy theories but on those who embrace them. Our principle of social influence below integrates psychological motivations, sociopolitical and situational factors and the role of media and one's social network media.

> **Principle of Social Influence.** Social influence (e.g., other people within a person's social network as well as the media) provides the content or stories of conspiracy beliefs. Exposure to these influence sources may also stem from relatively stable psychological motivations of belief defense, belief accuracy, and social integration, as well as sociopolitical factors and situational factors.

Several specific research questions and answers are relevant to this principle.

9.1.2.1 *What is the role of discussions with other people?*

Exchanges with others within our networks have the capacity to affect conspiracy beliefs. Discussing the conspiracy theory that illegal voting swayed the 2016 popular vote to Hillary Clinton was associated with endorsing that conspiracy belief. For the belief that the link between the MMR vaccine and autism has been covered up, close relationships are less important than occasional ones. In particular, discussing the conspiracy theory with people online and acquaintances but not with family correlates with this view. More generally, however, discussions with others can sometimes offset conspiracy beliefs.

What types of media exposure, if any, predispose people to believing in conspiracy theories? In our surveys, the associations between media use and holding accurate beliefs were consistent with the ideological bent of the media on which the respondent relied. So, for example, use of liberal media led to a lower likelihood of believing a statement we consider accurate: "Obama's inaction facilitated a crisis in Syria." When it comes to acceptance of political conspiracy theories, we found stronger associations with use of media than use of other media. Although conservative media use correlates strongly and positively with political conspiracy beliefs, the other media have small negative associations if any. We also found that reading, hearing, or viewing information about political or health conspiracy theories in print, radio, or television or online correlated with belief in them, as did the amount of media to which the respondent was exposed. This evidence supplements associations with the patterns of media use we report and lends credence to the social influence principle.

What types of media disseminate conspiracy theories on Twitter?
Our research found that a conspiracy tweet originating from a conservative media account handle is disproportionately more likely to be disseminated than is a conspiracy tweet originating from other sources.

What is the contribution of anxiety in combination with media use?
The third principle that we proposed concerns how anxiety and social influence can combine to catalyze conspiracy beliefs. The synergy principle specifies that:

> **Principle of Synergy.** The social influence on conspiracy beliefs may be amplified by anxiety. The influence of social communications that promote conspiracy theories may be more pronounced when an audience is experiencing anxiety.

When it comes to the impact of fear and media on endorsement of beliefs, our surveys and a meta-analysis (see Chapter 8) support the conclusion that fear can magnify the effects of social influences by increasing the impact of the conspiratorial content conveyed by the media. Thus, audiences that are anxious and that also use fear-inflected media are particularly vulnerable to their media effects.

Are there synergistic effects of different media sources and fear-inducing posts on dissemination of conspiracy theories on Twitter?
Our findings showed that conspiracy tweets were disseminated more when they were initially sent by a conservative media account, but there was no robust interaction with fear language. First, fear language predicted fewer rather than more retweets, and had only a marginal interaction with fear language, using the index of fear that allowed for conspiracy language to be included. When conspiracy synonyms were excluded from the fear language index, the marginal interaction disappeared.

9.1.3 Perceived Plausibility and Unfalsifiability

Our work also explored how beliefs about the plausibility and unfalsifiability of a theory correlate with conspiracy beliefs, as expressed in this principle:

> **Principle of perceived plausibility and unfalsifiability.** Conspiracy stories become plausible through (a) historic similarity, (b) psychological similarity (i.e., the audience's ability to understand the motives of others), and (c) normative plausibility (i.e., the audience's knowledge that others hold these beliefs). However, the device that protects conspiracy beliefs from falsification is the proposition that evidence

confirming the conspiracy has been covered up and that sources of disconfirming information are untrustworthy.

Our questions and answers about perceived plausibility and unfalsifiability follow.

Are beliefs in conspiracies supported by a sense of historical plausibility, psychological plausibility, as well as normative plausibility? According to our research, people who believe that history has many examples of people falsifying documents to achieve power are more likely to endorse the claim that Obama faked his birth certificate to become president. Likewise, people who have confidence that people like them believe that people fake documents to achieve power are more likely to endorse this belief as well. Furthermore, normative plausibility was more strongly correlated with conspiracy beliefs than with the accurate counterparts that served as a control, suggesting that norms, inferred from discussions with others as well as information in their media ecosystems, are particularly important sources of plausibility for conspiracy thoughts.

What is the role of perceived unfalsifiability in the creation of conspiracy beliefs? A scientific or investigative epistemology prescribes verification and falsification as methods to test conclusions about a phenomenon. By contrast, a conspiratorial epistemology is unfalsifiable because lack of evidence or evidence that disconfirms the conspiracy is taken instead as evidence for its validity. However, whether perceptions of unfalsifiability correlate with conspiracy beliefs was an empirical question before our research was conducted. Our survey measures of perceived falsifiability showed that, as one might expect in an empirically-grounded epistemology, for accurate beliefs such as one asserting that undocumented immigrants use false documents to work, the more people believed that the idea was unfalsifiable, the less they believed in it. In contrast, for conspiracy theories, unfalsifiability was either uncorrelated, or positively correlated with stronger beliefs. This contrast suggests that conspiracy theories have at the very least made the falsifiability of content irrelevant, which is key to the success of these theories in society.

9.1.4   How to Reduce the Political Risk of Conspiracy Beliefs and Structural Barriers to Dissemination

At a political and structural level, boosting social wellbeing seems to be a necessary but difficult precondition to preventing conspiracy beliefs (Cichoka, 2020). In addition, if information is the currency of democracy, the problem of misinformation in general, and conspiracy theories in particular present a serious challenge to the quality of democratic self-governance (Coddington, Molyneux, & Lawrence, 2014). However, where the First Amendment's right to freedom of speech limits the governmental actions that can be taken to stop the online spread of conspiracy theories, the platforms themselves have no obligation to carry content that violates their policies.

It is not our intent to exhaustively detail the efforts of the platforms to minimize the spread of conspiracy content. Instead, we want to highlight their capacity to do so and note that, despite their efforts, both COVID-19 and deep state election conspiracies have survived in their venues. As Romer and Jamieson (2021) state, in March 2020, Twitter pledged to remove content containing "a clear call to action that could directly pose a risk to people's health or well-being" and Facebook declared its plans to remove "false claims and conspiracy theories flagged by global health organizations." In August 2020, Facebook reported that it had removed "7 million posts pushing covid-19 misinformation from its main social media site and Instagram between April and June." In December, YouTube said that it had removed more than 700,000 misleading COVID-19 videos. Yet, before it was interdicted, conspiracy content nonetheless managed to reach sizeable audiences (Ahmed et al., 2020; Kearney, Chiang, & Massey, 2020).

As we noted in an earlier chapter, attempts by the platforms to shut down the Pizzagate conspiracy after the arrest and conviction of Edgar Welch ultimately failed as well. So too did moves by the platforms to quash political conspiracy content calling for violence. After publication of warnings from the FBI and American military researchers about the threat posed by extremist groups, in summer 2020, Twitter (Lerman & Dwoskin, 2020) and Facebook (Dwoskin & Stanley-Becker, 2020) began limiting the reach of some of these accounts and shuttering others in August 2020. A May 2019 bulletin from the FBI's Phoenix bureau not only assessed "conspiracy theory-driven domestic extremists" as a growing threat but singled out QAnon by name as cause for concern (J. Winter, 2019). The Combating Terrorism Center at West Point concluded that "QAnon represents a public security threat with the potential in the future to become a more impactful domestic terror threat. This is true especially given that conspiracy theories have a track record of propelling terrorist violence elsewhere in the West as well as QAnon's more recent influence on mainstream political discourse" (Amarasiggam & Argentino, 2020).

In mid-2020, Twitter barred high-traffic QAnon accounts and depressed QAnon-tied tweets in search results. By mid-September, those moves had reduced the number of QAnon-related tweets by half, according to a Twitter spokesperson (Collins, 2020). Meanwhile, QAnon adherents on Facebook responded to efforts to thwart its dissemination on that platform by "dropping explicit references to Q, and 'camouflaging' QAnon content under hashtags ostensibly about protecting children" (Collins and Zadrozny, 2020). In early October 2020, Facebook banned QAnon altogether from all of its platforms. The week before "the QAnon community ha[d] pushed the conspiracy theory that Trump [who had been hospitalized with COVID-19] is not sick with the coronavirus, but carrying out secret missions in a fictitious war that has been predicted by QAnon followers" (Collins and Zadrozny, 2020).

The government's forecasts that extremist groups would prove violent was prophetic. On January 6th, an appeal to insurrection by Donald J. Trump propelled a group of his supporters, among them QAnon adherents, to storm the United States Capitol to thwart the certification of the 2020 election for the Democratic ticket. Some who breached the perimeter of the building carried weapons. Others bore tie wraps presumably meant to restrain kidnapped lawmakers. By denying Trump's request that he refuse to certify the votes of key states that had gone to Biden, the vice president had elicited the ire of the incumbent and the enmity of the mob. In digital footage of the assault, the chant "Hang Pence" could be heard.

The violent assault on the building and the ensuing threat to elected representatives not only temporarily halted the certification process but also led to the deaths of five individuals, one of them an avowed QAnon supporter; it also elicited the second impeachment of the incumbent Republican days before the power of the presidency would transfer from his hands. In the wake of the insurrection provoked by Trump speech and online content. Facebook, Instagram, and Twitter suspended President Trump's accounts (BBC, 2021). Snapchat and Twitch also locked Trump's account until he left office, the latter saying that it did not want the account to be used "to incite further violence" (Klepper & O'Brien, 2021).

After the Russian interference in the 2016 presidential election in the United States, Facebook and other social media platforms came under increased scrutiny because of their reported inability or suspected reluctance to viral contents (Isaac & Wakabayashi, 2017). An estimated 126 million people were reached through Facebook alone in 2016 by Russian operations to interfere in the election (Isaac & Wakabayashi, 2017). Facebook and Twitter, but not Google, took steps to give the public more information about who buys and who views political advertising on their site (Solon and Siddiqui, 2017). These transparency initiatives were meant to bring the companies more in accordance with what is required of print and TV advertisers.

In 2020, civil rights groups, Democrats and Facebook's own employees called for the social media giant to hold Trump accountable for posts that critics said break Facebook's rules against inciting violence and spreading false information about voting (Bond, 2020). In September 2020, Facebook announced it would halt political advertising a week before the 2020 election, presumably because of its lack of ability to fact-check them (Bump, 2020). This measure, however, likely had limited impact because as Bump puts it, "The fundamental risk isn't that some nefarious actor is going to invest millions of dollars to persuade people to believe something false. The risk is that Facebook users themselves will seize upon false information and pass it around without restriction." The number of social media users for different platforms reached 4.14 billion in October 2020, with an annual growth of 12.3 percent a year and a user versus population penetration of 53 percent (DataReportal, 2020).

Controlling the content shared in social media by its users is much more difficult than keeping advertisers accountable. More recently, platforms are being developed to help people distinguish truthful from unreliable information. DisInfoNet was designed to help a wide spectrum of users understand the dynamics of disinformation dissemination in social networks (Guarino et al., 2019). DisInfoNet combines text-mining and classification with graph analysis and visualization to offer a comprehensive and user-friendly tool. If the use of these platforms becomes more widespread, fact-checking by users may become more common and guard the population from misinformation spread in social media.

Eroding the quality of information necessary for a well-functioning democracy, deception-inflected policy debates conveyed in stories and claims by political elites stretch the truth or fundamentally distort it (Coddington et al., 2014). In the 2000s, fact-checking in journalism has developed an evidence-based method for assessing political claims that may be exercising a growing influence on the news (Coddington et al., 2014). In turn, the rise of social media sites like Twitter has offered new possibilities for an instantaneous discussion of political claims. If well-harnessed, these capacities could be healthy for democracy and minimize the spread of conspiracy theories and misinformation.

Fact-checking has also been used in the health arena. Research shows that some exposure to fact-checking labels on misinformation can generate more positive attitudes toward vaccines in comparison to exposure to misinformation alone (Zhang, Featherstone, Calabrese, & Wojcieszak,

2020). Incorporating labels from trusted universities and health institutions on social media platforms is a promising direction for addressing the vaccine misinformation problem (Zhang et al., 2020). A different study built a classifier to detect fake news related to COVID-19 (Shahi & Nandini, 2020). Use of this classifier in 40 languages and 105 countries, which reflects widespread interest in curbing the misinformation epidemic.

As mentioned, after the January 6, 2021 storming of the Capitol by Trump supporters attempting to stop the Congressional certification of Joe Biden's victory in the presidential election, the incumbent president's Facebook and Twitter accounts were locked and later suspended. Both Facebook and Twitter had used fact-checks and warning labels increasingly throughout the year to flag inaccurate Trump posts about the novel coronavirus and the supposed rigging of votes in the presidential election (BBC, 2021). Although an extreme measure, flagging or suspending the account of a political figure who is spreading conspiracy theories and other forms of consequential misinformation about health science or the integrity of voting seems a reasonable step, especially during a pandemic or as votes are being certified in an election.

9.1.5   Inducing Trust in Trustworthy Sources

The finding that those who accept conspiracy theories are likely also to distrust the experts best equipped to debunk them makes it difficult to rely on such sources to persuade conspiracy believers. Bolstering trust in such source could correlatively reduce the susceptibility of the public. In other words, trusting science (Crease, 2004; Oreskes, 2019) and trustworthy media sources (Kohring, 2019; Schranz, Schneider, & Eisenegger, 2018) minimizes susceptibility to conspiracy beliefs. In our context, trust in science can prevent conspiracy theories from taking hold by making people more selective with respect of sources of information. It can also increase reliance on conventional scientific epistemologies to interpret reality. And of course, trust in science strengthens public support for this way of knowing, which in turn increases public funding of science, scientific discoveries, and societal wellbeing (Muñoz, Moreno, & Luján, 2012; National Science Foundation, 2016).

Unfortunately, however, as O'Brien, Palmer, and Albarracin (2021) showed, trust in science can be hijacked by conspiracy sources claiming to have scientific credentials or invoking pseudoscientific information (Hoffman et al., 2019). It can also be displaced from science to questionable claims made by politicians. One example is the continued reliance on

Wakefield's retracted study as a basis for claims of a link between the MMR vaccine and autism in children. The Wakefield incident is not an isolated one. Relying on hearsay and small, problem-ridden studies, Donald J. Trump advocated the use of the anti-malarial drug hydroxychloroquine to treat COVID-19, both before and after well-powered clinical trials confirmed that the risks of doing so outweighed the benefits (Dejong & Wachter, 2020).

9.1.6 Prebunking

Inducing resistance through use of inoculation has become popular as a way to curb misinformation (Banas & Richards, 2017; Jarche, 2020; Roozenbeek, van der Linden, & Nygren, 2020). Theorized by McGuire and Papageorgis (1961) as a means of reducing the likelihood of counter-persuasion, inoculation tries to induce resistance to attacks on beliefs that are deeply held but weakly supported (i.e., "truisms;" e.g., brushing one's teeth frequently is beneficial) by exposing the audience to the problematic content and presenting or having the audience generate a brief defense of it ahead of time. In their research, participants received a message attacking a truism after having defended the truism from a mild attack (a message) or after having received no such attack. They found that those exposed to the attack after being immunized by the exposure, defense, and rebuttal of earlier, milder version of it showed more resistance than those not previously inoculated.

The idea of "prebunking," which builds on McGuire and Papageorgis's (1961) concept of inoculation, is a promising tool for preventing the spread of conspiracy beliefs (Jarche, 2020; Lewandowsky & Cook, 2020). "Prebunking" has been used as an umbrella term to denote a treatment to confer resistance by warning, inoculating, or training an audience ahead of time. Banas and Miller (2013) investigated various techniques for doing so when dealing with conspiracy theories. Their focus was the 9/11 conspiracy theory, which claims that the United States was complicit in the attacks to the World Trade Center towers. They employed three treatments aimed at preventing persuasion as a result of exposure to a conspiracy-ridden film titled "Loose Change: Final Cut" that purports

> to prove the official story of 9/11 – "that the impact of two planes flying into two World Trade Center towers and the resulting fires caused three World Trade Center steel framed buildings to collapse" is false ... [and expose] the inconsistencies and lies put forward by the Bush administration

in the hours, days and weeks after 9/11, and their role in hoaxing the American people that 19 Islamic terrorists were the sole perpetrators of 9/11, the crime of the century ("Loose Change: Final Cut," n.d.).

One of the prebunking treatments focused on dispelling actual errors in the movie. Another concentrated on demonstrating that the 9/11 Truth conspiracy theory was not logically sound. The factual treatment concluded that:

> In the end, we were able to debunk each of these assertions with hard evidence and a healthy dose of common sense. We learned that a few theories are based on something as innocent as a reporting error on that chaotic day. Others are the byproducts of cynical imaginations that aim to inject suspicion and animosity into public debate. Only by confronting such poisonous claims with irrefutable facts can we understand what really happened on a day that is forever seared into world history (p. 202)

The logic-based inoculation ended by saying:

> Conspiracy theories may make for amusing entertainment, but they aren't logical, and you could look very foolish for believing in them. However, by employing Occam's razor, examining the methodology, and evaluating the whistleblowers, you can insure that logic will protect you from the psychological appeal of conspiracy theories. (p. 204)

A third meta-inoculative treatment attempted to insulate the 9/11 conspiracy theory from being falsified by warning participants that they may be manipulated by people who deny conspiracy theories:

> There are people out there who don't want you to be open to new ideas; they want you thinking their way about things. So, they warn against "dangerous ideas," and how easy it is with the Internet and editing to mess with your mind. They say "someone is going to try change your belief about X topic." They let you know a threatening message is likely coming your way, and they offer one or two reasons you shouldn't believe a word of it. So, you put your guard up, ready to dismiss any type of new idea or message that comes along. Sometimes that's a good thing; but, have you ever thought that you could be manipulated this way? (p. 204)

The results from this important study indicated that both the logic-based and factual inoculations reduced the persuasive impact of the conspiracy theory film, and of the two, the factual one was more effective. The inoculation reduced the likelihood that participants would be subsequently persuaded by the conspiracy film. Furthermore, the meta-inoculation thwarted the effect of the inoculation, although the inoculation continued to have some effect.

It is noteworthy that other "prebunking" manipulations have included more complex forms of resistance training (Roozenbeek et al., 2020). For example, Roozenbeek et al.'s (2020) study used a game ("Bad News") in which players adopt the role of somebody who wants to deceive others online. The study, which included misinformation involving conspiracy, found a small effect ($d = 0.17$) on a measure of reliability of information of the prebunking game in three countries.

9.1.7 Correcting Conspiracy Beliefs

The capacities and limitations of corrective information have been extensively studied. Although misbeliefs are remarkably tenacious, detailed corrections are more effective than less detailed ones, and making an audience question information through their own means has corrective power as well (Chan et al., 2017). When correcting misinformation, one should provide a clear explanation of why the prior information is false and offer a detailed explanation of what was wrong and what is known (Chan et al., 2017; Lewandowsky et al., 2020).

Some of the difficulties in correcting conspiracy beliefs, however, are related to the unfalsifiable nature of the propositions, which seal the theories off from disconfirming information. Whereas other beliefs may be corrected by presenting detailed, accurate information, displacing conspiracy beliefs may require immersion in corrective alternatives and reintegration of conspiracy believers into new media ecosystems and new social networks, akin to controversial forms of "deprogramming" for cult victims or "social reintegration" for terrorists (Introvigne, 1995; Richardson, 2011; Ungerleider & Wellisch, 1979; Webber et al., 2018).

Various methods of correcting conspiracy beliefs were tested by Orosz et al. (2016). These authors first exposed participants to a message about a conspiracy theory and then attempted three debunking approaches: (a) rationally counter arguing by pointing out the logical flaws of the message and correcting it in depth; (b) ridiculing the theory, which entailed deriding the logical inconsistencies and "ridiculous" aspects of the theory; and (c) empathizing with the group demonized by the theory, while calling attention to the dangers of engaging in scapegoating groups that are frequently persecuted. Compared to a control condition, the rational and the ridiculing condition weakened conspiracy beliefs ($ds = -0.27$ and $d = -0.20$), whereas the empathetic condition had no effect (Cohen's $d = 0.10$). These results suggest that well designed rational arguments and ridiculing can counter established conspiracy beliefs.

In addition, however, correcting fear- inducing content deserves attention and has been relatively neglected in the literature. For example, in the literature on correction, Ecker et al. (2011) conducted experiments presenting statements about a plane crash that was explained in either more or less threatening ways. In this research, a "high emotionality" explanation attributed the crash to a terrorist attack, whereas a "low emotionality" ascribed it to bad weather. Contrary to the possibility that more and less emotional information would differ in ease of correction, beliefs in these two messages did not differ following corrections ($Fs < 2.97$ in Experiment 1 and $Fs < 1$ in Experiment 2). The null findings in Ecker et al.'s research, however, may be the product of methodological decisions. For example, all information about a plane crash is negative by definition. Consistent with this possibility, participants reported above-midpoint negative affect even in the low-emotionality condition (e.g., $M = 6.40$, $SE = 0.40$ cm vs. a scale midpoint of 5.00 on a 0 to 10 cm visual analog scale in Experiment 2).

Despite these prior null findings, negative topics attract attention and elicit cognitive elaboration (Anderson, 1965; Baumeister, Bratslavsky, Finkenauer, & Vohs, 2001; Gilbert, Fridlund, & Sabini, 1987; Kramer, Guillory, & Hancock, 2014; Ohira, Winton, & Oyama, 1998; Peeters & Czapinski, 1990; Porter et al., 2010; Pratto & John, 1991; Rozin & Royzman, 2001; Skowronski & Carlston, 1989; Taylor, 1991). Thus, corrections may be scrutinized more when the information has negative emotional implications (Bless et al. 1990; Bohner, Crow, Erb, & Schwarz, 1992; Bower, 1981; Forgas, 2007, 2008; Mackie & Worth, 1989; Mitchell, 2000; Worth & Mackie, 1987). Greater scrutiny of corrections could in turn make them more or less efficacious than they would be if the corrected information were emotionally neutral. Strong corrections may be more convincing, and weak ones less so (see e.g., Bless et al., 1990).

Countering anxiety-inducing conspiracy beliefs may be more successful if one uses unconventional correction techniques inspired by anxiety research. For example, distracting individuals from thinking about negative topics or training audiences in emotion reappraisal may decrease anxiety (Moyal, Henik, & Anholt, 2014). Such techniques may in turn allow people to process corrections in a less anxious state.

9.1.8 Deciding When to Counter Conspiracy Beliefs

Because corrections are effortful and not always successful, whether and when these beliefs should be corrected are not straightforward questions (for another analysis of this issues, see Uscinski et al., 2020). We offer the following criteria for making these decisions on the basis of a determination of risk.

Criterion of clear risk to self or others. Conspiracy beliefs are in many ways cultural ones that, like systems of knowledge, religions, and cultural norms, deserve as much respect as other cultural creations. However, some of them should be addressed because they pose risk to the people who endorse them and/or to others. For example, the belief that vaccines are dangerous but the dangers have been covered up presents risk to individuals and societies, and therefore should be corrected. In contrast, the belief that the side effects of genetically modified organisms (GMOs) have been covered up poses little risk, other than increasing cost of purchasing foods that are certified to be GMO-free.

Criterion of actionability. In addition to the criterion of risk, when two potentially risky but equally prevalent beliefs are circulating, the one with more direct behavioral implications should be corrected first. For example, a belief that American elections are fraudulent is less actionable than a Facebook claim that, because the deep state will inevitably steal elections, would-be voters should forego voting. In short, given two risky conspiracy beliefs, those that are more actionable should be prioritized for correction.

Criterion of salience. Beliefs that are present in more than 10 percent of a population are typically deemed salient and as a result may be worth correcting. Thus, the prevalence of a belief is an important consideration as well. Higher incidence of the belief in a population can be defined as the increase in the popularity of a belief during a specified time period. Risky conspiracy beliefs with higher incidence should be prioritized by debunkers.

Criterion of dominance within a belief system. Attempts at countering conspiracy theories are often ineffective and occasionally backfire (Carey et al., 2020; Nyhan & Zeitzoff, 2018; Rao et al., 2014). Therefore, whether the risky behaviors produced by conspiracy beliefs have other belief bases should be another important consideration. For example, although people who believe in a deep state may be less likely to vote, a campaign that supports voting based on other beliefs associated with voting (e.g., others will be proud that I did; voting is easy; I will have an influence of local policy; I will post my "I voted" sticker on my office at work; etc.) may be a better investment than a campaign that counters the deep state conspiracy belief.

9.2   A Research Agenda for the Future

9.2.1   *The Path to Behavior*

There are important questions about the processes by which conspiracy beliefs guide behavior that are outside the scope of this book. In general terms, beliefs affect behavior only to the extent that they have evaluative implications for the behavior being considered. For example, believing that vaccines protect individuals from infection does not influence vaccination behavior for people who evaluate protection from infection as evaluatively neutral (Ajzen et al., 2018; Albarracin, Fishbein, & Middlestadt, 1998; Albarracín et al., 2001). However, positive attitudes toward vaccination and ultimately vaccination itself should result when the belief that vaccines prevent infections is combined with the evaluation that preventing infections is desirable.

In many cases, conspiracy theories and corresponding beliefs should be evaluatively neutral. For example, although fourteenth-century Europeans feared falling off the earth when navigating the Atlantic Ocean, the belief that the earth is flat has neither positive nor negative implications for most of us. By contrast, a conspiracy belief about the MMR vaccine may decrease vaccination through corresponding effects on attitudes toward or norms about vaccination (Ajzen et al., 2018; D. Albarracin et al., 1998; Albarracín et al., 2001).

In addition, many political conspiracy beliefs are relatively inconsequential for behavior not because of their neutral evaluation but because regular citizens have little power to change the political system. The notion that a deep state is sabotaging Donald J. Trump's presidency may be met with strong disapproval by his supporters but may have no behavioral implications during non-election years. During election years, however, these beliefs could either increase or decrease voter turn-out depending on whether people believe voting to be an adequate response against the conspiracy (for the role of response efficacy, (Floyd, Prentice-Dunn, & Rogers, 2000; Gerstlé & Nai, 2019; Maddux & Rogers, 1983; Tannenbaum et al., 2015). They can also lead a mob to storm the Capitol.

9.2.2   *Reduction or Increase in Anxiety as a Result of Conspiracy Beliefs*

The past scholarship on conspiracy theories assumes that the formation of conspiracy beliefs reduces anxiety in people who were anxious to begin with (see Chapter 4). Although our work tested this possibility in passing (see longitudinal analyses in Chapter 4), conspiracy beliefs are likely maintained because of this function. However, conspiracy thoughts are themselves anxiety-provoking, and have led people such as Welch to conduct criminal acts. Although such instances suggest that the conspiracy beliefs are not always effective at reducing anxiety, past research has not uncovered the mechanisms that separate their soothing from the energizing effects. More generally, what makes some people simply coexist with versus fight the conspiracies they believe surround them should be a focus of future research.

9.2.3 General versus Specific Anxiety

One of the theses of this book is that conspiracy beliefs are fueled by general anxiety (see Chapter 4). However, it is easy to imagine how highly specific anxieties might come into play. In the case of Pizzagate, the anxieties could have been consistent with the more mainstream conservative beliefs. For example, the conservatives in "Focus on the Family" are dedicated to "defending the God-ordained institution of the family and promoting biblical truths worldwide" ("Focus on the Family Website," n.d.). For them, "Marriage is intended by God to be a thriving, lifelong relationship between a man and a woman," not a same-sex couple. Conservative rhetoric is rich with language alleging that liberals support murder (i.e., abortion), destruction of the traditional family (i.e., support for same-sex marriage and adoption), and child endangerment (e.g., opposition of the human papillomavirus [HPV] vaccine and same-sex restrooms).

The Pizzagate theory also reinforced the ideological assumptions and electoral interests of the right-wing 4chan users and Trump supporters who originated the theory. At the same time, the theory counterbalanced charges that Republican Party presidential nominee Donald J. Trump had engaged in sexually predatory behavior. Those allegations gained credibility from his admission in the so-called Hollywood Access tape that he had kissed and groped women without their consent. Julian Assange released the first tranche of Podesta emails on October 7, 2016, within an hour of the emergence of the *Washington's Post*'s story about and posting of that hot mic conversation of Trump's (Jamieson, 2018).

The theory was responsive as well to the fears that conservatives share about the potential abuses of concentrated governmental power, and more recently, the broader deep state theory. In Pizzagate, these concerns included "fears over the trustworthiness of big government, big media, and elites that represent excessive authority and seem to threaten demo-cratic values" (Debbies-Carl, 2017). The scholarly literature has produced important evidence that a discernible part of the conservative population resents educated elites and feels threatened by cultural changes associated with the power and size of communities of color (Mutz, 2018; Sides, Tesler, & Vavreck, n.d.) and legally enforced acceptance of cultural, racial, sexual, and religious diversity (Cavalcante, 2015).

Comet Ping Pong was an all but tailor-made trigger for these bundles of anxieties. Characterized by *Slate* as both a family-friendly venue and a cultural haven for gays, punks, and alt art (Cauterucci & Fischer, 2016), Comet Ping Pong was, as (Debbies-Carl, 2017) put it, "a tangible emblem of inclusivity, tolerance, and other progressive values that are threatening to the conspiracy-prone alt-Right" (Debbies-Carl, 2017). The bands it features and even some of the food on its menu betray its liberal sensibil-ities. Its customers can feast on "honey-chili smoked squash rings" and "lamb sausage" (Cauterucci & Fischer, 2016) while enjoying the sounds of "Acid Mothers Temple & The Melting Paraiso U.F.O., ST 37" and "Des Demonas, Enablers, Kid Claws" ("Comet Ping Pong Event," n.d.).

For the people who believed the Pizzagate theory, Comet Ping Pong, its owner, and its activities also were anxiety-inducing because of their ties to Democratic elites and the gay community. Not only did Comet Ping Pong host fundraisers for Democrats, including both Obama and Hillary Clinton, but the restaurant owner James Alefantis dated David Brock (Winter, 2012) of the liberal watchdog group Media Matters for America that monitors conservative media for error and hypocrisy. Regarded by those on the right as a turncoat, Brock broke onto the national scene in the 1990s with salacious and questionably sourced allegations about both Bill and Hillary Clinton. Later, he disavowed that work and confessed that he had lied to discredit a key allegation of Anita Hill against Supreme Court nominee Thomas – that he was a consumer of pornography (Kuczynski & Glaberson, 2001). The year after chron-icling his conversation in his 2003 *Blinded by the right* book (Brock, 2003), Brock founded Media Matters. In the run-up to the 2016 presi-dential campaign, he headed up "Correct the Record," which was described by the *New York Times* as "a rapid-response squad dedicated to fending off attacks on Mrs. Clinton," and also served on the board of Priorities USA, the major super PAC supporting her presidential bid (Confessore, 2014).

Homophobia was a probable source of anxiety for the Pizzagate believer group as well, and could explain the focus of the conspiracy on pedophilia.

As the Southern Poverty Law Center notes, "Depicting gay men as a threat to children may be the single most potent weapon for stoking public fears about homosexuality" (Schlatter & Steinback, 2011). As social media activity shows, these fears resonated with conspiracy theorists. Accordingly, the Pizzagate proponents made much of a photo posted by Alefantis showing three adult males, two bare chested and the third wearing a black T-shirt reading "I (heart) L'Enfant." From the message on the T-shirt, they deduced that the owner of Comet Ping Pong, who was presumed to be the T-shirted individual, was not only promoting but also confessing to pedophilia. In fact, Alefantis was not in the photo. Instead, as the *Washington Post* confirmed, the man in the black T-shirt "was a co-owner of a different restaurant in Washington." Nor was the "I (heart)" wording a reference to loving an infant. Rather, the shirt was touting its wearer's restaurant, "L'Enfant Cafe-Bar," an establishment named in honor of "Pierre Charles L'Enfant, an American colonist from France who served under George Washington during the Revolutionary War" (Aisch et al., 2016).

Child trafficking is a made-to-order theme to elicit anxiety in an audience. Allegations that those involved in Pizzagate sexually abuse children presents the supposedly complicit Democratic elites and their Hollywood and media allies as evil. By capitalizing on the reality that some children actually are the victims of sex traffickers, and alleging that John Podesta and his brother kidnapped three-year-old Madeleine McCann, who was abducted in Portugal in May, 2007, the Pizzagate proponents melded real events and imagined ones into a coherent account of Democratic depravity. In the process, they fueled anxiety and outrage. We hear this in texts Edgar Maddison Welch sent to a friend before the incident (Yuhas, 2017):

> "Raiding a pedo ring, possibly sacraficing [sic] the lives of a few for the lives of many,"

> "Standing up against a corrupt system that kidnaps, tortures and rapes babies and children in our own back yard."

> "I'm sorry bro, but I'm tired of turning the channel and hoping someone does something and being thankful it's not my family. One day it will be our families. The world is too afraid to act and I'm too stubborn not to." (Yuhas, 2017)

That communication itself also provides evidence that belief in the conspiracy bonded Welch to at least one other person. More generally, he was connected to many other followers of Alex Jones and an active group of 4channers.

If general anxiety strengthens beliefs in conspiracy theories, it is easy to imagine how specific anxieties could have similar or even stronger effects. First, specific anxieties that arise in the context of a conspiracy theory may increase interest and attention to the theory. In addition, specific anxieties may be less likely to be discounted as irrelevant than more general uncertainty. However, no prior work, including the research presented in this book, has examined these possibilities.

9.2.4   Evolution of Conspiracy Theories

Conspiracy theories are updated with new events and storylines, and, in the process, may acquire new champions. In Chapter 2, we analyzed the case of Pizzagate, a theory that later evolved into QAnon and is immersed in the broader deep state theory. After Clinton's loss of the 2016 presidential election, interest in Pizzagate died down, only to resurface, first with a focus on the celebrity elites who were supposedly part of the plot, and later in a Q-driven narrative in which President Donald J. Trump is a secret crusader against the Democratic pedophiles (e.g., Hillary Clinton, and more recently Joe Biden; see McCarthy, 2020).

QAnon's progeniture, the pseudonymous Q, "who claimed to be a government insider with Q security clearance, the highest level in the Department of Energy" (Andrews, 2020), first emerged on 4chan in October 2017 but now inhabits 8kun formerly known as "8chan" (Harwell & Timberg, 2020). In the first 2017 post, "The Calm Before the Storm," Q revealed that Trump was fighting a deep state of Hollywood and Democratic pedophiles. Some speculate that those posting in the name of Q are in a "military intelligence team in the Trump administration (itself part of a global positive 'Alliance') ... opening up a back-channel with the public, bypassing the compromised mass media, to reach the 'anons' and 'autists' who populate 8chan" (Maresca, 2020). Others think Q may actually be Trump (Barkun, 2018), a Trump administration operative, (Zuckerman, 2019) or the late JFK Jr., who supposedly has been in hiding since surviving an assassination attempt by deep state operatives in 1999.

A number of factors drove the increase in Pizzagate web activity in 2020, including a film by a presumed Hollywood insider and seeming confirmation that one-time teen pop idol Justin Bieber was the victim of sex trafficking. Where Pizzagate presented a perpetrator, the 2020 information offered a plausible victim. In April 2020, a 77-minute documentary titled "Out of the Shadows" appeared on YouTube. Presented as the revelations of Hollywood insider and stuntman Mike Smith, the film's self-described purpose is to "wake up the general public by shedding light on how we all have been lied to and brainwashed by a hidden enemy with a sinister agenda." "Some of the ideas and theories touched on throughout the film are at times hard to hear," it warns, among them "the cannibalism-themed Hollywood dinners, trafficking of children in Hollywood, and child abuse as entertainment during Hollywood events" ("Out of Shadows," n.d.-a).

To the Pizzagate narrative, which focused on Washington, Hollywood, and media elites trafficking and abusing children, "Out of the Shadows" added details of Svengalian subversion of traditional values by Hollywood-based "Satanic pedophilia rings that distribute propaganda through films like Zoolander, the music videos of Katy Perry and Lady Gaga, and a discreet set of symbols, including the words 'television' (tell-a-vision), 'channel' (psychic communication), and 'Hollywood' (named, they say, for the holly plant—which is poisonous and was once used in Druid rituals)" ("Out of Shadows," n.d.-b). By the end of June 2020, "Out of the Shadows" had registered 15 million YouTube views, and, by early August, 20 million (Hitt, 2020). An attorney for Smith estimated in early August that across various websites, the film had been watched "roughly 100 million times" (Kang & Frenkel, 2020).

As "Out of the Shadows" was coming to light, in May 2020, the child sex abuse theory was expanded to identify former teen heartthrob Justin Bieber as a victim, a status inferred from a sign taken as a coded confession. As the *New York Times* reported (Hitt, 2020):

> [T]he pop star's innocuous gesture set off a flurry of online activity, which highlighted the resurgence of one of social media's early conspiracy theories . . . Fans then left thousands of comments on Mr. Bieber's social media posts asking him if he was safe. Within days, searches for "Justin and Pizzagate" soared on Google, and the hashtag #savebieber started trending.

Pizzagate's new list of global elites who served as villains or victims in the theory have recently expanded to include "Mr. Bieber, Bill Gates, Ellen DeGeneres, Oprah Winfrey and Chrissy Teigen" (Kang & Frenkel, 2020). Among those whose lives became fodder for the theory proponents was singer Celine Dion, whose weight loss was attributed by them to her "addiction to Adrenochrome, a real chemical compound that Pizzagate proponents claim is 'harvested' from tortured children, and taken by the political and Hollywood elite to get high" (Kang & Frenkel, 2020).

But what is the pattern of growth of these theories? We think this is an important question for future research. The process of theory development resembles the construction of anonymous literature in the Middle Ages, when communities contributed to the stories without a need to identify specific authors. In this case, the social media have provided a vehicle for collaboration of people who previously had no voice. However, the principles that explain this construction are understudied and constitute an important area for scholars to investigate in the future.

9.3   Final Note

The global COVID-19 pandemic has adjoined ten well-catalogued conspiracy theories (Lynas, 2020) to an already sizable set of false beliefs about all domains of life. Most of them are trivial, a large number are fantastic, a few have immediate real-world consequences, and most contribute to a cynical view of the world. At their root are anxiety and social influences woven within a larger system of psychological and political factors that have interested scholars for decades. At a fraught time in which large-scale uncertainty about the COVID-19 pandemic is fueling conspiracy beliefs, our book contributes an explanatory model that integrates psychological and political factors that can be dispositional or situational. Psychological and sociopolitical factors that activate the belief defense, belief accuracy, or social integration motivation can make people anxious and guide them toward the conservative media. In turn, this anxiety and exposure to conservative media cause the endorsement of conspiracy beliefs. We hope that a better understanding of these dynamics will prove useful in minimizing the spread of conspiracy beliefs such as those that prompted Edgar Welch to charge into Comet Ping Pong with a loaded weapon, Anthony Quinn Warner to blow up a part of downtown Nashville, and Ashli Babbitt to storm the Capitol to thwart the election of a person she believed was implicated in a pedophilia ring run by the deep state.

Methodology of Our Studies and Samples

Our research involved an instrument development phase, followed by the studies reported in this book. The developmental studies served to refine our selection of theories to study and the survey items to measure those theories and all of our variables. For example, one of the tested theories was that Hillary Clinton ran a pizza-parlor child-sex ring in Washington, DC. However, this theory was later replaced by its broader relative, the "deep state" theory. Both the pilot and later surveys retained the theories about Obama falsifying his birth certificate and undocumented immigrants deciding the popular vote in the 2016 presidential election. The final selection of items was based on the psychometric properties of the scales we constructed and the available space in the surveys.

Understanding conspiracy beliefs requires a broad approach that goes beyond a particular belief. Across four surveys, we measured five conspiracy beliefs that cut across domains, are more or less recent, and belong to either the political or health domain. The control beliefs served the purpose of disentangling part of the psychological and sociopolitical dynamic of conspiracy beliefs that is specific to "conspiracy theories" or applicable to the phenomenon of belief, or political belief, more generally. The methodology in our studies and the details about modeling are described in the coming sections. The complete details about modeling appear in the code in the Online Supplement.

A.1 Overview of Studies

Cross-Sectional Studies 1–3. Three cross-sectional surveys reported in this book were fielded in 2019. The platforms, type of sampling method, data collections, beliefs, and sample sizes appear in Table A.1, which includes the N and the estimated power to detect a small effect size

Table A.1. *Methodological characteristics of cross-sectional studies*
(Studies 1–3)

	Study 1	Study 2	Study 3
Platform	M-Turk	Dynata	Dynata
Type of sampling	Convenience	Nationally representative	Nationally representative
Form of data collection	Online	Online	Online
Theories	Conspiracy beliefs: Birther; undocumented immigrant vote; HIV virus cover-up; MMR vaccine cover-up Control Beliefs: Obama's inaction and crisis in Syria; undocumented immigrants use false documents to work; Tuskegee study; tobacco effects cover-up	Conspiracy beliefs: Birther; undocumented immigrant vote; HIV virus cover-up; MMR vaccine cover-up Control Beliefs: Obama's inaction and crisis in Syria; undocumented immigrants use false documents to work; Tuskegee study; tobacco effects cover-up cover-up	Conspiracy beliefs: Birther; undocumented immigrant vote; HIV virus cover-up; MMR vaccine cover-up Control Beliefs: Obama's inaction and crisis in Syria; undocumented immigrants use false documents to work; Tuskegee study; tobacco effects cover-up
Total number of respondents	765	1,054	1,014
Estimated power (based on $r = 0.1$ and alpha error = 0.05)	0.79	0.90	0.89

Note: r: Pearson correlation.

$(r = .10$ and alpha $= .05)$. The cross-sectional surveys measured conspiracy beliefs; factors associated with the belief defense, belief accuracy, and social integration motivation; anxiety; norms and discussions with other people; as well as exposure to conservative, mainstream, and liberal media.

Longitudinal Panel. We also ran a phone panel survey with a probability sample of adults living in the United States. The information about

Table A.2. *Longitudinal panel (online/phone hybrid; Study 4)*

	Theory	Date	N
Wave 1	Deep state	11/11/2019	1,000
Wave 2	Deep state	12/27/2019	969
Wave 3	Deep state	2/09/2020	849

this survey appears in Table A.2, which also includes the N and the estimated power to detect a small effect size ($r = .10$ and alpha $= .05$). It concerned primarily the belief that the "deep state," ostensibly a group of unelected government officials and intelligence officers, was conspiring against Donald J. Trump. The first wave was fielded in November 2019, the second in December 2019, and the third in February 2020. This survey measured the belief in the deep state, as well as anxiety, norms, and exposure to conservative, mainstream, and liberal media.

Experiment. We also conducted an experiment with 632 participants from Dynata. This experiment included a manipulation of fear experienced in another context by having participants recollect such an episode or not. We then measured the belief in the possibility that 5G technology was responsible for the COVID-19 pandemic, a belief salient in July 2020, when the experiment was conducted. In addition, we manipulated attention to the feelings of anxiety by asking participants to report their feelings either before or after they were asked whether they believed that 5G technology was responsible for the COVID-19 pandemic on a scale from 1 (definitely false) to 5 (definitely true). The design was a 2 (fear induction: Present versus absent) × 2 (fear questions order: Before versus after the belief measure). The same size was estimated to be adequate for an effect size $f = 2.62$, power $= 95\%$, and alpha $= .05$.

Social Media Study. To study the dissemination of posts about conspiracy theories via retweets, we also collected tweets. We crawled Twitter's Full Archive API with hashtags and keywords to identify tweets originating in the United States and written in English. Tweets were then grouped into two datasets (i.e., one for conspiracy theories and the other with accurate claims) based on their hashtags and keywords. For example, 2016–2017 tweets about Obama allegedly falsisying his birth certificate were obtained using #fakebirthcertificate, obamafakebirthcertificate, #obamafakebirthcertificate, fakeobama, and #fakeobama. Just as with the surveys, in addition to analyzing tweets supporting conspiracy beliefs, we analyzed those supporting accurate beliefs. This time, however, the tweets advocating the truth involved posts opposing the conspiracy beliefs, such as those with the hashtag "#birther."

We extracted four "root-level" attributes, including id, user, text or full_text, and retweet_count, to reconstruct tweet records. Next, we filtered out retweets (i.e., direct reposting of other Twitter users' tweets) by checking "RT @" the content in the text or full_text attribute. We were interested in determining the degree to which different media account handles, separated by ideology, participated in the online dissemination of messages about the conspiracy theories. Specifically, we used three lists of conservative, liberal, and mainstream media account handles to derive two sets of variables: (a) whether the account handle of the author is a conservative media, liberal media, mainstream media, or another account and (b) how many conservative, liberal, and mainstream media account handles were mentioned in the tweet. These variables, along with the fear sentiments of the tweets, were then included as independent variables in regressions to explain the number of retweets. Fear sentiments were used to gauge the source of anxiety-inducing contents in the dissemination of the tweets.

A.2   Cross-Sectional Survey Measures, Validity, and Sample Descriptions

A.2.1   Beliefs, Perceived Plausibility, and Perceived Unfalsifiability Measures

Table A.3 presents the theories measured in the cross-sectional surveys, including the conspiracy theories and the accurate statements used as controls. Table A.4 presents a summary of the belief, perceived plausibility, and perceived unfalsifiability measures included in each study.

Beliefs. In Studies 1–3, participants were first asked to report their belief in the theories in Table A.4. The theories were randomly presented. Participants rated statements such as "Obama was not born in the United States and faked his birth certificate to become president" on a scale with the following options: "Definitely True," "Probably True," "Neither True nor False," "Probably False," and "Definitely False." These were scored 1 ("Definitely False") to 5 ("Definitely True").

Perceived plausibility measures. Studies 1–3 included measures of perceived plausibility and unfalsifiability. In Studies 1 and 2, we measured the perceived plausibility of each theory in Table A.3. In Study 3, we included these measures for half of the theories addressed in the survey, namely undocumented immigrants deciding the popular vote and the

Table A.3. *Conspiracy and control beliefs measured in our survey research (Studies 1–4)*

Theory Designation	Conspiracy beliefs	Accurate control beliefs
Obama's birth certificate ("Birther")	Barack Obama was not born in the US; he faked his birth certificate to become president (Politico, 2011).	Obama's inaction facilitated the humanitarian crisis in Syria.
Undocumented immigrants voted in the 2016 election	Undocumented immigrants voting illegally prevented Republicans from winning the popular vote in 2016 (Business Insider, 2018).	Undocumented immigrants often obtain fake social security numbers in order to work in the United States.
HIV as a CIA creation	The United States government created the HIV epidemic by experimentally injecting the virus in people of African descent (Heller, 2015).	The United States government studied the natural course of syphilis by leaving African Americans untreated.
MMR vaccine cover-up	The MMR vaccine causes autism, but this has been covered up by the United States government (Eggertson, 2010).	The tobacco industry covered up the damaging effects of smoking.
Deep state	A "deep state" is a secret group of unelected government and intelligence officials who seek to illegally undermine the presidency of Donald Trump (Deep State, 2020).	NA

MMR vaccine cover-up. Perceived plausibility was measured with the following three items:

1. "Independently of your beliefs as to whether this occurred, please consider the situation described in this statement and answer the questions below: Obama was not born in the United States and faked his birth certificate to become president. – People like me believe it is common for some people to fake documents to achieve power."
2. "Independently of your beliefs as to whether this occurred, please consider the situation described in this statement and answer the questions below: Obama was not born in the United States and faked his birth certificate to become president. – I can imagine why somebody may want to fake documents to achieve power."

Table A.4. *Propositions in the measures of belief, perceived plausibility, and perceived unfalsifiability (Studies 1–4)*

Theory #	Conspiracy beliefs	Control beliefs	Study 1			Study 2			Study 3			Study 4		
			B	P	U	B	P	U	B	P	U	B	P	U
1	Barack Obama was not born in the US; he faked his birth certificate to become president (Politico, 2011).	Obama's inaction facilitated the humanitarian crisis in Syria.	Y	Y	Y	Y	Y	Y	Y	N	N	N	N	N
2	Undocumented immigrants voting illegally prevented Republicans from winning the popular vote in 2016 (Business Insider, 2018).	Undocumented immigrants often obtain fake social security numbers in order to work in the United States.	Y	Y	Y	Y	Y	Y	Y	Y	Y	N	N	N
3	The United States government created the HIV epidemic by experimentally injecting the virus in people of African descent (Heller, 2015).	The United States government studied the natural course of syphilis by leaving African Americans untreated.	Y	Y	Y	Y	Y	Y	Y	N	N	N	N	N
4	The MMR vaccine causes autism, but this has been covered up by the United States government (Eggertson, 2010).	The tobacco industry covered up the damaging effects of smoking.	Y	Y	Y	Y	Y	Y	Y	Y	Y	N	N	N
5	A "deep state" is a secret group of unelected government and intelligence officials who seek to illegally undermine the presidency of Donald Trump (Deep State, 2020).	NA	N	N	N	Y	N	N						

Note: B: Belief measures. P: Perceived plausibility measures. U: Perceived unfalsifiability measures. Y: Included in the survey. N: Not included in the survey.

3. "Independently of your beliefs as to whether this occurred, please consider the situation described in this statement and answer the questions below: Obama was not born in the United States and faked his birth certificate to become president. – History has provided many examples of people faking documents to achieve power."

Participants provided their responses using the following scale points: "Clearly describes my feelings," "Mostly describes my feelings," "Moderately describes my feelings," "Slightly describes my feelings," and "Does not describe my feelings." These points were scored 1 ("Does not describe my feelings") to 5 ("Clearly describes my feelings").

Unfalsifiability measures. Whenever we measured the subjective plausibility of a theory, we also measured its subjective unfalsifiability. Studies 1–3 included the following items, except that the first one was omitted in Study 3.

1. "Independently of your beliefs as to whether this occurred, please consider the situation described in this statement and answer the questions below: Obama was not born in the United States and faked his birth certificate to become president. – Some types of evidence (data, documents) can demonstrate if Obama was born in the United States or not."
2. "Independently of your beliefs as to whether this occurred, please consider the situation described in this statement and answer the questions below: Obama was not born in the United States and faked his birth certificate to become president. – No evidence can conclusively demonstrate if Obama was born in the United States or not."
3. "Independently of your beliefs as to whether this occurred, please consider the situation described in this statement and answer the questions below: Obama was not born in the United States and faked his birth certificate to become president. – There are no reliable sources to determine if Obama was born in the United States or not.

Participants provided their responses using the following scale points: "Clearly describes my feelings," "Mostly describes my feelings," "Moderately describes my feelings," "Slightly describes my feelings," and "Does not describe my feelings." These points were scored 1 ("Does not describe my feelings") to 5 ("Clearly describes my feelings").

A.2.2 Anxiety

All surveys included measures of anxiety at the time (Thyer & Westhuis, 1989). In addition, Studies 1 and 2 included anxiety specific to political

Table A.5. *Measures of norms and discussions with others: Studies 3–4*

Measures	Scales	Study 3	Study 4
Norms	People who are close to me believe that this is: Undocumented immigrants voting illegally prevented Republicans from winning the popular vote during the 2016 presidential elections. People close to me believe that this is (definitely true) to (definitely false)	Y	Y
Discussions	Regardless of whether you believe this to be true or not, have you ever talked about the issue of immigrants voted illegally in the 2016 election with the following people?		
	Friends and people close to you	Y	N
	People I only interact with online	Y	N
	Acquaintances	Y	N

Note: [a] In Study 3, questions were asked about illegal voting and the MMR vaccine conspiracy. In Studies 4 and 5, they were asked about the deep state conspiracy.

issues (i.e., political anxiety) and two included anxiety specific to health issues (i.e., health anxiety). The items included in each survey appear in Table A.6. Responses were given on Likert scales, as follows. "Strongly Agree," "Somewhat Agree," "Neither Agree nor Disagree," "Somewhat Disagree," and "Strongly Disagree." This scale was scored from 1 ("Strongly Disagree") to 5 ("Strongly Agree").

A.2.3   *Variables Associated with the Belief Defense Motivation*

Need for closure. Studies 1 and 2 included a short measure of need for closure (Kossowska et al., 2002). The two items were (a) "I don't like situations that are uncertain," and (b) "I enjoy having a clear and structured mode of life. For further validation." Study 3 included the full Need for Closure Scale. Including this and other complete scales in Study 3 allowed us to examine if our results were robust to the reduction in the number of items in the scales. Responses were provided on Likert scales, as follows. "Strongly Agree," "Somewhat Agree," "Neither Agree nor Disagree," "Somewhat Disagree," and "Strongly Disagree." This scale was scored from 1 ("Strongly Disagree") to 5 ("Strongly Agree").

Table A.6. *Anxiety measures (Studies 1–4)*

		Study			
		1	2	3	4
General Anxiety					
	I feel calm.	Y	N	N	N
	I am worried.	Y	N	N	N
	I am confused.	Y	N	N	N
	I sometimes don't feel safe.	Y	Y	Y	N
	I feel calm most of the time.	N	Y	Y	N
	I am worried most of the time.	N	Y	Y	N
	I am confused most of the time.	N	Y	Y	N
	Thinking about feeling calm or worried, in the past week, would you say you felt: very calm to very worried	N	N	Y	N
Political Anxiety	When it comes to politics, I feel calm.	Y	Y	N	N
	When it comes to politics, I am worried.	Y	Y	N	N
	When it comes to politics, I am confused.	Y	Y	N	N
	Politics makes me anxious.	Y	Y	N	N
	I am worried about contemporary politics.	Y	Y	N	N
Health Anxiety	Health issues make me anxious.	Y	Y	N	N
	I am worried about health issues.	Y	Y	N	N

Note: Y: Included in the survey. N: Not included in the survey.

Political ideology. Studies 1–3 included a 3-point measure of ideology, namely: "Do you think of yourself liberal, conservative, or neither?" (1) "liberal," (2) "neither," and (3) "conservative."

A.2.4   Variables association with the Belief Accuracy Motivation

Need for cognition. Studies 1 and 2 included short measures of need for cognition (Cacioppo et al., 1986) with Likert scales. Specifically, need for cognition was measured with the following items: (a) "I like to have responsibility for handling situations that require a lot of thinking," and (b) "I prefer simple to complex problems." Study 3 included the complete need for cognition scale (Cacioppo et al., 1986). Responses were given on Likert scales, as follows. "Strongly Agree," "Somewhat Agree," "Neither Agree nor Disagree," "Somewhat Disagree," and "Strongly Disagree." This scale was scored from 1 ("Strongly Disagree") to 5 ("Strongly Agree").

Political knowledge. In Studies 1 and 2, the measures of political knowledge were two knowledge items used by the Pew Center (Pew Center, The public, the political system and American Democract. Appendix A: Measures and scales. https://www.pewresearch.org/politics/2018/04/26/appendix-a-measures-and-scales-2/ Accessed July 1, 2018) from Delli-Carpini and Keeter's scale (1993), which appear in Table A.7. As shown, responses were given on multiple-choice scales.

Education. Education was measured with the following item: "What is the highest level of school you have completed or the highest degree you have received? Participants responded on the following scale: (1) "Less than high school degree," (2) "High school graduate (high school diploma or equivalent including GED)." (3) "Some college but no degree," (4) "Associate degree in college (two-year)," (5) "Bachelor's degree in college (four-year)," (6) "Master's degree," (7) "Doctoral degree," (8) "Professional degree (JD, MD)."

A.2.5   Variables Associated with the Social Integration Motivation

As variables associated with the social integration motivation, we measured need to belong, recent experience of a financial loss, and present employment status.

Need to belong. Need to belong (M. R. Leary et al., 2013) was similarly measured with the following items: (a) "I do not like being alone," and (b) "I want other people to accept me." Study 3 included the full Need to Belong scale. Responses were provided on Likert scales, as follows: "Strongly Agree," "Somewhat Agree," "Neither Agree nor Disagree," "Somewhat Disagree," and "Strongly Disagree." This scale was scored from 1 ("Strongly Disagree") to 5 ("Strongly Agree").

Cynicism. The measures of trust in government appear in Table A.7. Studies 1 and 2 included items developed by Foley (2015): (a) "Politicians are honest," (b) "Politicians genuinely try to keep their campaign promises;" and (c) "Politicians are incompetent."

Trust in Government. Study 3 added items developed in house, which were as follows: (a) "The US president is honest," (b) "The US Senate can be trusted," (c) "The Centers for Disease Control (CDC) can be trusted," (d) "The police can be trusted," (e) "The Federal Bureau of Investigation (FBI) can be trusted," and (f) "I trust the US government to do what's right." In all cases. responses were again provided on Likert scales, as follows: "Strongly Agree," "Somewhat Agree," "Neither Agree nor Disagree," "Somewhat Disagree," and

Table A.7. *Political knowledge and trust in government measures*
(Studies 1–4)

		Study			
		1	2	3	4
Political knowledge	In the case of a tied vote in the U.S. Senate, the deciding vote is cast by:	Y	Y	Y	N
	• The president • The vice president (Correct Response) • The Senate majority leader • The Senate parliamentarian				
	A filibuster in the U.S. Senate can be used to prevent legislation from coming to a vote. Of the 100 U.S. senators, how many votes are needed to end a filibuster?	Y	Y	Y	N
	• 51 • 60 • 67 (Correct Response) • 70				
	How is the number of terms a president can serve determined?	Y	Y	Y	N
	• There is no limit to the number of terms a president can serve. • Article II of the U.S. Constitution (Correct Response) • Custom and precedent • The 22nd Amendment of the Constitution.				
Cynicism	Politicians are honest.	Y	Y	Y	N
	Politicians genuinely try to keep their campaign promises.	Y	Y	Y	N
	Politicians are incompetent.	Y	Y	Y	N
Trust in government	The US House of Representatives can be trusted.	N	N	Y	N
	The US Senate can be trusted.	N	N	Y	N
	The Centers for Disease Control (CDC) can be trusted.	N	N	Y	N
	The police can be trusted.	N	N	Y	N
	The Federal Bureau of Investigation (FBI) can be trusted.	N	N	Y	N
Trust in the president	The US president is honest.	N	N	Y	N

Note: Y: Included in the survey. N: Not included in the survey.

"Strongly Disagree." This scale was scored from 1 ("Strongly Disagree") to 5 ("Strongly Agree").

A.2.6 Norms

Study 3 included one normative item (see Table A.5) for two of the theories (i.e., illegal voting during the 2016 election and MMR vaccine cover-up). An example of these items is: "People who are close to me believe that Obama was not born in the United States and faked his birth certificate to become president." Participants provided their response on a scale with the following points 1 ("People Close to Me Believe This is Definitely true"), 2 ("People Close to Me Believe This is Probably true"), 3 ("People Close to Me Believe This is Neither true nor false"), 4 ("People Close to Me Believe This is Probably false"), and 5 ("People Close to Me Believe This is Definitely false").

A.2.7 Discussions with Others

For two of the theories (i.e., voting of undocumented immigrants during the 2016 election and MMR vaccine cover-up), Study 3 also included an item measuring discussions with other people, including family and close friends, people online, and acquaintances. These items are described in Table A.5 and served to understand social influences.

A.2.8 Media Exposure

Media use. The media measures appear in Table A.8. Studies 1 and 2 had a set of detailed measures used in past research (Jamieson & Albarracín, 2020; Stecula, Kuru, Albarracin, & Jamieson, 2020). Study 3 had those same measures but added far-right and far-left sources (see Table 6.1) catalogued with community impact.

Exposure to information about the conspiracy beliefs. In Study 3, for the illegal voting during the 2016 election and MMR vaccine cover-up, participants were asked "Regardless of whether you believe this to be true or not, have you read or watched news about the autism effects of the MMR vaccine being covered up?" Participants were then presented, "Read news about this," "Watched news," and "Heard on radio" For each one, they used a scale with the points: "Very frequently," "Frequently," "Somewhat," "Rarely," and "Never," which were scored on a scale from 1 ("Never") to 5 ("Very Frequently").

Table A.8. *Media measures (Studies 1–3)*

Type of Media	Items	Study 1	2	3
Frequency news media use	How many days in the past week did you get information from each of the following sources? 0–7			
Conservative media use				
Conservative cable	Cable news channels Fox News or One America News	Y	Y	Y
Conservative radio	Talk Radio (such as The Rush Limbaugh Show, The Mark Levin Show, or The Sean Hannity Show)	Y	Y	Y
Conservative online outlets	Online news and blogs such as the Drudge Report or Breitbart	Y	Y	Y
Liberal Media Use				
Liberal cable	Cable news channel MSNBC	Y	Y	Y
Liberal cable	Cable news channel CNN	Y	Y	Y
Liberal conservative outlets	Online news and blogs such as Vox, or HuffPost	Y	Y	Y
Mainstream Media Use				
Mainstream broadcast	Broadcast news (such as ABC, CBS, or NBC)	Y	Y	Y
Local broadcast	Your local (e.g., county) television news	Y	Y	Y
NPR	Public Radio (such as NPR)	Y	Y	Y
Local newspaper	Your local (e.g., county) newspaper (including online)	Y	Y	Y
Mainstream newspapers	National newspapers (such as the New York Times, *USA Today*, or the *Wall Street Journal* (including online)	Y	Y	Y
Social media use				
Social media	Social media (such as Facebook, Twitter, or Reddit)	Y	Y	Y
Far-right media use				
Conspiratorial online outlets	Websites like DavidIcke.com, WhatReallyHappened.com, thetruthseeker.co.uk, bilderbergmeetings.org, nexusmagazine.com, conspiracyarchive.com, serendipity.it, propagandamatrix.com, thethreewars.com or the like?	N	N	Y
	www.infowars.com	N	N	Y
	Websites like Radix Journal, American Renaissance, Vdare, The Right Stuff, Daily Stormer, or similar publication.	N	N	Y
	Ben Shapiro's The Daily Wire.	N	N	Y

Table A.8. (*cont.*)

Type of Media	Items	Study I	2	3
Conservative magazines	Magazines like *National Review*, *the Weekly Standard*, *American Spectator*, *American Thinker*, *The Washington Examiner*, *The American Conservative*, or *Newsmax Magazine*	N	N	Y
Conservative online outlets	Blogs like Power Line, Captain Quarters, Red State, Power Line, Hot Air, Instapundit, or Michelle Malkin's	N	N	Y
Conservative cable	Cable news from Blaze Media, Newsmax TV, or Sinclair Broadcast Group	N	N	Y
Conservative newspapers	The *New York Post*, or the *Washington Times*	N	N	Y
Far-left media use				
Left online outlet	slate.com	N	N	Y
Left online outlets	Websites like Indymedia, truthdig, US Uncut, World Socialist Web Website, or The Real News	N	N	Y
Liberal radio shows	Radio shows like • Pacifica Radio, The David Pakman Show, Democracy Now!, The Majority Report with Sam Seder, Chapo Trap House, and The Jimmy Dore Show	N	N	Y
Social or traditional media preference				
Preference for social or traditional media	If you had to choose between traditional sources of information, such as newspapers or television, and social media, such as Facebook or Twitter, which one would you prefer to get your information from?	Y	Y	Y
Other cultural media Frequency of consumption of other cultural products	How often do you do the following? Every day, several times a week, several times a month, several times a year, never.			
	Watch movies	Y	Y	Y
	Watch sports	Y	Y	Y
	Read fiction	Y	Y	Y
	Watch television	N	N	Y

Note: Y: Included. No: Not included.

A.2.9 Demographics Not Already Covered

We also included census measures for demographics, including age, income, sex, race, and ethnicity.

A.2.9.1 Descriptive Statistics and Measurement Consistency

The full instruments used in Studies 1–3 appear in the Online Appendix. The descriptive statistics of all variables appear in Table A.10. Importantly, Table A.10 presents Cronbach's alphas for each variable, which were high (>0.70) for variables other than political knowledge. However, Cronbach's alpha is not ideal for knowledge measures, as those items are designed to cover different aspects of a topic. For that reason, inter-item correlations greater than $r = 0.30$ are considered acceptable for belief and knowledge scales (Ajzen & Fishbein, 1980). All in all, and considering that the measures were previously validated, we concluded that our measures had satisfactory internal consistency.

Table A.9. *Media measures (Study 4)*

Measure		Baseline	Follow-ups
News Media Frequency	Thinking about a typical week, how frequently, if ever, do you get information from sources such as?		
	1. Never 2. One or two days a week 3. 3–4 days a week 4. 5–6 days a week[a] 5. Everyday		
	IF IDENT1=1,2: 9 (DO NOT READ) Refused IF IDENT1=3: 9 Web Blank		
Conservative media	Fox News, Rush Limbaugh, or One America News	Y	Y
Liberal media	MSNBC, Bill Maher, or Huffington Post	Y	Y
Mainstream media	ABC News, CBS News, or NBC News	Y	Y
	Breitbart News and websites like DavidIcke.com, WhatReallyHappened.com, thetruthseeker.co.uk.		

Note: [a] This option was only available in the follow-ups of Study 4.

Table A.10. Descriptive statistics of variables (Studies 1–3)

	Study 1			Study 2			Study 3		
	M	SD	α	M	SD	α	M	SD	α
Belief									
Obama's birth certificate	2.13	1.34	—	2.22	1.38	—	2.21	1.38	—
Obama's inaction and crisis in Syria	2.87	1.26	—	2.99	1.25	—	2.94	1.25	—
Undocumented immigrants voted in 2016 election	2.3	1.32	—	2.5	1.35	—	2.45	1.36	—
Immigrants use false documents to work	3.51	1.25	—	3.67	1.18	—	3.71	1.15	—
HIV virus cover-up	2.22	1.3	—	2.43	1.33	—	2.48	1.31	—
Tuskegee study	3.06	1.37	—	3.22	1.27	—	3.26	1.22	—
MMR vaccine cover-up	2.32	1.31	—	2.41	1.29	—	2.46	1.29	—
Tobacco cover-up	4.07	1.14	—	4.1	1.1	—	4.11	1.07	—
Perceived Plausibility									
Obama's birth certificate	2.67	1.17	0.83	2.78	1.2	0.82	—	—	—
Obama's inaction and crisis in Syria	2.86	1.08	0.78	2.86	1.07	0.73	—	—	—
Undocumented immigrants voted in 2016 election	2.69	1.18	0.8	2.77	1.21	0.78	3.21	1.05	0.74
Immigrants use false documents to work	3.24	1.14	0.83	3.18	1.16	0.8	3.64	0.9	0.65
HIV virus cover-up	2.55	1.15	0.81	2.69	1.16	0.78	—	—	—
Tuskegee study	2.69	1.18	0.81	2.76	1.15	0.77	—	—	—
MMR vaccine cover-up	3.07	1.23	0.87	3.05	1.18	0.81	3.63	0.95	0.76
Tobacco cover-up	3.54	1.13	0.85	3.47	1.13	0.8	3.96	0.91	0.77
Perceived Unfalsifiability									
Obama's birth certificate	2.21	1.35	0.87	2.18	1.24	0.79	—	—	—
Obama's inaction and crisis in Syria	2.57	1.31	0.88	2.49	1.33	0.82	—	—	—
Undocumented immigrants voted in 2016 election	2.48	1.36	0.85	2.46	1.27	0.83	2.75	1.23	0.74
Immigrants use false documents to work	2.09	1.2	0.84	2.27	1.2	0.83	2.53	1.22	0.81
HIV virus cover-up	2.71	1.38	0.86	2.61	1.3	0.82	—	—	—
Tuskegee study	2.39	1.34	0.88	2.4	1.23	0.81	—	—	—

	M	SD	α	M	SD	α	M	SD	α
MMR vaccine cover-up	2.57	1.37	0.85	2.5	1.29	0.81	2.5	1.24	0.75
Tobacco cover-up	1.91	1.16	0.85	2.11	1.23	0.85	2.1	1.23	0.86
Anxiety	2.28	0.91	0.76	2.52	0.86	0.69	2.5	0.89	0.72
Political anxiety	3.06	0.89	0.86	3.06	0.8	0.7	–	–	–
Health anxiety	3.25	1.18	0.86	3.31	1.09	0.82	–	–	–
Need for cognition	3.4	0.86	0.7	3.22	0.69	0.55	3.1	0.54	0.82
Need for structure	3.72	0.93	0.59	3.71	0.85	0.53	3.3	0.54	0.75
Need to belong	3.25	0.71	0.6	3.17	0.68	0.53	2.9	0.65	0.76
Cynicism	3.49	0.92	0.66	3.6	0.82	0.62	3.5	0.84	0.63
Political knowledge	1.67	1.07	0.53	1.29	0.99	0.38	1.2	0.97	0.36
Conservative media use (day)	1.76	1.84	0.76	1.39	1.64	0.73	1.5	1.9	0.8
Liberal media use (day)	1.95	1.86	0.78	1.54	1.73	0.77	1.5	1.78	0.8
Mainstream media use (day)	2.41	1.71	0.76	2.18	1.53	0.69	2.3	1.68	0.74
Social media use (day)	3.41	2.58	–	2.65	2.56	–	2.94	2.7	–
Gender	1.47	0.5	–	1.53	0.5	–	1.55	0.5	–
Age group	3.12	0.85	–	3.1	1.13	–	3.02	1.16	–
Education level attained	3.54	0.64	–	3.1	0.83	–	3.05	0.85	–
Employment status	0.74	0.67	–	0.23	0.97	–	0.22	0.98	–
Income level	0.24	0.97	–	0.25	0.97	–	0.17	0.98	–
Political ideology	1.94	0.87	–	1.56	0.5	–	2.04	0.76	–

Note. M: Mean, *SD*: Standard deviation. Cronbach's alpha was not relevant when a measure was single item. α = Cronbach's alpha. Study 3 included a measure of trust in government, $M = 3.08$, $SD = 0.80$, alpha = 0.76. The same study had a measure of trust in the president, $M = 2.43$, $SD = 1.36$.

The demographic description of our survey samples appears in Table A.11, which also includes United States Census statistics for comparison. There was considerable diversity in all samples and the nationally representative panels provided reasonable approximation of the American population. In addition, the use of multiple studies provided the opportunity for us to replicate our findings.

A.3   Experimental Measures, Validity and Sample Description

A.3.1   *Manipulation and Measures*

The experiment we conducted manipulated fear experienced in another context by having participants recollect a fear-inducing instance or not. We then measured the belief in the truth and falsity of the statement that 5G technology was responsible for the COVID-19 pandemic. Participants reported their belief that "The novel coronavirus is caused by cell towers delivering 5G connectivity" on a scale from 1 ("definitely true") to 5 ("definitely false"), which we reverse scored.

We also manipulated participants' attention to their anxiety by either asking a question about how calm, worried, and confused they felt, as well as how much they experienced fear and how much fear and anxiety dominated their feelings. For example, participants were first asked: "How did you feel while writing about the experience?" They then provided their response to "While I was writing, I felt anxious" on a scale from 1 ("strongly disagree") to 5 ("strongly agree"). For participants in the fear questions first condition, these items appeared before the belief measures; for participants in the fear questions second condition, they appeared after the belief measures.

A.3.2   *Validity and Sample Characteristics*

The affect manipulation has been used successfully in the past and is considered valid (Albarracín & Kumkale, 2003; Albarracín & Wyer Jr., 2001). The main dependent measure was single item, thus precluding an analysis of internal consistency. The demographic description of this sample appears in Table A.11. Again, there was considerable diversity in all samples, and the representativeness was acceptable.

Table A.11. *Demographics (Studies 1–4)*

Demographic	Study 1 n (%)	Study 2 n (%)	Study 3 n (%)	Experiment n (%)	Study 4 n (%)	2019 United States Census Bureau (%)
Gender						
Male	388 (52%)	470 (46%)	433 (44%)	273 (43%)	473 (47%)	49%
Female	348 (47%)	527 (52%)	551 (56%)	292 (46%)	525 (53%)	51%
Age (years)						
15–24	28 (4%)	149 (15%)	180 (18%)	69 (11%)	107 (11%)	13%
25–29	142 (19%)	101 (10%)	83 (8%)	53 (8%)	116 (12%)	7%
30–39	272 (37%)	184 (18%)	187 (19%)	98 (16%)	163 (16%)	13%
≥40	287 (39%)	495 (49%)	534 (54%)	347 (55%)	575 (58%)	48%
Education level attained						
Less than high school degree	0 (0%)	24 (2%)	33 (3%)	19 (3%)	11 (1%)	17%
High school graduate (high school diploma or equivalent including GED)	59 (8%)	232 (23%)	228 (23%)	98 (16%)	26 (3%)	28%
Some college or technical degree	220 (30%)	373 (37%)	374 (38%)	161 (25%)	430 (43%)	25%
College degree or postgraduate education	461 (62%)	376 (37%)	353 (36%)	289 (46%)	527 (53%)	32%
Race/ethnicity						
White, non-Hispanic	495 (67%)	678 (67%)	663 (67%)	385 (61%)	578 (58%)	60%
Black, non-Hispanic	45 (6%)	115 (11%)	125 (13%)	80 (13%)	114 (11%)	13%
Asian, non-Hispanic	26 (4%)	47 (5%)	42 (4%)	15 (2%)	47 (5%)	6%
Hispanic	135 (18%)	93 (9%)	93 (9%)	42 (7%)	62 (6%)	15%
Other or multiple races	25 (3%)	48 (3%)	42 (4%)	46 (7%)	67 (7%)	2%
Employment status						
Not working	95 (13%)	384 (38%)	381 (39%)	67 (11%)	356 (36%)	—
Working	642 (87%)	617 (61%)	593 (60%)	307 (49%)	644 (64%)	—
Financial loss						
Strongly disagree	119 (16%)	171 (17%)	205 (21%)	—	—	—
Somewhat disagree	164 (22%)	196 (20%)	200 (20%)	—	—	—
Neither agree nor disagree	156 (21%)	316 (32%)	255 (26%)	—	—	—

Table A.11. (cont.)

Demographic	Study 1 n (%)	Study 2 n (%)	Study 3 n (%)	Experiment n (%)	Study 4 n (%)	2019 United States Census Bureau
Somewhat agree	173 (23%)	176 (18%)	190 (19%)	—	—	—
Strongly agree	127 (17%)	144 (14%)	135 (14%)	—	—	—
Income level						
Less than $10,000	39 (5%)	88 (9%)	78 (8%)	44 (7%)	113 (11%)	2%
$10,000 to $19,999	55 (7%)	93 (9%)	103 (10%)	65 (10%)		7%
$20,000 to $29,999	84 (11%)	113 (11%)	108 (11%)	93 (15%)	97 (10%)	42%
$30,000 to $39,999	105 (14%)	84 (8%)	112 (11%)	43 (7%)	97 (10%)	
$40,000 to $49,999	88 (12%)	76 (8%)	96 (10%)	46 (7%)	92 (9%)	
$50,000 to $59,999	87 (12%)	118 (12%)	96 (10%)	38 (6%)	84 (8%)	34%
$60,000 to $69,999	57 (8%)	67 (7%)	61 (6%)	22 (3%)	79 (8%)	
$70,000 to $79,999	64 (9%)	88 (9%)	57 (6%)	44 (7%)	148 (15%)	
$80,000 to $89,999	40 (5%)	54 (5%)	47 (5%)	23 (4%)		
$90,000 to $99,999	38 (5%)	42 (4%)	49 (5%)	35 (6%)		
$100,000 to $149,999	51 (7%)	111 (11%)	104 (11%)	65 (10%)	159 (16%)	15%
$150,000 or more	32 (4%)	76 (8%)	77 (8%)	48 (8%)	115 (12%)	
Political party						
Republican	275 (37%)	290 (29%)	264 (27%)	170 (27%)	226 (23%)	—
Democrat	254 (34%)	376 (37%)	384 (39%)	202 (32%)	376 (38%)	—
Independent	182 (25%)	256 (25%)	256 (26%)	163 (26%)	338 (34%)	—
Other	9 (1%)	16 (2%)	12 (1%)	11 (2%)	50 (5%)	—
No preference	20 (3%)	70 (7%)	71 (7%)	21 (3%)	5 (1%)	—
Political ideology						
Liberal	306 (41%)	327 (32%)	270 (27%)	201 (32%)	338 (34%)	—
Independent	172 (23%)	394 (39%)	411 (42%)	315 (50%)	349 (35%)	—
Conservative	261 (35%)	289 (29%)	305 (31%)	116 (18%)	293 (29%)	—

Note: Entries are frequencies and percentages in parentheses.

244

A.4   Longitudinal Survey of the Deep State Belief

A.4.1   Conspiracy Belief

In Study 4, participants rated the statement "Unelected U.S. government officials including some in the U.S. intelligence services have secretly conspired to illegally undermine the candidacy and presidency of Donald Trump." This belief item was introduced at baseline and reintroduced in the two follow-ups of the survey. Ratings were provided on a scale with the following points 1 ("Definitely true"), 2 ("Probably true"), 3 ("Probably false"), 4 ("Definitely false"), and 8 ("Not sure"). "Not Sure" was scored as the middle point of the scale and everything was mapped onto a 1 ("Definitely false") to 5 ("Definitely true").

A.4.2   Norms

We measured norms with respect to the deep state belief with the item presented in Table A.5, which was as follows: "Still thinking about the statement that unelected U.S. government officials including some in the U.S. intelligence services have secretly conspired to illegally undermine the candidacy and presidency of Donald Trump ... How about people close to you? Do people who are close to you believe this is: Ratings were provided on a scale with the following points 1 ("Definitely true"), 2 ("Probably true"), 3 ("Probably false"), 4 ("Definitely false"), and 8 ("Not sure"). "Not Sure" was scored as the middle point of the scale and everything was mapped onto a 1 ("Definitely false") to 5 ("Definitely true").

A.4.3   Discussions with Others

To measure discussions with others, participants were asked: "Regardless of what you believe with respect to this group of unelected U.S. government officials, how frequently, if ever, have you talked about this issue with other people before today." Participants answered on a scale with the following points 1 ("never"), 2 ("rarely"), 3 ("somewhat"), and 4 ("frequently").

A.4.4   Anxiety

As shown in Table A.6, the anxiety question was "Thinking about feeling calm or worried. In the past week, would you say you felt." Participants provided responses on the following scale: 1 ("Very calm most of the time"), 2 ("Fairly calm most of the time"), 3 ("Fairly worried most of the time"), 4 ("Very worried most of the time"), and 5 ("Neither calm nor worried"). Responses were rescored onto a 1 ("Very calm most of the time") to 5 ("Very worried most on the time"), with "Neither calm nor worried" scored a 3. This item was rotated to appear either before or after the other measures.

A.4.5   Media Exposure

General media use. As shown in Table A.8, all three times of the survey of Study 4 included one item measuring conservative media use (Table A.9), which was: "Thinking about a typical week, how frequently, if ever, do you get information from sources such as Fox News, Rush Limbaugh, or One America News?" In addition, the second and third time points of Study 4 included measures of mainstream and liberal media (see Table A.9). In wave 1, responses were provided on this scale: 1 ("Never"), 2 ("One or two days a week"), 3 ("3-4 days a week"), and 4 ("Everyday"). In waves 2 and 3, responses were provided on this scale: 1 ("Never"), 2 ("One or two days a week"), 3 ("3 or 4 days a week"), 4 ("5 or 6 days a week"), and 5 ("Everyday").

Exposure to information about the conspiracy beliefs. Study 4 included the following items measuring exposure to information about the deep state belief: (a) "And how frequently, if ever, have you heard or read about this issue on TV, radio or cable?" and (b) "And how frequently, if ever, have you heard or read about this issue in Internet communities or social media?" Participants answered on a scale with the following points 1 ("never"), 2 ("rarely"), 3 ("somewhat"), and 4 ("frequently").

A.4.6   Political Ideology

Study 4 included a frequently used the 5-point scale of political ideology: 1 ("Very conservative"), 2 ("Somewhat conservative"), 3 ("Moderate"), 4 ("Somewhat liberal"), 5 ("Very liberal"), and 8 ("Don't know"). These responses were rescored with 1 and 2 as 3 ("conservative"), 3 as 2 ("neutral"), and 4 and 5 as 1 ("liberal"), so that a higher score represented higher conservatism.

A.4.7   Validity and Sample Characteristics

Following survey research traditions and given the need to keep the survey short, our measures were single item, thus preventing an analysis of internal consistency. The demographic description of this sample appears in Table A.11, and was again close to the general United States population.

A.5 Social Media Study

A.5.1 Data Collection

We purchased our Twitter data through the Twitter Premium Full Archive API, which provides complete access to tweets dating to the first tweet in March 2006. We searched English-language tweets that matched hashtags and keywords associated with conspiratorial and control posts about (a) Obama's birth certificate and (b) deep state; and conspiratorial posts about (c) the MMR-vaccine and autism link, (d) Pizzagate, (e) Chemtrails, (f) lizard people, (g) flat earth, (h) Agenda 21, (i) GMOs, and (j) Bush's knowledge of the 9/11 attacks. We chose tweets posted between 2016 and 2017 because that period offered the most complete coverage of all our hashtags based on the volume of tweets in the past five years using the social media tool Brandwatch (also known as Crimson Hexagon). We extracted four "root-level" attributes from each tweet JSON object obtained from the Twitter Premium API (i.e., id, user, text or full_text, and retweet_count; see Tweet Data Dictionary; "Twitter: Data Dictionary Standard v1.1," n.d.) for conspiratorial theories in 2016 and 2017 (see Table A.12). We removed retweets (i.e., direct reposting of other Twitter users' tweets) from the collected data by checking "RT @" in the tweets. We obtained 407,697 relevant tweets that were from the United States and publicly available (i.e., 391,935 tweets for conspiracy theories and 15,762 control tweets). In response to growing attention to the deep state theory during Trump's presidency, we decided to collect additional tweets in random periods of 2018, 2019, and 2020 (see Table A.12). In the final dataset, each row represented a unique record for each tweet, which included retweets as the primary outcome variable. We next used R code to derive three additional variables, including whether (a) the user account handle of the author of each tweet was a conservative, liberal, or mainstream account; (b) whether the tweet mentioned a conservative, liberal, or mainstream media account handle (e.g., @Fox News); and (c) the fear sentiments of each tweet. Details of these variables are provided next.

A.5.2 Media or Other Author

We were interested in determining the degree to which conservative, liberal, and mainstream media account handles (e.g., @FoxNews)

Table A.12. *Summary of Twitter data collected for conspiracy and control posts for each conspiracy*

Conspiracy	Category	Hashtag	Search period	Number of tweets
Conspiratorial posts				
Obama's birth certificate	political	#fakebirthcertificate, #obamafakebirthcertificate, #fakeobama	2016–2017	1,243
Deep state	political	#deepstate, #spygate, #Qanon, #thegreatawakening, #DeepStateFiles*, #DrainTheDeepState*, #QanonPosts*	2017, Jun 2018, Oct 2019, Jan 2020	191,945
MMR autism link cover-up	health	#CDCwhistleblower, #mmrautism, #AutismMMR*, #Vaccines CauseAUTISM*	2017	7,962
Pizzagate	political	#hillarypizzaparlor, #hillarysexring, #pizzagate*, #pedogate*	Nov–Dec 2017	27,337
Chemtrails	science	#chemtrails, #geoengineering, #wedonotconsent, #WeaponizingWeather	Nov–Dec 2017	69,885
Lizard people	science	#lizardpeople OR #reptilians OR #annunaki	2017	39,504
Flat earth	science	#flatearth	Dec 2017	13,101
Agenda 21	science	#Agenda21	2017	16,122
GMO cover-up	science	#banGMOs, #labelGMOs, #GMOs	Nov–Dec 2017	20,687
Bush knew about 9/11	political	#911truth	May–Dec 2017	4,149
Control posts				
Obama birth certificate	political	#birther	2017	14,168
Deep state	political	#deepstatehoax, #QAnonHoax, #Qhoax, #Spygatehoax, #WalkAwayMAGA, #WalkAwayQanon, #QAnonLOL, #MAGAlol	2017	1,594

Note: * indicates hashtag was not included in the query search of Nov 2017.

participated in the dissemination of conspiratorial tweets. Thus, we developed three lists of conservative, liberal, and mainstream media account handles corresponding to the media measured in our national surveys (see Table A.8). Conservative media account handles included: "FoxNews," "BreitbartNews," "marklevinshow," "hughhewitt," "seanhannity," "davidicke," "realalexjones," "benshapiro," "dcexaminer," "MIRedState," "AmericaNewsroom," "Fox10_NicoleG," "Fox10Danielle," "foxandfriends," "FoxBusiness," "foxnation," "DailyLimbaugh," "OANN," "DRUDGE," "glennbeck," "ASavageNation," "MedvedSHOW," "nexusmagazine," "infowars," "RadixJournal," "RichardBSpencer," "_AltRight_," "realDailyWire," "michaeljknowles," "JeremyDBoreing," "MattWalshBlog," "vdare," "NRO," "amspectator," "americanthinker," "amconmag," "newsmax," "powerlineUS," "RedState," "hotairblog," "instapundit," "michellemalkin," "WeAreSinclair," "nypost," and "WashTimes." *Liberal media account handles* included: "MSNBC," "CNN," "CNNPolitics," "HuffPostPol," "Voxdotcom," HuffPost," "Slate," "Truthdig," "WSWS_Updates," "therealnews," "davidpakmanshow," "democracynow," "majorityfm," "jimmy_dore," "CHAPOTRAPHOUSE," "RadioPacifica." *Mainstream media account handles* included: "ABC," "CBS," "NBC," "NPR," "nytimes," "USATODAY," and "WSJ." We then derived a nominal variable with four values (i.e., 1 = conservative media account account handle, 2 = liberal media account handle, 3 = mainstream media account handle, and -1 = another account handle) by checking whether each tweet's author was one of the account handles on our lists.

A.5.3   Fear Sentiments

We also assessed the fear-content level of each tweet using the R package *tidytext*. Words associated with fear were those included in the NRC Word-Emotion Association Lexicon (a.k.a., NRC Emotion Lexicon). Introduced by Saif Mohammad and Peter Turney in 2010, the lexicon is a list of English words (i.e., unigrams) and their manually annotated associations with eight basic emotions (anger, fear, anticipation, trust, surprise, sadness, joy, and disgust) and two sentiments (negative and positive). We applied the NRC Emotion Lexicon to the tokens of tweets ("Emotion Lexicon," n.d.) and counted the number of fear words. As tweets vary in the number of words and a shorter tweet as a result conveys a higher level of fear sentiment than a longer tweet, we calculated percentages of words associated with fear over all tokens within that tweet. Examples of actual tweets and their scoring are:

> "#GeoEngineering Above #MountRainier #washingtonstate Notice The Two Obvious #Chemtrail **Lines** In Top, Right Corner Of Picture. #WEDONOTCONSENT #Poison Poison Poison Poison\nPoison Poison Poison\nPoison Poison Poison\nPoison Poison Poison\n \"Geoengineering Is A Fancy Word For **Murder!**\"... https://t.co/ sBtUqU4rmT" (Bold is ours to represent fear words; Number of fear words: 15; Token: 40; Percentage of fear sentiment: 37.50)

> "chemtrails are **death** chemtrails are **death** chemtrails are **death** chemtrails are **death** chemtrails are **death** chemtrails are **death** chemtrails are **death** chemtrails are **death** chemtrails are **death** chemtrails are **death** chemtrails are **death** chemtrails are **death** chemtrails are **death**" (Bold is ours to represent fear words; Number of fear words: 13; Token: 39; Percentage of fear sentiment: 33.33)

> "SATAN IS AN **ALIEN** FROM **HELL DANGER DANGER** SATAN WILL **KILL** EVERYONE ATOM BOMBS – CHEMTRAILS BIOLOGICAL **WARFARE DISEASE** – SATAN IS ALL **DISEASE** BLACK **DEATH** BLACK **CANCER**" (Bold is ours to represent fear words; Number of fear words: 10; Token: 26; Percentage of fear sentiment: 38.46154)

The descriptive statistics for the Twitter data appear in Table A.13.

A.6   Model Equations

A.6.1   Chapter 4

The model concerning associations of the general measure of anxiety and health anxiety with conspiracy beliefs (Study 1) was as follows:
Level 1:

$$\hat{Y}_{ij} = \beta_{oj} + \varepsilon_{ij}$$

Level 2:

$$\beta_{oj} = \gamma_{oo} + \gamma_{o1}(Anxiety_j) + \gamma_{o2}(Health\ Anxiety_j) + u_{oj}$$

The above equations can be expressed as the single-level model below:

$$\hat{Y}_{ij} = \gamma_{oo} + \gamma_{o1}(Anxiety_j) + \gamma_{o2}(Health\ anxiety_j) + u_{ok} + \varepsilon_{ij},$$

where $\hat{Y}_{ij}$ is the belief in a specific conspiracy theory i nested within participant j. *Anxiety$_j$* and *Health Anxiety$_j$* represents explanatory variables for participant j.

Table A.13. Descriptive statistics of Twitter data

Variable	N	Missing percent	Mean	SD	Range	Skew
Conspiratorial tweets						
Agenda 21						
Retweets	16122	0	0.89	8.36	829 (0-829)	70.3
Account handle	16122	0	-1	0	0 (-1-1)	–
Fear percent	4730	70.66	6.73	3.62	32.07 (1.27-33.33)	2.15
Fear percent (centered)	4730	70.66	0.19	1.01	8.96 (-1.34-7.62)	2.15
Obama's birth certificate						
Retweets	1243	0	1.73	18.28	603 (0-603)	29.24
Account handle	1243	0	-1	0	0 (-1-1)	–
Fear percent	363	70.8	7.88	4.8	38 (2-40)	2.42
Fear percent (centered)	363	70.8	0.51	1.34	10.62 (-1.13-9.48)	2.42
Bush 9/11						
Retweets	4149	0	1.38	7.66	197 (0-197)	13.83
Account handle	4149	0	-1	0.05	3 (-1-2)	64.41
Fear percent	1134	72.67	6.76	3.38	26.27 (1.32-27.59)	1.7
Fear percent (centered)	1134	72.67	0.2	0.94	7.34 (-1.32-6.01)	1.7
Chemtrails						
Retweets	69885	0	0.65	14.73	3746 (0-3746)	235.99
Account handle	69885	0	-1	0.01	2 (-1-1)	186.93
Fear percentage	24470	64.99	6.9	3.45	49.04 (0.96-50)	2.01
Fear percentage (centered)	24470	64.99	0.24	0.96	13.7 (-1.42-12.28)	2.01
Deep state						
Retweets	191945	0	3.44	60.67	16520 (0-16520)	136.82
Author media	191945	0	-1	0.02	3 (-1-2)	132.9
Fear percentage	67956	64.6	5.54	3.51	59.07 (0.93-60)	2.32
Fear percentage (centered)	67956	64.6	-0.15	0.98	16.5 (-1.43-15.07)	2.32
Flat earth						
Retweets	13101	0	0.95	15.14	1668 (0-1668)	102.39
Account handle	13101	0	-1	0	0 (-1-1)	–
Fear percentage	2762	78.92	5.39	3.26	32.36 (0.97-33.33)	1.56
Fear percentage (centered)	2762	78.92	-0.19	0.91	9.04 (-1.42-7.65)	1.56

Table A.13. (cont.)

Variable	N	Missing percent	Mean	SD	Range	Skew
GMO						
Retweets	20687	0	1.08	9.29	753 (0–753)	55.06
Account handle	20687	0	–1	0.02	3 (–1–2)	143.83
Fear percentage	6677	67.72	6.48	3.7	41.85 (1.01–42.86)	1.52
Fear percentage (centered)	6677	67.72	0.12	1.03	11.69 (–1.41–10.28)	1.52
Pizzagate						
Retweets	27337	0	2.87	42.03	4022 (0–4022)	54.06
Account handle	27337	0	–1	0.02	2 (–1–1)	116.91
Fear percentage	9731	64.4	5.79	3.39	36.54 (0.96–37.5)	1.98
Fear percentage (centered)	9731	64.4	–0.08	0.95	10.21 (–1.42–8.78)	1.98
Lizard people						
Retweets	39504	0	0.32	6.07	688 (0–688)	74.93
Account handle	39504	0	–1	0.02	2 (–1–1)	81.13
Fear percentage	8344	78.88	7.14	3.79	48.77 (1.23–50)	2.48
Fear percentage (centered)	8344	78.88	0.3	1.06	13.62 (–1.35–12.28)	2.48
MMR vaccine cover-up						
Retweets	7962	0	1.82	4.28	110 (0–110)	8.08
Account handles	7962	0	–1	0.02	2 (–1–1)	89.23
Fear percentage	2234	71.94	7.23	3.28	22.42 (1.11–23.53)	1.3
Fear percentage (centered)	2234	71.94	0.33	0.91	6.26 (–1.38–4.88)	1.3
Nonconspiratorial tweets						
Obama's birth certificate						
Retweets	14168	0	1.6	28.2	2468 (0–2468)	57.91
Account handles	14168	0	–1	0	0 (–1–1)	–
Fear percentage	4523	68.08	6.27	3.14	55.71 (1.43–57.14)	2.7
Fear percentage (centered)	4523	68.08	–0.02	0.98	17.37 (–1.53–15.84)	2.7
Deep state						
Retweets	1594	0	0.27	3.04	115 (0–115)	33.96
Account handles	1594	0	–1	0	0 (–1–1)	–
Fear percentage	405	74.59	7.11	3.79	22.87 (2.13–25)	1.66
Fear percentage (centered)	405	74.59	0.24	1.18	7.13 (–1.31–5.82)	1.66

Note: N refers to the sample size and SD refers to the standard deviation. –: Index could not be calculated due to zero variance.

A.6.2   Chapter 6

The multilevel negative binomial regression analysis of post type and fear on retweets was as follows:
Level 1:

$$\hat{Y}_{ij} = \beta_{0j} + \beta_{1j}\,Conspiracy_{ij} + \beta_{2j}\,Fear_{ij} + r_{ij}$$

Level 2:

$$\beta_{0j} = \gamma_{00} + u_{0j}$$
$$\beta_{1j} = \gamma_{10}$$
$$\beta_{2j} = \gamma_{20}$$

These equations can be redistributed to the following single equation:

$$\hat{Y}_{ij} = \gamma_{00} + \gamma_{10}\,Conspiracy_{ij} + \gamma_{20}\,Fear_{ij} + u_{0j} + r_{ijw}$$

where $\hat{Y}_{ij}$ is the number of retweets for post i nested within user account handle j (Twitter user account handle, i.e., @[username]; level 2 unit). *Conspiracy*$_{ij}$ (i.e., a binary variable classifying each post as pertaining a conspiracy or control theory) and *Fear*$_{ij}$ (i.e., the percentage of fear words) are explanatory variables for individual post i nested within user account handle j (Twitter user account handle, i.e., @[username]; level 2 unit).

A.6.3   Chapter 7

The model predicting retweets from media account handle types and fear is as follows:
Level 1:

$$\hat{Y}_{ij} = \beta_{0j} + \beta_{1j}(Theory_{ij}) + \beta_{2j}(Fear_{ij}) + \varepsilon_{ij}$$

Level 2:

$$\beta_{0j} = \gamma_{00} + \gamma_{01}(Author\ type_{j}) + u_{0j}$$
$$\beta_{1j} = \gamma_{10}$$
$$\beta_{2j} = \gamma_{20} + \gamma_{21}(Author\ type_{j})$$

The above equations can be expressed as a single-level model.

$$\hat{Y}_{ij} = \gamma_{00} + \gamma_{01}(Author\ type_{j}) + \gamma_{10}(Theory_{ij}) + \gamma_{20}(Fear_{ij})$$
$$+ \gamma_{21}(Author\ type_{j}) * (Fear_{ij}) + u_{0j} + \varepsilon_{ij},$$

where $\hat{Y}_{ij}$ is the number of retweets for post i nested within user account handle j (Twitter user account handle, i.e., @[username]; level 2 unit).

Theory$_{ij}$ (i.e., a nominal variable of different conspiracy theories and Agenda 21 theory was included as the comparison theory) represents a control variable and *Fear$_i$* (i.e., the percentage of fear words) represents an explanatory variable for individual post i nested within account handle j, and *Account type$_j$* (i.e., a nominal variable of the type of the user account handle [i.e., conservative, liberal, mainstream, and other]) represents an explanatory variable for account j.

A.6.4   Chapter 8

The model of the **meta-analysis** of influence of conservative media use and anxiety was as follows:

Level 1:

$$\hat{Y}_{ijk} = \pi_{ojk} + e_{ijk}$$

Level 2:

$$\pi_{ojk} = \beta_{ook} + \beta_{o1k}\,(Gender_{jk}) + \beta_{o2k}\,(Age\ group_{jk}) + \beta_{o3k}\,(Education\ level_{jk})$$
$$+ \beta_{o4k}\,(Ideology_{jk}) + \beta_{o5k}\,(Time_{jk}) + \beta_{o6k}\,(Anxiety_{jk})$$
$$+ \beta_{o7k}\,(Conservative\ media\ use_{jk})$$
$$+ \beta_{o8k}\,(Social\ media\ use_{jk})$$
$$+ \beta_{o9k}\,(Conservative\ media\ use_{jk}) * (Anxiety_{jk}) + \varepsilon_{ojk}$$

Level 3:

$$\beta_{ook} = \gamma_{ooo} + u_{ok}$$
$$\beta_{o1k} = \gamma_{o1o}$$
$$\beta_{o2k} = \gamma_{o2o}$$
$$\beta_{o3k} = \gamma_{o3o}$$
$$\beta_{o4k} = \gamma_{o4o}$$
$$\beta_{o5k} = \gamma_{o5o}$$
$$\beta_{o6k} = \gamma_{o6o}$$
$$\beta_{o7k} = \gamma_{o7o}$$
$$\beta_{o8k} = \gamma_{o8o}$$
$$\beta_{o9k} = \gamma_{o9o}$$

The above equations can be expressed as the single-level model below:

$$\hat{Y}_{ijk} = \gamma_{ooo} + \gamma_{o1o}\,(Gender_{jk}) + \gamma_{o2o}\,(Age\ group_{jk}) + \gamma_{o3o}\,(Education\ level_{jk})$$
$$+ \gamma_{o4o}\,(Ideology_{jk}) + \gamma_{o5o}\,(Time_{jk}) + \gamma_{o6o}\,(Anxiety_{jk})$$
$$+ \gamma_{o7o}\,(Conservative\ media\ use_{jk}) + \gamma_{o8o}\,(Social\ media\ use_{jk})$$
$$+ \gamma_{o9o}\,(Conservative\ media\ use_{jk}) * (Anxiety_{jk}) + u_{ok} + \varepsilon_{ojk} + e_{ijk},$$

where $\hat{Y}_{ijk}$ is belief in a specific conspiracy theory i is nested within participant j and participant is nested within study k. The main effects of nine factors, including *Gender*$_{jk}$, *Age group*$_{jk}$, *Education level*$_{jk}$, *Ideology*$_{jk}$, *Anxiety*$_{jk}$, *Conservative media use*$_{jk}$, *Social media use*$_{jk}$, and *Time*$_{jk}$ (with 1 being assigned to Studies 1, 2, and 3 because they had only one time point), together with an interaction term *Conservative media use*$_{jk}$*Anxiety*$_{jk}$ as explanatory variables at the level of participant j nested within study k.

The multilevel model of **deep state beliefs as a function of anxiety and media use over time** (Study 4) was as follows:

Level 1:

$$\hat{Y}_{ij} = \beta_{0j} + \beta_{1j}(Liberal\ media\ use_{ij}) + \beta_{2j}(Mainstream\ media\ use_{ij})$$
$$+ \beta_{3j}(Conservative\ media\ use_{ij}) + \beta_{4j}(Anxiety_{ij}) + \beta_{5j}(Time_{ij})$$
$$+ \beta_{6j}(Conservative\ media\ use_{ij}) * (Time_{ij})$$
$$+ \beta_{7j}(Anxiety_{ij}) * (Time_{ij})$$
$$+ \beta_{8j}(Conservative\ media\ use_{ij}) * (Anxiety_{ij}) * (Time_{ij}) + \varepsilon_{ij},$$

Level 2:

$$\beta_{0j} = \gamma_{00} + u_{0j}$$
$$\beta_{1j} = \gamma_{10}$$
$$\beta_{2j} = \gamma_{20}$$
$$\beta_{3j} = \gamma_{30}$$
$$\beta_{4j} = \gamma_{40}$$
$$\beta_{5j} = \gamma_{50}$$
$$\beta_{6j} = \gamma_{60}$$
$$\beta_{7j} = \gamma_{70}$$
$$\beta_{8j} = \gamma_{80}$$

The above equations can be expressed as the single-level model below:

$$\hat{Y}_{ij} = \gamma_{00} + \gamma_{10}(Liberal\ media\ use_{ij}) + \gamma_{20}(Mainstream\ media\ use_{ij})$$
$$+ \gamma_{30}(Conservative\ media\ use_{ij}) + \gamma_{40}(Anxiety_{ij}) + \gamma_{50}(Time_{ij})$$
$$+ \gamma_{60}(Conservative\ media\ use_{ij}) * (Time_{ij}) + \gamma_{70}(Anxiety_{ij}) * (Time_{ij})$$
$$+ \gamma_{80}(Conservative\ media\ use_{ij}) * (Anxiety_{ij}) * (Time_{ij}) + u_{0k} + \varepsilon_{ij},$$

where $\hat{Y}_{ij}$ is belief in the deep state conspiracy theory at time point i nested within participant j. The main effects of *Liberal media use*$_{ij}$, *Mainstream media use*$_{ij}$, *Conservative media use*$_{ij}$, *Anxiety*$_{ij}$, and *Time*$_{ij}$, and the three interaction terms *(Conservative media use*$_{ij}$)*(Time*$_{ij}$)*, *(Anxiety*$_{ij}$)*(Time*$_{ij}$)*, *(Conservative media use*$_{ij}$)* (Anxiety*$_{ij}$)*(Time*$_{ij}$)* were explanatory variables at time i nested within participant j.

The analyses of **media use in the context of norms, discussions with other people, and trust in the president in Study 3** followed this model:

$$\hat{Y} = \beta_0 + \beta_1(Conservative\ media\ use) + \beta_2(Liberal\ media\ use)$$
$$+ \beta_3(Mainstream\ media\ use) + \beta_4(Discussion\ with\ others)$$
$$+ \beta_5(Trust\ in\ the\ president) + \beta_6(Norm) + \varepsilon,$$

where $\hat{Y}$ is belief in either voting by undocumented immigrants deciding the popular vote or the MMR vaccine cover-up. *Conservative media use, Liberal media use, Mainstream media use, Discussion with others, Trust in the president,* and *Norm* represent explanatory variables.

The model **media use in the context of norms, discussions with other people, and trust in the president** in Study 4 was as follows:
Level 1:

$$\hat{Y}_{ij} = \beta_{0j} + \beta_{1j}(Conservative\ media\ use_{ij}) + \beta_{2j}(Liberal\ media\ use_{ij})$$
$$+ \beta_{3j}(Mainstream\ media\ use_{ij}) + \beta_{4j}(Discussion\ with\ others_{ij})$$
$$+ \beta_{5j}(Norm_{ij}) + \varepsilon_{ij}$$

Level 2:

$$\beta_{0j} = \gamma_{00} + u_{0j}$$
$$\beta_{1j} = \gamma_{10}$$
$$\beta_{2j} = \gamma_{20}$$
$$\beta_{3j} = \gamma_{30}$$
$$\beta_{4j} = \gamma_{40}$$
$$\beta_{5j} = \gamma_{50}$$

The above equations can be expressed as the single-level model below.

$$\hat{Y}_{ij} = \gamma_{00} + \gamma_{10}(Conservative\ media\ use_{ij}) + \gamma_{20}(Liberal\ media\ use_{ij})$$
$$+ \gamma_{30}(Mainstream\ media\ use_{ij}) + \gamma_{40}(Discussion\ with\ others_{ij})$$
$$+ \gamma_{50}(Norm_{ij}) + u_{0k} + \varepsilon_{ij},$$

where $\hat{Y}_{ij}$ is belief in the deep state conspiracy theory for time i nested within participant j. *Conservative media use$_{ij}$, Liberal media use$_{ij}$, Mainstream media use$_{ij}$, Discussion with others$_{ij}$,* and *Norm$_{ij}$* were explanatory variables for time i nested within participant j.

A.7 Final Note

This supplement presented the measurement and experimental methodology used in this book. All code, data, and materials are linked to the Online Supplement for the convenience of our readers.

References

Abrams, S. J., & Fiorina, M. P. (2012). "The big sort" that wasn't: A skeptical reexamination. *PS: Political Science & Politics*, *45*(2), 203–210.

Adorno, T. W., Frenkel-Brunswik, E., Levinson, D. J., & Sanford, R. N. (1950). *The authoritarian personality*. New York, NY: Harper & Brothers.

Ahmed, W., Vidal-Aballi, J., Downing, J., & Seguí, F. L. (2020). COVID-19 and the 5G conspiracy theory: Social network analysis of twitter data. *Journal of Medical Internet Research*, *22*(5), e19458. DOI: https://doi.org/10.2196/19458

Aisch, G., Jon, H., & Kang, C. (2016). Dissecting the #PizzaGate conspiracy theories. Retrieved January 1, 2021, from www.nytimes.com/interactive/2016/12/10/business/media/pizzagate.html

Aistrope, T. (2016). *Conspiracy theory and American foreign policy*. Manchester: Manchester University Press.

AJMC. (2020). Dr Fauci tackles the issue of antiscience sentiments. *American Journal of Managed Care*, August 30.

Ajzen, I., & Fishbein, M. (1980). *Understanding attitudes and predicting social behavior* (Vol. 278). Englewood Cliffs, NJ: Prentice-Hall.

Ajzen, I., Fishbein, M., Lohmann, S., & Albarracín, D. (2018). The influence of attitudes on behavior. In D. Albarracín & B. T. Johnson (Eds.), *The handbook of attitudes, volume 1: Basic principles* (2nd ed.). New York, NY: Routledge. DOI: https://doi.org/10.1007/BF02294218

Al-Rawi, A. (2019). Networked emotional news on social media. *Journalism Practice*. DOI: https://doi.org/10.1080/17512786.2019.1685902

Albarracin, D. (2021). *Action and inaction in a social world: Predicting and changing attitudes and behaviors*. Cambridge: Cambridge University Press.

Albarracín, D. (2002). Cognition in persuasion: An analysis of information processing in response to persuasive communications. *Advances in Experimental Social Psychology*, *34*, 61–130. Retrieved from www.sciencedirect.com/science/article/pii/S0065260102800041

Albarracin, D., Fishbein, M., & Middlestadt, S. (1998). Generalizing behavioral findings across times, samples, and measures: A study of condom use. *Journal of Applied Social Psychology*, *28*(8). DOI: https://doi.org/10.1111/j.1559-1816.1998.tb01725.x

Albarracín, D., Johnson, B. T., Fishbein, M., & Muellerleile, P. A. (2001). Theories of reasoned action and planned behavior as models of condom use: A meta-analysis. *Psychological Bulletin, 127*(1), 142.

Albarracín, D., & Kumkale, G. T. (2003a). Affect as information in persuasion: A model of affect identification and discounting. *Journal of Personality and Social Psychology, 84*(3), 453.

(2003b). Affect as information in persuasion: A model of affect identification and discounting. *Journal of Personality and Social Psychology, 84*(3), 453. DOI: https://doi.org/10.1037/0022-3514.84.3.453

Albarracín, D., McNatt, P. S., Klein, C. T. F., Ho, R. M., Mitchell, A. L., & Kumkale, G. T. (2003). Persuasive communications to change actions: An analysis of behavioral and cognitive impact in HIV prevention. *Health Psychology, 22*(2), 166–177. DOI: https://doi.org/10.1037/0278-6133.22.2.166

Albarracín, D., & Mitchell, A. L. (2004). The role of defensive confidence in preference for proattitudinal information: How believing that one is strong can sometimes be a defensive weakness. *Personality and Social Psychology Bulletin*. DOI: https://doi.org/http://dx.doi.org/10.1177/0146167204271180

Albarracín, D., & Shavitt, S. (2018). Attitudes and attitude change. *Annual Review of Psychology* (Vol. 69, pp. 299–327). DOI: https://doi.org/10.1146/annurev-psych-122216-011911

Albarracin, D., & Vargas, P. (2010). Attitudes and persuasion: From biology to social responses to persuasive intent. In S. T. Fiske, D. T. Gilbert, & G. Lindzey (Eds.), *Handbook of social psychology* (Vol. 57, pp. 394–427). Wiley. DOI: https://doi.org/10.1146/annurev.psych.57.102904.190034

Albarracín, D., & Wyer Jr., R. S. (2001). Elaborative and nonelaborative processing of a behavior-related communication. *Personality and Social Psychology Bulletin, 27*(6), 691–705. DOI: https://doi.org/10.1177/0146167201276005

Albarracin, J., & Valeva, A. (2011). Political participation and social capital among Mexicans and Mexican Americans in Central Illinois. *Hispanic Journal of Behavioral Sciences, 33*(4), 507–523.

Alexander, H. (2020). "They didn't want me to get a vaccine WIN": Donald Trump accuses the FDA of holding up Pfizer vaccine until after the election – and says decision to delay it will cost lives. *Daily Mail*. Retrieved from www.dailymail.co.uk/news/article-8931911/Donald-Trump-accuses-FDA-holding-Pfizer-vaccine-election.html

Alford, J. R., & Hibbing, J. R. (2004). The origin of politics: An evolutionary theory of political behavior. *Perspectives on Politics, 2*(4), 707–723.

Allcott, H., & Gentzkow, M. (2017). Social media and fake news in the 2016 election. *Journal of Economic Perspectives, 31*(2), 211–236.

Altemeyer, B. (1988). *Enemies of freedom: Understanding right-wing authoritarianism*. Jossey-Bass.

(2002). Dogmatic behavior among students: Testing a new measure of dogmatism. *Journal of Social Psychology, 142*(6). DOI: https://doi.org/10.1080/00224540209603931

Amarasiggam, A., & Argentino, M.-A. (2020). The QAnon conspiracy theory: A security threat in the making? Retrieved from https://ctc.usma.edu/the-qanon-conspiracy-theory-a-security-threat-in-the-making/

Anderson, N. H. (1965). Averaging versus adding as a stimulus-combination rule In impression formation. *Journal of Experimental Psychology, 70*(4), 394–400. DOI: https://doi.org/10.1037/h0021280

Andrews, T. M. (2020). QAnon is tearing families apart. Retrieved January 1, 2021, from www.washingtonpost.com/technology/2020/09/14/qanon-families-support-group/

Arti, S. S., & Gandhar, S. S. (2021). A cross sectional study to assess the willingness and hesitancy regarding COVID-19 vaccination. Journal of Cardiovascular Disease Research, 12 (4), 486–494.

NBC News (2019, February). Arrest of Mr. Welch. Retrieved January 1, 2021, from www.nbcwashington.com/news/local/body-cam-video-shows-arrest-of-pizzagate-gunman_washington-dc/4525/

Baker, P. (2020, August). Trump embraces bringe theories about protests and the Coronavirus. *New York Times.*

Baker, P., & Shear, M. D. (2019, August). El Paso shooting supect's manifesto echoes Trump's language. *New York Times.*

Bakshy, E., Messing, S., & Adamic, L. A. (2015). Exposure to ideologically diverse news and opinion on Facebook. *Science, 348*(6239), 1130–1132.

Bale, J. M. (2007). *Political paranoia v. political realism: On distinguishing between bogus conspiracy theories and genuine conspiratorial politics. Patterns of Prejudice* (Vol. 41). Graduate School of International Policy Studies, Monterey Institute of International Studies, Monterey, CA, US: Taylor & Francis. DOI: https://doi.org/http://dx.doi.org/10.1080/00313220601118751

Banas, J. A., & Miller, G. (2013). Inducing resistance to conspiracy theory propaganda: Testing inoculation and metainoculation strategies. *Human Communication Research, 39*(2), 184–207. DOI: https://doi.org/http://dx.doi.org/10.1111/hcre.12000

Banas, J. A., & Richards, A. S. (2017). Apprehension or motivation to defend attitudes? Exploring the underlying threat mechanism in inoculation-induced resistance to persuasion. *Communication Monographs, 84*(2), 164–178. DOI: https://doi.org/http://dx.doi.org/10.1080/03637751.2017.1307999

Barkun, M. (2013). *A culture of conspiracy: Apocalyptic visions in contemporary America* (Vol. 15). Berkeley, CA: University of California Press.

Barkun, M. (2018). Failed Prophecies Won't Stop Trump's True Believers. Retrieved January 1, 2021, from https://foreignpolicy.com/2018/11/08/failed-prophecies-wont-stop-trumps-true-believers/

Barnes, J. E., & Sanger, D. E. (2020, July). Russian intelligence agencies push disinformation on pandemic. *New York Times.*

Barreto, M. A., Cooper, B. L., Gonzalez, B., Parker, C. S., & Towler, C. (2011). The Tea Party in the age of Obama: Mainstream conservatism or out-group anxiety? In *Rethinking Obama* (pp. 105–137). Emerald Group Publishing Limited.

Barron, D., Furnham, A., Weis, L., Morgan, K. D., Towell, T., & Swami, V. (2018). The relationship between schizotypal facets and conspiracist beliefs via cognitive processes. *Psychiatry Research, 259,* 15–20. DOI: https://doi .org/http://dx.doi.org/10.1016/j.psychres.2017.10.001

Barron, D., Morgan, K., Towell, T., Altemeyer, B., & Swami, V. (2014). Associations between schizotypy and belief in conspiracist ideation. *Personality and Individual Differences, 70,* 156–159. DOI: https://doi.org/ http://dx.doi.org/10.1016/j.paid.2014.06.040

Bartlett, J., & Miller, C. (2010). *The power of unreason: Conspiracy theories, extremism and counter-terrorism.* London: Demos.

Basham, L. (2003). Malevolent global conspiracy. *Journal of Social Philosophy, 1* (34), 91–103.

(2006). Afterthoughts on conspiracy theory: Resilience and ubiquity. In D. Coady (Ed.), *Conspiracy theories: The philosophical debate.* Hampshire, England: Ashgate.

Baumeister, R. F. (1997). Identity, self-concept, and self-esteem: The self lost and found. In *Handbook of personality psychology* (pp. 681–710). San Diego, CA, US: Academic Press.

Baumeister, R. F., Bratslavsky, E., Finkenauer, C., & Vohs, K. D. (2001). Bad is stronger than good. *Review of General Psychology, 5*(4), 323–370. DOI: https://doi.org/10.1037//1089-2680.5.4.323

BBC. (2017, January). Reality Check: Did millions vote illegally in the US? *BBC News.* (2021, January). Twitter permanently suspends Trump's account. *BBC News.*

BBC Reality Check team. (2020, November). US election 2020: Fact-checking Trump team's main fraud claims. *BBC News.*

Becker, J., Porter, E., & Centola, D. (2019). The wisdom of partisan crowds. *Proceedings of the National Academy of Sciences, 116*(22), 10717–10722. DOI: https://doi.org/10.1073/pnas.1817195116

Beckett, L., & Ho, V. (2021). "She was deep into it": Ashli Babbitt, killed in Capitol riot, was devoted conspiracy theorist. Retrieved January 14, 2021, from www.theguardian.com/us-news/2021/jan/09/ashli-babbitt-capitol-mob-trump-qanon-conspiracy-theory

Benkler, Yochai, Faris, R., & Roberts, H. (2018). *Network Propaganda: Manipulation, Disinformation, and Radicalization in American Politics.* Oxford Scholarship Online. DOI: https://doi.org/10.1093/oso/ 9780190923624.001.0001

Berkowitz, M. (2014). zionist ConsPiraCy theories racism and the formation of israel. *Hidden Religion,* 29.

Bessi, A., Coletto, M., Davidescu, G. A., Scala, A., Caldarelli, G., & Quattrociocchi, W. (2015). Science vs conspiracy: Collective narratives in the age of misinformation. *PLoS ONE, 10*(2), e0118093. DOI: https://doi .org/10.1371/journal.pone.0118093

Biblarz, A., Brown, R. M., Biblarz, D. N., Pilgrim, M., & Baldree, B. F. (1991). Media influence on attitudes toward suicide. *Suicide and Life Threatening Behavior, 21*(4), 374–384.

Biddlestone, M., Green, R., & Douglas, K. M. (2020). Cultural orientation, power, belief in conspiracy theories, and intentions to reduce the spread of COVID-19. *British Journal of Social Psychology*, *59*, 663–673

Bird, S. T., & Bogart, L. M. (2005). Conspiracy Beliefs about HIV/AIDS and Birth Control among African Americans: Implications for the Prevention of HIV, Other STIs, and Unintended Pregnancy. *Journal of Social Issues*, *61*(1), 109–126. DOI: https://doi.org/http://dx.doi.org/10.1111/j.0022-4537.2005.00396.x

Bless, H., Bohner, G., Schwarz, N., & Strack, F. (1990). Mood and persuasion. *Personality and Social Psychology Bulletin*, *16*(2), 331–345. DOI: https://doi.org/10.1177/0146167290162013

Bogart, L. M., Galvan, F. H., Wagner, G. J., & Klein, D. J. (2011). Longitudinal association of HIV conspiracy beliefs with sexual risk among Black males living with HIV. *AIDS and Behavior*, *15*(6), 1180–1186. DOI: https://doi.org/http://dx.doi.org/10.1007/s10461-010-9796-7

Bogart, L. M., Wagner, G. J., Green Jr., H. D., Mutchler, M. G., Klein, D. J., McDavitt, B., ... Hilliard, C. L. (2016). Medical mistrust among social network members may contribute to antiretroviral treatment nonadherence in African Americans living with HIV. *Social Science & Medicine*, *164*, 133–140. DOI: https://doi.org/http://dx.doi.org/10.1016/j.socscimed.2016.03.028

Bohner, G., Crow, K., Erb, H.-P., & Schwarz, N. (1992). Affect and persuasion: Mood effects on the processing of message content and context cues and on subsequent behaviour. *European Journal of Social Psychology*, *22*(6), 511–530. DOI: https://doi.org/10.1002/ejsp.2420220602

Bohrer, J. (2019). Tape shows Donald Trump and Jeffrey Epstein discussing women at 1992 party. Retrieved January 1, 2021, from www.nbcnews.com/news/us-news/tape-shows-donald-trump-jeffrey-epstein-discussing-women-1992-party-n1030686

Boltanski, L. (2014). *Mysteries and Conspiracies: Detective Stories, Spy Novels and the Making of Modern Societies*. Cambridge, UK: Polity Press.

Bond, S. (2020, June). Facebook Begins Labeling "State-Controlled" Media. *NPR*.

Bouie, J. (2016). How Trump Happened. *Slate, March*, *13*.

Bovet, A., & Makse, H. A. (2019). Influence of fake news in Twitter during the 2016 US presidential election. *Nature Communications*, *10*(1), 7. DOI: https://doi.org/10.1038/s41467-018-07761-2

Bower, G. H. (1981). Mood and memory. *American Psychologist*, *36*(2), 129–148. DOI: https://doi.org/10.1037/0003-066X.36.2.129

Brader, T., Valentino, N. A., & Suhay, E. (2008). What Triggers Public Opposition to Immigration? Anxiety, Group Cues, and Immigration Threat. *American Journal of Political Science*, *52*(4), 959–78.

Bradley, M. M., Codispoti, M., Cuthbert, B. N., & Lang, P. J. (2001). Emotion and motivation I: Defensive and appetitive reactions in picture processing. *Emotion*, *1*(3), 276.

Bradley, M. M., Hamby, S., Löw, A., & Lang, P. J. (2007). Brain potentials in perception: Picture complexity and emotional arousal. *Psychophysiology, 44* (3), 364–373.

Brashier, N. M., & Marsh, E. J. (2020). Judging Truth. *Annual Review of Psychology.* DOI: https://doi.org/10.1146/annurev-psych-010419 050807

Brock, D. (2003). *Blinded by the right: The conscience of an ex-conservative.* (B. Books., Ed.). Portland, OR.

Brooks, R. A., Allen Jr, V. C., Regan, R., Mutchler, M. G., Cervantes-Tadeo, R., & Lee, S.-J. (2018). HIV/AIDS conspiracy beliefs and intention to adopt preexposure prophylaxis among black men who have sex with men in Los Angeles. *International Journal of STD & AIDS, 29*(4), 375–381.

Brotherton, R., & Eser, S. (2015). Bored to fears: Boredom proneness, paranoia, and conspiracy theories. *Personality and Individual Differences, 80,* 1–5. DOI: https://doi.org/10.1016/j.paid.2015.02.011

Brotherton, R., French, C. C., & Pickering, A. D. (2013). Measuring belief in conspiracy theories: The generic conspiracist beliefs scale, *4*(May), 1–15. DOI: https://doi.org/10.3389/fpsyg.2013.00279

Bruder, M., Haffke, P., Neave, N., Nouripanah, N., & Imhoff, R. (2013). Measuring individual differences in generic beliefs in conspiracy theories across cultures: Conspiracy mentality questionnaire. *Frontiers in Psychology, 4* (April), 225. DOI: https://doi.org/10.3389/fpsyg.2013.00225

Brugha, T., Bebbington, P., Tennant, C., & Hurry, J. (1985). The List of Threatening Experiences: a subset of 12 life event categories with considerable long-term contextual threat. *Psychological Medicine.* DOI: https://doi .org/10.1017/S003329170002105X

Bruns, A., Harrington, S., & Hurcombe, E. (2020). 'Corona? 5G? or both?': The dynamics of COVID-19/5G conspiracy theories on Facebook. *Media International Australia,* 1329878X2094611. DOI: https://doi.org/10.1177/ 1329878X20946113

Buchman, B. (2017). Pizzagate Shooter Gets 4-Year Prison Stretch. Retrieved January 1, 2021, from www.courthousenews.com/pizzagate-shooter-gets-4-year-prison-stretch/

Bump, P. (2020, September). Facebook made change that could help control election misinformation.. It isn't the ban on ads. *The Washington Post.*

Business Insider. (2018). 19 outlandish conspiracy theories Donald Trump has floated on the campaign trail and in the White House. Retrieved from www .businessinsider.com/donald-trump-conspiracy-theories-2016-5#claims-3000-people-didnt-die-in-puerto-rico-after-hurricane-maria-and-that-democrats-inflated-the-death-toll-19

Byford, J. (2011). *Conspiracy theories: A critical introduction.* London: Palgrave Macmillan

Cacioppo, J T, Kao, C. F., Petty, R. E., & Rodriguez, R. (1986). Central and peripheral routes to persuasion. An individual difference perspective. *Journal of Personality and Social Psychology, 51*(5), 1032–1043. DOI: https://doi.org/ 10.1037/0022-3514.51.5.1032

Cacioppo, John T, Gardner, W. L., & Berntson, G. G. (1997). Beyond bipolar conceptualizations and measures: The case of attitudes and evaluative space. *Personality and Social Psychology Review, 1*(1), 3–25.

Campaign, B. (2020). Barack Obama and Kamala Harris: "So tell me about Joe" | Joe Biden For President 2020, YouTube. Retrieved from www.youtube .com/watch?v=BXbPa73skxQ

Campbell, A., Miller, P. E., Converse, W. E., & Stokes, D. E. (1960). *The American Voter.* New York: Wiley.

Carey, J. M., Chi, V., Flynn, D. J., Nyhan, B., & Zeitzoff, T. (2020). The effects of corrective information about disease epidemics and outbreaks: Evidence from Zika and yellow fever in Brazil. *Science Advances, 6*(5). DOI: https:// doi.org/10.1126/sciadv.aaw7449

Carleton, R. N., Norton, M. A. P. J., & Asmundson, G. J. G. (2007). Fearing the unknown: A short version of the Intolerance of Uncertainty Scale. *Journal of Anxiety Disorders.* DOI: https://doi.org/10.1016/j.janxdis.2006.03.014

Carmichael, V., & Whitley, R. (2019). Media coverage of Robin Williams' suicide in the United States: A contributor to contagion? *PLOS ONE, 14* (5), e0216543. DOI: https://doi.org/doi: 10.1371/journal.pone.0216543.

Carpini, M. X. D., & Keeter, S. (1993a). Measuring Political Knowledge: Putting First Things First. *American Journal of Political Science, 37*(4), 1179–1206. DOI: https://doi.org/10.2307/2111549

(1993b). Measuring Political Knowledge: Putting First Things First. *American Journal of Political Science, 37*(4), 1179–1206. DOI: https://doi.org/10 .2307/2111549

Carrington, P., Scott, J., & Wasserman, S. (2005). *Models and methods in social network analysis.* (P. J. Carrington, J. Scott, & S. Wasserman, Eds.), *Cambridge University Press* (Vol. 29). Cambridge: Cambridge University Press. DOI: https://doi.org/10.1017/CBO9780511811395

Carver, C. S., & White, T. L. (1994). Behavioral inhibition, behavioral activation, and affective responses to impending reward and punishment: The BIS/BAS Scales. *Journal of Personality and Social Psychology.* DOI: https://doi .org/10.1037/0022-3514.67.2.319

Cassidy, J., & Berlin, L. J. (1994). The Insecure/Ambivalent Pattern of Attachment: Theory and Research. *Child Development.* DOI: https://doi .org/10.1111/j.1467-8624.1994.tb00796.x

Cassidy, J., & Kobak, R. R. (1988). Avoidance and its relation to other defensive process. In J. Belsky & T. Nezworski (Eds.), *Clinical implications of attachment* (pp. 300–323). Hillsdale, NJ: Lawrence Erlbaum Associates, Inc.

Castanho Silva, B., Vegetti, F., & Littvay, L. (2017). The elite is up to something: Exploring the relation between populism and belief in conspiracy theories. *Swiss Political Science Review, 23*(4), 423–443.

Cauterucci, C., & Fischer, J. L. (2016). Comet is D.C.'s weirdo pizza place. Maybe that's why it's a target. *Slate.* Retrieved from https://slate.com/ human-interest/2016/12/comet-ping-pong-is-a-haven-for-weirdos-and-now- a-target.html

Cavalcante, A. (2015). Anxious displacements: The representation of gay parenting on modern family and the new normal and the management of cultural anxiety. *Television & New Media, 16*(5), 454–471.

Čavojová, V., Šrol, J., & Jurkovič, M. (2020). Why should we try to think like scientists? Scientific reasoning and susceptibility to epistemically suspect beliefs and cognitive biases. *Applied Cognitive Psychology, 34*(1), 85–95. DOI: https://doi.org/10.1002/acp.3595

Chaiken, S. R. (1980). Heuristic versus systematic information processing and the use of source versus message cues in persuasion. *Journal of Personality and Social Psychology*. DOI: https://doi.org/10.1037/0022-3514.39.5.752

Chaiken, S. R., & Eagly, A. H. (1976). Communicatioon modality as a determinant of message persuasiveness and message comprehensibility. *Journal of Personality and Social PsychologyI, 34*(4), 605–614. DOI: https://doi.org/10.1037//0022-3514.34.4.605

Chamorro-Premuzic, T., & Furnham, A. (2007). Personality and music: Can traits explain how people use music in everyday life? *British Journal of Psychology, 98*, 175–185.

Chan, M.-P. S., Jones, C. R., Hall Jamieson, K., & Albarracín, D. (2017). Debunking: A meta-analysis of the psychological efficacy of messages countering misinformation. *Psychological Science, 28*(11). DOI: https://doi.org/10.1177/0956797617714579

Chan, M. S., Jamieson, K. H., & Albarracin, D. (2020). Prospective associations of regional social media messages with attitudes and actual vaccination: A big data and survey study of the influenza vaccine in the United States. *Vaccine, 38*(40), 6236–6247.

Chan, M. S., Jones, C. R., Jamieson, K. H., & Albarracín, D. (2017). Debunking: A meta-analysis of the psychological efficacy of messages countering misinformation. *Psychological Science, 28*(11), 1531–1546. DOI: https://doi.org/10.1177/0956797617714579

Chen, L., Zhang, Y., Young, R., Wu, X., & Zhu, G. (2020). Effects of vaccine-related conspiracy theories on Chinese young adults' perceptions of the HPV vaccine: An experimental study. *Health Communication*, April 20, 1–11.

Cheng, J. W., Mitomo, H., Otsuka, T., & Jeon, S. Y. (2016). Cultivation effects of mass and social media on perceptions and behavioural intentions in post-disaster recovery: The case of the 2011 Great East Japan Earthquake. *Telematics and Informatics, 33*(3), 753–772.

Save the Children. (2021). Child trafficking: Myth vs. fact. Retrieved January 1, 2021, from www.savethechildren.org/us/charity-stories/child-trafficking-myths-vs-facts

Chiricos, T., Eschholz, S., & Gertz, M. (1997). Crime, news and fear of crime: Toward an identification of audience effects. Social problems. *Social Problems, 44*(3), 342–357.

Chouchani, N., & Abed, M. (2020). Online social network analysis: Detection of communities of interest. *Journal of Intelligent Information Systems*, *54*(1), 5–21. DOI: https://doi.org/10.1007/s10844-018-0522-7

Cialdini, R. B., & Goldstein, N. J. (2004). Social influence: Compliance and conformity. *Annual Review of Psychology*, *55*, 591–621. DOI: https://doi.org/10.1146/annurev.psych.55.090902.142015

Cichocka, A., Marchlewska, M., De, A. G., & Olechowski, M. (2016). "They will not control us": Ingroup positivity and belief in intergroup conspiracies. *British Journal of Pschology*, *107*(3), 556–576. DOI: https://doi.org/10.1111/bjop.12158

Cichocka, A., Marchlewska, M., & Golec de Zavala, A. (2016). Does self-love or self-hate predict conspiracy beliefs? Narcissism, self-esteem, and the endorsement of conspiracy theories. *Social Psychological and Personality Science*, *7*(2), 157–166. DOI: https://doi.org/http://dx.doi.org/10.1177/1948550615616170

Cichoka, A. (2020). To counter conspiracy theories, boost well-being. *Nature*, *177*. Retrieved from www.nature.com/articles/d41586-020-03130-6

Civettini, A. J. W., & Redlawsk, D. P. (2009). Voters, emotions, and memory. *Political Psychology*, *30*, 125–151.

Clore, G. L., & Schnall, S. (2005). The influence of affect on attitude. In D. Albarracin, B.T. Johnson, and M.P. Zanna (Eds.), *The handbook of attitudes, volume 1: Basic principles* (2nd ed.) (pp. 437–489). New York, NY: Routledge. DOI: https://doi.org/10.1007/BF02294218

Coan, T. G., Merolla, J. L., Zechmeister, E. J., & Zizumbo-Colunga, D. (2020). Emotional responses shape the substance of information seeking under conditions of threat. *Political Research Quarterly*. DOI: https://doi.org/10.1177/1065912920949320

Coddington, M., Molyneux, L., & Lawrence, R. G. (2014). Fact checking the campaign: How political reporters use Twitter to set the record straight (or not). *The International Journal of Press/Politics*, *19*(4), 391–409.

Cohen, S., Kamarck, T., & Mermelstein, R. (1983). A global measure of perceived stress. *Journal of Health and Social Behavior*, 24, 385–396.

Collett, M. (2021). #PIZZAGATE – A Review so far. Retrieved January 1, 2021, from https://steemit.com/pizzagate/@michael.collett/pizzagate-a-review-and-message

Collins, B. (2020, September). QAnon leaders look to rebrand after tech crack downs. *NBC News*. Retrieved from https://urldefense.com/v3/__www.nbcnews.com/tech/tech-news/qanon-leaders-look-rebrand-after-tech-crack-downs-n1241125__;!!DZ3fjg!oeFn6DBQ2pTormAeQKGz_EuxgXkcHKqo3EVboz4twqajqJayJQf8jVUqqxklLncM5Q$

Collins, B. and Zadrozny, B. C. (2020, October 6). Facebook bans QAnon across its platforms. *NBC News*. Retrieved from www.nbcnews.com/tech/tech-news/facebook-bans-qanon-across-its-platforms-n1242339

Comet Ping Pong Event. (n.d.). Retrieved January 2, 2021, from www.eventbrite.com/v/comet-ping-pong-598

Confessore, N. (2014, January 23). Huge "Super PAC" is moving early to back Clinton. Retrieved from www.nytimes.com/2014/01/24/us/politics/biggest-liberal-super-pac-to-fund-possible-clinton-bid.html

Converse, P. E. (1964). The nature of belief systems in mass publics. In D. E. Apter (Ed.), *Ideology and Discontent* (pp. 206–261). New York, NY: The Free Press.

Crano, W. D., & Hannula-Bral, K. A. (1994). Context/Categorization model of social influence: Minority and majority influence in the formation of a novel response norm. *Journal of Experimental Social Psychology*. DOI: https://doi.org/10.1006/jesp.1994.1012

Crease, R. P. (2004). The paradox of trust in science. *Physics World* (March), 18.

Darwin, H., Neave, N., & Holmes, J. (2011). Belief in conspiracy theories. The role of paranormal belief, paranoid ideation and schizotypy. *Personality and Individual Differences, 50*(8), 1289–1293. DOI: https://doi.org/10.1016/j.paid.2011.02.027

DataReportal. (2020). Global social media overview. Retrieved from https://datareportal.com/social-media-users

Daugherty-Brownrigg, B. (2013). Tuskegee syphilis study. In S. Loue (Ed.), *Mental health practitioner's guide to HIV/AIDS* (pp. 454–426). New York, NY: Springer Science + Business Media. DOI: https://doi.org/http://dx.doi.org/10.1007/978-1-4614-5283-6_90

De keersmaecker, J. et al. (2020). Investigating the robustness of the illusory truth effect across individual differences in cognitive ability, need for cognitive closure, and cognitive style. *Personality and Social Psychology Bulletin*. DOI: https://doi.org/10.1177/0146167219853844

Debbies-Carl, J. S. (2017). Pizzagate and beyond: Using social research to understand conspiracy legends. *Skeptical Inquirer, 41*(6). Retrieved from https://skepticalinquirer.org/2017/11/pizzagate-and-beyond/

deHaven-Smith, L. (2010). Beyond conspiracy theory: Patterns of high crime in American government. *American Behavioral Scientist,* 2010;53(6):795–825. DOI: https://doi.org/10.1177/0002764209353274

DeHaven-Smith, L. (2013). *Conspiracy theory in America* (Vol. 6). Austin, TX: University of Texas Press.

deHaven-Smith, L., & Witt, M. T. (2013). Conspiracy theory reconsidered: Responding to mass suspicions of political criminality in high office. *Administration & Society, 45*(3). Sage Publications. DOI: https://doi.org/http://dx.doi.org/10.1177/0095399712459727

Dejong, C., & Wachter, R. M. (2020, August). The risks of prescribing hydroxychloroquine for treatment of COVID-19: First, do no harm. *JAMA Internal Medicine*. American Medical Association. DOI: https://doi.org/10.1001/jamainternmed.2020.1853

Del Vicario, M. et al. (2016). The spreading of misinformation online. *Proceedings of the National Academy of Sciences, 113*(3), 554–559. DOI: https://doi.org/10.1073/pnas.1517441113

Deliso, M., & Date, J. (2020, December 29). Nashville bombing suspect possibly interested in various conspiracy theories: Sources. *ABC News*. Retrieved from https://abcnews.go.com/US/nashville-bombing-suspect-possibly-interested-conspiracy-theories-sources/story?id=74958506

Department of State. (2017). 274. Memorandum From the Deputy under Secretary of State for Political Affairs (Kohler) to Secretary of State Rusk Retrieved from https://history.state.gov/historicaldocuments/frus1964-68v28/d274

Detoc, M., Bruel, S., Frappe, P., Botelho-Nevers, E., & Gagneux-Brunon, A. (2020). Intention to participate in a COVID-19 vaccine clinical trial and to get vaccinated against COVID-19 in France during the pandemic. *Vaccine*, *38*(45), 7002–7006. Epub 09/17. pmid:32988688

Deutsch, M., & Gerard, H. B. (1955). A study of normative and informational social influences upon individual judgment. *The Journal of Abnormal and Social Psychology*, *51*(3), 629.

Dickinson, T. (2020). How Roger Ailes built the Fox News fear factory. Retrieved October 11, 2020, from www.rollingstone.com/politics/politics-news/how-roger-ailes-built-the-fox-news-fear-factory-244652/

Dickson, C. (2017). Agenda 21: The Unconspiracy that just won't die. Retrieved from www.thedailybeast.com/agenda-21-the-un-conspiracy-that-just-wont-die

Dillard, J. P., Plotnick, C. A., Godbold, L. C., Freimuth, V. S., & Edgar, T. (1996). The multiple affective outcomes of AIDS PSAs: Fear appeals do more than scare people. *Communication Research*, *23*(1), 44–72. DOI: https://doi.org/10.1177/009365096023001002

Dodd, R. H., Cvejic, E., Bonner, C., Pickles, K., & McCaffery, K. J. (2020). Willingness to vaccinate against COVID-19 in Australia. *The Lancet. Infectious Diseases*, *21*(5), E 110, doi: 10.1016/S1473-3099(20)30559-4

Doubek, J. (2017). Conspiracy theorist Alex Jones apologizes for promoting "Pizzagate." *NPR*. Retrieved January 1, 2021, from www.npr.org/sections/thetwo-way/2017/03/26/521545788/conspiracy-theorist-alex-jones-apolo gizes-for-promoting-pizzagate

Douglas, K. M., & Sutton, R. M. (2015). Climate change: Why the conspiracy theories are dangerous. *Bulletin of the Atomic Scientists*, *71*(2), 98–106.

(2018). Why conspiracy theories matter: A social psychological analysis. *European Review of Social Psychology*, *29*(1), 256–298. DOI: https://doi.org/10.1080/10463283.2018.1537428

Douglas, K. M., Sutton, R. M., Callan, M. J., Dawtry, R. J., & Harvey, A. J. (2016). Someone is pulling the strings: Hypersensitive agency detection and belief in conspiracy theories. *Thinking & Reasoning*, *22*(1), 57–77. DOI: https://doi.org/http://dx.doi.org/10.1080/13546783.2015.1051586

Douglas, K. M., Sutton, R. M., & Cichocka, A. (2017). The psychology of conspiracy theories. *Current Directions in Psychological Science*, *26*(6), 538–542. DOI: https://doi.org/http://dx.doi.org/10.1177/0963721417718261

Douglas, K. M., Uscinski, J. E., Sutton, R. M., Cichocka, A., Nefes, T., Ang, C. S., & Deravi, F. (2019). Understanding conspiracy theories. *Political Psychology, 40*, 3–35.

Dunning, D., Anderson, J. E., Schlösser, T., Ehlebracht, D., & Fetchenhauer, D. (2014). Trust at zero acquaintance: More a matter of respect than expectation of reward. *Journal of Personality and Social Psychology, 107*(1), 122–141. DOI: https://doi.org/http://dx.doi.org/10.1037/a0036673

Durden, T. (2016). Reddit Bans "Pizzagate" – "We Don't Want Witchhunts On Our Site." Retrieved January 1, 2021, from https://kundaliniandcelltowers .com/Reddit Bans %22Pizzagate%22 - %22We Don't Want Witchhunts On Our Site%22 %7C Zero Hedge - 2016-11-24.pdf

Dwoskin, E., & Stanley-Becker, I. (2020, August). Facebook says it will crack down on QAnon conspiracy theory but stops short of full ban. *The Washington Post.* Retrieved from https://www.washingtonpost.com/technol ogy/2020/08/19/facebook-crackdown-qanon/

Eady, G., Nagler, J., Guess, A., Zilinsky, J., & Tucker, J. A. (2019). How many people live in political bubbles on social media? Evidence from linked survey and Twitter data. *Sage Open, 9*(1), 2158244019832705.

Eagly, A.H., & Chaiken, S. (1993). Psychology of attitudes. In *Psychology of Attitudes.* New York, NY: Harcourt, Brace, & Janovich.

Eagly, Alice H, Chen, S., Chaiken, S., & Shaw-Barnes, K. (1999). The impact of attitudes on memory: An affair to remember. *Psychological Bulletin, 125*(1), 64–89. DOI: https://doi.org/10.1037/0033-2909.125.1.64

Ecker, U. K. H., Lewandowsky, S., & Apai, J. (2011). Terrorists brought down the plane!—No, actually it was a technical fault: Processing corrections of emotive information. *The Quarterly Journal of Experimental Psychology, 64*(2), 283–310. DOI: https://doi.org/http://dx.doi.org/10.1080/17470218.2010.497927

Edwards, G. S., & Rushin, S. (2018). The effect of President Trump's election on hate crimes. Retrieved from https://papers.ssrn.com/sol3/papers.cfm? abstract_id=3102652

Eggertson, L. (2010). Lancet retracts 12-year-old article linking autism to MMR vaccines. *Canadian Medical Association Journal (Journal de l'Association Medicale Canadienne), 182*(4), 2010. DOI: https://doi.org/10.1503/cmaj.109-3179

Einstein, K. L., & Glick, D. M. (2015). *Cynicism, conspiracies, and contemporaneous conditions moderating experimental treatment effects.* Unpublished manuscript, Boston University, Department of Political Science.

Enders, A. M. (2017). *Conspiracy theory and partisan politics. Dissertation Abstracts International Section A: Humanities and Social Sciences.* Michigan State University. Retrieved from https://search.proquest.com/docview/1903672226? accountid=14553

Engelmann, T., & Hesse, F. W. (2011). Fostering sharing of unshared knowledge by having access to the collaborators' meta-knowledge structures. *Computers and Human Behavior, 27*(6), 2078–2087. DOI: https://doi.org/10.1016/j .chb.2011.06.002

Epstein, Z., Pennycook, G., & Rand, D. (2020). *Will the crowd game the algorithm? Using layperson judgments to combat misinformation on social media by downranking distrusted sources.* Proceedings of the 2020 CHI Conference on Human Factors in Computing Systems. April 2020, pp. 1–11. DOI: https://doi.org/10.1145/3313831.3376232

Etzersdorfer, E., & Sonneck, G. (1998). Preventing suicide by influencing mass-media reporting: The Viennese experience 1980–1996. *Archives of Suicide Research*, *4*(1), 67–74. DOI: https://doi.org/doi: 10.1023/A:1009691903261

Fahlman, S. A., Mercer, K. B., Gaskovski, P., Eastwood, A. E., & Eastwood, J. D. (2009). Does a lack of life meaning cause boredom? Results from psychometric, longitudinal, and experimental analyses. *Journal of Social and Clinical Psychology*, *28*(3), 307–340. DOI: https://doi.org/10.1521/jscp.2009.28.3.307

Fahri, P. (2017). Conspiracy theorist Alex Jones backs off 'Pizzagate' claims. *The Washington Post*. Retrieved from www.washingtonpost.com/lifestyle/style/conspiracy-theorist-alex-jones-backs-off-pizzagate-claims/2017/03/24/6f0246fe-10cd-11e7-ab07-07d9f521f6b5_story.html?utm_term=.de2c3a8d07f0

Fazio, L. K., Brashier, N. M., Payne, B. K., & Marsh, E. J. (2017). Knowledge does not protect against illusory truth. *Journal of Experimental Psychology: General*, *144*(5), 993.

Feehan, D. M., & Salganik, M. J. (2016). Generalizing the network scale-up method. *Sociological Methodology*, *46*(1), 153–186. DOI: https://doi.org/10.1177/0081175016665425

Fenigstein, A., & Vanable, P. A. (1992). Paranoia and Self-Consciousness. *Journal of Personality and Social Psychology*. DOI: https://doi.org/10.1037/0022-3514.62.1.129

Fenster, M. (1999). *Conspiracy theories: Secrecy and power in American culture.* Minneapolis, MN: University of Minnesota Press.

   (2008). *Conspiracy theories: Secrecy and power in American culture* (2nd ed.). Minneapolis, MN: University of Minnesota Press.

Ferrara, E., Chang, H., Chen, E., Muric, G., & Patel, J. (2020). Characterizing social media manipulation in the 2020 U.S. presidential election. *First Monday*. DOI: https://doi.org/10.5210/fm.v25i11.11431

Festinger, L. (1954). A theory of social comparison processes. *Human Relations*. DOI: https://doi.org/10.1177/001872675400700202

   (1957). An introduction to the theory of dissonance. *A Theory of Cognitive Dissonance.* DOI: https://doi.org/10.1037/10318-001

Fink, D. S., Santaella-Tenorio, J., & Keyes, K. M. (2018). Increase in suicides the months after the death of Robin Williams in the US. PLOS ONE. *PLOS ONE*, *13*(2), e0191405. DOI: https://doi.org/doi: 10.1371/journal.pone.0191405

Fiorina, M. P., & Abrams, S. J. (2008). Political polarization in the American public. *Annual Review of Political Science*, *11*, 563–588.

Fishbein, M., & Ajzen, I. (1975). Belief, attitude, intention, and behavior. Addison-Wesley series in social psychology. *Ecological Economics*. DOI: https://doi.org/10.1016/j.ecolecon.2004.07.008

(2011). Attitudes, norms, and control as predictors of intentions and behavior. In *Predicting and changing behavior: The reasoned action approach* (pp. 179–219).

Fiske, S. T., & Taylor, S. E. (1991). *Social cognition* (2nd ed.). New York, NY: McGraw-Hill.

Florian, V., Mikulincer, M., & Taubman, O. (1995). Does hardiness contribute to mental health during a stressful real-life situation? The roles of appraisal and coping. *Journal of Personality and Social Psychology*. DOI: https://doi.org/10.1037/0022-3514.68.4.687

Floyd, D. L., Prentice-Dunn, S., & Rogers, R. W. (2000). A meta-analysis of research on protection motivation theory. *Journal of Applied Social Psychology*. DOI: https://doi.org/10.1111/j.1559-1816.2000.tb02323.x

Focus on the Family Website. (n.d.). Retrieved January 4, 2021, from www.focusonthefamily.com/

Foley, J. (2015). *Political cynicism: A critical re-examination*. Wake Forest University.

Ford, D. (2020). Fact check: There are no "pedophilia code words" in a conversation about Joe Biden that took place between Kamala Harris and Barack Obama. Retrieved January 1, 2021, from https://leadstories.com/hoax-alert/2020/09/fact-check-there-are-no-%27pedophilia-code-words%27-in-a-conversation-about-joe-biden-between-kamala-harris-and-barack-obama.html

Forgas, J. P. (2007). When sad is better than happy: Negative affect can improve the quality and effectiveness of persuasive messages and social influence strategies. *Journal of Experimental Social Psychology*, *43*(4), 513–528. DOI: https://doi.org/10.1016/J.JESP.2006.05.006

(2008). The role of affect in attitudes and attitude change. In W. D. Crano & R. Prislin (Eds.), *Frontiers of Social Psychology*. (pp. 158–439). New York, NY: Psychology Press.

Forgas, J. P., & Bower, G. H. (1987). Mood effects on person-perception judgments. *Journal of Personality and Social Psychology*, *53*(1), 53–60. DOI: https://doi.org/10.1037/0022-3514.53.1.53

Franks, B., Bangerter, A., & Bauer, M. W. (2013). Conspiracy theories as quasi-religious mentality: An integrated account from cognitive science, social representations theory, and frame theory. *Frontiers in Psychology*, *4*(JUL), 1–12. DOI: https://doi.org/10.3389/fpsyg.2013.00424

Fraser, S. (2009). Phantom menace? Are conspirators using aircraft to pollute the sky? *Current Science*, *94*, 8–9.

Freedman, J. L., & Sears, D. O. (1966). Selective exposure. *Advances in Experimental Social Psychology*. DOI: https://doi.org/10.1016/S0065-2601(08)60103-3

Freeman, D., & Bentall, R. P. (2017). The concomitants of conspiracy concerns. *Social Psychiatry and Psychiatric Epidemiology*, *52*(5), 595–604. DOI: https:// doi.org/http://dx.doi.org/10.1007/s00127-017-1354-4

Freeman, D., et al. (2019). The revised Green et al. Paranoid Thoughts Scale (R-GPTS): Psychometric properties, severity ranges, and clinical cut-offs. *Psychological Medicine*, *51*(2), 244–253. DOI. https://doi.org/10.1017/S0033291719003155

Freeston, M. H., Rhéaume, J., Letarte, H., Dugas, M. J., & Ladouceur, R. (1994). Why do people worry? *Personality and Individual Differences*. DOI: https://doi.org/10.1016/0191-8869(94)90048-5

Freiman, J. (2021, January 3). Nashville bomber sent writings espousing conspiracy theories to multiple people days before blast. Retrieved January 14, 2021, from www.cbsnews.com/news/nashville-bomber-anthony-quinn-sent-conspiracy-the ories-to-people-before-explosion/

Freud, S. (1961). The ego and the id. In J. Strachey et al. (Trans.), The Standard Edition of the Complete Psychological Works of Sigmund Freud, Volume XIX (1923–1925): *The Ego and the Id and Other Works* (pp. 1–66). London: Hogarth Press.

Frey, D. (1986). Recent research on selective exposure to information. *Advances in Experimental Social Psychology*. DOI: https://doi.org/10.1016/S0065-2601 (08)60212-9

Gabbatt, A. (2020). Hysteria and dismay: Fox hosts spend evening fear-monger- ing over Kamala Harris. Retrieved October 11, 2020, from www.theguardian .com/us-news/2020/aug/19/fox-news-kamala-harris-sean-hannity-tucker-carlson

Gadarian, S. K., & Albertson, B. (2014). Anxiety, immigration, and the search for information. *Political Psychology*, *35*(2), 133–164.

Gaines, B. J., Kuklinski, J. H., Quirk, P. J., Peyton, B., & Verkuilen, J. (2007). Same facts, different interpretations: Partisan motivation and opinion on Iraq. *The Journal of Politics*, *69*(4), 957–974.

Galliford, N., & Furnham, A. (2017). Individual difference factors and beliefs in medical and political conspiracy theories. *Scandinavian Journal of Psychology*, *58*(5), 422–428. DOI: https://doi.org/http://dx.doi.org/10.1111/sjop.12382

Garrett, R. K. (2009). Echo chambers online?: Politically motivated selective exposure among Internet news users. *Journal of Computer-Mediated Communication*, *14*(2), 265–285.

Garrett, R. Kelly, & Weeks, B. E. (2017). Epistemic beliefs' role in promoting misperceptions and conspiracist ideation. *PLoS ONE*, *12*(9), 17.

Gasper, K., & Clore, G. L. (2000). Do you have to pay attention to your feelings to be influenced by them? *Personality and Social Psychology Bulletin*, *26*(6), 698–711. DOI: https://doi.org/10.1177/0146167200268005

Georgiou, N., Delfabbro, P., & Balzan, R. (2019). Conspiracy beliefs in the general population: The importance of psychopathology, cognitive style and educational attainment. *Personality and Individual Differences*, *151*(March), 109521. DOI: https://doi.org/10.1016/j.paid.2019.109521

Gerber, A., & Green, D. (1999). Misperceptions about perceptual bias. *Annual Review of Political Science*, 2(1), 189–210.

Gerbner, G., & Gross, L. (1976). Living with television: The violence profile. *Journal of Communication*, 26(2), 172–199.

Gerstlé, J., & Nai, A. (2019). Negativity, emotionality and populist rhetoric in election campaigns worldwide, and their effects on media attention and electoral success*. *European Journal of Communication*, 34(4), 410–444. DOI: https://doi.org/10.1177/0267323119861875

Gigone, D., & Hastie, R. (1993). The common knowledge effect: Information sharing and group judgment. *Journal of Personality and Social Psychology*, 65 (5), 959–974. DOI: https://doi.org/10.1037/0022-3514.65.5.959

Gilbert, A. N., Fridlund, A. J., & Sabini, J. (1987). Hedonic and social determinants of facial displays to odors. *Chemical Senses*, 12(2), 355–363. DOI: https://doi.org/10.1093/chemse/12.2.355

Gillin, J. (2016, December 9). "Pizzagate" makes leap from conspiracy theory to reality. *Tampa Bay Times*. Retrieved from www.tampabay.com/news/pizza gate-makes-leap-from-conspiracy-theory-to-reality/2305705/

Glenski, M., Weninger, T., & Volkova, S. (2018). Propagation from Deceptive News Sources Who Shares, How Much, How Evenly, and How Quickly? *IEEE Transactions on Computational Social Systems*, 5(4), 1071–1082. DOI: https://doi.org/10.1109/TCSS.2018.2881071

Goel, S., Anderson, A., Hofman, J., & Watts, D. J. (2015). The structural virality of online diffusion. *Management Science*, 62(1), 180–196. DOI: https://doi .org/10.1287/mnsc.2015.2158

Goertzel, T. (1994). Belief in conspiracy theories. *Political Psychology*, 15(4), 731–742. DOI: https://doi.org/10.2307/3791630

   (2010). Conspiracy theories in science: Conspiracy theories that target specific research can have serious consequences for public health and environmental policies. *EMBO Reports*, 11(7), 493–499.

Goldman, A. (2016, December 7). The Comet Ping Pong Gunman Answers Our Reporter's Questions. *New York Times*. Retrieved from www.nytimes.com/ 2016/12/07/us/edgar-welch-comet-pizza-fake-news.html

González-Bailón, S., Borge-Holthoefer, J., & Moreno, Y. (2013). Broadcasters and hidden influentials in online protest diffusion. *American Behavioral Scientist*, 57(7), 943–965. DOI: https://doi.org/10.1177/ 0002764213479371

Goreis, A., & Voracek, M. (2019). A systematic review and meta-analysis of psychological research on conspiracy beliefs: Field characteristics, measurement instruments, and associations with personality traits. *Frontiers in Psychology*, 10, 205.

Gould, M., Jamieson, P., & Romer, D. (2003). Media contagion and suicide among the young. *American Behavioral Scientist*, 46(9), 1269–1284.

Gould, M. S. (2001). Suicide and the media. In J. Hendin, H and Mann (Ed.), *Clinical Science of Suicide Prevention* (Vol. 932, pp. 200–224). New York, NY: New York Academy of Sciences.

Grabe, M. E., & Kamhawi, R. (2006). Hard wired for negative news? Gender differences in processing broadcast news. *Communication Research*, *33*(5), 346–369.

Graeupner, D., & Coman, A. (2017). The dark side of meaning-making: How social exclusion leads to superstitious thinking. *Journal of Experimental Social Psychology*, *69*, 218 222. DOI: https://doi.org/http://dx.doi.org/10.1016/j.jesp.2016.10.003

Granovetter, M. S. (1973). The strength of weak ties. *American Journal of Sociology*, *78*(6), 1360–1380.

Graton, A., Ric, F., & Gonzalez, E. (2016). Reparation or reactance? The influence of guilt on reaction to persuasive communication. *Journal of Experimental Social Psychology*, *62*, 40–49. DOI: https://doi.org/http://dx.doi.org/10.1016/j.jesp.2015.09.016

Gray, J. A., & McNaughton, N. (2000). Fundamentals of the septo-hippocampal system. *The neuropsychology of anxiety: An enquiry into the functions of septo-hippocampal system, 2nd Ed.* (pp. 204–232). Oxford: Oxford University Press.

Gray, Jeffrey A. (1991). The neuropsychology of temperament. In *Explorations in temperament* (pp. 105–128). Springer.

Gray, M. (2010). The situated focus theory of power. In A. Guinote & T. K. Vescio (Eds.), *The social psychology of power* (pp. 141–176). New York, NY: Guilford Press.

Green, C. E. L. et al. (2008). Measuring ideas of persecution and social reference: The Green et al. Paranoid Thought Scales (GPTS). *Psychological Medicine*, *38*(1), 101–111.

Green, R., & Douglas, K. M. (2018). Anxious attachment and belief in conspiracy theories. *Personality and Individual Differences*, *125*, 30–37. DOI: https://doi.org/10.1016/j.paid.2017.12.023

Gruzd, A., & Mai, P. (2020). Going viral: How a single tweet spawned a COVID-19 conspiracy theory on Twitter. *Big Data & Society*, *7*(2), 2053951720938405. DOI: https://doi.org/10.1177/2053951720938405

Grzesiak-Feldman, M. (2015). Are the high authoritarians more prone to adopt conspiracy theories? The role of right-wing authoritarianism in conspiratorial thinking. In M. Bilewicz, A. Cichocka, & W. Soral (Eds.), *The psychology of conspiracy BT – The psychology of conspiracy* (pp. 99–121). New York, NY: Routledge/Taylor & Francis Group.

Grzesiak-Feldman, M., & Ejsmont, A. (2008). *Paranoia and conspiracy thinking of Jews, Arabs, Germans, and Russians in a Polish sample. Psychological Reports* (Vol. 102). University of Warsaw, Warsaw, Poland. DOI: https://doi.org/http://dx.doi.org/10.2466/PR0.102.3.884-886

Guarino, S., Trino, N., Chessa, A., & Riotta, G. (2019). Beyond fact-checking: Network analysis tools for monitoring disinformation in social media. In *International conference on complex networks and their applications* (pp. 436–447). Springer.

Guess, A., Lyons, B., Nyhan, B., & Reifler, J. (2018). Avoiding the echo chamber about echo chambers: Why selective exposure to like-minded political news is less prevalent than you think. Retrieved from https://kf-site-production.s3 .amazonaws.com/media_elements/files/000/000/133/original/Topos_KF_ White-Paper_Nyhan_V1.pdf

Hacker News. (2016). Retrieved January 1, 2021, from https://news.ycombinator .com/item?id=13031138

Hamada, C. (2018, September 8). Trustworthy studies on the trustworthiness of media? *Medium*. Retrieved from https://medium.com/media-theory-and-criti cism-fall-2018/trustworthy-studies-on-the-trustworthiness-of-media-9f2ec2f00e77

Hamilton, W. et al. (1973). The strength of weak ties. *Advances in Neural Information Processing Systems*, 929–934. DOI: https://doi.org/10.1111/j .1467-9280.2007.01917.x

Harambam, J., & Aupers, S. (2015). Contesting epistemic authority: Conspiracy theories on the boundaries of science. *Public Understanding of Science (Bristol, England)*, 24(4), 466–480. DOI: https://doi.org/10.1177/0963662514559891

Harris, K. (2018). What's epistemically wrong with conspiracy theorising? *Royal Institute of Philosophy Supplement*, 84, 235–257. DOI: https://doi.org/DOI: 10.1017/S1358246118000619

Hart, W., Albarracín, D., Eagly, A. H. A. H., Brechan, I., Lindberg, M. J., & Merrill, L. (2009). Feeling validated versus being Correct: A Meta-analysis of selective exposure to information. *Psychological Bulletin*, 135(4). DOI: https://doi.org/10.1037/a0015701

Hartmann, H. (1958). *Ego psychology and the problem of adaptation. Trans. David Rapaport*. New York, NY: International Universities Press.

Harvard T.H. Chan. (2017). *Discrimination in America: Experiences and views of African Americans*. Retrieved from https://media.npr.org/assets/img/2017/ 10/23/discriminationpoll-african-americans.pdf

Harvey, A. M., Thompson, S., Lac, A., & Coolidge, F. L. (2019). Fear and derision: A quantitative content analysis of provaccine and antivaccine internet memes. *Health Education & Behavior*, 46(6), 1012–1023. DOI: https://doi.org/10.1177/1090198119866886

Harwell, D., & Timberg, C. (2020). 'My faith is shaken': The QAnon conspiracy theory faces a post-Trump identity crisis. Retrieved January 3, 2021, from www.washingtonpost.com/technology/2020/11/10/qanon-identity-crisis/

Haselton, T. (2019). Alex Jones was banned from Facebook, but an hour later he was back on Facebook livestreaming. Retrieved January 1, 2021, from www.cnbc.com/2019/05/02/alex-jones-banned-from-face book-but-hes-already-back.html

Hasher, L., Goldstein, D., & Toppino, T. (1977). Frequency and the conference of referential validity. *Journal of Verbal Learning and Verbal Behavior*, 16(1), 107–112. DOI: https://doi.org/10.1016/S0022-5371(77)80012-1

Hawton, K., Simkin, S., Deeks, J. J., O'Connor, S., Keen, A., et al. (1999). Effects of a drug overdose in a television drama on presentations to hospital for self-poisoning: time series and questionnaire study. *BMJ*, 318(972–977). DOI: https://doi.org/doi: 10.1136/bmj.318.7189.972

Hawton, K., & Williams, K. (2001). The connection between media and suicidal behavior warrants serious attention. *Crisis, 22,* 137–140. DOI: https://doi.org/10.1027//0227-5910.22.4.137

Heath, C. (1996). Do people prefer to pass along good or bad news? Valence and relevance of news as predictors of transmission propensity. *Organizational Behavior and Human Decision Processes, 68*(1), 79 94. DOI: https://doi.org/ DOI: https://doi.org/10.1006/obhd.1996.0091

Heimbach, I., & Hinz, O. (2016). The impact of content sentiment and emotionality on content virality. *International Journal of Research in Marketing, 33*(3), 695–701. DOI: https://doi.org/http://dx.doi.org/10.1016/j.ijresmar.2016.02.004

Heine, S. J., Proulx, T., & Vohs, K. D. (2006). The meaning maintenance model: On the coherence of social motivations. *Personality and Social Psychology Review, 10*(2), 88–110. DOI: https://doi.org/10.1207/s15327957pspr1002_1

Heller, J. (2015). Rumors and realities: Making sense of HIV/AIDS conspiracy narratives and contemporary legends. *American Journal of Public Health, 105* (1), e43–e50. DOI: https://doi.org/10.2105/AJPH.2014.302284

Hellinger, D. C. (2018). *Conspiracies and conspiracy theories in the age of Trump.* London: Springer.

Hendriks Vettehen, P., & Kleemans, M. (2018). Proving the obvious? What sensationalism contributes to the time spent on news video. *Electronic News, 12*(2), 113–127. DOI: https://doi.org/10.1177/1931243117739947

Henley, J., & McIntyre, N. (2020, October). Survey uncovers widespread belief in "dangerous" Covid conspiracy theories. *The Guardian.*

Hernáiz, H. A. P., & Antonio, P. (2008). The uses of conspiracy theories for the construction of a political religion in Venezuela. *International Journal of Human and Social Sciences, 3*(4).

Hetherington, M. J., & Nelson, M. (2003). Anatomy of a rally effect: George W. Bush and the war on terrorism. *PS: Political Science & Politics, 36*(1), 37–42.

Higham, L., Piracha, I., & Crocombe, J. (2016). *Asperger syndrome, internet and fantasy versus reality – A forensic case study. Advances in Mental Health and Intellectual Disabilities* (Vol. 10). St Andrews Healthcare, Birmingham, United Kingdom: Emerald Group Publishing Limited. DOI: https://doi.org/http://dx.doi.org/10.1108/AMHID-07-2015-0034

Hilgard, J., & Jamieson, K. H. (2017). Does a scientific breakthrough increase confidence in science? News of a zika vaccine and trust in science. *Scientific Communication, 39*(4), 548–560. DOI: https://doi.org/DOI: https://doi.org/10.1177/1075547017719075

Hitt, T. (2020). Inside 'Out of Shadows': The bonkers Hollywood-pedophilia 'documentary' QAnon loves. Retrieved January 2, 2020, from www.thedailybeast.com/inside-out-of-shadows-the-bonkers-hollywood-pedophilia-documentary-qanon-loves

Hoffman, B. L. et al. (2019). It's not all about autism: The emerging landscape of anti-vaccination sentiment on Facebook. *Vaccine*, *37*(16), 2216–2223. DOI: https://doi.org/10.1016/j.vaccine.2019.03.003

Hofstadter, R. (1964, November). The paranoid style in American politics. *Harpers Magazine*.

Hofstyzer, M. K. (2013). *Narrative, ethos, and artificial fluoridation: The "storying" of a public health policy. Dissertation Abstracts International Section A: Humanities and Social Sciences*. Retrieved from https://search.proquest.com/docview/1466095441?accountid=14553

Holbert, R. L., Shah, D. V., & Kwak, N. (2004). Fear, authority, and justice: Crime-related TV viewing and endorsements of capital punishment and gun ownership. *Journalism & Mass Communication Quarterly*, *81*(2), 343–363.

How Fontes Media Ranks News Sources. (n.d.). Retrieved October 1, 2020, from www.adfontesmedia.com/how-ad-fontes-ranks-news-sources/

Howe, D. W., & Finn, P. E. (1974). Richard Hofstadter: The ironies of an American historian. *The Pacific Historical Review*, 1–23.

Howe, L. C., & Krosnick, J. A. (2015). Attitude strength. *Annual Review of Psychology*. DOI: https://doi.org/10.1146/annurev-psych-122414-033600

Hsu, S. S. (2017, June 14). "Pizzagate" gunman says he was foolish, reckless, mistaken – and sorry. *The Washington Post*. Retrieved from www.washingtonpost.com/local/public-safety/pizzagate-shooter-apologizes-in-handwritten-letter-for-his-mistakes-ahead-of-sentencing/2017/06/13/f35126b6-5086-11e7-be25-3a519335381c_story.html

Huberman, B. A., Romero, D. M., & Wu, F. (2009). Social networks that matter Twitter under the microscope. *First Monday*, *14*(1). DOI: https://doi.org/10.5210/fm.v14i1.2317

Husting, G., & Orr, M. (2007). Dangerous machinery: "Conspiracy theorist" as a transpersonal strategy of exclusion. *Symbolic Interaction*, *30*(2), 127–150. DOI: https://doi.org/http://dx.doi.org/10.1525/si.2007.30.2.127

Hyman, H. H., & Sheatsley, P. B. (1947). Some reasons why information campaigns fail. *Public Opinion Quarterly*, *11*(3), 412–423.

Illing, S. (2020, May). The "deep state" is real. But it's not what Trump thinks it is. *Vox*.

Imhoff, R., & Lamberty, P. (2018). How paranoid are conspiracy believers? Toward a more fine-grained understanding of the connect and disconnect between paranoia and belief in conspiracy theories. *European Journal of Social Psychology*. DOI: https://doi.org/http://dx.doi.org/10.1002/ejsp.2494

Introvigne, M. (1995). The evolution of the Christian "movement against cults" 1978–1993. *Social Compass*, *42*(2), 237–247. DOI: https://doi.org/10.1177/003776895042002007

Invernizzi, G., & Mohamed, A. E. (2020). *Trust nobody: How voters react to conspiracy theories*. Unpublished manuscript. Retrieved from https://papers.ssrn.com/sol3/papers.cfm?abstract_id=3507190

Inverse. (2016). Science: The 10 most popular climate change conspiracy theories. Retrieved January 14, 2021, from www.inverse.com/article/24714-10-most-pop

ular-climate-change-conspiracy-theories#:~:text=The 10 Most Popular Climate Change Conspiracy Theories,Forced Into Cities. 6 ... %28more items%29

Ipsos. (2020). More than 1 in 3 Americans believe a "deep state" is working to undermine Trump. Retrieved January 1, 2021, from www.ipsos.com/en-us/news-polls/npr-misinformation-123020

Isaac, M., & Wakabayashi, D. (2017). Russian influence reached 126 million through facebook alone. *New York Times*.

Isbell, L. M., & Wyer, R. S. (1999). Correcting for mood-induced bias in the evaluation of political candidates: The roles of intrinsic and extrinsic motivation. *Personality & Social Psychology Bulletin, 25*(2), 237–249. DOI: https://doi.org/10.1177/0146167299025002009

Izadi, E. (2020, September). The QAnon problem facing local journalism this election season. *The Washington Post*.

Jaiswal, J., Singer, S. N., Siegel, K., & Lekas, H.-M. (2018). *Hiv-related "conspiracy beliefs"': Lived experiences of racism and socio-economic exclusion among people living with HIV in New York City. Culture, Health & Sexuality.* New York: Taylor & Francis. DOI: https://doi.org/http://dx.doi.org/10.1080/13691058.2018.1470674

Jamison, A. M., Broniatowski, D. A., Dredze, M., Sangraula, A., Smith, M. C., & Quinn, S. C. (2020). Not just conspiracy theories: Vaccine opponents and proponents add to the COVID-19 "infodemic" on Twitter. *Harvard Kennedy School Misinformation Review, 1*(3). DOI: https://doi.org/10.37016/mr-2020-38

Jamieson, Kathleen H., & Cappella, J. N. (2008). *Echo chamber: Rush Limbaugh and the conservative media establishment.* New York, NY: Oxford University Press.

Jamieson, Kathleen Hall. (2018). *Cyberwar: How Russian hackers and trolls helped elect a president – What we don't, can't, and do know.* Oxford University Press.

Jamieson, Kathleen Hall, & Albarracín, D. (2020). The Relation between Media Consumption Misinformation at the Outset of the COVID-19 Pandemic in the US. *Harvard Kennedy School Misinformation Review, 1*. Retrieved from https://misinforeview.hks.harvard.edu/wp-content/uploads/2020/04/April19_FORMATTED_COVID-19-Survey.pdf

Jamieson, Kathleen Hall, & Dunn, J. (2008). The "B" word in traditional news and on the web. *Nieman Reports, 31*.

Jamieson, P. E., & Romer, D. (2017). Cultivation theory and the construction of political reality. In K. H. Kenski, K., Jamieson (Ed.), *Oxford Handbook of Political Communication* (pp. 595–604). New York, NY: Oxford University Press.

Janoff-Bulman, R. (1989). Assumptive worlds and the stress of traumatic events: Applications of the schema construct. *Social Cognition.* DOI: https://doi.org/10.1521/soco.1989.7.2.113

Jarche, H. (2020). Prebunking the conspiracy theorists. Retrieved from https://jarche.com/2020/05/prebunking-the-conspiracy-theorists/

Jerit, J., & Barabas, J. (2012). Partisan perceptual bias and the information environment. *The Journal of Politics, 74*(3), 672–684.

Jerit, J., & Zhao, Y. (2020). Political misinformation. *Annual Review of Political Science, 23,* 77–94.

Jolley, D. (2013). The detrimental nature of conspiracy theories. *Psychology Postgraduate Affairs Group Quarterly, 88,* 35–39.

Jolley, D., & Douglas, K. M. (2014a). The effects of anti-vaccine conspiracy theories on vaccination intentions. *PLoS ONE, 9*(2), e89177. DOI: https://doi.org/10.1371/journal.pone.0089177

(2014b). The social consequences of conspiracism: Exposure to conspiracy theories decreases intentions to engage in politics and to reduce one's carbon footprint. *British Journal of Psychology, 105*(1), 35–56. DOI: https://doi.org/http://dx.doi.org/10.1111/bjop.12018

Jolley, D., Douglas, K. M., Leite, A. C., & Schrader, T. (2019). Belief in conspiracy theories and intentions to engage in everyday crime. *British Journal of Social Psychology, 58*(3), 534–549.

Jolley, D., Meleady, R., & Douglas, K. M. (2020). Exposure to intergroup conspiracy theories promotes prejudice which spreads across groups. *British Journal of Psychology, 111*(1), 17–35.

Jost, J., Stern, C., Rule, N., & Sterling, J. (2017). The Politics of Fear: Is There an Ideological Asymmetry in Existential Motivation? *Social Cognition, 35,* 324–353.

Jost, J. T., Glaser, J., Kruglanski, A. W., & Sulloway, F. J. (2003). Political conservatism as motivated social cognition. *Psychological Bulletin, 129*(3), 339–375. DOI: https://doi.org/10.1037/0033-2909.129.3.339

Jurkowitz, M., Mitchell, A., Shearer, E., & Walker, M. (2020). Americans are divided by party in the sources they turn to for political news. Retrieved January 10, 2021, from www.journalism.org/2020/01/24/americans-are-divided-by-party-in-the-sources-they-turn-to-for-political-news/

Kang, C. (2016). Fake news onslaught targets pizzeria as nest of child-trafficking. Retrieved January 1, 2021, from www.mediapicking.com/medias/files_medias/fake-news-onslaught-targets-pizzeria-as-nest-of-child-trafficking—the-new-york-times-004028800148172917.pdf

Kang, C., & Frenkel, S. (2020). 'PizzaGate' conspiracy theory thrives anew in the TikTok era. *New York Times.* Retrieved from www.nytimes.com/2020/06/27/technology/pizzagate-justin-bieber-qanon-tiktok.html

Kay, A. C., Whitson, J. A., Gaucher, D., & Galinsky, A. D. (2009). Compensatory control: Achieving order through the mind, our institutions, and the heavens. *Current Directions in Psychological Science, 18*(5), 264–268. DOI: https://doi.org/http://dx.doi.org/10.1111/j.1467-8721.2009.01649.x

Kearney, M. D., Chiang, S. C., & Massey, P. M. (2020). The Twitter origins and evolution of the COVID-19 "plandemic" conspiracy theory. *Harvard Kennedy School Misinformation Review, 1*(October), 1–18. DOI: https://doi.org/10.37016/mr-2020-42

Kennedy, M. (2017, June). "Pizzagate" gunman sentenced to 4 years in prison. *NPR*.

Kessler, G., Rizzo, S., & Kelly, M. (2020, April). President Trump made 18,000 false or misleading claims in 1,170 days. *The Washington Post*.

Kilgo, D. K., & Sinta, V. (2016). Six things you didn't know about headline writing: Sensationalistic form in viral news content from traditional and digitally native news organizations. *Official Journal of the International Symposium on Online Journalism*, *6*(1), 111–130.

Kinder, D. R., & Kalmoe, N. P. (2017). *Neither liberal nor conservative: Ideological innocence in the American public*. University of Chicago Press.

Klapper, J. T. (1960). The effects of mass communication. London: Free Press.

Klein, A. (2012). Slipping racism into the mainstream: A theory of information laundering. *Communication Theory*, *22*(4), 427–448. DOI: https://doi.org/10.1111/j.1468-2885.2012.01415.x

Klein, C., Clutton, P., & Dunn, A. G. (2019). Pathways to conspiracy: The social and linguistic precursors of involvement in Reddit's conspiracy theory forum. *PLoS ONE*, *14*(11), e0225098. DOI: https://doi.org/10.1371/journal.pone.0225098

Klepper, D., & O'Brien, M. (2021, January). Social platforms flex their power, lock down Trump accounts. *Associated Press*. Retrieved from https://urldefense.com/v3/__https://apnews.com/article/facebook-ban-trump-3e9a00e791f9806a4d925ec9a2fbe9f3__;!!DZ3fjg!oeFn6DBQ2pTormAeQKGz_EuxgXkcHKqo3EVboz4twqajqJayJQf8jVUqqxn8rUzOXg$

Knight, P. (2002). *Conspiracy nation: The politics of paranoia in postwar America*. New York, NY: New York University Press. Retrieved from https://search.proquest.com/docview/619757876?accountid=14553

Knobloch, S., & Zillmann, D. (2002). Mood management via the digital jukebox. *Journal of Communication*, *52*(2), 351–366.

Koehler, F. et al. (2020). Music therapy in the psychosocial treatment of adult cancer patients: A systematic review and meta-analysis. *Frontiers in Psychology*, *11*. DOI: https://doi.org/10.3389/fpsyg.2020.00651

Kofta, M., Soral, W., & Bilewicz, M. (2020). What breeds conspiracy antisemitism? The role of political uncontrollability and uncertainty in the belief in Jewish conspiracy. *Journal of Personality and Social Psychology*, *118*(5), 900–918. DOI: https://doi.org/10.1037/pspa0000183.

Kohring, M. (2019). Public trust in news media. *The International Encyclopedia of Journalism Studies* (April). DOI: https://doi.org/10.1002/9781118841570.iejs0056

Korta, S. (2018). *Fake news, conspiracy theories, and lies: An information laundering model for homeland security*. Homeland Security Affairs.

Kossowska, M., Van Hiel, A., Chun, W. Y., & Kruglanski, A. W. (2002). The Need for Cognitive Closure Scale: Structure, cross-cultural invariance, and comparison of mean ratings between European-American and East Asian samples. *Psychologica Belgica*, *42*(4), 267–286.

Kramer, A. D. I., Guillory, J. E., & Hancock, J. T. (2014). Experimental evidence of massive-scale emotional contagion through social networks. *Proceedings of the National Academy of Sciences of the United States of America*, *111*(24), 8788–8790. DOI: https://doi.org/10.1073/pnas.1320040111

Kuczynski, A., & Glaberson, W. (2001). Book author says he lied in his attacks on Anita Hill in bid to aid Justice Thomas. *New York Times*. Retrieved from www.nytimes.com/2001/06/27/us/book-author-says-he-lied-his-attacks-anita-hill-bid-aid-justice-thomas.html

Kuklinski, J. H., Quirk, P. J., Jerit, J., Schwieder, D., & Rich, R. F. (2000). Misinformation and the currency of democratic citizenship. *The Journal of Politics*, *62*(3), 790–816.

Kunda, Z. (1987). Motivated inference: Self-serving generation and evaluation of causal theories. *Journal of Personality and Social Psychology*. DOI: https://doi.org/10.1037/0022-3514.53.4.636

(1990). The case for motivated reasoning. *Psychological Bulletin*. DOI: https://doi.org/10.1037/0033-2909.108.3.480

Kunda, Z., & Sanitioso, R. (1989). Motivated changes in the self-concept. *Journal of Experimental Social Psychology*. DOI: https://doi.org/10.1016/0022-1031(89)90023-1

Landau, M. J., Kay, A. C., & Whitson, J. A. (2015). Compensatory control and the appeal of a structured world. *Psychological Bulletin*, *141*(3), 694–722. DOI: https://doi.org/http://dx.doi.org/10.1037/a0038703

Lantian, A., Muller, D., Nurra, C., & Douglas, K. M. (2017). "I know things they don't know!": The role of need for uniqueness in belief in conspiracy theories. *Social Psychology*, *48*(3), 160–173. DOI: https://doi.org/http://dx.doi.org/10.1027/1864-9335/a000306

Lantian, A., Muller, D., Nurra, C., Klein, O., Berjot, S., & Pantazi, M. (2018). Stigmatized beliefs: Conspiracy theories, anticipated negative evaluation of the self, and fear of social exclusion. *European Journal of Social Psychology*. DOI: https://doi.org/http://dx.doi.org/10.1002/ejsp.2498

Larose, S., Bernier, A., Soucy, N., & Duchesne, S. (1999). Attachment style dimensions, network orientation and the process of seeking help from college teachers. *Journal of Social and Personal Relationships*. DOI: https://doi.org/10.1177/0265407599162006

Larsen, E. M., Donaldson, K., & Mohanty, A. (2020). *Conspiratorial thinking during COVID-19: The roles of paranoia, delusion-proneness, and intolerance to uncertainty*. Unpublished manuscript. Retrieved from https://europepmc.org/article/PPR/PPR320856

Laughlin, P. R. (2011). *Group problem solving*. Princeton, NJ: Princeton University Press.

Lazarsfeld, P., Berelson, B., & Gaudet, H. (1948). *The people's choice: How the voter makes up his mind in a presidential campaign*. New York, NY: Columbia University Press.

Lazer, D. M. J. et al. (2018). The science of fake news. *Science*, *359*(6380), 1094–1096. DOI: https://doi.org/10.1126/science.aao2998

Leary, M. R., Kelly, K. M., Cottrell, C. A., & Schreindorfer, L. S. (2013). *Individual differences in the need to belong: Mapping the nomological network.* Unpublished manuscript, Duke University.

Leary, Mark R, & Baumeister, R. F. (2000). The nature and function of self-esteem: Sociometer theory. In *Advances in experimental social psychology* (Vol. 32, pp. 1-62). New York, NY: Academic Press. Elsevier.

Leavitt, A., Burchard, E., Fisher, D., Gilbert, S., Ecology, W., & Pub, P. (2009). The Influentials: New approaches for analyzing influence on Twitter. *Web Ecology Project, 4*(2), 1-18.

Leman, P. J., & Cinnirella, M. (2013). Beliefs in conspiracy theories and the need for cognitive closure. *Frontiers in Psychology, 4.* DOI: https://doi.org/10.3389/fpsyg.2013.00378

Lerman, R., & Dwoskin, E. (2020, July). Twitter bans 7,000 QAnon accounts as conspiracy theorists gather offline. *The Washington Post.*

Lerner, M. J. (1980). The belief in a just world. In *The belief in a just world: A fundamental delusion.* DOI: https://doi.org/10.1007/978-1-4899-0448-5_2

Levine, L. J., & Edelstein, R. S. (2009). Emotion and Memory Narrowing: A Review and Goal-Relevance Approach. *Cognition & Emotion, 23*(5), 833-75.

Lewandowsky, S. et al. (2020). *The debunking handbook 2020.* Retrieved from https://www.cssn.org/the-debunking-handbook-2020-a-consensus-based-handbook-of-recommendations-for-correcting-or-preventing-misinformation/

Lewandowsky, Stephan, & Cook, J. (2020). *The handbook of conspiracy theories.* Retrieved from www.climatechangecommunication.org/conspiracy-theory-handbook/

Lewandowsky, Stephan, Gignac, G. E., & Oberauer, K. (2015). The robust relationship between conspiracism and denial of (climate) science. *Psychological Science, 26*(5), 667-670. DOI: https://doi.org/http://dx.doi.org/10.1177/0956797614568432

Lewis-Beck, M. S., & Stegmaier, M. (2009). American voter to economic voter: Evolution of an idea. *Electoral Studies, 28*(4), 625-631.

Liang, H. (2018). Broadcast versus viral spreading: The structure of diffusion cascades and selective sharing on social media. *Journal of Communication, 68*(3), 525-546. DOI: https://doi.org/10.1093/joc/jqy006

Liang, H., Fung, I. C. H., Tse, Z. T. H., Yin, J., Chan, C. H., Pechta, L. E., ... Fu, K. W. (2019). How did Ebola information spread on twitter: Broadcasting or viral spreading? *BMC Public Health, 19*(1), 438. DOI: https://doi.org/10.1186/s12889-019-6747-8

Lipton, E. (2016, December). Man motivated by "pizzagate" conspiracy theory arrested in Washington gunfire. *New York Times.*

Lohmann, S. et al. (2018). HIV messaging on Twitter. An analysis of current practice and data-driven recommendations. *AIDS, 32*(18), 2799-2805. DOI: https://doi.org/10.1097/QAD.0000000000002018

Loose Change: Final Cut (2007). Retrieved June 9, 2021, from https://www.imdb .com/title/tt0914809/

Lord, C. G., Ross, L., & Lepper, M. R. (1979). Biased assimilation and attitude polarization: The effects of prior theories onsubsequently considered evidence. *Journal of Personality and Social Psychology*. DOI: https://doi.org/ 10.1037/0022-3514.37.11.2098

Lu, X., Yi, F., & Hu, L. (2020). Music-induced analgesia: An adjunct to pain management. *Psychology of Music*. DOI: https://doi.org/10.1177/ 0305735620928585

Luskin, R. C., Sood, G., & Blank, J. (2013). *The waters of Casablanca: Political misinformation (and knowledge and ignorance)*. Unpublished manuscript.

Lynas, M. (2020). COVID: Top 10 current conspiracy theories. Retrieved January 2, 2020, from https://allianceforscience.cornell.edu/blog/2020/04/ covid-top-10-current-conspiracy-theories/

Lynch, C. (2016). Paranoid politics: Donald Trump's style perfectly embodies the theories of renowned historian. Retrieved January 6, 2021, from www.salon .com/2016/07/07/paranoid_politics_donald_trumps_style_perfectly_ embodies_the_theories_of_renowned_historian/

Lynn, M., & Snyder, C. R. (2002). Uniqueness seeking. In C. R. Snyder & S. J. Lopez (Eds.), *Handbook of positive psychology* (pp. 395–410). Oxford: Oxford University Press.

Mackie, D. M., & Worth, L. T. (1989). Processing deficits and the mediation of positive affect in persuasion. *Journal of Personality and Social Psychology*, *57* (1), 27–40.

Madden, T. J., Ellen, P. S., & Ajzen, I. (1992). A comparison of the theory of planned behavior and the theory of reasoned action. *Personality and Social Psychology Bulletin*, *18*(1), 3–9. DOI: https://doi.org/10.1177/ 0146167292181001

Maddux, J. E., & Rogers, R. W. (1983). Protection motivation and self-efficacy: A revised theory of fear appeals and attitude change. *Journal of Experimental Social Psychology*, *19*(5), 469–479. DOI: https://doi.org/10.1016/0022-1031 (83)90023-9

Mak, T. (2016). "Pizzagate" gunman liked Alex Jones. Retrieved January 2, 2021, from www.thedailybeast.com/pizzagate-gunman-liked-alex-jones

Makkonen, A. et al. (2020). Fear-triggering effects of terrorism threats: Cross-country comparison in a terrorism news scenario experiment. *Personality and Individual Differences*, *161*. DOI: https://doi.org/10.1016/j.paid.2020 .109992

Mancosu, M., Vassallo, S., & Vezzoni, C. (2017). Believing in conspiracy theories: Evidence from an exploratory analysis of Italian survey data. *South European Society and Politics*, *22*(3), 327–344.

Marchlewska, M., Cichocka, A., & Kossowska, M. (2017). Addicted to answers: Need for cognitive closure and the endorsement of conspiracy beliefs. *European Journal of Social Psychology*, *48*(2), 109–117. DOI: https://doi .org/http://dx.doi.org/10.1002/ejsp.2308

Marcus, G. E., Neuman, W. R., & MacKuen, M. (2000). *Affective intelligence and political judgment*. Chicago, IL: University of Chicago Press.

Maresca, S. (2020). WWG1WGA: The greatest communications event in history. Retrieved January 3, 2020, from https://goldenageofgaia.com/2020/10/24/wwg1wga-the-greatest-communications-event-in-history-2/

Martel, J. (2011). *Textual conspiracies: Walter Benjamin, idolatry, and political theory*. University of Michigan Press.

Martin, L. L., Ward, D. W., Achee, J. W., & Wyer, R. S. (1993). Mood as Input: People have to interpret the motivational implications of their moods. *Journal of Personality and Social Psychology, 64*(3), 317–326. DOI: https://doi.org/10.1037/0022-3514.64.3.317

Marx, K., Engels, F., More, S., & Engels, F. (2013). *Manifesto of the communist party*. New York, NY: Simon and Schuster.

Mashuri, A., & Zaduqisti, E. (2015). The effect of intergroup threat and social identity salience on the belief in conspiracy theories over terrorism in Indonesia: Collective angst as a mediator. *International Journal of Psychological Research, 8*(1), 24–35. Retrieved from https://search.proquest.com/docview/1712598535?accountid=14553

Mays, V. M., Coles, C. N., & Cochran, S. D. (2012). Is there a legacy of the U.S. Public Health Syphilis Study at Tuskegee in HIV/AIDS-related beliefs among heterosexual African Americans and Latinos? *Ethics & Behavior, 22*(6), 461–471. DOI: https://doi.org/http://dx.doi.org/10.1080/10508422.2012.730805

McCarthy, B. (2020). PolitiFact: QAnon hoax has been linked to violence. Fox News' Greg Gutfeld falsely claimed it hasn't. Retrieved January 1, 2021, from www.tampabay.com/florida-politics/buzz/2020/08/26/politifact-qanon-hoax-has-been-linked-to-violence-fox-news-greg-gutfeld-falsely-claimed-it-hasnt/

Mccauley, C., & Jacques, S. (1979). *Personality Social Psychology, 37*(5), 637–644.

MGraw, M. (2017). Alex Jones apologizes for propagating 'Pizzagate' conspiracy theory. ABC News. Accessed January 3, 2020., from www.kvue.com/article/news/local/alex-jones-apologizes-for-propagating-pizzagate-conspiracy-theory/269-425599420

McGregor, I., Hayes, J., & Prentice, M. (2015). Motivation for aggressive religious radicalization: Goal regulation theory and a personality× threat× affordance hypothesis. *Frontiers in Psychology, 6*, 1325.

McGuire, W. J., & Papageorgis, D. (1961). The relative efficacy of various types of prior belief-defense in producing immunity against persuasion. *Journal of Abnormal and Social Psychology*. DOI: https://doi.org/10.1037/h0042026

McHoskey, J. W. (1995). *Case closed? On the John F. Kennedy assassination: Biased assimilation of evidence and attitude polarization. Basic and Applied Social Psychology* (Vol. 17). Clemson U, Dept of Psychology, SC, US: Lawrence Erlbaum Taylor & Francis. DOI: https://doi.org/http://dx.doi.org/10.1207/s15324834basp1703_7

McNaughton-cassill, M. E. (2001). The news media and psychological distress. *Anxiety, Stress, & Coping, 14*(2), 193–211. DOI: https://doi.org/10.1080/10615800108248354

Mcshane, B. B., & Böckenholt, U. (2017). Single paper meta-analysis: Benefits for study summary, theory-testing, and replicability. *Journal of Consumer Research*, *43*, ucw085. DOI: https://doi.org/10.1093/jcr/ucw085

Media Bias Fact Check Methodology. (n.d.). Retrieved October 1, 2020, from https://mediabiasfactcheck.com/methodology/

Media Bias Rating Method of AllSides Index. (n.d.). Retrieved October 1, 2020, from www.allsides.com/media-bias/media-bias-rating-methods

Mehra, M. R., Desai, S. S., Ruschitzka, F., & Patel, A. N. (2020). RETRACTED:Hydroxychloroquine or chloroquine with or without a macrolide for treatment of COVID-19: A multinational registry analysis. *The Lancet*. DOI: https://doi.org/10.1016/S0140-6736(20)31180-6

Melley, T. (2000). *The empire of conspiracy: The culture of paranoia in postwar America*. Cornell University Press.

Menn, J. (2020, August). Russian-backed organizations amplifying QAnon conspiracy theories, researchers say. *Reuters*.

Mikulincer, M., Shaver, P. R., & Pereg, D. (2003). Attachment theory and affect regulation: The dynamics, development, and cognitive consequences of attachment-related strategies. *Motivation and Emotion*. DOI: https://doi.org/10.1023/A:1024515519160

Miller, J. (2020). Do COVID-19 Conspiracy Theory Beliefs Form a Monological Belief System? *Canadian Journal of Political Science*, *53*(2), 319–326. DOI: https://doi.org/doi:10.1017/S0008423920000517

Miller, J. M., Saunders, K. L., & Farhart, C. E. (2016). Conspiracy endorsement as motivated reasoning: The moderating roles of political knowledge and trust. *American Journal of Political Science*, *60*(4), 824–844.

Mills, D. (2018). Robert F. Kennedy Jr.: Q&A About Vaccine Safety.

Miranda, D., & Blais-Rochette, C. (2020). Neuroticism and emotion regulation through music listening: A meta-analysis. *Musicae Scientiae*, *24*(3), 342–355. DOI: https://doi.org/10.1177/1029864918806341

Mitchell, M. M. (2000). Able but not motivated? The relative effects of happy and sad mood on persuasive message processing. *Communication Monographs*, *67*(2), 215–226. DOI: https://doi.org/10.1080/03637750009376505

Mohammad, S. M. (2020, June 3). Sentiment and emotion lexicons. National Research Council Canada. Retrieved from https://nrc.canada.ca/en/research-development/products-services/technical-advisory-services/sentiment-emotion-lexicons

Monin, B., & Norton, M. I. (2003). Perceptions of a fluid consensus: Uniqueness bias, false consensus, false polarization, and pluralistic ignorance in a water conservation crisis. *Personality and Social Psychology Bulletin*, *29*(5), 559–567.

Mooney, T. (2020, April 14). Anti-vaxxers spread fear about future coronavirus vaccine. *CBS News*. Retrieved from www.cbsnews.com/news/anti-vaxxer-fear-coronavirus-vaccine/

Morgan, M., Shanahan, J. (1997). Two decades of cultivation research: An appraisal and meta-analysis. *Annals of the International Communication Association*, *20*(1), 1–45.

Morse, A. (2021). Twitter bans high-profile QAnon accounts in wake of Capitol Hill attack. MSN.com. Retrieved January 14, 2021, from www.msn.com/en-us/news/technology/twitter-bans-high-profile-qanon-accounts-in-wake-of-capitol-hill-attack/ar-BB1cASsk?c=11419836265968585248?mkt&ocid=uxbndlbing

Morss, R. E., Cuite, C. L., Demuth, J. L., Hallman, W. K., & Shwom, R. L. (2018a). Is storm surge scary? The influence of hazard, impact, and fear-based messages and individual differences on responses to hurricane risks in the USA. *International Journal of Disaster Risk Reduction, 30,* 44–58. DOI: https://doi.org/DOI: https://doi.org/10.1016/j.ijdrr.2018.01.023

    (2018b). Is storm surge scary? The influence of hazard, impact, and fear-based messages and individual differences on responses to hurricane risks in the USA. *International Journal of Disaster Risk Reduction, 30,* 44–58. DOI: https://doi.org/DOI: https://doi.org/10.1016/j.ijdrr.2018.01.023

Motta, M., Stecula, D., & Farhart, C. (2020). How right-leaning media coverage of COVID-19 facilitated the spread of misinformation in the early stages of the pandemic in the U.S. *Canadian Journal of Political Science, 53,* 335–342. DOI: https://doi.org/doi:10.1017/S0008423920000396

Moulding, R., Nix-Carnell, S., Schnabel, A., Nedeljkovic, M., Burnside, E. E., Lentini, A. F., & Mehzabin, N. (2016). Better the devil you know than a world you don't? Intolerance of uncertainty and worldview explanations for belief in conspiracy theories. *Personality and Individual Differences, 98,* 345–354. DOI: https://doi.org/http://dx.doi.org/10.1016/j.paid.2016.04.060

Moyal, N., Henik, A., & Anholt, G. E. (2014). Cognitive strategies to regulate emotions-current evidence and future directions. *Frontiers in Psychology, 4,* 1019. DOI: https://doi.org/10.3389/fpsyg.2013.01019

Mueller, J. E. (1970). Presidential popularity from Truman to Johnson 1. *American Political Science Review, 64*(1), 18–34.

Mueller, P., & Schulz, A. (2019). Alternative media for a populist audience? Exploring political and media use predictors of exposure to Breitbart, Sputnik, and Co. *Information, Communication & Society.* DOI: https://doi.org/10.1080/1369118X.2019.1646778

Müller, K., & Schwarz, C. (2019). *From hashtag to hate crime: Twitter and anti-minority sentiment.* Unpublished manuscript. https://papers.ssrn.com/sol3/papers.cfm?abstract_id=3149103.

Muñoz, A., Moreno, C., & Luján, J. L. (2012). Who is willing to pay for science? On the relationship between public perception of science and the attitude to public funding of science. *Public Understanding of Science, 21*(2), 242–253. DOI: https://doi.org/10.1177/0963662510373813

Mutz, D. (2018). Status threat, not economic hardship, explains the 2016 presidential vote. *Proceedings of National Academy of Sciences, 115*(19), E4330–E4339.

National Science Foundation. (2016). Science and technology: Public attitudes and understanding. Retrieved January 7, 2021, from https://www.nsf.gov/statistics/seind14/index.cfm/chapter-7/c7h.htm

Needle, S. (2016, July). How does Twitter decide what is trending? Retrieved January 7, 2021, from https://rethinkmedia.org/blog/how-does-twitter-decide-what-is-trending

Nettler, G. (1957). A measure of alienation. *American Sociological Review*, 22(6), 670–677.

Neville-Shepard, R. (2019). Post-presumption argumentation and the post-truth world: On the conspiracy rhetoric of Donald Trump. *Argumentation and Advocacy*, 55(3), 175–193.

Newheiser, A.-K., Farias, M., & Tausch, N. (2011). The functional nature of conspiracy beliefs: Examining the underpinnings of belief in the Da Vinci Code conspiracy. *Personality and Individual Differences*, 51(8), 1007–1011. DOI: https://doi.org/http://dx.doi.org/10.1016/j.paid.2011.08.011

Newman, E. J., Jalbert, M. C., Schwarz, N., & Ly, D. P. (2020). Truthiness, the illusory truth effect, and the role of need for cognition. *Consciousness and Cognition*. DOI: https://doi.org/10.1016/j.concog.2019.102866

Newman, M. E. J. (2001). The structure of scientific collaboration networks. *Proceedings of the National Academy of Sciences of the United States of America*, 98(2), 404–409. DOI: https://doi.org/10.1073/pnas.98.2.404

Newman, N. (2011). Mainstream media and the distribution of news in the age of social discovery. *Reuters Institute for the Study of Journalism*, 1–58.

New York Times. (2016). Election 2016: Exit polls. Retrieved May 27, 2021, from www.nytimes.com/interactive/2016/11/08/us/politics/election-exit-polls.html

Newsweek Staff. (2010). Tea Party movement is full of conspiracy theories. *Newsweek*, February 8, 2010. Retrieved January 17, 2021, from www.newsweek.com/tea-party-movement-full-conspiracy-theories-75153

Niederkrotenthaler, T., Fu, K. W., Yip, P. S., Fong, D. Y., & Stack, S., et al. (2012). Changes in suicide rates following media reports on celebrity suicide: A meta-analysis. *Journal of Epidemiology and Community Health*, 66(11), 1037–1042. DOI: https://doi.org/doi: 10.1136/jech-2011-200707

Niederkrotenthaler, Thomas, Braun, M., Pirkis, J., Till, B., Stack, S., Sinyor, M., ... Spittal, M. (2020). Association between suicide reporting in the media and suicide: systematic review and meta-analysis. *BMJ*, 368, m575. DOI: https://doi.org/10.1136/bmj.m575

Nyhan, B., Reifler, J., Richey, S., & Freed, G. L. (2014). Effective messages in vaccine promotion: A randomized trial. *Pediatrics*, 133(4), e835–42. DOI: https://doi.org/10.1542/peds.2013-2365

Nyhan, B., & Zeitzoff, T. (2018). Fighting the Past: Perceptions of Control, Historical Misperceptions, and Corrective Information in the Israeli-Palestinian Conflict. *Political Psychology*, 39(3), 611–631. DOI: https://doi.org/10.1111/pops.12449

O'Brien, T. C., Palmer, R. P., & Albarracin, D. (2021). *Misplaced trust: When trust in science fosters belief in pseudoscience and the benefits of critical evaluation*. Urbana, IL.

Ohiheiser, A. (2016, November 23). Fearing yet another witch hunt, Reddit bans 'Pizzagate'. *The Washington Post*. Retrieved from https://www

.washingtonpost.com/news/the-intersect/wp/2016/11/23/fearing-yet-another-witch-hunt-reddit-bans-pizzagate/

Ohira, H., Winton, W. M., & Oyama, M. (1998). Effects of stimulus valence on recognition memory and endogenous eyeblinks: Further evidence for positive-negative asymmetry. *Personality and Social Psychology Bulletin, 24* (9), 906 993.

Oliver, J. E., & Wood, T. (2014). Medical conspiracy theories and health behaviors in the United States. *JAMA Internal Medicine, 174*(5), 817–818.

Orden, E., & Scannell, K. (2020). Steve Bannon, three others charged with fraud in border wall fundraising campaign. Retrieved December 29, 2020, from www.cnn .com/2020/08/20/politics/bannon-build-the-wall-indictment/index.html

Oreskes, N. (2019, October 24). Science isn't always perfect – but we should still trust it. *Time Magazine.* Retrieved from https://time.com/5709691/why-trust-science/

Orosz, G., Krekó, P., Paskuj, B., Tóth-Király, I., Bothe, B., Roland-Lévy, C., ... Roland-Lévy, C. (2016). Changing conspiracy beliefs through rationality and ridiculing. *Frontiers in Psychology, 7*(October), 9. DOI: https://doi.org/ 10.3389/fpsyg.2016.01525

Ortmann, S., & Heathershaw, J. (2012). Conspiracy theories in the post-soviet space. *The Russian Review, 71*(4), 551–564.

Ostroff, R. B., Behrends, R. W., Lee, K., & Oliphant, J. (1985). Adolescent suicides modeled after television movie. *American Journal of Psychiatry, 142*(8), 989–989.

Out of Shadows. (2020). Movie, 78 min. Retrieved January 4, 2021, from https:// documentaryheaven.com/out-of-shadows/

Ovide, S. (2020, August). A playbook for combating QAnon. *New York Times.*

Owens, J. (2019, Dec) I worked for Alex Jones. *NYT Magazine.*

Pacini, R., & Epstein, S. (1999). The relation of rational and experiential information processing styles to personality, basic beliefs, and the ratio-bias phenomenon. *Journal of Personality and Social Psychology, 76*(972–987).

Pal, S., & Ghosh, I. (2021). A mechanistic model for airborne and direct human-to-human transmission of COVID-19: Effect of mitigation strategies and immigration of infectious persons. arXiv preprint arXiv:2107.12785.

Pariser, E. (2011). *The filter bubble: What the Internet is hiding from you.* London: Penguin Books Limited.

Park, C. L. (2010). Making sense of the meaning literature: An integrative review of meaning making and its effects on adjustment to stressful life events. *Psychological Bulletin.* DOI: https://doi.org/10.1037/a0018301

Parsons, S., Simmons, W., Shinhoster, F., & Kilburn, J. (1999). A test of the grapevine: An empirical examination of conspiracy theories among African Americans. *Sociological Spectrum, 19*(2), 201–222. DOI: https://doi.org/ http://dx.doi.org/10.1080/027321799280235

Patry, A. L., & Pelletier, L. G. (2001). Extraterrestrial beliefs and experiences: An application of the theory of reasoned action. *Journal of Social Psychology, 141* (2), 199–217. DOI: https://doi.org/10.1080/00224540109600547

Pearce, L. J., & Field, A. P. (2016). The impact of "scary" TV and film on children's internalizing emotions: A meta-analysis. *Human Communication Research, 42*(1), 98–121. DOI: https://doi.org/10.1111/hcre.12069

Peeters, G., & Czapinski, J. (1990). Positive-negative asymmetry in evaluations: The distinction between affective and informational negativity effects. *European Review of Social Psychology, 1*(1), 33–60. DOI: https://doi.org/10.1080/14792779108401856

Pennycook, G., McPhetres, J., Zhang, Y., Lu, J. G., & Rand, D. G. (2020). Fighting COVID-19 misinformation on social media: Experimental evidence for a scalable accuracy-nudge intervention. *Psychological Science, 31*(7), 770–780. DOI: https://doi.org/10.1177/0956797620939054

Pennycook, G., & Rand, D. G. (2019). Lazy, not biased: Susceptibility to partisan fake news is better explained by lack of reasoning than by motivated reasoning. *Cognition, 188,* 39–50.

Perry, J. C., Presniak, M. D., & Olson, T. R. (2013). Defense mechanisms in schizotypal, borderline, antisocial, and narcissistic personality disorders. *Psychiatry: Interpersonal and Biological Processes, 76*(1), 32–52. DOI: https://doi.org/10.1521/psyc.2013.76.1.32

Petty, R. E., & Cacioppo, J. T. (1986). The elaboration likelihood model of persuasion. *Advances in Experimental Social Psychology.* DOI: https://doi.org/10.1016/S0065-2601(08)60214-2

Petty, R. E., Wells, G. L., & Brock, T. C. (1976). Distraction can enhance or reduce yielding to propaganda: Thought disruption versus effort justification. *Journal of Personality and Social Psychology.* DOI: https://doi.org/10.1037/0022-3514.34.5.874

Pew Research Center. (2018). The public, the political system and American democracy.
  (2017). The partisan divide grows even wider. https://www.pewresearch.org/politics/2017/10/05/the-partisan-divide-on-political-values-grows-even-wider/
  (2016). The parties on the eve of the 2016 election: Two coalitions, moving further apart. https://www.pewresearch.org/politics/2016/09/13/the-parties-on-the-eve-of-the-2016-election-two-coalitions-moving-further-apart/. All retrieved August 2, 2021.

Pham, M. T. (1998). Representativeness, relevance, and the use of feelings in decision making. *Journal of Consumer Research, 25*(2), 144–159. DOI: https://doi.org/10.1086/209532

Phillips, D. P., Lesyna, K., & Paight, D. J. (1992). Suicide and the media. In R. W. Maris, A. L. Berman, & J. Malstberger (Eds.), *Assessment and prediction of suicide.* New York, NY: Guilford Press.

Pierce, S., Bolter, J., & Selee, A. (2018). US immigration policy under Trump: Deep changes and lasting impacts. *Migration Policy Institute, 9.*

Pierri, F., Piccardi, C., & Ceri, S. (2020). Topology comparison of Twitter diffusion networks effectively reveals misleading information. *Scientific Reports, 10*(1), 1–9. DOI: https://doi.org/10.1038/s41598-020-58166-5

Pipes, D. (1997). *Conspiracy: How the paranoid style flourishes and where it comes from.* New York: Free Press.

Politico. (2011). Birthersim: Where it all began. *Politico.* Retrieved from www .politico.com/story/2011/04/birtherism-where-it-all-began-053563

Pollard, J. (2016). Skinhead culture: The ideologies, mythologies, religions and conspiracy theories of racist skinheads. *Patterns of Prejudice, 50*(4–5), 398–419.

Popper, Karl R. (1949). Prediction and prophecy and their significance for social theory. *Proceedings of the Tenth International Congress of Philosophy, 1,* 82–91.

(2005). *The logic of scientific discovery.* Abingdon: Routledge.

(2006). The conspiracy theory of society. In David Coady (Ed.), *Conspiracy theories: The philosophical debate* (pp. 13–16). Abingdon: Routledge.

(2012). *The Open Society and Its Enemies.* Abingdon: Routledge.

Porter, S., Bellhouse, S., McDougall, A., ten Brinke, L., & Wilson, K. (2010). A prospective investigation of the vulnerability of memory for positive and negative emotional scenes to the misinformation effect. *Canadian Journal of Behavioural Science, 42*(1), 55–61. DOI: https://doi.org/10.1037/a0016652

Pratto, F., & John, O. P. (1991). Automatic vigilance: The attention-grabbing power of negative social information. *Journal of Personality and Social Psychology, 61*(3), 380–391.

Prentice, D. A., & Miller, D. T. (1993). Pluralistic ignorance and alcohol use on campus. Some consequences of misperceiving the social norm. *Journal of Personality and Social Psychology, 64*(2), 243–256. DOI: https://doi.org/10 .1037/0022-3514.64.2.243

Prislin, R., & Wood, W. (2005). Social influence in attitudes and attitude change. In D. Albarracín, B. T. Johnson, & M. P. Zanna (Eds.), *The handbook of attitudes* (pp. 671–705). Mahwah, NJ: Lawrence Erlbaum Associates Publishers.

Raban, D. R., & Rabin, E. (2007). The power of assuming normality. In *Proceedings of the European and Mediterranean Conference on Information Systems, EMCIS 2007.*

(2009). Statistical inference from power law distributed web-based social interactions. *Internet Research, 19*(3). DOI: https://doi.org/10.1108/ 10662240910965342

Räikkä, J. (2009). On political conspiracy theories. *Journal of Political Philosophy, 17*(2), 185–201.

Rao, Y., Li, Q., Mao, X., & Wenyin, L. (2014). Sentiment topic models for social emotion mining. *INFORMATION SCIENCES, 266,* 90–100. DOI: https:// doi.org/10.1016/j.ins.2013.12.059

Recalde, L., Nettleton, D. F., Baeza-Yates, R., & Boratto, L. (2017). Detection of trending topic communities: Bridging content creators and distributors. In *HT 2017 – Proceedings of the 28th ACM Conference on Hypertext and Social Media.* DOI: https://doi.org/10.1145/3078714.3078735

Redlawsk, D. P., Civettini, A. J. W., & Lau, R. R. (2007). Affective intelligence and voting: Information processing and learning in a campaign. In W. R.

Neuman, G. E. Marcus, A. N. Crigler, & M. MacKuen (Eds.), *The affect effect: Dynamics of emotion in political thinking* (pp. 152–179). Chicago, IL: University of Chicago Press.

Reinecke, L. (2017). Mood management. In P. Rössler (Ed.), *The international encyclopedia of media effects* (pp. 1271–1284). Hoboken, NJ: Wiley-Blackwell.

Rettner, R. (2020). COVID-19 has fueled more than 2,000 rumors and conspiracy theories. Retrieved January 7, 2021. https://www.livescience .com/covid-19-rumors-conspiracy-theories-infodemic.html

Richard-Lalonde, M. et al. (2020). The effect of music on pain in the adult intensive care unit: A systematic review of randomized controlled trials. *Journal of Pain and Symptom Management, 59*(6), 1304+. DOI: https://doi .org/10.1016/j.jpainsymman.2019.12.359

Richardson, J. T. (2011). Deprogramming: from private self-help to governmental organized repression. *Crime Law and Social Change, 55*(4, SI), 321–336. DOI: https://doi.org/10.1007/s10611-011-9286-5

Rico, G., Guinjoan, M., & Anduiza, E. (2017). The emotional underpinnings of populism: How anger and fear affect populist attitudes. *Swiss Political Science Review, 23*(4), 444–461. DOI: https://doi.org/10.1111/spsr .12261

Riehm, K. E., Holingue, C., Kalb, L. G., Bennett, D., Kapteyn, A., Jiang, Q., . . . Thrul, J. (2020). Associations between media exposure and mental distress among U.S. adults at the beginning of the COVID-19 pandemic. *American Journal of Preventive Medicine,* S0749–3797(20)30274-9. DOI: https://doi .org/10.1016/j.amepre.2020.06.008

Robins, R. S., & Post, J. M. (1997). *Political paranoia: The psychopolitics of hatred.* New Haven, CT: Yale University Press.

Rocklage, M. D. et al. (2017). An examination of the factorial and convergent validity of four measures of conspiracist ideation, with recommendations for researchers. *PLoS ONE, 12*(4), 27. DOI: https://doi.org/10.1177/ 0146167207312527

Roets, A., & Van Hiel, A. (2011). Item selection and validation of a brief, 15-item version of the Need for Closure Scale. *Personality and Individual Differences.* DOI: https://doi.org/10.1016/j.paid.2010.09.004

Rogers, P., Fisk, J. E., & Lowrie, E. (2018). Paranormal belief, thinking style preference and susceptibility to confirmatory conjunction errors. *Consciousness and Cognition, 65*(January), 182–196. DOI: https://doi.org/ 10.1016/j.concog.2018.07.013

Romer, D., Jamieson, K. H., & Aday, S. (2014). Television news and the cultivation of fear of crime. Jo. *Journal of Communication, 53*(1), 88–104.

Romer, Dan, Jamieson, P. E., & Jamieson, K. H. (2006). Are news reports of suicide contagious? A stringent test in six US cities. *Journal of Communication, 56*(2), 253–270.

Romer, Daniel, & Jamieson, K. H. (2020). Conspiracy theories as barriers to controlling the spread of COVID-19 in the U.S. *Social Science & Medicine.* DOI: https://doi.org/doi.org/10.1016/j.socscimed.2020.113356.

(2021). *Unpublished manuscript.* Philadelphia, PA.

Romero, D. (2019). Authorities seek man in arson fire at "Pizzagate" eatery. Retrieved January 1, 2021, from www.nbcnews.com/news/us-news/authorities-seek-man-arson-fire-pizzagate-eatery-n963206

Roose, K. (2020, August). What is QAnon, the viral pro-Trump Conspiracy theory? *New York Times.*

Roozenbeek, J., van der Linden, S., & Nygren, T. (2020). Prebunking interventions based on "inoculation" theory can reduce susceptibility to misinformation across cultures. *The Harvard Kennedy School (HKS) Misinformation Review.* DOI: https://doi.org/10.37016//mr-2020-008

Rose, J. (2017). Brexit, Trump, and post-truth politics. *Public Integrity,* 19:6, 555–558, DOI: 10.1080/10999922.2017.1285540.

Ross, K. (2020, August 24). Why QAnon is attracting so many followers in Australia – and how it can be countered. *The Conversation.* Retreived from https://theconversation.com/why-qanon-is-attracting-so-many-followers-in-australia-and-how-it-can-be-countered-144865

Ross, M. W., Essien, E. J., & Torres, I. (2006). Conspiracy beliefs about the origin of HIV/AIDS in four racial/ethnic groups. *Journal of Acquired Immune Deficiency Syndromes (1999), 41*(3), 342.

Rozin, P., & Royzman, E. B. (2001). Negativity bias, negativity dominance, and contagion. *Personality and Social Psychology Review, 5*(4), 296–320. DOI: https://doi.org/10.1207/S15327957PSPR0504_2

Rupar, A. (2020, May). Eric Trump used his latest Fox News appearence to push an absurd conspiracy theory about Covid-19. *Vox.*

Russell, J. A. (2003). Core affect and the psychological construction of emotion. *Psychological Review, 110*(1), 145.

Safire, W., & Gardner, W. (2005). *Before the fall: An inside view of the pre-Watergate White House.* New York, NY: Routledge

Salathé, M., Vu, D. Q., Khandelwal, S., & Hunter, D. R. (2013). The dynamics of health behavior sentiments on a large online social network. *EPJ Data Science, 2*(1), 1–12. DOI: https://doi.org/10.1140/epjds16

Sanawi, J. B., Samani, M. C., & Taibi, M. (2017). #Vaccination: Identifying influencers in the vaccination discussion on Twitter through social network visualisation. *International Journal of Business and Society, 18*(S4), 718–26.

Sanders, A., Stogner, J., Seibert, J., & Miller, B. L. (2014). Misperceptions of peer pill-popping: The prevalence, correlates, and effects of inaccurate assumptions about peer pharmaceutical misuse. *Substance Use and Misuse.* DOI: https://doi.org/10.3109/10826084.2014.880485

Sandler, D., Connell, P., Welsh, K., & Daniels, R. G. (1986). Emotional crises imitating television. *The Lancet, 327*(8485), 856.

Sapountzis, A., & Condor, S. (2013). Conspiracy accounts as intergroup theories: challenging dominant understandings of social power and political legitimacy. *Political Psychology, 34*(5), 731–752.

Satariano, A., & Alba, D. (2020, April 20). Burning cell towers, out of baseless fear they spread the virus. *New York Times.* Retrieved from www.nytimes.com/2020/04/10/technology/coronavirus-5g-uk.html

Saunders, K. L. (2017). The impact of elite frames and motivated reasoning on beliefs in a global warming conspiracy: The promise and limits of trust. *Research & Politics*, *4*(3), 2053168017717602.

Schachter, S. (1951). Deviation, rejection, and communication. *Journal of Abnormal and Social Psychology*, *46*(2), 190–207. DOI: https://doi.org/10 .1037/h0062326

Schaeffer, K. (2020). A look at the Americans who believe there's some truth to the conspiracy theory that covid was planned. Retrieved January 7, 2021. https://www.pewresearch.org/fact-tank/2020/07/24/a-look-at-the-ameri cans-who-believe-there-is-some-truth-to-the-conspiracy-theory-that-covid- 19-was-planned/

Scherr, S., & Steinleitner, A. (2017). Between Werther and Papageno effects: A propositional meta-analysis of ambiguous findings for helpful and harmful media effects on suicide contagion. In S. Niederkrotenthaler, T and Stack (Ed.), *Media and suicide: International perspectives on research, theory, and policy* (pp. 183–195). Abingdon: Routledge.

Schimmack, U., & Crites, S. L. (2005). The structure of affect. In D. Albarracin, B.T. Johnson, & M.P. Zanna (Eds.), *Handbook of attitudes* (pp. 397–435). Mahwah, NJ: Lawrence Earlbaum.

Schlatter, E., & Steinback, R. (2011). 10 anti-gay myths debunked. Retrieved January 1, 2020, from www.splcenter.org/fighting-hate/intelligence-report/ 2011/10-anti-gay-myths-debunked

Schmidt, A. L. et al. (2017). Anatomy of news consumption on Facebook. *Proceedings of the National Academy of Sciences*, *114*(12), 3035–3039. DOI: https://doi.org/10.1073/pnas.1617052114

Schmidtke, A., & Häfner, H. (1988). The Werther effect after television films: New evidence for an old hypothesis. Psychological Medicine. *Psychological Medicine*, *18*(3), 665–676. DOI: https://doi.org/doi: 10.1017/S0033291700008345.

Schneider, A. (2018). Twitter bans Alex Jones and InfoWars; cites abusive behavior. Retrieved January 1, 2021, from www.npr.org/2018/09/06/ 645352618/twitter-bans-alex-jones-and-infowars-cites-abusive-behavior

Schranz, M., Schneider, J., & Eisenegger, M. (2018). Media trust and media use. In K. Otto & A. Köhler (Eds.), *Trust in media and journalism*. Wiesbaden: Springer VS. DOI: https://doi.org/10.1007/978-3-658-20765-6_5

Schroeder, C. M., & Prentice, D. A. (1998). Exposing pluralistic ignorance to reduce alcohol use among college students. *Journal of Applied Social Psychology*, *28*(23), 2150–2180. DOI: https://doi.org/10.1111/j.1559-1816 .1998.tb01365.x

Schudson, M. (1993). *Watergate in American memory: How we remember, forget, and reconstruct the past.* New York, NY: Basic Books.

Schwarz, N., & Clore, G. L. (1983). Mood, misattribution, and judgments of well-being: Informative and directive functions of affective states. *Journal of Personality and Social Psychology*, *45*(3), 513–523. DOI: https://doi.org/10 .1037/0022-3514.45.3.513

(2007). Feelings and Phenomenal Experiences. In A. Kruglanski & E. T. Higgins (Eds.), *Social psychology. Handbook of basic principles* (2nd ed.) (pp. 385–407). New York, NY: Guilford.

Schwarz, N., & Lee, S. W. S. (2019). Embodied cognition and the construction of attitudes. In D. Albarracín & B. T. Johnson (Eds.), *The handbook of attitudes, volume 1: Basic principles* (2nd ed.). New York, NY: Routledge.

Sears, D. O., & Freedman, J. L. (1967). Selective Exposure to Information. A Critical Review. *Public Opinion Quarterly, 31*(2), 194. DOI: https://doi.org/10.1086/267513

Sen, A., & Zadrozny, B. (2010, August 10). *QAnon groups have millions of members on Facebook, documents show. NBC News.* www.nbcnews.com/tech/tech-news/qanon-groups-have-millions-members-facebook-documents-show-n1236317

Sesso, G., & Sicca, F. (2020). Safe and sound: Meta-analyzing the Mozart effect on epilepsy. *Clinical Neurophysiology, 131*(7), 1610–1620. DOI: https://doi.org/10.1016/j.clinph.2020.03.039

Shacham, S. (1983). A shortened version of the profile of mood states. *Journal of Personality Assessment.* DOI: https://doi.org/10.1207/s15327752jpa4703_14

Shahi, G. K., & Nandini, D. (2020). FakeCovid – A multilingual cross-domain fact check news dataset for COVID-19. *ArXiv Preprint ArXiv:2006.11343.*

Shao, C., Hui, P.-M., Wang, L., Jiang, X., Flammini, A., Menczer, F., & Ciampaglia, G. L. (2018). Anatomy of an online misinformation network. *PLOS ONE, 13*(4), e0196087. DOI: https://doi.org/10.1371/journal.pone.0196087

Shapiro, R. Y., & Bloch-Elkon, Y. (2008). Do the facts speak for themselves? Partisan disagreement as a challenge to democratic competence. *Critical Review, 20*(1–2), 115–139.

Sharma, L. L., Teret, S. P., & Brownell, K. D. (2010). The Food Industry and Self-Regulation: Standards to Promote Success and to Avoid Public Health Failures. *American Journal of Public Health, 100*(2), 240–246. DOI: https://doi.org/10.2105/AJPH.2009.160960

Sharp, P. M., & Hahn, B. H. (2011). Origins of HIV and the AIDS pandemic. *Cold Spring Harbor Perspectives in Medicine, 1*(1), 1–22. DOI: https://doi.org/10.1101/cshperspect.a006841

Shelbourne, M. (2017). Infowars'' Alex Jones apologizes for pushing "Pizzagate" conspiracy theory. Retrieved January 1, 2021, from https://thehill.com/homenews/325761-infowars-alex-jones-apologizes-for-pushing-pizzagate-conspiracy-theory

Shermer, M. (2011). *The believing brain: From ghosts and gods to politics and conspiracies – how we construct beliefs and reinforce them as truths.* New York, NY: Times Books.

Shoemaker, P. J., & Cohen, A. A. (2006). News around the world: Content. *Practitioners, and the Public.* New York, NY: Routledge.

Shoemaker, P. J., & Reese, S. D. (2014). *Mediating the Message in the 21st Century: Theories of influence on mass media content.* New York, NY: Routledge.

Shooman, Y. (2016). Between everyday racism and conspiracy theories (pp. 136–154). *Media and minorities.* Berlin: Vandenhoeck & Ruprecht.

Shore, J., Back, J., & Dellarocas, C. (2018). Twitter is not the echo chamber we think it is. *MIT Sloan Management Review, 60*(1), 1–5.

Siani, A. (2019). Measles outbreaks in Italy: A paradigm of the re-emergence of vaccine-preventable diseases in developed countries. *Preventive Medicine, 121,* 99–104.

Sides, J., Tesler, M., & Vavreck, L. (2018). *Identity crisis: The 2016 presidential campaign and the battle for the meaning of America. 2019.* Princeton, NJ: Princeton University Press.

Simmons, W. P., & Parsons, S. (2005). Beliefs in conspiracy theories among African Americans: A comparison of elites and masses. *Social Science Quarterly, 86*(3), 582–598. DOI: https://doi.org/http://dx.doi.org/10.1111/j.0038-4941.2005.00319.x

Sisask, M., & Värnik, A. (2012). Media roles in suicide prevention: A systematic review. *International Journal of Environmental Research and Public Health, 9* (1), 123–138. DOI: https://doi.org/doi: 10.3390/ijerph9010123

Skowronski, J. J., & Carlston, D. E. (1989). Negativity and extremity biases in impression formation: A review of explanations. *Psychological Bulletin, 105* (1), 131–142. DOI: https://doi.org/10.1037/0033-2909.105.1.131

Skurka, C., Niederdeppe, J., & Romero-canyas, R. (2018). Pathways of influence in emotional appeals: Benefits and tradeoffs of using fear or humor to promote climate change-related intentions and risk perceptions, *Journal of Communication 68,* 169–193. DOI: https://doi.org/10.1093/joc/jqx008

Sloan, A. (2017, August 20). Brexit Britain: A United Kingdom of hate and denial. *Al Jazeera.* Retrieved from https://www.aljazeera.com/opinions/2017/8/20/brexit-britain-a-united-kingdom-of-hate-and-denial/

Smallman, S. (2018). Conspiracy theories and the zika epidemic. *Journal of International and Global Studies, 9*(2), 1–13.

Solon, O. and Siddiqui, S. (2017, October). Russia-backed Facebook posts "reached 126m Americans" during US election. *The Guardian.* Retrieved from https://www.theguardian.com/technology/2017/oct/30/facebook-russia-fake-accounts-126-million

Sonneck, G., Etzersdorfer, E., & Nagel-Kuess, S. (1994). Imitative suicide on the Viennese subway. *Social Science & Medicine, 38*(3), 453–457. DOI: https://doi.org/doi: 10.1016/0277-9536(94)90447-2

Sorrentino, R. M., & Short, J. A. C. (1986). Uncertainty orientation, motivation, and cognition. In R. M. Sorrentino & E. T. Higgins (Eds.), *Handbook of motivation and cognition: Foundations of social behavior* (pp. 379–403). New York, NY: Guilford Press.

Spielberger, C. D., Gorsuch, R. L., Lushene, R., Vagg, P. R., & Jacobs, G. A. (1983). *Manual for the State-Trait Anxiety Inventory (STAI Form Y).*

Consulting Psychologists Palo Alto. DOI: https://doi.org/10.1002/9780470479216.corpsy0943

Spring, M., & Wendling, M. (2020). How Covid-19 myths are merging with the QAnon conspiracy theory. https://www.bbc.com/news/blogs-trending-53997203 Retrieved December 20, 2020.

Stecula, D., Kuru, O., Albarracin, D., & Jamieson, K. H. (2020). Policy views and negative beliefs about vaccines in the United States, 2019. *American Journal of Public Health, 110*(10), 1561–1563..

Steele, C. M. (1988). The Psychology of Self-Affirmation: Sustaining the Integrity of the Self. *Advances in Experimental Social Psychology.* DOI: https://doi.org/10.1016/S0065-2601(08)60229-4

Stein, J. (2016). What 20,000 pages of hacked WikiLeaks emails teach us about Hillary Clinton. Retrieved January 1, 2021, from www.vox.com/policy-and-politics/2016/10/20/13308108/wikileaks-podesta-hillary-clinton

Stelter, B. (2020). *Hoax: Donald Trump, Fox News, and the Dangerous Distortion of Truth.* New York: Atria/One signal Publishers.

Stempel, C., Hargrove, T., & Stempel, G. (2007). Media Use, Social Structure, and Belief in 9/11 Conspiracy Theories. *Journalism and Mass Communication Quarterly, 84*(2), 353–372.

Stewart, I. (2020, August). One year after Walmart Massacre, El Paso Mourn – At a distance. *NPR News.*

Stojanov, A., & Halberstadt, J. (2019). The Conspiracy Mentality Scale: Distinguishing between irrational and rational suspicion. *Social Psychology, 50*(4), 215–232. DOI: https://doi.org/10.1027/1864-9335/a000381

Stossel, J., & Jaquez, N. D. (2007). The "fear industrial complex." *ABC News.* USA.

Stroud, N. J. (2010). Polarization and partisan selective exposure. *Journal of Communication, 60*(3), 556–576.

Sun, S., Lin, D., & Operario, D. (2020). Need for a population health approach to understand and address psychosocial consequences of COVID-19. *Psychological Trauma: Theory, Research, Practice, and Policy, 12*(S1), S25.

Sunstein, C. R. (2009). *Republic.com 2.0.* Princeton University Press.

(2014). *Conspiracy theories and other dangerous ideas. Conspiracy theories and other dangerous ideas.* New York: Simon & Schuster. Retrieved from https://search.proquest.com/docview/1518033925?accountid=14553

Sunstein, C. R., & Vermeule, A. (2008). *Conspiracy theories.* Harvard Public Law Working Paper No. 08-03, University of Chicago, Chicago.

(2009). Conspiracy theories: Causes and cures. *Journal of Political Philosophy, 17*(2), 202–227.

Surian, D., Nguyen, D. Q., Kennedy, G., Johnson, M., Coiera, E., & Dunn, A. G. (2016). Characterizing twitter discussions about HPV vaccines using topic modeling and community detection. *Journal of Medical Internet Research, 18*(8), e232. DOI: https://doi.org/10.2196/jmir.6045

Swami, V. (2012). Social psychological origins of conspiracy theories: The case of the Jewish conspiracy theory in Malaysia. *Frontiers in Psychology, 3* (August). DOI: https://doi.org/10.3389/fpsyg.2012.00280

Swami, V., Barron, D., Weis, L., & Furnham, A. (2018). To Brexit or not to Brexit: The roles of Islamophobia, conspiracist beliefs, and integrated threat in voting intentions for the United Kingdom European Union membership referendum. *British Journal of Psychology, 109*(1), 156–179. DOI: https://doi.org/http://dx.doi.org/10.1111/bjop.12252

Swami, V., Chamorro-Premuzic, T., & Furnham, A. (2010). Unanswered questions: A preliminary investigation of personality and individual difference predictors of 9/11 conspiracist beliefs. *Applied Cognitive Psychology, 24*(6), 749–761. DOI: https://doi.org/http://dx.doi.org/10.1002/acp.1583

et al. (2011). Conspiracist ideation in Britain and Austria: Evidence of a monological belief system and associations between individual psychological differences and real-world and fictitious conspiracy theories. *British Journal of Psychology, 102*(3), 443–463. DOI: https://doi.org/10.1111/j.2044-8295.2010.02004.x

Swami, V., & Furnham, A. (2014). Political paranoia and conspiracy theories. In J. Prooijen & P. Lange (Eds.), *Power, politics, and paranoia: Why people are suspicious of their leaders* (pp. 218–236). Cambridge: Cambridge University Press. DOI: https://doi.org/10.1017/CBO9781139565417.016

Swami, V., Furnham, A., Smyth, N., Weis, L., Lay, A., & Clow, A. (2016). Putting the stress on conspiracy theories: Examining associations between psychological stress, anxiety, and belief in conspiracy theories. *Personality and Individual Differences, 99*, 72–76. DOI: https://doi.org/http://dx.doi.org/10.1016/j.paid.2016.04.084

Swami, V., Voracek, M., Stieger, S., Tran, U. S., & Furnham, A. (2014). Analytic thinking reduces belief in conspiracy theories. *Cognition, 133*(3), 572–585. DOI: https://doi.org/10.1016/j.cognition.2014.08.006

Swire, B., Berinsky, A. J., Lewandowsky, S., & Ecker, U. K. H. (2017). Processing political misinformation: Comprehending the Trump phenomenon. *Royal Society Open Science, 4*(3), 160802.

Symbols and Logos Used by Pedophiles to Identify Sexual Preferences. (2016).

Tang, X., & Yang, C. C. (2010). Identifing influential users in an online healthcare social network. In *ISI 2010 – 2010 IEEE International Conference on Intelligence and Security Informatics: Public Safety and Security* (pp. 43–48). DOI: https://doi.org/10.1109/ISI.2010.5484779

Tannenbaum, M. B., Hepler, J., Zimmerman, R. S. R. S., Saul, L., Jacobs, S., Wilson, K., & Albarracín, D. (2015). Appealing to fear: A meta-analysis of fear appeal effectiveness and theories. *Psychological Bulletin, 141*(6), 1178–1204. DOI: https://doi.org/10.1037/a0039729

Tappin, B., Pennycook, G., & Rand, D. G. (2020). Bayesian or biased?Analytic thinking and political belief updating. *Cognition* (Forthcoming).

Taylor, S. E. (1991). Asymmetrical effects of positive and negative events: The mobilization-minimization hypothesis. *Psychological Bulletin, 110*(1), 67–85.

Tempey, N. (2016). What on earth is Pizzagate and how did it result in gunfire at Comet Ping Pong? Retrieved January 1, 2021, from https://web.archive.org/

web/20161208075242/http://dcist.com/2016/12/what_on_earth_is_pizza gate_why_did.php

Tesser, A. (2001). On the plasticity of self-defense. *Current Directions in Psychological Science.* DOI: https://doi.org/10.1111/1467-8721.00117

The Flat Earth Society. (n.d.). Retrieved January 2, 2020, from www.tfes.org/

The republian elite. (2020). Retrieved January 2, 2020, from http://content.time.com/ time/specials/packages/article/0,28804,1860871_1860876_1861029,00.html

Thomas, E. (2020). QAnon deploys "Information Warfare" to influence the 2020 election. *WIRED.*

Thresher-Andrews, C. (2013). An introduction into the world of conspiracy. *The British Psychological Society. Special Issue: The Psychology of Conspiracy Theories,* (88), 5.

Thunstrom, L., Ashworth, M., Finnoff, D., & Newbold, S. (2020). *Hesitancy towards a COVID-19 vaccine and prospects for herd immunity.* Unpublished manuscript. https://papers.ssrn.com/sol3/papers.cfm?abstract_id=3593098

Thyer, B. A., & Westhuis, D. (1989). Test-retest reliability of the Clinical Anxiety Scale. *Phobia Practice and Research, 2,* 111–113.

Till, B., Strauss, M., Sonneck, G., & Niederkrotenthaler, T. (2015). Determining the effects of films with suicidal content: A laboratory experiment. *British Journal of Psychiatry, 207*(1), 72–78. DOI: https://doi.org/10.1192/bjp.bp .114.152827

Tobacyk, J., & Milford, G. (1983). Belief in paranormal phenomena: Assessment instrument development and implications for personality functioning. *Journal of Personality and Social Psychology.* DOI: https://doi.org/10.1037/ 0022-3514.44.5.1029

Tomasello, M., Carpenter, M., Call, J., Behne, T., & Moll, H. (2005). Understanding and sharing intentions: The origins of cultural cognition. *Behavioral and Brain Sciences, 28*(5). DOI: https://doi.org/10.1017/ S0140525X05000129

Tomljenovic, H., Bubic, A., & Erceg, N. (2020). It just doesn't feel right: The relevance of emotions and intuition for parental vaccine conspiracy beliefs and vaccination uptake. *Psychology & Health, 35*(5), 538–554.

Towers, S. et al. (2015). Mass media and the contagion of fear: The case of Ebola in America. *PLOS ONE, 10*(6), e0129179.

Turner, J. C. (1985). Social categorization and the self-concept: A social cognitive theory of group behavior. In E. J. Lawler (Ed.), *Advances in group processes: Theory and research* (Vol. 2, pp. 77–122). Greenwich, CT: JAI Press.

Turner, P. A. (1993). *I heard it through the grapevine: Rumor in African-American culture.* University of California Press.

Tuters, M., Jokubauskaitė, E., & Bach, D. (2016). Post-truth protest: How 4chan cooked up the Pizzagate bullshit. *M/C Journal, 21*(3). Retrieved from https:// journal.media-culture.org.au/index.php/mcjournal/article/view/1422

Twitter: Data Dictionary Standard v1.1. (n.d.). Retrieved October 1, 2020, from https://developer.twitter.com/en/docs/twitter-api/v1/data-dictionary/object-model/tweet

Ungerleider, J. T., & Wellisch, D. K. (1979). Coercive persuasion (brainwashing), religious cults, and deprogramming. *American Journal of Psychiatry, 136* (3), 279–282.

Unkelbach, C., & Rom, S. C. (2017). A referential theory of the repetition-induced truth effect. *Cognition.* DOI: https://doi.org/10.1016/j.cognition .2016.12.016

United States Department of Justice (2017). North Carolina man sentenced to four-year prison term for armed assault at Northwest Washington Pizza restaurant. Retrieved January 1, 2021, from www.justice.gov/usao-dc/pr/ north-carolina-man-sentenced-four-year-prison-term-armed-assault-north west-washington

U.S. Department of Health & Human Services (n.d.). Does depression increase the risk of suicide? Retrieved January 9, 2021, from www.hhs.gov/answers/ mental-health-and-substance-abuse/does-depression-increase-risk-of-suicide/ index.html

Uscinski, J. E. (2016). If Trump's rhetoric around conspiracy theories follows him to the White House, it could lead to the violation of rights on a massive scale. *Impact of American Politics & Policy Blog.*

et al. (2020). Why do people believe COVID-19 conspiracy theories? *Harvard Kennedy School Misinformation Review, 1*(3).

Uscinski, J. E., & Parent, J. M. (2014). *American conspiracy theories* (Vol. 1789). Oxford: Oxford University Press. DOI: https://doi.org/10.1093/acprof:oso/ 9780199351800.001.0001

Valente, T. W. (2010). *Social networks and health: Models, methods, and applications* (1st ed.). Oxford University Press.

Valentino, N. A., Hutchings, V. L., Banks, A. J., & Davis, A. K. (2008). Is a worried citizen a good citizen? Emotions, political information seeking, and learning via the internet. *Political Psychology, 29*(2), 247–273.

Valentino, Nicholas A., Banks, A. J., Hutchings, V. L., & Davis., A. K. (2009). Selective exposure in the internet age: The interaction between anxiety and information utility. *Political Psychology, 30*(4), 591–613.

Valentino, Nicholas A., Brader, T., Groenendyk, E. W., Gregorowicz, K., & Hutchings, V. L. (2011). Election night's alright for fighting: The role of emotions in political participation. *Journal of Politics, 73*(1), 156–170. DOI: https://doi.org/10.1017/S0022381610000939

Van Alstyne, M., & Brynjolfsson, E. (1996). Could the Internet balkanize science? *Science, 274*(5292), 1479–1480. DOI: https://doi.org/10.1126/ science.274.5292.1479

Van Assche, J. et al. (2018). Positive neighborhood norms buffer ethnic diversity effects on neighborhood dissatisfaction, perceived neighborhood disadvantage, and moving intentions. *Personality and Social Psychology Bulletin, 44*(5), 700–716. DOI: https://doi.org/http://dx.doi.org/10.1177/0146167217744767

van den Bos, K. (2009). Making sense of life: The existential self trying to deal with personal uncertainty. *Psychological Inquiry.* DOI: https://doi.org/10 .1080/10478400903333411

Van der Linden, S. (2015). The conspiracy-effect: Exposure to conspiracy theories (about global warming) decreases pro-social behavior and science acceptance. *Personality and Individual Differences, 87,* 171–173. DOI: https://doi.org/10.1016/j.paid.2015.07.045

van Harreveld, F., Rutjens, B. T., Schneider, I. K., Nohlen, H. U., & Keskinis, K. (2014). In doubt and disorderly: Ambivalence promotes compensatory perceptions of order. *Journal of Experimental Psychology. General, 143*(4), 1666–1676. DOI: https://doi.org/http://dx.doi.org/10.1037/a0036099

van Prooijen, J.-W., & Acker, M. (2015). The influence of control on belief in conspiracy theories: Conceptual and applied extensions. *Applied Cognitive Psychology, 29*(5), 753–761. DOI: https://doi.org/http://dx.doi.org/10.1002/acp.3161

van Prooijen, J.-W., Douglas, K. M., & De Inocencio, C. (2018). Connecting the dots: Illusory pattern perception predicts beliefs in conspiracies and the supernatural. *European Journal of Social Psychology, 48,* 320–335.

van Prooijen, J.-W., Douglas, K. M., De Inocencio, C., Prooijen, J., Douglas, K. M., & De Inocencio, C. (2017). *Connecting the dots: Illusory pattern perception predicts belief in conspiracies and the supernatural. European Journal of Social Psychology* (Vol. 48). Ashgate: John Wiley & Sons. DOI: https://doi.org/http://dx.doi.org/10.1002/ejsp.2331

van Prooijen, J.-W., & Jostmann, N. B. (2013). *Belief in conspiracy theories: The influence of uncertainty and perceived morality. European Journal of Social Psychology* (Vol. 43). Amsterdam: John Wiley & Sons. DOI: https://doi.org/http://dx.doi.org/10.1002/ejsp.1922

van Prooijen, J.-W., & Krouwel, A. P. M. (2015). Mutual suspicion at the political extremes. In M. Bilewicz, A. Cichocka & W. Soral (Eds.), *The psychology of conspiracy* (pp. 79–99). London: Routledge.

van Prooijen, J.-W., & van Dijk, E. (2014). When consequence size predicts belief in conspiracy theories: The moderating role of perspective taking. *Journal of Experimental Social Psychology, 55,* 63–73. DOI: https://doi.org/10.1016/j.jesp.2014.06.006

van Prooijen, J.-W., & van Lange, P. A. M. (2014). The social dimension of belief in conspiracy theories. In *Power, politics, and paranoia: Why people are suspicious of their leaders.* DOI: https://doi.org/10.1017/CBO9781139565417.017

van Prooijen, J.-W., & van Vugt, M. (2018). Conspiracy theories: Evolved functions and psychological mechanisms. *Perspectives on Psychological Science, 13*(6), 770–788.

van Prooijen, J. (2017). Why education predicts decreased belief in conspiracy theories. *Applied Cognitive Psychology, 31*(1), 50–58. DOI: https://doi.org/http://dx.doi.org/10.1002/acp.3301

van Prooijen, J. W. (2016). Sometimes inclusion breeds suspicion: Self-uncertainty and belongingness predict belief in conspiracy theories. *European Journal of Social Psychology, 46*(3), 267–279. DOI: https://doi.org/10.1002/ejsp.2157

Vosoughi, S., Roy, D., & Aral, S. (2018). The spread of true and false news online. *Science, 1151*(March), 1146–1151. DOI: https://doi.org/10.1126/science.aap9559

Walter, D., Ophir, Y., & Jamieson, K. H. (2020). Russian Twitter accounts and the partisan polarization of vaccine discourse, 2015–2017. *American Journal of Public Health, 110*(5), 718–724. DOI: https://doi.org/10.2105/ajph.2019.305564

Watson, K. (2020). Trump banks on fear and anxiety to motivate voters. Retrieved October 11, 2020, from www.cbsnews.com/news/trumps-use-of-fear-and-anxiety-to-motivate-his-voters/

Webber, D. et al. (2018). Deradicalizing detained terrorists. *Political Psychology, 39*(3), 539–556. DOI: https://doi.org/10.1111/pops.12428

Webster, D. M., & Kruglanski, A. W. (1994). Individual Differences in Need for Cognitive Closure. *Journal of Personality and Social Psychology*. DOI: https://doi.org/10.1037/0022-3514.67.6.1049

Welbers, K., & Opgenhaffen, M. (2019). Presenting news on social media. *Digital Journalism, 7*(1), 45–62. DOI: https://doi.org/10.1080/21670811.2018.1493939

Welles, B. F., & González-Bailón, S. (Eds.) (2020). *The Oxford handbook of networked communication*. Oxford: Oxford University Press. DOI: https://doi.org/10.1093/oxfordhb/9780190460518.001.0001

Whitson, J. A., & Galinsky, A. D. (2008). Lacking control increases illusory pattern perception. *Science*. DOI: https://doi.org/10.1126/science.1159845

Wiedeman, E. A. (2020). *Terministic screening and conspiracy theory in political communication: A critical analysis of trump's rhetorical ties to fair and alex jones through "invasion" immigration discourse.* Upublished thesis. Retrieved from https://thekeep.eiu.edu/cgi/viewcontent.cgi?article=5792&context=theses

Wikipedia. (n.d.-a). Alternative media: U.S. political left. Retrieved July 1, 2019, from https://en.wikipedia.org/wiki/Alternative_media_(U.S._political_left

(n.d.-b). Alternative media: U.S. political left. Retrieved June 9, 2021, from https://en.wikipedia.org/wiki/Alternative_media_(U.S._political_left)

(n.d.-c). Alternative media: U.S. political right. Retrieved June 9, 2021, from https://en.wikipedia.org/wiki/Alternative_media:_U.S._political_right.

(n.d.-d). News media in the United States. Retrieved July 1, 2019, from https://en.wikipedia.org/wiki/News_media_in_the_United_States

(2018). /Tectonic weapon. Retrieved September 15, 2018, from https://en.wikipedia.org/wiki/Tectonic_weapon

(2020a). Deep State in the United States. Retrieved June 2, 2020, from https://en.wikipedia.org/wiki/Deep_state_in_the_United_States

(2020b). Sandy Hook Elementary School shooting. Retrieved from https://en.wikipedia.org/wiki/Sandy_Hook_Elementary_School_shooting

Wilder, D. A. (1977). Perception of groups, size of opposition, and social influence. *Journal of Experimental Social Psychology*. DOI: https://doi.org/10.1016/0022-1031(77)90047-6

Williams, J. M. G., Lawton, C., Ellis, S. J., Walsh, S., & Reed, J. (. (1987). Copycat suicide attempts. *The Lancet. Infectious Diseases, 330*(8550), 102–103.

Wilner, T. (n.d.). We can probably measure media bias. But do we want to? Retrieved January 7, 2021, from https://www.cjr.org/innovations/measure-media-bias-partisan.php

Wilson, G. D. (1973). *The psychology of conservatism.* London, UK: Academic Press.

Wilson, M. S., & Rose, C. (2014). *The role of paranoia in a dual-process motivational model of conspiracy belief.* Cambridge University Press. DOI: https://doi.org/10.1017/CBO9781139565417.019

Winter, J. (2012, February 27). Media Matters boss paid former partner $850G "blackmail" settlement. *Fox News.* Retrieved January 1, 2021, from www.foxnews.com/politics/media-matters-boss-paid-former-partner-850g-blackmail-settlement

Winter, J. (2019). Exclusive: FBI document warns conspiracy theories are a new domestic terrorism threat. *Yahoo!News.* Retrieved from https://urldefense.com/v3/__https://news.yahoo.com/fbi-documents-conspiracy-theories-terrorism-160000507.html__;!!DZ3fjg!oeFn6DBQ2pTormAeQKGz_EuxgXkcHK qo3EVboz4twqajqJayJQf8jVUqqxnU1oojUA$

Winter, S., Metzger, M. J., & Flanagin, A. J. (2016). Selective use of news cues: A multiple-motive perspective on information selection in social media environments. *Journal of Communication, 66*(4), 669–693. DOI: https://doi.org/10.1111/jcom.12241

Winter, T., Kosnar, M., and Wong, W. (2010, December 30). Feds probing whether Nashville bomber believed in lizard people conspiracy. NBC News. Retrieved May 31, 2021, from www.nbcnews.com/news/us-news/girlfriend-nashville-bomber-warned-police-he-was-building-explosives-2019-n1252536

Wise, K., Eckler, P., Kononova, A., & Littau, J. (2009). Exploring the hardwired for news hypothesis: How threat proximity affects the cognitive and emotional processing of health-related print news. *Communication Studies, 60*(3), 268–287.

WNYC Studios. (n.d.). The United States of Anxiety. Retrieved October 11, 2016, from www.wnycstudios.org/podcasts/otm/episodes/united-states-anxiety

Wood, M. J. (2018). Propagating and debunking conspiracy theories on Twitter during the 2015–2016 zika virus outbreak. *Cyberpsychology, Behavior, and Social Networking, 21*(8), 485–490. DOI: https://doi.org/10.1089/cyber.2017.0669

Wood, M. J., & Douglas, K. M. (2013). "What about building 7?" A social psychological study of online discussion of 9/11 conspiracy theories. *Frontiers in Psychology, 4,* 9. DOI: https://doi.org/http://dx.doi.org/10.3389/fpsyg.2013.00409

Wood, W., Lundgren, S., Ouellette, J. A., Busceme, S., & Blackstone, T. (1994). Minority influence. A meta-analytic review oof social-influence processes.

Psychological Bulletin, 115(3), 323–345. DOI: https://doi.org/10.1037/0033-2909.115.3.323

Wood, W., Pool, G. J., Leck, K., & Purvis, D. (1996). Self-Definition, defensive processing, and influence: The normative impact of majority and minority groups. *Journal of Personality and Social Psychology.* DOI: https://doi.org/10.1037/0022-3514.71.6.1181

Wormwood, J. B., Devlin, M., Lin, Y.-R., Barrett, L. F., & Quigley, K. S. (2018). When words hurt: Affective word use in daily news coverage impacts mental health. *Frontiers in Psychology, 9.* DOI: https://doi.org/10.3389/fpsyg.2018.01333

Worth, L. T., & Mackie, D. M. (1987). Cognitive mediation of positive affect in persuasion. *Social Cognition, 5*(1), 76–94. DOI: https://doi.org/10.1521/soco.1987.5.1.76

Wray-Lake, L., Wells, R., Alvis, L., Delgado, S., Syvertsen, A. K., & Metzger, A. (2018). Being a Latinx adolescent under a Trump presidency: Analysis of Latinx youth's reactions to immigration politics. *Children and Youth Services Review, 87,* 192–204.

Wu, Q., Liu, Z., Pang, X., & Cheng, L. (2020). Efficacy of five-element music interventions in perinatal mental health and labor pain: A meta-analysis. *Complementary Therapies in Clinical Practice, 40.* DOI: https://doi.org/10.1016/j.ctcp.2020.101217

Wyer Jr., R. S., & Shrum, L. J. (2015). The role of comprehension processes in communication and persuasion. *Media Psychology, 18*(2, SI), 163–195. DOI: https://doi.org/10.1080/15213269.2014.912584

Wyer, R. S., & Adaval, R. (2004). Pictures, words, and media influence: The interactive effects of verbal and nonverbal information on memory and judgments. In L. J. Shrum (Ed.), *Blurring the Lines Between Entertainment and Persuasion: The Psychology of Entertainment Media* (pp. 137–159). Mahwah, NJ: Erlbaum.

Wyer, R. S., & Albarracín, D. (2005). Belief formation, organization, and change: Cognitive and motivational influences. In D. Albarracín, B. T. Johnson, & M. P. Zanna (Eds.), *Handbook of attitudes* (pp. 273–322). Hillsdale, NJ: Lawrence Erlbaum.

Wyer, R. S. J., Clore, G. L., & Isbell, L. M. (1999). Affect and information processing. *Advances in Experimental Social Psychology, 31,* 1–77. DOI: 10.1016/S0065-2601(08)60271-3.

YouTube. (2014, August). CDC whistleblower revealed. Retrieved from www.youtube.com/watch?v=sGOtDVilkUc&feature=youtu.be&list=UUflZ2PofuUgEM79W3fOc6Mg.

Yuhas, A. (2017, March 25). "Pizzagate" gunman pleads guilty as conspiracy theorist apologizes over case. *The Guardian.* Retrieved from www.theguardian.com/us-news/2017/mar/25/comet-ping-pong-alex-jones

Zadrozny, B. (2019). Fire at "pizzagate" shop reignites conspiracy theorists who find a home on Facebook. *NBC News.* Retrieved from https://www.nbcnews

.com/tech/social-media/fire-pizzagate-shop-reignites-conspiracy-theorists-who-find-home-facebook-n965956

Zaller, J. R. (1992). *The nature and origins of mass opinion*. Cambridge University Press.

Zhang, J., Featherstone, J. D., Calabrese, C., & Wojcieszak, M. (2020). Effects of fact-checking social media vaccine misinformation on attitudes toward vaccines. *Preventive Medicine*, 145, 106408. DOI: https://doi.org/10.1016/j.ypmed.2020.106408

Zhao, K., Greer, G. E., Yen, J., Mitra, P., & Portier, K. (2015). Leader identification in an online health community for cancer survivors: A social network-based classification approach. *Information Systems and E-Business Management*, 13(4), 629–645. DOI: https://doi.org/10.1007/s10257-014-0260-5

Zhao, N., & Zhou, G. (2020). Social media use and mental health during the covid-19 pandemic: Moderator role of disaster stressor and mediator role of negative affect. *Applied Psychology: Health and Well-Being*. DOI: https://doi.org/10.1111/aphw.12226

Zia-Ebrahimi, R. (2018). When the Elders of Zion relocated to Eurabia: Conspiratorial racialization in antisemitism and Islamophobia. *Patterns of Prejudice*, 52(4), 314–337.

ZIillmann, D., Hezel, R. T., & Medoff, N. J. (1980). The effect of affective states on selective exposure to televised entertainment fare. *Journal of Applied Social Psychology*, 10(4), 323–339. DOI: https://doi.org/10.1111/j.1559-1816.1980.tb00713.x

Zillmann, D. (1988a). Mood management: Using entertainment to full advantage. In L. Donohew, H. E. Sypher, & E. T. Higgins (Eds.), *Communication, social cognition, and affect* (pp. 147–171). Hillsdale, NJ: Lawrence Erlbaum Associates.

(1988b). Mood management through communication choices. *American Behavioral Scientist*, 31(3), 327–341.

(2000). Mood management in the context of selective exposure theory. In M. F. Roloff (Ed.), *Communication yearbook 23* (pp. 103–123). Thousand Oaks, CA: Sage.

Zillmann, D., & Bryant, J. (1985). Affect, mood, and emotion as determinants of selective exposure. In D. Zillmann & J. Bryant (Eds.), *Selective exposure to communication* (pp. 157–190). Hillsdale, NJ: Lawrence Erlbaum Associates.

Zillmann, D., Hezel, R. T., & Medoff, N. J. (1980). The effect of affective states on selective exposure to televised entertainment fare. *Journal of Applied Social Psychology*, 10(4), 323–339.

Zollo, F. et al. (2017). Debunking in a world of tribes. *PLoS ONE*, 12(7). DOI: https://doi.org/10.1371/journal.pone.0181821

Zuckerman, E. (2019). QAnon and the emergence of the unreal. *Journal of Design and Science*, 6. Retrieved from https://jods.mitpress.mit.edu/pub/tliexqdu/release/4

Index